Gender Perspectives and Gender Impacts of the Global Economic Crisis

With the full effects of the Great Recession still unfolding, this collection of essays analyses the gendered economic impacts of the crisis. The volume, from an international set of contributors, argues that gender-differentiated economic roles and responsibilities within households and markets can potentially influence the ways in which men and women are affected in times of economic crisis.

Looking at the economy through a gender lens, the contributors investigate the antecedents and consequences of the ongoing crisis as well as the recovery policies adopted in selected countries. There are case studies devoted to Latin America, transition economies, China, India, South Africa, Turkey, and the USA. Topics examined include unemployment, the job-creation potential of fiscal expansion, the behavioral response of individuals whose households have experienced loss of income, social protection initiatives, food security and the environment, shedding of jobs in export-led sectors, and lessons learned thus far. From these timely contributions, students, scholars, and policymakers are certain to better understand the theoretical and empirical linkages between gender equality and macroeconomic policy in times of crisis.

Rania Antonopoulos is Senior Scholar and Director of the *Gender Equality and the Economy* program area of the Levy Economics Institute of Bard College, USA and co-director of the Global Network on Gender, Macroeconomics and International Economics (GEM-IWG).

Routledge frontiers of political economy

Gender Perspectives and Gender Impacts of the Global Economic Crisis

Edited by Rania Antonopoulos

Routledge
Taylor & Francis Group

LONDON AND NEW YORK

First published 2014
by Routledge
2 Park Square, Milton Park, Abingdon, Oxfordshire OX14 4RN

and by Routledge
711 Third Avenue, New York, NY 10017, USA

First issued in paperback 2016

Routledge is an imprint of the Taylor & Francis Group, an informa business

British Library Cataloguing in Publication Data
A catalogue record for this book is available from the British Library

Library of Congress Cataloging in Publication Data
Gender perspectives and gender impacts of the global economic crisis / edited by Rania Antonopoulos.
    pages cm. – (Routledge frontiers of political economy ; 180)
    1. Sex role and globalization. 2. Global Financial Crisis, 2008–2009.
    I. Antonopoulos, Rania, 1960– editor of compilation.
    HQ1075.G46456 2014
    305.3–dc23
                                                                2013025210

ISBN 13: 978-1-138-67445-5 (pbk)
ISBN 13: 978-0-415-65817-1 (hbk)

Typeset in Times
by Wearset Ltd, Boldon, Tyne and Wear

Contents

Figures

Tables

Contributors

Diana Alarcón is a senior economic affairs officer at UNDESA and contributor to its annual flagship publication *World Economic and Social Survey*. She holds a PhD in Economics from the University of California at Riverside and specializes in development economics.

Rania Antonopoulos is director of the Gender Equality and the Economy Program (GEEP) of the Levy Economics Institute of Bard College. Her recent research is on empirical applications of employment/job guarantee policies and on the poverty inducing effects of time deficits.

Christina Bodouroglou, previously with UNDESA, is currently an economist at UNCTAD. Her main areas of research include gender economics, food security, and sustainable development. She holds an MSc from SOAS, University of London, and a BA from the University of Cambridge.

Serkan Değirmenci is a research assistant at Istanbul Technical University (ITU), Faculty of Management and PhD candidate in Economics at Marmara University. He received his MA in Economics from ITU. His current research interests are supply- and demand-side analyses of labor markets.

Corina Rodriguez Enriquez is researcher at the National Council of Scientific and Technical Research (Conicet) and at the Interdisciplinary Centre for the Study of Public Policy (Ciepp) in Buenos Aires, Argentina. Her research centers on fiscal and social policy, care economy, and labor market issues.

Valeria Esquivel is Associate Professor of Economics at the Universidad Nacional de General Sarmiento, Argentina and Research Associate at the Levy Economics Institute. She has published extensively on time-use methods and on the care economy. Her current research focuses on macroeconomic policy and gender inequalities.

Jayati Ghosh is Professor of Economics at the Centre for Economic Studies and Planning at the Jawaharlal Nehru University in New Delhi, India. Her specialities include globalization, international finance, employment patterns in developing countries, and macroeconomic policy.

Indira Hirway is Director and Professor of Economics at the Centre for Development Alternatives (CFDA), India and Research Associate at the Levy Economics Institute. Major areas of her interest and published work are in development alternatives; poverty, employment, and labour market structures.

Sara Hsu has been an Assistant Professor of Economics at SUNY New Paltz in New York for two years. Her research interests include the Chinese economy, unseen financial flows, and financial crises. She earned her PhD from the University of Utah in 2006.

İpek İlkkaracan is Associate Professor of Economics at Istanbul Technical University, Faculty of Management and research associate at the Levy Economics Institute. Her current research entails macroeconomics of unemployment and wages, labor market inequalities, and work–family reconciliation policies.

Tamar Khitarishvili is a research scholar at the Levy Economics Institute of Bard College. Her research interests include gender economics, human capital and economic development, and the economics of transition countries. She received her PhD from the University of Minnesota.

Kijong Kim is a research scholar in the Gender Equality and the Economy program at the Levy Economics Institute. His research areas are feminist economics and active labor market policies and involve use of input–output analysis. He received his PhD from the University of Minnesota.

David Kucera received a PhD in Economics from the New School for Social Research and has been a research economist at the ILO since 2000. He is the author of *Gender, Growth and Trade* (2001, Routledge) and researches labor standards, informal employment, trade, and structural transformation.

Yan Liang is an associate professor at Willamette University. Her research expertise includes development financing, international finance, and the political economy of China. She earned a PhD in Economics from University of Missouri–Kansas City.

Tom Masterson is Director of Applied Micromodeling and a research scholar working primarily on the Levy Institute Measure of Economic Well-Being (LIMEW) within the Distribution of Income and Wealth program at Levy Economics Institute of Bard College.

Leanne Roncolato is an Economics PhD candidate at American University in Washington, DC. Her research interests are in gender, development, and labor. Leanne has had journal articles published on informal employment and trade liberalization in South Africa and India.

Erik von Uexkull holds an MA from Johns Hopkins School of Advanced International Studies. Previously with the ILO's Trade and Employment Programme, he is presently an economist in the World Bank's Africa region. He has published on trade, economic diversification, and development.

Ajit Zacharias is the director of the Distribution of Income and Wealth program at the Levy Economics Institute. His main areas of research are economic measurement and political economy. He received his PhD from the New School for Social Research.

Acknowledgments

The idea of putting this edited volume together dates back to initial discussions in 2009 held among colleagues who are members of the global capacity-development and knowledge-sharing network on Gender, Macroeconomics and International Economics (GEM-IWG), many of whom are also affiliated with the Levy Institute's Gender Equality and the Economy Program. The commitment to revamp this initiative and publish our collective research was renewed again in late 2011. In addition to feedback individual authors sought on earlier versions of their work, the chapters included here have received the benefit of comments provided by Nilüfer Çağatay, the co-director of GEM-IWG, Manuel Butch, Xiao-yuan Dong, Sara Hsu, Tamar Khitarishvili, Emel Memis and Ajit Zacharias. My deep appreciation must also be extended to Jonathan Hubschman, my colleague at the Levy Institute, for his substantive comments and overall support. To the authors I remain grateful for their contributions, camaraderie, and cooperation in carrying out the proposed revisions. Additionally, I must gratefully acknowledge the International Development Research Center of Canada (IDRC) and, especially, senior program specialist Francisco Cos-Montiel, whose support provided what was instrumental for the completion of this volume. Above all, I am indebted to Kate Lasko, whose able assistance in all matters, including editing, proofreading, and communicating with authors, was invaluable.

The Levy Economics Institute of Bard College

Founded in 1986, the Levy Economics Institute of Bard College is an autonomous nonprofit public policy research organization. It is nonpartisan, open to the examination of diverse points of view and dedicated to public service.

The Levy Institute believes in the potential for economic study to improve the human condition. Its purpose is to generate viable, effective public policy responses to important economic problems. It is concerned with issues that profoundly affect the quality of life in the USA, in other highly industrialized nations and in countries with developing economies.

The Levy Institute's present research programs include such issues as financial instability, economic growth and employment, international trade, problems associated with the distribution of income and wealth, the measurement of economic well-being, and gender equality, globalization and poverty.

The opinions expressed in this volume are those of the authors and do not necessarily represent those of the Levy Institute, its Board of Governors or the Trustees of Bard College.

Abbreviations and acronyms

ARRA	American Recovery and Reinvestment Act of 2009
ASEC	Annual Social and Economic Supplement of the Current Population Survey
BDS	Bono de Desarrollo Social (Social Development Allowance)
BEA	Bureau for Economic Analysis
BID	Banco Interamericano de Desarrollo (Inter-American Development Bank)
BIE	Banco de Información Económica (Economic Information Bank)
BLS	Bureau of Labor Statistics
CCT	conditional cash transfer
CDA	Child Development Associate
CEE/FSU	Central and Eastern Europe/Former Soviet Union
CFDA	Centre for Development Alternatives
CGE	computable general equilibrium
CGIAR	Consultative Group on International Agricultural Research
CIEPP	Centro Interdisciplinario para el Estudio de Políticas Públicas (Interdisciplinary Centre for the Study of Public Policies)
CIMMYT	International Centre for Maize and Wheat Improvement
CMIE	Centre for Monitoring Indian Economy
CONAMU	Comisión Nacional de las Mujeres (National Commission for Women)
CONICET	Consejo Nacional de Investigaciones Científicas y Técnicas (National Council for Scientific and Technical Research)
DESA	Department of Economic and Social Affairs
DWE	discouraged worker effect
EBRD	European Bank for Reconstruction and Development
ECLAC	Economic Commission for Latin America and the Caribbean
ECOSOC	Economic and Social Council
EG	employment guarantee
EU	European Union
FAO	Food and Agriculture Organization
FDI	foreign direct investment
FDIC	Federal Deposit Insurance Corporation

FFS	Farm Field Schools
FTE	full-time equivalent
GDP	gross domestic product
GEMLAC	Grupo Género y Macroeconómica de América Latina (Latin American Gender and Macroeconomic Group)
GHG	greenhouse gas
GIPS	Greece, Ireland, Portugal, and Spain
HDI	Human Development Index
HH	household
HIV/AIDS	human immunodeficiency virus/acquired immunodeficiency syndrome
HLFS	Household Labor Force Survey
IAASTD	International Assessment of Agricultural Science and Technology for Development
IFAD	International Fund for Agricultural Development
IFPRI	International Food Policy Research Institute
ILO	International Labour Organization
IMF	International Monetary Fund
INEGI	Instituto Nacional de Estadística y Geografía (National Institute of Statistics and Geography)
INMUJERES	Instituto Nacional de las Mujeres (National Women Institute)
I–O	input–output
IPCC	Intergovernmental Panel on Climate Change
IPM	integrated pest management
IRRI	International Rice Research Institute
LABORSTA	ILO Labour Statistics databases
MDG	Millennium Development Goal
NAFTA	North American Free Trade Agreement
NAHC	National Association for Home Care and Hospice
NAICS	North American Industry Classification System
NCEUS	National Commission for the Unorganized Sector (India)
NERICA	New Rice for Africa
NGO	nongovernmental organization
NHHCS	National Home Health Aide Survey
NREGA	National Rural Employment Guarantee Act
OECD	Organisation for Economic Co-operation and Development
PEMEX	Petróleos Mexicanos (Mexican Oil Company)
PET	Programa de Empleo Transitorio (Program of Short-term Employment)
PICE	Programa para Impulsar el Crecimiento y el Empleo (Program to Promote Growth and Employment)
PNRT	National Plan for Work Regularization
PSU	primary sampling unit
PW	public works
R&D	research and development

RBI	Reserve Bank of India
REPRO	Programa de Reconversión Productiva (Productive Recovery Program)
RMB	renminbi
SAIS	sustainable agricultural innovation system
SAMs	social accounting matrices
SAPs	structural adjustment programmes
SDA	Surat Diamond Association
SIPA	Sistema Integrado Previsional Argentino (Argentine Integrated Retirement System)
SOE	state-owned enterprise
SRI	System of Rice Intensification
TRIPS	Trade-Related Aspects of Intellectual Property Rights
UN	United Nations
UNAIDS	Joint United Nations Programme on HIV/AIDS
UNCTAD	United Nations Conference on Trade and Development
UNDESA	United Nations Department of Economic and Social Affairs
UNFPA	United Nations Population Fund
UNGS	Universidad Nacional de General Sarmiento (National University of General Sarmiento)
UN-INSTRAW	United Nations International Research and Training Institute for the Advancement of Women
US	United States
WDI	World Development Indicators
WTO	World Trade Organization

1 Introduction to the book

Rania Antonopoulos

1 Introduction

The context of this edited volume is the recent global economic crisis. More than five years have now elapsed since the subprime mortgage debacle first erupted in the United States. Within a few months, its global reach indicated that it could become the worst financial and economic crisis in recent history, earning it the name "Great Recession" – a term reminiscent of the Great Depression. Since 2008, over 38 million people have dropped out of the labor market due to discouraging prospects of finding paid work, with an additional 29 million still looking for a job. Last year alone, that is, in 2012, unemployment increased by an additional four million persons, three-quarters of them from regions other than the advanced economies – with marked effects in East Asia, South Asia, and Sub-Saharan Africa (ILO 2013a).

At the onset of the crisis, while the Northern countries tried to avoid a total financial meltdown, developing and emerging market countries had high hopes that they were sufficiently "decoupled" and expectations of remaining unscathed ran high. This did not come to pass. Instead, spillovers of the crisis hit the Global South hard through a severe international trade slowdown and outflows of finance capital. In 2009, for instance, while global output dropped by 2.2 percent, trade worldwide dropped by 12.2 percent (Kucera *et al.*, Chapter 5, this volume; WTO 2010). Exports in Asia declined by 18 percent; South and Central America by 23 percent; Africa and the Middle East by roughly 30 percent each; and in the Commonwealth of Independent States, countries located in the former Soviet Union region, by 36 percent (WTO 2012).

Yet, despite the crisis, and while admitting great variation in depth of impact and speed of recovery, there is evidence that developing countries have been emerging from the crisis much faster than their developed country counterparts (ILO 2013b). It is indeed telling that the 2013 Human Development Report of the United Nations is titled "The Rise of the South." Many reasons may account for that, but two of them must be noted. First, most developing countries were not directly implicated in investment products linked to bundled subprime mortgage derivatives, and therefore avoided the immediate wrath of the financial collapse. Second, many economies in the Global South, and the larger-scale emerging economies among them, were better prepared to weather the storm. High growth rates prior to the crisis – fueled for some of them, in part, by favorable commodity prices and current account surpluses together with favorable fiscal balance positions – provided the fiscal space to engage in typically Keynesian countercyclical policy. Political will, therefore, for an expanded role of a clearly interventionist state was backed by adequate domestic finances. With ample international reserves, and without fiscal constraints, China, for example, introduced a fiscal stimulus package of approximately US$600 billion, corresponding to 13 percent of its GDP. Other examples of fiscal interventions include Indonesia, Argentina, and Brazil, all of which intervened at a scale ranging from 4 to 10 percent of GDP (UNCTAD 2011).

In contrast, in the immediate aftermath of the crisis, developed countries were primarily concerned with the danger of a financial meltdown and focused their expansionary policy on saving financial institutions that were "too big to fail," providing liquidity infusion, mostly via bank bailouts including recapitalization. Fiscal expansion also took place in high-income developed countries, but from the outset, the scale of interventions did not match the challenge at hand. In the United States, for instance in 2009, the stimulus package introduced was US$787 billion, to be spent over the next two years, which represented a mere 2.6 percent of GDP per annum. Still, the worst was yet to come. Beginning in 2010, the policy climate changed dramatically. The genuine threat of a collapse of the real economy and massive increase of unemployment faded away. While recovery was still weak, concerns in the epicenter of the crisis, that is, in the United States and Europe, were suddenly shifted toward the impending dangers of fiscal deficits and debt accumulation. The fact that, in recessionary periods with declining output, tax revenue necessarily also declines was pushed aside. Even if government spending is maintained at pre-crisis levels, let alone expanded in a countercyclical manner as it should, budget deficits are set to rise and this necessarily results in higher levels of sovereign debt. There are two views as to the impact of rising debt to GDP. One view holds that when the government borrows and spends with the aim of introducing stimulus packages and reigniting the economy, employment and growth will take place and business activity will recover. As output and incomes increase, tax revenue will increase, too, and the need for government stimulus spending dissipates. This is what Keynes advocated more than 70 years ago.

The opposite view holds that high debt-to-GDP ratios slow down growth and prevent recovery from taking hold, mostly because when government borrows it "crowds out" private-sector borrowing, but also because as sovereign debts rise, borrowing in a country becomes more expensive, reflecting the higher risk premium imposed because financial markets start to doubt the ability of the country to pay back its creditors. For recovery, according to this view, prudence dictates that government spending, even in the midst of a crisis, observes a "sustainable" debt-to-GDP ratio. Hence, the prescription dictates spending cuts and stringent imposition of austerity measures. A little or a lot of pain now will pay off later. This view has been contested in the past with research-based evidence.

Przeworski and Vreeland (2000) have in fact shown that austerity measures imposed on countries with high deficit-to-GDP ratios lead to a decline in growth rates. The same controversy has erupted again now. In a recent study, Herndon *et al.* (2013) have decidedly refuted Reinhart and Rogoff's (2010) previously influential findings, especially in policy circles, that had claimed that median growth rates for countries are negatively affected with public debt over 90 percent of GDP.

But old habits and ideologies die hard. Post-2010, austerity won the day and procyclical trends soon settled in (Ortiz and Cummins 2012). Greece, Ireland, Portugal, Spain, and Italy provide examples of the disastrous effects of a "balance the budget at any cost" approach. Structural adjustment programs imposed in Latin America and Sub-Saharan Africa in the 1980s and 1990s have been revamped as the only pathway to (eventual) growth. Small government, privatization of public assets, cut-backs of social services, increasing taxes, and a fixation on export-led growth as panacea, which is based on promoting export competitiveness via severe labor rights curtailment and (private-sector) wage reductions, are already leading member countries of the European Union to a wage race to the bottom, double-digit unemployment rates, and deepening recessions of domestic economies. These economic downturns, besides devastating living standards and creating a double dip in some countries with a real danger of a "lost decade" in view (Latin American for some countries and Japanese-style for others) for Europe, in today's globalized context of finance, production, and trade, are also creating a dangerous overall global drag.

The fact that some countries in the Global South have taken the opposite view engenders optimism. The lesson learned – and discussed in different national contexts by the contributing chapters to this volume – is that a more balanced approach to development requires attention to at least three issues: rebalancing domestic production with an orientation toward domestic consumption, instead of exclusive dependence on export-led growth; sustained wage growth that reduces income inequalities, enhances consumption demand, and generates more employment; and gradual strengthening of social protection institutions that not only ensure access to basic necessities for all, but can also be scaled up for crisis mitigation and economic stabilization as needed. The closer a country is to meeting these criteria, the stronger the resilience it would show against the danger of collapse of its economy and living standards. This stands in sharp contrast to beliefs that still place all hopes in the ability of unfettered markets to self-regulate and produce optimal outcomes. The contributed essays highlight that developing countries' overall development strategies have differed substantially over the years; and that in turn influenced, on the one hand, the ways individual countries had been linked with the global economy prior to the crisis and, on the other, the policy options they chose to combat it, once the crisis erupted.

Developing countries also differ in terms of their gendered structures of production and distribution, which is the central theme of this book. Patterns of employment, ownership of productive assets, housework and other unpaid household production, and care responsibilities show very clearly that, in aggregate terms, women are at a disadvantage. It is precisely this recognition that has led governments around the world to national commitments and international agreements to implement policies that close the gender gap. While the crisis has been unfolding, there has been a grave concern that progress made in women's equality may come to a halt. The 2012 ILO report on Global Employment Trends for Women provides evidence that while gender gaps in unemployment, employment, insecure vulnerable employment, and labor force participation were closing during 2002–07, they have now stagnated and in many instances have shown reversals in the crisis period of 2008–12 (ILO, December 2012, p. 2).

Gender equality is about improving women's lives, but, as many of the chapters highlight, this is better achieved under macroeconomic circumstances and labor market conditions that promote the attainment of adequate living standards and decent work conditions for *all*. A closing of the gap between men and women is sometimes not cause for celebration, as this may reflect deteriorating trends for men instead of women's enhanced sharing of benefits. The wide range of gender differences and inequalities between men and women implies that the paths of transmission of the crisis may differ across gender lines (Antonopoulos 2009) and this cautions us to also avoid overgeneralizations as to whether women or men bear the larger share of the brunt of a crisis. Sometimes, gendered outcomes may be contradictory. An initially low female labor force participation may be rising, for example, but women may be accepting the most unprotected and precarious of jobs or may be working as (unpaid) contributing family workers. Statistics about the crisis also show that unemployment has hit men harder than women in some regions. Yet, if we do not have adequate information – and for the most part we do not – to understand how women and men cope differently when household incomes decline in terms of, for example, their paid *and* unpaid work responses, consumption patterns, health and educational outcomes of male and female children etc., it is hard to draw conclusions. To complicate matters further, women may be able to show more resilience. Past experience, such as the Asian crisis and the years immediately following the dissolution of the Soviet Union, has shown that in times of economic shocks, self-destructive behavior and suicide rates are more prevalent among men.

From the perspective of this book, it is important to understand the differentiated pathways through which men and women are affected by economic shocks and to implement mindful and responsive policy to these differences. In this regard, there are two key issues to keep in mind. The first concerns the fact that the immediate and second-round impacts of these shocks on men and women accumulate on top of pre-existing inequities, and hence are particularly harsh to those who were the least privileged, such as those least well-off households with women being at higher risk of poverty. Second, economic recovery from a crisis neither automatically translates to gains in decent job creation for women, nor ensures social provisioning that reduces their unpaid work burdens and allows for greater reconciliation of work and family life. Furthermore, it does not provide automatically an expanded social security and protection system – not independently of labor market and family ties conditionalities. Hence, it is important to understand not only the immediate crisis impacts and policy responses, but also the type of economic (re)orientation that is emerging in different national contexts since this will influence future developments that can have positive or negative effects for gender equality.

The above issues are addressed, to varying degrees, in the chapters that follow. Written with a wide range of audiences in mind, the book combines analytical description, methodological and technical analysis, and policy-oriented discussion. The focus of this compendium is primarily on developing countries, with the exception of two chapters, one dealing with the United States exclusively and the other with Europe's response to the crisis as part of a chapter, so as to provide a context for delving into global issues. The remaining contributions are devoted to China, India, South Africa, and Turkey as well as Latin America, exemplified by Mexico, Argentina, and Ecuador – three countries that represent a diversity of experiences in the region – and on transition economies countries.

The book's chapters concretize and contextualize the necessity for "gender perspectives" in analyzing the crisis in a variety of ways. Two essays provide syntheses of emerging regional employment trends, comparing them along the way with past experiences that include crisis mitigation interventions. Other chapters present research insights based on primary and secondary data that deepen our understanding of how the male and female content of employment in the various sectors of an economy influences gender-differentiated labor market outcomes in times of crisis. Beyond exploring the immediate gender-differentiated unemployment effects of the crisis, we also present findings from studies on women's decisions to look for paid work (or not) when incomes decline due to men's job losses. An additional theme deals with policies that aim at crisis mitigation via job creation. As direct job-creation government programs constitute a significant policy intervention in times of crisis, a theme highlighted by several authors in this book, an empirical study on this topic, from a gender perspective, is also included. The financial and economic crisis came at a time when a severe food crisis had already affected millions of people; thus, a chapter looking forward is also included on food security and environmental sustainability in a post-crisis environment.

Finally, across the board, the contributions in this volume allude to the fact that changes in both women's and men's world of work cannot be assessed without data on time allocation between paid and unpaid forms of labor activities. Incomes in times of crisis decline due to loss of paid work and, oftentimes, reduced wages. Public services and various in-kind and in-cash subsidies, which also contribute to the standard of living that households enjoy, increase or decrease depending on policy decisions. It has been argued convincingly in the past that when earned income and public-sector provisioning decline, women's time becomes severely strained in that they provide substitutes for market purchases by stressing their own time to fill in newly created task gaps. We therefore need to go beyond anecdotal evidence but rely more on small sample surveys of time-use allocation that can be of great value in this regard. Second, as this Introduction was written, many developed countries were still immersed in recession, while growth predictions for emerging economies were being downgraded.

The expectation is that policies to be undertaken from now and beyond will move the global economy and its people into a firm recovery era. But the current state of affairs in terms of revealed choices among policy options in Europe and the United States, still the key drivers for global growth, do not allow for much optimism. The opportunity may indeed be stronger than ever before for the Global South to fill in the policy vacuum.

2 About this book

The book opens with Jayati Ghosh's "Financial Crises and Their Gendered Employment Impact: Emerging Trends and Past Experiences." The chapter begins by showing that in recent decades, global labor markets have been increasingly characterized by part-time, informal, and self-employed work (i.e., less stable, more precarious employment). This trend has been particularly strong for women workers. Against this backdrop, the author reviews annual unemployment rates by sex and region and notes that while in some parts of the developing world women have been hit harder than men, there is a clear divide in that in developed countries the financial crisis and its aftermath so far have primarily affected male-dominated sectors. Consequently, unemployment rates for men exceeded those of women in developed countries in 2010. Moreover, it is very likely that ongoing austerity policies will soon impact sectors in which women workers are dominant and increase unemployment for women as well as for men. In contrast, unemployment rates for men and women in developing countries have improved since 2010, but lower unemployment rates for women in some regions do not imply that the impacts of the financial crisis have been less severe for women: female workers have also experienced wage cuts, reductions in hours, reduced progress in closing gender gaps, and increased burdens of unpaid work. Drawing on the experience of the Asian crisis of 1997–98, we are reminded that it produced deterioration in the level of full-time employment for women and an increase in the gender wage gap. Furthermore, employment impacts during the recovery phase of the Asian crisis were the result of policy choices that depressed domestic consumption and investment in favor of protecting exchange rates to support an export-led recovery. The author warns that this may be the foreshadowing of things to come in the European context, because, as many of the countries in the region use the same currency, internal devaluation will mean that wages will be decimated, which in turn will reinforce already depressed levels of consumption demand. Ghosh next evaluates the results of fiscal policy responses to the 2008 crisis, observing that most policy responses have failed to deliver adequate employment growth, and, in particular, have undercut the economic position of women engaged in paid and unpaid work. The chapter then concludes with examples of gender-sensitive economic policies implemented in Argentina and Sweden. These governments incorporated targeted policies (e.g., expanded social protection spending, job creation, collective labor agreements, etc.) to reduce gender disparities in labor markets as part of their overall macroeconomic recovery strategy. Such examples are crucial: they prove that well-integrated gender-sensitive policy responses can be enacted even in times of crisis and that, in fact, they are an effective means to reduce the impacts of financial crises while promoting economic recovery and gender equality simultaneously.

Chapter 3, "Investing in Care in the Midst of a Crisis: A Strategy for Effective and Equitable Job Creation in the United States," co-authored by Rania Antonopoulos, Kijong Kim, Tom Masterson, and Ajit Zacharias, expands on the last idea of the previous chapter and reaffirms that, in fact, gender awareness in crisis remediation interventions can reinforce positive outcomes. The authors of the chapter, which was written in 2010, advocated through their research an increase of a previously introduced fiscal stimulus by the Obama Administration through the American Recovery and Reinvestment Act – but this time, they proposed that directing funds to social service provisioning should be given priority as an effective and equitable means to job creation in the United States. According to the authors, in times of crisis when the private sector sheds jobs, the government ought indeed to provide job-creation programs. As a first criterion, so that public funds are not wasted, the identification of meaningful work projects that benefit society must be observed. A second criterion that must be met is that the selected public works be labor intensive, i.e., have the potential for as massive a public job creation as possible. Finally, such programs ought to be equitable, ensuring that all groups that face greater vulnerability, women included, have access to job opportunities. Traditionally, the focus of the majority of public works concentrates on physical infrastructure. The authors posit that all too often a set of alternative work projects remains invisible: unpaid care provisioning, work that women often perform under unpaid conditions for their households and communities, can become regularized paid work. With this idea at hand, they set out to simulate an investment of US$50 billion on projects that enhance social care and compare the results with a commensurate investment aimed at infrastructure (construction). A macro–micro simulation model is developed to account for spillover effects of inter-industry supply–demand linkages, through which new jobs in a variety of occupations are created throughout the economy. The model then assigns the jobs to individuals among the unemployed with relevant skills and other characteristics pertinent to employment by a series of statistical propensity score matching and imputation, using the annual social and economic supplement of the Current Population Survey. The method enables the authors to assess not only aggregate but also distributional impacts of the expansion of social care services. Their findings provide evidence that social care investment produces more than twice the number of jobs as infrastructure spending, and almost one-and-a-half times the number of jobs that green energy generates. This type of stimulus investment (as compared to infrastructure and green energy projects) is particularly beneficial for women, as new jobs are concentrated in the female-intensive sectors of teaching, child care, and home health care and reach individuals who are members of low-income households and people with lower levels of educational attainment. Further, expanding social sector services also creates more jobs that require some college education and are geared toward the middle- and top-income groups. While Obama's proposals were part of the solution to mitigating double-digit unemployment, he seems to have overlooked the relative job creation effects of comparable investments in various sectors of the US economy. The authors note that the government had allocated vast amounts of resources to rescuing Wall Street and the banks – who were the main beneficiaries during times of economic prosperity – rather than low-income households, who continue to lose their jobs and houses. They therefore conclude by recommending a second stimulus package, one aimed at state and local governments that currently lack the resources to deliver increased levels of social care. Their recommendation remains valid to date. Despite recent progress made in growth recovery and job creation in the United States, with 11.6 million unemployed today as compared to 7.6 million back in December 2007, just months before the subprime mortgage debacle engulfed the world, much remains to be done.

Chapter 4, Valeria Esquivel and Corina Rodríguez Enríquez's "Macroeconomic Policies and Gender Equality in Latin America: Assessing the Gender Impact of the Global Economic Crisis," returns to the topic of crisis responses in the context of macroeconomic trajectories and compares three national cases from the region, namely, Mexico, Argentina, and Ecuador. The specific countries are chosen as they are considered to represent well the variation of effects that the global economic crisis has had in Latin America. The three countries are quite different regarding their initial pre-crisis positions and the policy space they occupied, in two respects. First, in the past they have followed different approaches to their macroeconomic policy, which has shaped their pre-crisis economic paths in distinct ways. Second, the crisis responses that each country deemed as most appropriate and the ability to implement them also differed. Mexico, whose government has adopted orthodox economic policies over the last two decades, was the most severely hit economy in the region due to the combined effect of its links to the United States and its oil and manufacturing export orientation. The emphasis on "fiscal responsibility" (and the belief in the market) prevented the Mexican government from intervening expeditiously and more forcefully in the economy – even though it had the financial resources and bureaucracy to do so. The results in terms of growth and employment (worse than the worst scenario forecast at the beginning of 2009) have proven that the policy responses to crisis have been weak and transitory relative to the shock. Argentina, on the other hand, has explicitly departed from the neoliberal policy since 2002, adjusting its exchange rate and fiscal policies and therefore granting the state an interventionist role in the economy. The fiscal and external space gained in previous years allowed the government to implement countercyclical policies and sustain already existing social and labor market policies without much external support. Strong institutions made it possible for the government to implement the initiatives in a timely fashion. Finally, Ecuador was impacted by the crisis due to its heavy dependence on exports (with an important share of oil exports) and remittances. On top of this, Ecuador's left-of-center government had to deal with a dollarized economy (the most "orthodox" monetary framework). In a paradoxical mix of political transformation, weak institutional fabric, and an inherited dollarized economy, Ecuador showed the tensions between political discourse and space to exercise an effective fiscal and monetary policy in a small and open economy. The review of these experiences shows that when governments did not entrust recovery to market forces, but instead implemented policy initiatives that prioritized employment generation and sustained household income, there was a greater potential to favor gender equality in macroeconomic policy. For this potential to be realized, however, it is required that gender considerations are explicitly introduced in the policy agenda. A striking result of this chapter's review is that the countercyclical policy packages in all three countries studied have had no explicit consideration of the gender dimensions involved.

The next three chapters, Chapters 5, 6, and 7, concentrate on the impacts of trade on employment. As indicated earlier in the book, it is well established that most developing countries had limited exposure to the crisis through financial channels. But the global crisis of 2008–09 was unprecedented in the role that trade played as a transmission channel, a result of what has been referred to as the "Great Trade Collapse."

Chapter 5, "Trade Contraction in India and South Africa during the Global Crisis: Examining Gender and Skill Biases in Job Loss," is co-authored by David Kucera, Leanne Roncolato, and Erik von Uexkull. The authors estimate empirically the effects of trade contraction on employment in India and South Africa, two of the major emerging economies of the South. In particular, using social accounting matrices (SAMs) in a Leontief multiplier model, they focus on declining exports from India and South Africa to the European Union and United States. The motivation for such a study, according to the authors, is partly based on the fact that developing a detailed understanding – beyond aggregates – of how specific industries and different types of workers may be affected by trade contraction can usefully inform government responses to crisis. As such, this chapter evaluates employment impacts at both aggregate and industry levels, with breakdowns by skills and – central to this volume – gender. Their empirical results are discussed with reference to actual changes in employment in the two countries during the crisis, along with the governments' crisis responses. Regarding gender-differentiated effects, this analysis does not explore the potentially biased responses of employers during the economic crisis, i.e., the buffer versus substitution hypotheses. Nor does it examine the labor supply response of men and women, i.e., the added worker or discouraged worker effect, a topic that is explored later in this volume. Rather, this analysis addresses the extent to which patterns of gender segregation among industries may lead to disproportionate employment losses for men or women as a result of the trade collapse. The chapter finds that declining exports to the European Union and United States during the "Great Trade Collapse" had a substantial negative effect on employment in India and particularly so in South Africa. Even though the shock originated in the tradable goods sector, a large share of total estimated employment declines resulted from ripple effects in non-tradable industries. A large share of estimated employment declines is income-induced, which has an important policy implication: stabilizing household incomes, in addition to its social benefits, can be an effective means of reducing job loss. From a gender perspective, Kucera *et al.* find that for India, there was essentially no gender or skills bias in employment resulting from trade contraction in the crisis. For South Africa, there was somewhat of a gender bias, but it was in favor of women workers and there was a stronger bias against less-educated workers. The result of gender bias in favor of women workers during the crisis is usefully set against a prior study's findings of gender bias against women workers during the period of trade liberalization from 1993 to 2006 (Kucera and Roncolato 2011). An important determinant of the gender bias against women workers prior to the crisis was the large number of jobs lost in the clothing industry as a result of trade expansion with developing countries combined with the high share of women workers in the industry. This same study also found no skills bias against less-educated workers during the period of trade liberalization prior to the crisis. In this sense, both the gender and skills biases observed in South Africa as a result of the 2008–09 trade contraction represent breaks from previous trends. The chapter concludes with a policy discussion on export-led growth. The global crisis has revealed with ample clarity that greater trade openness can be a source of vulnerability in a volatile global economy. This presents a significant challenge to policy-makers and emphasizes the importance of governments' ability to deliver timely and effective responses to external shocks in open economies.

In Chapter 6, "Impacts of Financial Crisis and Post-Crisis Policies on China: A Gendered Analysis," Yan Liang and Sara Hsu turn our attention to trade and employment impacts in China, another emerging economy whose role in terms of size and economic evolution has been expanding globally. The authors begin with a general overview of the impacts of the financial crisis on Asian economies and highlight some studies that examine the experience of other Asian countries that share similar levels of economic openness and development with China. Following that, they describe in some detail the employment patterns of women in China prior to the crisis, ranging from labor force participation and sectoral concentration to their regional location, migration, and access to social security. Having discussed China's role in global trade and production as well as the impacts of the global crisis on its export production, Liang and Hsu proceed to investigate the impacts of the crisis on female workers, especially in the export production sector. Finally, the authors critically assess the gendered impacts of the Chinese government's policies that were implemented both to stem the crisis and to reach long-term development goals. Through descriptive statistics, making use of national sources and International Labour Organization regional surveys, Liang and Hsu find that there existed unequal and biased employment and social protection policies against migrant workers even prior to the crisis. As a result, the crisis has had a significant negative impact on women workers who were disproportionally concentrated in the export production sector as migrant workers. In addition, they find evidence suggesting that the crisis and the subsequent income losses heightened the burden of unpaid, care, and household production work that was disproportionally shouldered by women. Regarding policies, while the stimulus package that sought to counter the worst effects of the crisis can be viewed as pro-male in terms of job creation, other aspects of the package, such as extension of social benefits and subsidization of basic goods, benefit women more significantly as compared to men. Liang and Hsu conclude with a section that discusses long-term impacts of the crisis in general, and for women in particular, in the context of the latest 12th Five-Year Plan. The government's plan seeks to redress economic inequalities resulting from the economy's orientation toward exports and to enhance domestic demand in inland areas. This excites optimism, as proposed improvements and progressive expansion in the universal pension system, unemployment benefits, and welfare systems will undoubtedly also positively impact women's economic conditions and living standards. Currently, there is mixed evidence as to whether the Chinese government will successfully move onto a growth path along a different development trajectory that balances reliance on exports with strengthening of domestic demand. Nonetheless, the recent financial and economic crisis has provided ample evidence that gender equality and sustainable growth require a fundamental overhaul of China's growth model.

Next, we turn to Chapter 7, "Has India Learned Any Lessons from the Global Crisis? The Case of a Less Well-Known but Most Globalized Industry from a Gender Perspective." Indira Hirway's contribution presents the findings of a case study on the impact of the global crisis on one of the most globalized sectors of the Indian economy, the diamond cutting and polishing industry. In order to gain a better understanding of the gender dimension of the impact, it focuses on the impact of the crisis on small producers and informal workers as well as on women homemakers. The chapter also provides evidence on the status of the sector and its workers two years after the crisis to determine whether any lessons have been learned from it. For this study, original data was collected through a quick survey that was conducted in 2009 to understand the impact of the global crisis on the diamond industry, its workers, and women employed in the industry. This was backed by in-depth discussions with concerned industry leaders, producers, and exporters; concerned policy-makers and government officials; and prominent labor leaders. Surat, the most prominent diamond industry center, was selected for the in-depth study. A sample of migrant workers who returned to their native villages during the crisis was also selected for the study. A quick review of the industry and workers in Surat was also done two years after this first survey to determine the status of the workers and small producers in the industry in 2011. The first study showed that the global crisis impacted all dimensions of diamond workers' employment, reducing their incomes by almost half. Their coping strategies adversely affected not only their levels of living but also their children's education. The conditions for the returned migrants were even worse. Being thrown back to the place they had left to escape poverty and unemployment a few years before was both depressing and frustrating for them. While unemployment has affected men quite severely, the study shows that women have also emerged as shock absorbers of the crisis. Women have suffered as wage earners, as self-employed individuals, and as homemakers. However, no policy has been designed to bail women out of the crisis. The crisis has laid bare a number of weak points of India's trade and industrial policy as well as its lack of protection for workers. In the context of the crisis, this study has opened up space for specific recommendations for the industry and its workers, and a special bailout package has been advocated for women – as wage earners, small producers, and as unpaid female workers engaged in household services. Since the crisis was short-lived, the industry jumped back to almost the same position in 2011 as it was in before the crisis. In fact, the industry did learn some lessons for reducing risks in terms of (1) diversifying export markets and developing domestic markets and (2) moving upward in the value chain by manufacturing diamond ornaments in the country. However, Hirway concludes that almost no lessons have been learned for protecting workers and small producers as well as protecting women. If a crisis were to occur again, workers and women would go through the same painful experiences.

Chapters 8 and 9 explore an employment-related issue whose focus is on the behavior – or the reaction – of women (and men) who were previously outside the labor market in the face of crisis-induced loss of income in the household. For example, do women (and previously "inactive" men) enter the labor market looking for paid work as a distress coping strategy so as to replace the income loss their households experience when a previously employed member experiences a job loss? Or do they, alternatively, abstain from labor market participation because the prevailing crisis conditions discourage them? The added-versus-discouraged worker effect controversy dates back to the Great Depression of 1929, and although data requirements are challenging, the authors below explore the issue in innovative ways and produce very interesting insights.

In Chapter 8, "The Economic Crisis of 2008 and the Added Worker Effect in Transition Countries," Tamar Khitarishvili indicates from the outset that following the financial crisis of 2008, transition countries experienced an increase in female labor force participation rates and a decrease in male labor force participation rates in part because male-dominated sectors were hit the hardest. These developments have prompted many to argue that women have been spared the full-blown effects of the crisis. In this chapter, Khitarishvili critically evaluates this claim by investigating the extent to which the increase in the female labor force participation rate may have reflected a distress labor-supply response to the crisis via the added worker effect, broadly defined as an increase in labor supply due to a household income shock. To answer this question, the author uses data for 28 transition countries from the 2010 Life in Transition Survey conducted by the European Bank for Reconstruction and Development. The survey contains observations on 32,084 households and includes a range of demographic and socioeconomic characteristics, and, pertinent to this analysis, it contains an economic crisis module. In this investigation, the dependent variable is the labor force participation status of an individual and the explanatory variable that represents the household income shock is the loss of another household member's job. A number of other individual and household-level variables are also used in the estimation, and to account for macroeconomic heterogeneity among countries included in the sample, the author supplements these variables with unemployment rates, per capita GDP, and differences in the structure of each economy proxied by the shares of services, industry, government, and exports in GDP. The author finds the presence of the female added worker effect in the context of both spousal relationships and in the broader household setup, highlighting the importance of the extended household structure in the region. The effect is driven by married 45- to 54-year-old women with no children in the household and is especially pronounced in vulnerable households. This effect is the strongest among the region's middle-income countries, potentially due the presence of a well-developed social insurance system among the more affluent transition countries and by the low odds of finding a job in the poorer countries of the region. Among men, the evidence points to a negative relationship between labor force participation and household-specific income shocks. This result is arguably due to the negative correlation in the labor force status of men because they tend to concentrate in the industries that experienced greatest job losses during this crisis. Unlike the differences in the response to household-specific income shocks, the labor-supply response to a weaker macroeconomic environment is negative for both men and women – hinting at the presence of the "discouraged worker" effect, which cuts across gender lines. Khitarishvili concludes that for women, the distress labor-supply response in the form of the added worker effect was indeed present, counteracting the discouraged worker effect and contributing to the rise in their labor force participation rate. The decrease in men's labor force participation, on the other hand, was likely a combined result of the initial sectoral contraction and the subsequent impact of the discouraged worker effect. The findings highlight the presence of heterogeneity in the way in which household-specific shocks, as opposed to economy-wide conditions, affect both female and male labor force participation rates.

Serkan Değirmenci and İpek İlkkaracan explore the same subject matter in the context of Turkey in their contribution, titled "Economic Crises and the Added Worker Effect in the Turkish Labor Market" (Chapter 9). Given the phenomenally low female labor force participation rate in Turkey (one of the lowest in the world) and the limited scope of the unemployment insurance scheme, the authors propose that there appears to be ample room for a female added worker as a household strategy against unemployment shocks during economic crises. Using micro data from household labor force surveys for the 2004–10 period, the authors examine the extent to which an unemployment shock to the primary male earner instigates female members of the household to move from non-participant status to labor market participation. Rather than simply basing the analysis on a static association between women's observed participation status and men's observed unemployment status in the survey period, the chapter explores whether there is a dynamic relationship between transitions of women and men across labor market states. To do this, Değirmenci and İlkkaracan make use of a question introduced to the Household Labor Force Survey in 2004 on previous year's labor market status. This allows the authors to explore transitions by female members of households from non-participant in the previous year to participant status in the current year in response to male members making a transition from employed in the previous period to unemployed in the current period. They explore whether and to what extent primary male earners moving from employed to unemployed status determines the probability of married or single female full-time homemakers entering the labor market. The authors estimate the marginal effect of the unemployment shock on labor market transition probability for the overall sample as well as for different groups of women. Hence, they are able to demonstrate that the added worker effect varies widely depending on particular characteristics of the woman, such as her education level, age, urban/rural residence, or marital and parental status. Değirmenci and İlkkaracan find that at the micro level, an unemployment shock to the household increases the probability of a female homemaker entering the labor market, but the marginal effects vary substantially across different groups of women by age, rural/urban residence, and education. For instance, a household unemployment shock increases the probability that a university graduate homemaker in the 20–45 age group will enter the labor market by as much as 34 percent and for a high school graduate 17 percent, while for her counterpart with a secondary education, the marginal effect is only 7 percent. At the same time, Değirmenci and İlkkaracan estimate that of the total (weighted) number of female added workers in the crisis years, only roughly 9 percent of the homemakers in households experiencing an unemployment shock enter the labor market. This corresponds to a relatively small share, which the authors attribute to the deeply embedded structural constraints against female labor force participation in Turkey.

The book concludes with Chapter 10, "Agricultural Innovation for Food Security and Environmental Sustainability in the Context of the Recent Economic Crisis: Why a Gender Perspective?," a forward-looking essay that draws the reader's attention to the food crisis. Diana Alarcón and Christina Bodouroglou begin by reminding us that living standards were already severely affected by the 2007–08 world food-price crisis and that the ensuing economic crisis added to the already limited purchasing power of swathes of the population in many developing countries, exacerbating poverty and food insecurity. Surging international food prices saw the number of undernourished people reach an unprecedented high, surpassing one billion in 2009. In unraveling the causes of soaring food prices, Alarcón and Bodouroglou reveal deep structural problems in the global food system, which will have to be transformed in order to double food production by mid-century to feed a forecasted future population of nine billion people. With current agricultural technology, practices, and land-use patterns, this cannot be achieved without further contributing to greenhouse gas emissions, land degradation, biodiversity loss, and water scarcity and pollution. But the consequent environmental damage will, in turn, undermine long-term food productivity and sustainability. There is therefore, the authors propose, an urgent need for rapid diffusion of sustainable agricultural technology and practices in order to combat hunger and malnutrition in a sustainable manner. In this endeavor, there is growing consensus over the centrality of small-scale farmers, a large share of whom are women. This stems from the reality that 75–90 percent of staple foods are produced and consumed locally. In addition, women comprise, on average, over 40 percent of the agricultural labor force and are the ones who are chiefly responsible for food processing and preparation in developing countries. Nevertheless, women often face discrimination in their access to agricultural land, credit, inputs, education and extension services, markets, and technology. Improving women's relative access to productive resources and technological opportunities could yield important benefits in terms of increased food productivity and output and reduced poverty and hunger. Alarcón and Bodouroglou argue that meeting the food security challenge while protecting the environment will require explicit national policies to build sustainable agricultural innovation systems, drafted through a gender-sensitive lens. This would entail the establishment of an integrated national framework for sustainable natural resource management, alongside the harnessing of the technology and innovation needed to increase the productivity, profitability, resilience, and climate change mitigation potential of rural production systems. The authors suggest that we already know what is needed. A wide range of sustainable agricultural technology options (including traditional knowledge and practices, enhanced seed varieties of the type emerging from the green revolution, and modern technologies) as well as supporting services (including access to rural infrastructure, inputs, finance, insurance, and training) can and should be made available to small-scale farm holders, with a particular emphasis on meeting the needs of female farmers. But improving women's access to productive resources, technologies, and markets will require gender-informed analysis in policy-making and targeted support. This will necessitate not only technocratic economic and technological solutions, but also the combating of gender bias in rural contexts through changes in legislation, policies, and institutions – including changes in deeply rooted patriarchal attitudes and norms.

In addition to policy action taken at the national level, the international community also has much to contribute to a global agenda for food security and environmental sustainability. Notably, Alarcón and Bodouroglou, in their concluding remarks, put forward six specific recommendations that require that international agreements be reached: (1) reform agricultural subsidies (including for biofuels), (2) increase investment in agricultural R&D, (3) provide payments for environmental services to small farm holders in developing countries, (4) re-examine non-tariff barriers to food trade, (5) effectively regulate commodity futures markets, and (6) call upon donors to deliver on financial pledges.

The chapters in this book present ideas, findings, and policy recommendations about the global onslaught of the financial crisis of 2007, drawn from the specific theoretical predilections and gender perspectives of its authors. While many readers may not agree with all of them, I hope that they help place gender equality center stage in the policy agenda.

References

Antonopoulos, R. (2009) "The current economic and financial crisis: a gender perspective," United Nations Development Programme, Gender Team, Working Paper 562, Levy Economics Institute.

Herndon T., Ash, M., and Pollin, R. (2013) "Does high public debt consistently stifle economic growth? A critique of Reinhart and Rogoff," Working Paper No. 322, Political Economy Research Institute, University of Massachusetts, Amherst.

ILO (International Labour Organization) (2013a) *Global Employment Trends 2013: recovering from a second jobs dip*, Geneva: ILO.

ILO (2013b) *World of Work Report 2013: repairing the economic and social fabric*, Geneva: ILO.

Kucera, D. and Roncolato, L. (2011) "Trade liberalization, employment and inequality in India and South Africa," *International Labour Review*, 150: 1–41.

Kucera, D., Roncolato, L., and von Uexkull, E. (2013) "Trade contraction in India and South Africa during the global crisis: examining gender and skill biases in job loss," in R. Antonopoulos (ed.), *Gender Perspectives on the Global Economic Crisis*, Abingdon: Routledge. This volume.

Ortiz, I. and Cummins, M. (2012) *A Recovery for All: rethinking socio-economic policies for children and poor households*, New York: UNICEF.

Przeworski, A. and Vreeland, J.R. (2000) "The effect of IMF programs on economic growth," *Journal of Development Economics*, 62: 385–421

Reinhart, C.M. and Rogoff, K.S. (2010) "Growth in a time of debt," *American Economic Review*, 100: 573–8.

UNCTAD (United Nations Conference on Trade and Development) (2011) *Trade and Development Report*, New York: United Nations.

World Bank (2010) *Global Economic Prospects 2010: crisis, finance, and growth*, Washington, DC: World Bank.

WTO (World Trade Organization) (2010, 2012) *World Trade Report*, Geneva: World Trade Organization.

2 Financial crises and their gendered employment impact

Emerging trends and past experiences

*Jayati Ghosh**

1 Changes in global labor markets in the current global crisis

Well before the financial implosion of 2008, the impact of financial instability was reflected in increased volatility of global commodity prices, which increased massively in the previous two years to generate a world food crisis (Ghosh 2009a).[1] While this was experienced widely, it obviously had particularly adverse effects on the nutrition of women and girls in developing countries. But when the crisis erupted, the real economic impacts of the crisis were felt not only in drastic falls in output in some countries, but also most quickly in employment (ILO 2009), and the effects of the crisis were widespread and serious. Employment declined sharply in export-oriented sectors, creating negative multiplier effects across other sectors. In addition, the effects on social sectors and on human development conditions, in general, were marked (Chhibber *et al.* 2009; Green *et al.* 2010), largely due to the fiscal responses to the crisis, which in many countries resulted in cutbacks in social spending (Ortiz *et al.* 2011). As economies slowed down, people faced open or disguised unemployment, loss of livelihood, and deteriorating living conditions. In the temporary recovery, even though output rebounded in most regions, employment expansion has remained sluggish and labor market conditions in most countries continue to remain adverse for workers.

Of course, it is well known that over the standard business cycle, as well as in past experiences of financial crises, employment tends to recover more slowly and to a lesser extent than output (Reinhart and Rogoff 2008). To that extent, the delayed recovery of employment would seem to be normal and not cause for excessive concern. But this current crisis has followed a boom in which, despite rapid increases in economic activity, employment – especially in the formal sector – had simply not kept pace with either output expansion or the requirements of the expanding labor force in most countries. So labor markets across the world were increasingly characterized by more casual non-formal contracts and the growth of precarious forms of self-employment rather than "decent work." In other words, the

* This chapter draws from a report prepared by the author for UN-Women, titled "Economic Crises and Women's Work: Exploring Progressive Strategies in a Rapidly Changing Global Environment," which was originally issued in January 2013.

boom did not generate enough decent work, yet the crisis has already had severe effects in reducing even those inadequate levels of employment across the world.

While the effects of the crisis on paid employment tend to be more noticeable, the impact of the crisis on unpaid work remains underrecognized in official discussions (both national and international). Such work, which still tends to be performed largely by women in most societies, is usually a critical part of the economic activity undertaken in all countries, and especially in developing ones. It is very common for crisis-adjustment measures to involve adding to such burdens as a means of ensuring some economic stabilization even on segments of the population at lower levels of household income. This is especially evident through the effects of fiscal policies that involve reductions in public provision of amenities and social services.

As Table 2.1 indicates, the recent crisis has been somewhat different from standard predictions in terms of overall employment results. Open unemployment rates did indeed increase globally and in all the regions described in the table. And for the world as a whole, female open unemployment rates were generally higher than male rates, although not significantly more so. However, there are some significant regional and other variations in this regard – open

Table 2.1 Unemployment rates by region and sex

		2000	2005	2006	2007	2008	2009	2010
World	Males	6.1	5.8	5.6	5.2	5.4	6	5.8
	Females	6.6	6.6	6.2	5.8	5.9	6.4	6.5
Developed economies and EU	Males	6.3	6.6	6.1	5.5	6	8.7	9.1
	Females	7.3	6.7	6.1	6.2	7.9	8.4	7.9
Central and Southeast Europe and CIS	Males	10.6	9.4	9.2	8.6	8.6	10.6	9.8
	Females	9	8.8	8	8.1	9.7	9.2	8.2
East Asia	Males	4.9	4.6	4.5	4.3	4.8	4.9	4.7
	Females	3.8	3.4	3.3	3.1	3.6	3.6	3.5
Southeast Asia and Pacific	Males	5.1	6	5.7	5.3	5.2	5.2	4.5
	Females	4.9	7	6.6	5.8	5.5	5.2	5.2
South Asia	Males	4.4	4.2	4.1	3.6	3.5	3.7	3.5
	Females	4.6	5.7	4.4	4.3	4.2	4.4	5
Latin America and Caribbean	Males	7.3	6.4	6.1	5.6	5.3	6.4	5.9
	Females	10.8	10.1	9.8	9	8.6	9.6	9.1
Middle East	Males	8.8	9.3	9	8.4	8.6	8.2	8.1
	Females	18.9	19.3	19.3	18.6	18.9	18.7	18.5
North Africa	Males	11.5	9	8.2	8.1	7.5	7.3	7.4
	Females	20.8	19.6	18	16.1	16	16.5	16.4
Sub-Saharan Africa	Males	8.5	7.8	7.7	7.6	7.6	7.7	7.7
	Females	10	9	8.9	8.8	8.8	8.7	8.7

Source: ILO, Global Employment Trends 2012 (ILO 2012b, p. 92, Appendix Table A2).

unemployment rates did not increase for women in the Middle East, and showed relatively minor increases in East Asia and Latin America. It is also important to see these patterns in the broader and more long-term context of much greater involvement of women in what the International Labour Organization (ILO) has termed "vulnerable employment" – an overwhelming proportion of women workers in developing countries as well as the majority in much of the developed world is involved in such work (ILO 2011).

For developed countries as a whole, including all of the European Union, female unemployment rates were higher than male rates until 2008, but in the course of the crisis male rates rose faster, such that they became and have remained higher. The difference was particularly marked in 2010: the male unemployment rate increased significantly, whereas the female rate actually declined slightly compared to the previous year, although it was still much higher than before. In two regions (Central and Southeastern Europe and East Asia) male unemployment rates were higher than female rates throughout, while in some other regions (Southeast and South Asia as well as Sub-Saharan Africa) the rates were broadly similar. However, Latin America and the Caribbean, the Middle East, and North Africa all exhibit much higher rates of open unemployment for women than for men – and these regions showed a slight decrease (*not* the expected increase) after the global crisis.

The previous analysis already suggests that more recent monthly trends in unemployment rates exhibited in Figure 2.1 (which shows the change in the unemployment rate in that month compared to the same month in the previous year) should be treated with some caution: first, because they refer only to the sample of countries for which such data are available; and second, because they incorporate large regional and national variations within each group. Even so, they point to slightly different patterns from those indicated by the annual trends

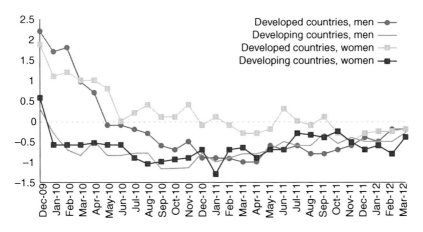

Figure 2.1 Recent monthly changes in unemployment rates by sex (source: ILO, *Global Short-Term Trends in Labor Markets*, various issues).

described in Table 2.1. In the more recent period, while male unemployment rates were higher to start with in the developed countries, they have come down faster than female rates, and the rates of change have stayed negative in all months, suggesting an improvement in employment conditions. However, for women in developed countries, the rates of change have remained positive or near zero for much of the recent period, so that unemployment conditions continued to deteriorate well into the middle of 2011. For developing countries as a group, unemployment rates have continued to improve for both men and women from January 2010.

This reflects the fact that the negative consequences of recessions in developed countries may impact overall more strongly on male than on female employment levels, especially in cyclically dependent sectors such as manufacturing and construction. In advanced countries, men are often employed in cyclically unstable industries or industries in long-term decline, while women tend to be employed in more stable service industries (Singh and Zammit 2000).

This confirms some arguments about the possible gender-differentiated impact of a crisis on employment, indicating the particular nature of the recent crisis in advanced economies, which has affected first of all financial activity, and then manufacturing and construction – all economic activities in which male workers are predominantly employed. The crisis has only more recently been transmitted to the other service activities in which most women in the developed world are employed. Now that fiscal austerity has become the most evident manifestation of the policy response to the crisis in many developed and some developing countries, it is likely that public employment will be adversely affected, and this too is likely to have direct implications for female jobs.

Ortiz and Cummins (2012) have noted that thus far in different parts of the world there have been broadly two phases of response to the crisis: an initial reaction to the crisis in 2008–09 during which the focus was on "promoting employment," and the subsequent phase from 2010 to the present, which they describe as "abandoning labour." This has been particularly evident in terms of fiscal strategy, with fiscal expansion dominating in the first phase and contraction in the second.

In any case, the evidence provided here does not necessarily indicate that labor market conditions for women have been better than for men, or that women workers have not been affected as much in the recent global crisis. Table 2.2 describes the movement of employment rates (or the ratio of workers to total population of working age) by region and sex. It is evident that in the world as a whole and in every single region, women have lower recorded employment rates than men (and, as noted earlier, even this is more likely to be in vulnerable forms of employment). This should not be mistaken for actual lack of involvement in economic activity, since most women are engaged in some and usually substantial amounts of unpaid labor, particularly in social reproduction and the care economy but also in other productive activities. However, it does give some indication of the fact that lower proportions of women are actually recognized as working. Furthermore, in most regions (with the exception of the Middle East and North Africa, which had extremely low female employment rates) these already low employment rates of women have been falling further – though it is not clear the extent to which this can be exclusively attributed to the impact of the global crisis.

Figure 2.2 shows the recent monthly changes in employment rates, which show some improvement in the very recent past – except for women in the developed countries, for whom it has remained the same or continued to increase in certain months. This tends to confirm the argument made earlier, that as the crisis sets in and fiscal austerity bites, the employment of women in a range of public and other social services will be specifically hit. This need not always be reflected in higher open unemployment figures, especially as the discouraged worker effect is known to be particularly strong for women. The decision to leave the labor market in bad times is often not a purely individual decision for women; it can reflect gender norms that encourage women to leave the "productive" space to husbands, brothers, etc.

Another major way in which crises alter the conditions of labor markets is by increasing the importance of non-regular work contracts. These include a variety of different types of contracts, including part-time work, temporary agency

Table 2.2 Employment rates (worker to population ratios) by region and sex

		2000	2005	2006	2007	2008	2009	2010
World	Males	73.8	73.4	73.4	73.6	73.4	72.6	72.6
	Females	48.6	48.9	48.9	48.9	48.6	48.1	47.8
Developed economies and EU	Males	65.8	64.4	64.9	65.2	64.9	62.5	61.8
	Females	48	48.4	49	49.5	49.7	48.9	48.6
Central and Southeast Europe and CIS	Males	62.1	61.8	62	63	63.6	62.3	63.1
	Females	44	44.1	44.5	45.1	45.3	44.7	45.1
East Asia	Males	78.1	76.9	76.9	76.9	76.2	75.9	75.9
	Females	67.1	65.7	65.6	65.6	64.8	64.6	64.6
Southeast Asia and Pacific	Males	78.6	77.7	77.7	77.7	77.6	77.6	78.2
	Females	55.6	54.3	54.4	55.1	55.5	55.5	55.5
South Asia	Males	79.6	79.9	79.7	79.7	79.3	78.7	78.5
	Females	33.4	35.2	34.7	33.6	32.5	31.4	30.1
Latin America and Caribbean	Males	74.8	75.1	75.2	75.4	75.7	74.6	75.1
	Females	42.9	46.1	46.5	47.2	47.7	47.5	48.4
Middle East	Males	67.4	67.1	67	67.3	66.6	67.1	67.6
	Females	13.2	15.3	15.1	15.1	14.3	14.5	14.8
North Africa	Males	66.3	68.4	68.1	68.1	68.6	68.7	68.6
	Females	17.5	18.2	18.6	19.8	19.9	19.8	20
Sub-Saharan Africa	Males	70.4	70	70.1	70.3	70.4	70.3	70.2
	Females	56.4	58.3	58.5	58.6	58.8	58.8	58.7

Source: ILO (2012b, p. 94, Appendix Table A5).

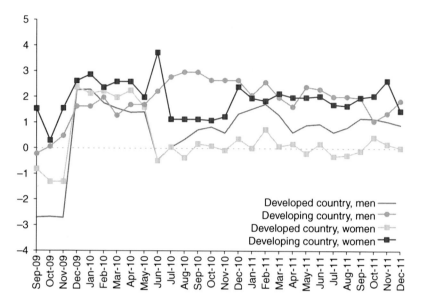

Figure 2.2 Recent monthly changes in employment rates by sex (source: ILO, *Global Short-Term Trends in Labor Markets*, various issues).

work, piece-rate work, and so on. Women tend to be disproportionately associated with such labor contracts (Seguino 2009; Chen *et al.* 2006; Elson 1993; Kabeer 1994). Of course, the increasing reliance on such contracts by employers cannot be attributed solely or even largely to the global crisis, but rather reflects the overall and more medium-term process of globalization, which generated a premium on labor market flexibility for employers. Thus, the growing significance of non-regular work, especially for women, has been an important feature of the past two decades, in both advanced and developing economies, and this process was quite far advanced well before the crisis broke.

In Japan, for example, the proportion of regular workers decreased from 83.4 percent in 1986 to 65.9 percent in 2008, while the share of non-regular workers (part-time workers, temporary agency workers, contract workers, and so on) increased from 16.6 percent in 1986 to 34.1 percent in 2008. Women dominated among non-regular workers, accounting for 63 percent of this category, and nearly three-quarters of part-time workers were female (Futagami 2010). What is more, the majority of women workers (57.4 percent) were found to be non-regular workers.

The growing incidence of non-regular work has been evident even in very "dynamic" emerging markets. In India, the lack of adequate paid employment generation despite more than a decade of rapid growth means that the proportion of informal workers remains very high at around 95 percent, while the share of self-employed workers in petty enterprises now accounts for more than half of the work force even in non-agricultural activities (Chandrasekhar and Ghosh 2011). In China, non-regular work is now estimated to account for anywhere between one-quarter and one-third of the work force, but it is hard to estimate because much of it is based on migrant workers without urban residence permits. In both these countries, non-regular work is much higher for women.

Given the wide regional and national variation in labor market structures and processes that is already evident, proceeding with the analysis in such general terms is likely to be relatively less illuminating. Accordingly, it is worth considering the nature of changes in particular countries and regions – some of which have been particularly badly hit by the crisis, and others that have managed to withstand some of the worst effects and preserve both the level and working conditions of women's paid employment.

1.1 Gendered employment patterns in the eurozone crisis

At the time of writing, the crisis in the eurozone has not yet reached its climax, and therefore it may be premature to talk of the impact on employment since the process is still unfolding. There is absolutely no doubt that things are likely to get much worse before there is any possibility of getting better. The financial stress is obviously part of the problem. Yields on government bond markets not just for Greece but for other economies under stress, such as for Spain, Italy, and others, keep rising to ridiculously unsustainable levels despite all the declarations of further government austerity measures, as would-be investors fear that future repayments will either be incomplete or perhaps even in another currency altogether. Bank deposits are being run down in all the European "periphery" countries, even as they rise sharply in Germany, Austria, Switzerland, and other supposedly "safe havens." Investors in productive activities are cutting back on expanding capacity or even ensuring more production – partly because of the uncertainty and depressed expectations about the future, but also in the case of small and medium enterprises because they cannot access bank credit for investment and sometimes even for working capital. In most European countries, banks have not resumed their normal role of providing loans to the real economy. In 2011, private investment as a percentage of GDP fell in all eurozone countries except one, despite low interest rates and the ample liquid assets held by large firms. This tendency has been especially problematic for small firms, which account for over two-thirds of employment in the eurozone (ILO 2012, p. 13).

The policy response thus far has been in the direction of reinforcing these negative trends. The fiscal austerity measures that are being imposed on these countries make everything that much worse, compounding the problem by reducing current economic activity and effective demand and creating a deflationary spiral. The reductions in income and employment that result not only reduce living standards and welfare, but also have strongly negative multiplier effects that cause economic activity to decline further. This then creates a negative feedback loop with the financial system, since all the indicators that financial markets look at (such as the fiscal deficit-to-GDP ratio or the public debt-to-GDP ratio) become even worse as the denominator shrinks. This, in turn, makes the banks' investment portfolios look even more fragile. The process is now so far advanced that it is no longer confined to those European countries that are seen to have "unsustainable" public debt positions. Even some of the "strongest" surplus countries in the eurozone, including Germany, are now coming under the scrutiny of credit rating agencies and bond markets that question the viability of the debt held by German banks in assets of periphery countries. The only way to break this is through a reversal of strategy to focus on economic expansion including through more public spending to break this negative spiral, but the prospects of this are currently not very bright.

These unfavorable financial and real economic variables are already being reflected in labor markets in the crisis countries. While the worst may be yet to come, the evidence already collected on European countries (Vaughan-Whitehead 2012) shows since 2008 that certain categories of workers have been hit more than others, particularly temporary workers (for example, 90 percent of employment losses in Spain); low-skilled workers especially in manufacturing and construction; and younger people, who typically have experienced double the rate of unemployment of other age categories. This sectoral impact is important in understanding why male workers in Europe have thus far been worse affected by job cuts and layoffs, such that the unemployment rate for men increased more than for women. This has also been in strong evidence in the three Baltic countries, Lithuania, Latvia, and Estonia, as well as in Ireland and Spain. In Iceland, the unemployment rate for women was higher than that for men throughout the 1990s. However, in the 2008–09 crisis, the overall unemployment rate increased significantly, but the unemployment rate for men did so faster such that it became higher than that for women (Olafsdottir 2009, p. 5).

However, women workers have also been affected adversely. Within male-dominated sectors, women workers have often been the first to be dismissed. Evidence from the Baltic countries (even "success stories" like Estonia) indicates that women workers have experienced more wage cuts than men (Vaughn-Whitehead 2012), and then is some evidence that gender gaps have stopped declining or have even increased in some countries. There is evidence of not only real wage cuts, but also nominal wage cuts, as in Estonia, Latvia, Lithuania, and other new EU member states, some of which have been made easier by labor market deregulation that allows employers to unilaterally recategorize jobs as part-time and thereby reduce working hours even marginally so as to reduce nominal wages. A third impact has been on unpaid labor, as fiscal austerity measures and attempts by employers to reduce costs have led to the reduction or removal of arrangements to reconcile work and family life, which typically has the maximum negative impact on female workers. Since more men have lost their jobs thus far in Europe than women, it may even come about that overall in the labor market there may be more women than men in paid jobs. However, the gender construction of societies is still such that women bear the largest share of the burden of household responsibilities and the care economy, whether or not they are employed elsewhere, so that the "double burden" of paid and unpaid work (Elson 1993) may become an even starker reality.

These trends are strongly related to policy measures. As noted in Vaughan-Whitehead (2012, p. 3):

> The policy shift that occurred in the second half of 2009 – from anti-crisis expansionary packages to restrictive budgetary policies – may also change the outcome in terms of inequalities. Employment cuts have generally been higher in the private sector, but have extended recently to public sector employees. While men have been hardest hit in the first phase, employment and wage cuts in the public sector and in services, which are female-dominated, will mainly impact upon women, thus reversing the narrowing gender pay gap and unemployment gap generated by the crisis so far. Other categories of employees – more skilled and older, but also disabled, and lone parents – are also likely to be directly affected by the cuts in budgetary expenditure. Employees from ethnic minority groups will also be hit because of their concentration in certain segments of the public sector.

It is worth examining trends in some of the more crisis-hit countries of the euro-zone in more detail. To that end, some gender-disaggregated data for Greece, Ireland, Portugal, and Spain ("GIPS" for short) are analyzed here, in comparison with other countries that have been less affected by the crisis so far. These four countries are chosen because they have already experienced significant recession in output and employment (in the case of Greece, substantially negative GDP growth for nearly five years) and because the process of fiscal tightening has already been under way for some time.

Consider labor force participation rates, as shown in Figures 2.3 and 2.4. One of the interesting features of the past decade has been the gradual increase in female participation rates even as male rates have remained stagnant or declined slightly. This is true for the Organisation for Economic Co-operation and Development (OECD) as a whole (Figure 2.3) as well as for the GIPS countries. Further, the process clearly began well before the 2007–08 crisis, so it cannot be attributed solely to the crisis. Indeed, during the previous boom, the increase in female labor force participation was attributed to the process of economic expansion that was drawing more and more women into paid economic activities. However, it is worth noting that the process was much more marked in the GIPS countries (Figure 2.4), where female labor force participation rates have increased by 8.5 percentage points over the decade as a whole. What is more interesting is that they continued to increase even after GDP started declining, and even in the period of deep recession they have gone up even as male rates have declined. (Only in Ireland did both female and male rates decrease.) In Greece, for example, female labor force participation rates increased by 2.6 percentage points between 2007 and 2010, while the male labor force participation rates fell slightly by 0.2 percentage points.

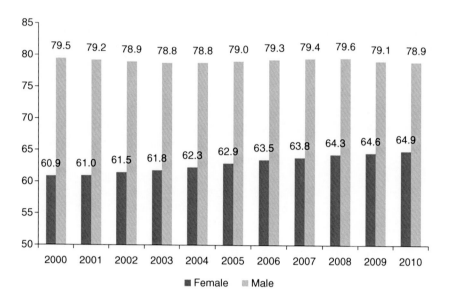

Figure 2.3 Labor force participation rates in OECD countries (average) by sex (source: OECD Gender Initiative data browser (OECD 2012)).

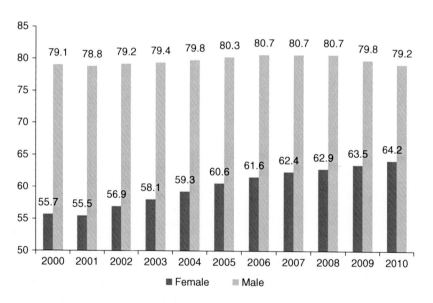

Figure 2.4 Labor force participation rates in GIPS countries (average) by sex (source: OECD Gender Initiative data browser (OECD 2012)).

Another concern relates to gender wage gaps, which, as noted earlier, are typically expected to increase in the wake of the crisis. In Southeast Asia, gender wage gaps increased in the aftermath of the crisis of 1997–98, as is discussed below. However, in Europe, a somewhat different process has been occurring, as indicated in Table 2.3. In Greece and Ireland, gender wage gaps actually decreased quite significantly after the crisis, even as they increased in Portugal and Spain. Meanwhile, even in the countries that have not yet really experienced the crisis, such as Germany and Austria (which incidentally have some of the highest such gaps of all OECD countries), gender wage gaps also decreased.

One important caveat must be borne in mind: the data presented in Table 2.3 refer to full-time work only, and women workers tend to be much more heavily represented in part-time work, which has also increased after the crisis. So the full extent of the gender wage gap or its trend over time may not be accurately portrayed here. Even so, such a diverse pattern deserves consideration. The explanation for these varying trends can be found in the occupational segregation by gender in different countries, relative to the sectors that have been most affected by crisis. This particular crisis has affected banking and financial sectors (even though not as much as could be expected given the gravity of the crisis and the culpabilities involved) and employment in these sectors is still predominantly male. This has been a high-remuneration sector, and even though it remains so, the returns have come down somewhat in the wake of the crisis, thus reducing wage dispersion among skilled and professional workers. The other activity that has been significantly hit is construction, which is another sector that male workers (of the semi-skilled variety) tend to be more concentrated in, and therefore as this has come down, wage dispersion in semi-skilled activities has also possibly come down. Since most women workers tend to be at the bottom of the wage distribution anyway, their wages may remain intact or decline only slightly compared to male workers. Indeed, in several cases, declining wage gaps actually reflect the negative trend of men's wages declining while women's wages (already lower) stay the same or decline a bit less.

Table 2.3 Gender wage gaps in some European countries (unadjusted gender gap in median earnings of full-time employees, %)

	2004	2005	2006	2007	2008	2009
Greece	14.2	16.5	12.2	12.2	9.6	9.6
Ireland	18.2	13.8	14.4	18	15	10.4
Portugal	13.3	16	14	15.5	15.6	15.6
Spain	12.7	12.5	10.4	8.8	11.8	11.8
Germany	25.4	23.1	23.9	22.8	24	21.6
Austria	22.4	22	21.9	21.6	20.9	19.4
France	9.7	12.1	11.9	12	13.1	13.1
Sweden	15.3	14.4	14.6	16.4	15.4	14.9
OECD average	17.1	16.7	15.8	16.3	16.4	15.9

Source: OECD Gender Initiative data browser.

Figure 2.5 describes the changes in part-time work (which is one of the forms of non-regular work, even though some of it may be formal) in the GIPS countries as well as in the OECD as a whole. As noted above, women are much more heavily represented in such contracts, with more than one-fifth of all women workers in such work, and the proportion has been rising. However, the proportion has been rising in both the OECD as a whole and in the GIPS countries – and indeed it has also been rising in the countries relatively unaffected by the crisis, such as Germany. If anything, the GIPS average for the incidence of part-time work (for both men and women) is slightly lower than for the OECD average, although the rate of increase has been marginally faster. There is no doubt, however, that the incidence of part-time employment has continued to rise throughout the crisis. If all forms of non-regular employment (including self-employment) are added to this, the outcome would probably appear to be much more stark.

What is certainly clear is that the combination of fiscal austerity, deleveraging of private debtors, and pressure on wages is creating a deadly mix of policies that combine to create or perpetuate economic slump. In such conditions, not only does economic activity get into a downward spiral, but the labor market conditions tend to deteriorate, particularly for women workers, to such an extent that the ultimate macroeconomic goals of the strategy – to achieve macroeconomic balance and external competitiveness – are actually hindered.

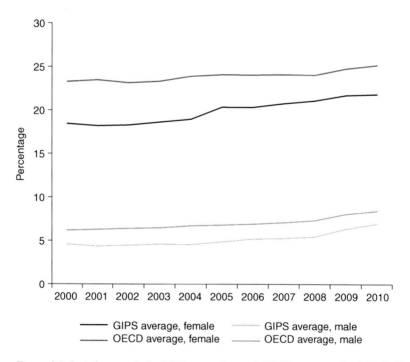

Figure 2.5 Part-time work in GIPS countries and OECD average (as % of all work) (source: OECD Gender Initiative data browser (OECD 2012)).

According to ILO (2012, p. 14), in the eurozone,

> Deficit countries ... have restored cost-competitiveness to some extent. On average, half of the relative increase in unit labour costs since the introduction of the Euro has been reversed since 2008. This has come about through real wage cuts and labour productivity improvements. Prices, on the other hand, have adjusted only slightly, thereby weakening the effect of reduced unit labour costs on competitiveness in deficit countries and adding to the hardship of those whose incomes have fallen.... 13 out of 17 Eurozone countries have carried out labour market flexibility reforms, often in the direction of easing dismissals. However, in a depressed macroeconomic context, these reforms are likely to lead to increased numbers of layoffs without any boost to job creation at least until economic recovery gathers momentum.

The point that is forgotten in these is that the presence of various public programs and interventions in the labor market and social protection are not just welfare measures; they are actually important countercyclical buffers that reduce or prevent downturns and enable faster recovery.

Even active labor market policies that promote employment or prevent excessive job cuts in downswings are under threat with fiscal austerity packages that do not allow governments the freedom to engage in such measures. Yet these can also be crucial, as the experience within Europe currently shows. For example, what is often characterized as "the German miracle" of rising labor productivity and near full employment is not only a tribute to technological progress within the German economy, it is also closely related to significant public provision for active labor market policies, as well as emphasis on policies to encourage short-term work contracts for the young and to prevent long-term unemployment from taking root. Similar schemes that seek to encourage employment also exist in Sweden and Finland, first and foremost, but also in France and Italy, all of which also engage in active industrial policies to support ailing industries such as construction, engineering, and the automobile sector.

Similarly, strong trade unions and wage bargaining have proved to be beneficial in preserving employment and thereby creating effective demand to prevent freefalls in economic activity, for example in Germany and France. Employment and wages therefore have to be seen not only as costs, but also as sources of demand, which may prove to become crucial to ensure macroeconomic viability in such periods. As the ILO (2012a) notes, in many other countries of Europe,

> the companies and workers not covered by social dialogue were unable to benefit from these possibilities and generally relied on immediate employment cuts to cope with declining activity. In countries with limited wage bargaining, such as Estonia, Latvia and Lithuania, wage cuts were immediate and substantial.

2 Employment patterns after the Asian crisis of 1997–98

It may be worth comparing this experience with that of the crisis-hit Southeast Asian countries after the Asian crisis of the late 1990s. It is interesting to note that the pattern in terms of employment was varied among these countries, but still similar to the current experience of some eurozone crisis countries. This reflects not just the impact of the crisis itself, but also the post-crisis trajectory that was followed, in terms of a broadly deflationary strategy that was focused on exports as the engine of growth and suppression of domestic consumption in consequence.

The East and Southeast Asian economies that were hit by the crisis were all previously among the best performers among developing countries in terms of both GDP growth and exporting ability. Their governments had embraced not only export orientation but also very extensive trade liberalization and, more recently, financial liberalization. The five countries that were particularly affected by the financial crisis – Thailand, South Korea, Indonesia, Malaysia, and the Philippines – had all been characterized by rapid export growth, espe-cially in "sunrise" newer manufacturing industries such as IT hardware and related electronic items, and were substantial recipients of private foreign capital. In general, they were characterized by "prudent" macroeconomic policies – three of them were running government budget surpluses and the other two had budget deficits that could be considered as moderate rather than excessive. They were regularly lauded by the Bretton Woods institutions as positive examples for other developing countries to follow, and cited as success stories of global integration.

Therefore, when the crisis struck, the first response was to find causes for the crisis that were not based on global integration as such, but other features such as "crony capitalism" and opaque financial systems that distorted the pattern of investment, and exchange rate rigidity because of the practice of pegging exchange rates to the appreciating US dollar, all of which adversely affected export competitiveness. However, there are more plausible reasons for the crisis, such as the structural problem of fallacy of composition that made the excessive focus on exports as the engine of growth more difficult as competing developing country exporters entered the scene. This was exacerbated by the more proxi-mate impact of external financial liberalization – in terms of allowing inflows of capital that enabled short-term borrowing for long-term projects, breaking the link between the ability to access foreign exchange and the need to earn it, and causing appreciation of the real exchange rate that shifted incentives within the economy from tradables to non-tradables (as elaborated in Jomo 1998; Ghosh and Chandrasekhar 2001, 2009). These countries also formed a fairly typical tra-jectory of global integration in which capital inflows create movements of the real exchange rate that generate internal shifts away from tradable to non-tradable activities, which in turn are associated with current account deficits that eventually become unsustainable (Ghosh 2006).

In the aftermath of the crisis, the five countries that were most affected by the crisis (Thailand, Malaysia, South Korea, Indonesia, and the Philippines) all experienced drops – substantial in some countries – in worker population rates. This is evident in Table 2.4, which shows that both male and female work participation rates tended to decline, although they showed somewhat divergent trends in the different countries. In Indonesia, male worker population rates fell from an average of 79 percent in the three years preceding the crisis to 77 percent over 2003–05. For women, the decline was from 47 percent to 45 percent. For South Korea, the decline was not so marked between the two periods – there was a very sharp drop for both men and women in the period just after the crisis, but a recovery thereafter. Male worker participation rates in 2003–05, when output recovery was more than complete, at 71 percent were still below the pre-crisis rate of 73 percent; however, for females, the rate actually increased between these two periods by 1 percentage point, to 48.6 percent. There is evidence that for women, more of this was part-time work. In Malaysia, aggregate worker population rates showed no change, but this reflected a decline for men and an increase for women (both by 2 percentage points). In Thailand, female rates remained broadly unchanged at 65 percent, but male rates fell substantially from 83.5 percent to 79.8 percent between the two periods. The Philippines is the clear outlier in this case – aggregate worker population rates actually increased between the two periods, and this is even though male rates remained unchanged, since female rates moved sharply up from a pre-crisis average of 44 percent to 50 percent in 2005. Once again, in the Philippines, there is other qualitative evidence suggesting that much of the new work was in the form of part-time and less formal employment.

Table 2.4 Worker-population rates in East and Southeast Asia before and after the East Asian crisis (%)

	Indonesia		South Korea		Malaysia		Philippines		Thailand	
	Male	Female	Male	Female	Male	Female	Male	Female	Male	Female
1991	78.9	47.4	72.0	46.2	78.9	42.6	76.2	42.0	84.7	70.4
1992	79.8	47.1	72.3	46.1	78.7	42.3	76.5	43.0	85.1	68.9
1993	78.9	47.1	71.8	46.0	79.4	42.6	75.7	42.8	84.3	66.4
1994	78.1	46.9	72.8	46.9	79.4	42.5	76.3	42.8	83.9	63.7
1995	78.5	46.7	73.4	47.7	79.4	42.4	76.8	44.4	83.6	65.3
1996	80.1	47.0	73.5	48.4	79.9	42.5	77.6	44.9	83.0	66.5
1997	79.8	46.6	73.0	49.0	79.9	42.4	76.8	44.7	82.9	66.8
1998	79.1	46.6	68.3	44.7	79.4	41.9	75.9	44.5	80.4	63.9
1999	79.9	47.2	68.2	45.5	78.6	42.2	75.1	45.3	79.6	63.0
2000	80.1	47.1	69.4	46.9	79.2	44.1	73.3	43.6	80.1	63.9
2001	78.7	46.1	69.5	47.5	79.0	43.9	75.4	46.8	80.4	63.4
2002	77.8	45.5	70.6	48.2	78.9	43.8	74.9	46.8	80.7	63.7
2003	77.5	45.2	70.3	47.1	78.6	43.6	74.7	46.8	80.5	63.7
2004	77.1	45.1	71.0	48.5	78.7	44.4	74.4	47.5	80.0	64.8
2005	77.7	44.3	70.9	48.6	78.6	44.8	76.9	50.7	79.9	65.0

Source: ILO Key Indicators of Labour Markets (ILO 2011).

Even in the sectors where export growth was buoyant, such as manufacturing, employment did not pick up commensurately. Indeed, in South Korea and Malaysia, manufacturing employment actually fell in absolute numbers during the recovery when compared to the pre-crisis years. Overall, survey and other micro evidence suggests that even where employment did not fall or has even increased, the quality of employment deteriorated in that there was a greater proportion of insecure casual contracts, low-grade self-employment, and part-time work in total employment, especially for women workers (Ghosh 2009b).

These employment outcomes (which also included higher rates of open unemployment in the past-crisis trajectory) were the result of deflationary policies on the part of the governments of these countries, which sought to suppress domestic consumption and investment. The "excess savings" that were generated as a result were then stored as foreign exchange reserves – partly as insurance against future crises and partly to prevent exchange rate appreciation that would damage the export-driven model. This obviously had effects on current levels of economic activity relative to the potential. But it also negatively affected future growth prospects because of the long-term potential losses of inadequate infrastructure investment, etc. These policies have had adverse implications for women as paid and unpaid workers, by worsening labor market conditions and forcing more of them into informal contracts or self-employment, rather than regular formal work in factories and services.

What emerges from these cases is that policy responses are absolutely crucial in determining the extent to which not just output but more importantly employment is preserved through and after a financial crisis. In the next section, some positive examples of progressive policies that contribute to post-crisis recovery while maintaining employment and social welfare as much as possible are briefly considered.

3 An overview of fiscal responses after the 2008 crisis

The initial impact of the 2008 crisis in terms of causing government revenues to fall in most of the world was quite marked and surprisingly rapid. For many countries, this decline was not related to proactive tax cuts as part of stimulus or recovery measures, but simply reflected the decline in economic activity that affected both indirect and direct taxes. It has been estimated that government revenues fell by 1.8 percent of GDP, or 8 percent of 2008 revenue, in 2009, in all regions except Latin America and the Caribbean, with the sharpest falls occurring in South Asia, Europe and Central Asia, and the Middle East and North Africa (Kyrili and Martin 2010). It is also worth noting that the fiscal deficits that have emerged as a result of the global crisis (either because of falling revenues or because of stimulus measures in response to the crisis) have come after a period of fairly disciplined fiscal behavior. In fact, except for a few countries, most developing countries had low deficits or fiscal surpluses in the years preceding the crisis. Figure 2.6 shows that among developing and transition countries in Latin America and the Caribbean, Sub-Saharan Africa, and

Europe, public sector balances were either in surplus on average, or had very low deficits.

The deterioration in government balances consequent upon the crisis (or increase in overall fiscal deficits) did not necessarily reflect more expansionary fiscal stances, since interest payments tend to account for a significant chunk of the overall deficit in most countries. Further, the composition of the deficit can matter as much as, if not even more than, the level. Thus, even where fiscal deficits have increased as part of the planned stimulus package, a major question is how this has happened. Thus far, apart from monetary policies, the various stimulus packages have included some combination of the following measures:

- bailouts of banks, finance companies, and other struggling corporate players;
- quantitative easing strategies to provide liquidity to banks to enable/encourage them to revive real sector lending;
- direct tax cuts to boost private spending;
- indirect tax cuts directed toward promoting particular industries or sectors;
- special packages, including tax holidays, credit subsidies, loan write-offs or guarantees and infrastructure provision, usually directed toward export sectors as well as direct/indirect subsidies to some manufacturing sectors (such as the automobile industry in the United States and Europe);

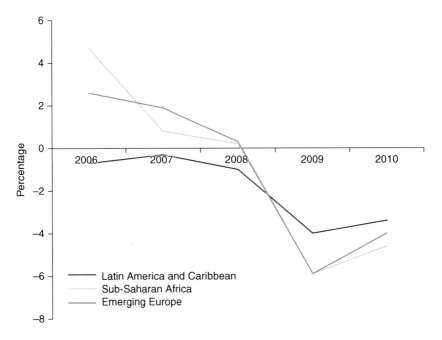

Figure 2.6 Public sector balance (% of GDP) (source: IMF Regional Economic Outlooks (data in simple unweighted averages of countries across region)).

- policies directed toward agriculture, such as trying to ensure continued flows of bank credit, input provision, and access to markets;
- tax credits for employment;
- public investment in physical infrastructure;
- public spending in social sectors (health and education) to increase access to and reduce costs for consumers of such services.

It was noted earlier that globally there have been two distinct phases of fiscal response to the ongoing crisis: expansion followed by contraction. A study of 130 developing countries by Ortiz and Cummins (2012) showed that 120 increased spending (by an average of 25 percent) in 2008–09 compared to 2005–07, while only 10 reduced it (by an average of 8.6 percent). However, for the subsequent period (2010–12 compared to 2008–09), only 70 countries increased public spending by an average of just 2.6 percent, while 60 countries reduced spending, also by an average of 2.6 percent. The point to note is that the phase of fiscal expansion typically emphasizes infrastructural investments that do not always specifically benefit women, while the phase of fiscal contraction is more likely to generate cuts both in female employment and in the goods and services that are important for women in their roles as household provisioners and unpaid care workers.

The largest fiscal stimulus package in terms of absolute amounts of funds outside the United States was that of China. A study of the Chinese fiscal stimulus (Kang and Wei 2010) noted that the overwhelming part of the RMB 4,000 billion public expenditure package was spent on infrastructure, with less than 4 percent being allocated for health care and education. There were incentives to increase some forms of consumption, such as tax cuts on consumer durables and easing of credit, which in turn fueled a boom in consumer credit and housing finance. This suggests a strong gender bias in the pattern of the fiscal response, with less emphasis being given to strategies either to expand/maintain good-quality female employment or to improve the conditions of women's lives through expanded and improved provision of public social services. This strategy can operate to increase output and productivity in the economy, but not necessarily to increase consumption and raise the living standards of the bulk of the population, which is more necessary even from the point of view of macroeconomic balance. Of course, it is true that improved transportation infrastructure and greater connectivity have positive implications for human development, conditions of living, and access to education, and therefore also for the conditions facing women and girls. However, specific measures in these areas are also clearly required. The proposed health care reform to ensure basic medical security and access to drugs for the entire population (which is planned to require an additional RMB 850 billion in government spending over five years) is designed to decrease the need for out-of-pocket health expenditures of households and the associated need for precautionary savings, but its impact is yet to be felt. While the Chinese fiscal stimulus was effective in maintaining aggregate growth and causing employment to recover quickly, it did not help to improve the macroeconomic imbalance, and did not address the specific concerns of women as paid and unpaid workers. This is likely to become even more of a concern as the latest slowdown in exports affects women workers in China.

Quite often, the fiscal dilemma is not the easier one of how to allocate more money, but the more difficult one of preventing cuts in important areas in conditions of fiscal stringency. The crisis was associated with declining revenues in many countries, especially in the developing world, and a major problem facing governments has been that of trying to maintain and increase public spending in critical areas that affect livelihoods and conditions of living, such as nutrition, sanitation, health, and education. Ortiz and Cummins (2012) point out that in the first phase, social protection measures formed an important part of the stimulus packages of governments, accounting for an average of 27 percent of the total announced amount in high-income countries and 24 percent in developing countries. However, in the subsequent period, budget cuts have also included allocations to sectors like education, health, agriculture, and social protection. The negative effects of this on women, not only as unpaid workers, but also as citizens with rights, are only too obvious.

This confirms the point made by Kyrili and Martin (2010) from a study of 28 low-income countries that in 2010, on average, social protection spending as a share of GDP fell by 0.2 percentage points of GDP compared to the 2008 level. The budgetary stringency associated with a downswing because of falling state revenues gets reflected in a reduction in such expenditure, so that social protection spending is cut when it is most needed. Spending on education has clearly suffered in the low-income countries, falling in terms of GDP (and in several cases, in absolute amounts as well, since GDP fell in 2009 for a number of countries). Spending on health was far more consistently maintained, with most of the low-income countries showing slightly higher levels of such expenditure relative to GDP. In general, spending on infrastructure and agriculture was initially maintained and even increased as proportions of GDP.

Another study (Ortiz *et al.* 2010) was based on a rapid desk review of IMF country reports dated between March 3, 2009 and March 16, 2010, which covered 86 countries (28 low income, 37 lower-to-middle income, and 21 upper-to-middle income). Fiscal trends in these 86 countries showed that nearly 40 percent of governments were planning to cut total spending in 2010–11, compared to 2008–09, with the average size of the projected expenditure contraction amounting to 2.6 percent of GDP. Very large cuts (4–13 percent of GDP) were expected in seven countries (Algeria, Marshall Islands, Republic of Congo, Belarus, Angola, Chad, and Maldives). This could be related to the fact that the impact of the global crisis was to worsen fiscal balances everywhere, and in developing countries with pre-existing balance of payments imbalances and limited or declining access to private international capital markets, this created a situation that could not be sustained despite the need for more spending in the absence of some increase in external resources. The fiscal cuts were therefore forced onto countries by the absence of adequate funding, including from the IMF. It should be borne in mind that many of these are countries that have predominantly poor populations and very inadequate provision of infrastructure and public services that provide minimum socioeconomic rights for the majority of the people. Therefore, cutbacks in fiscal spending in such countries are likely to have direct implications for economic and humanitarian conditions.

Even within supposedly protected social spending, a significant number of countries have been advised to make cuts in the form of limiting/reducing subsidies (including on food and health); "reforms" in pension and health systems, which essentially reduce pensions and make public health care services more expensive; and reducing the spread of social spending by emphasizing targeted rather than universal provision. The only "positive" recommendation for a significant number of countries is the expansion of targeted transfer programs. While this may appear to be a positive sign, the many problems associated with targeting in developing countries (problems of unfair exclusion or unjustified inclusion, higher administrative costs, diversion, and overall reduction in quality) suggests that such increases are unlikely to benefit or even counter the negative impact of other measures for much of the population, including vulnerable groups.

A very important recommendation that can have negative effects on both growth and human development is the very frequently posited requirement of putting caps on or inducing cuts in public sector wages. It has been found that erosion of pay and arrears in wage payments can have significant adverse effects on public service delivery in such essential areas as health and education, through greater absenteeism, internal and external brain drain, and loss of motivation (UNICEF 2010). In many of the countries in which such measures have been proposed, large numbers of public servants already have incomes that are at or below the official poverty line, and constraining or further reducing them is bound to have an effect on public service delivery as well as health and education outcomes.

Assessment by the ILO (2009) of fiscal responses in 2008–09 found that in the immediate aftermath of the crisis, many governments responded by:

- increasing spending on infrastructure and offering subsidies and tax reductions for small and medium-sized enterprises to stimulate labor demand;
- expanding public employment services, training programs and labor market intermediation facilities to support the unemployed as well as job seekers;
- increasing benefits for unemployed persons and others like the elderly, as well as cash transfers and social assistance programs to provide income support;
- attempting to achieve greater social dialogue by engaging with workers' and employers' organizations.

These measures, in turn, were estimated to have generated anywhere from 7 to 11 million jobs in 2009, even though globally, employment conditions deteriorated in the aftermath of the crisis. So they did operate to mitigate the worst effects, particularly in some countries. Table 2.5 provides some details of the kind of employment-generating measures in 54 countries in 2008–09. (These countries include both rich and developed countries as well as poor developing countries, and so obviously the nature and implications of these measures vary greatly within this group.)

Among the measures outlined in Table 2.5, those in the second and third categories generally tend to have more relevance and benefits for women workers, along with public employment, which is a measure in the first category. It is

Table 2.5 Fiscal employment-generating measures, 2008–09

Type of measure	Incidence (% of countries using this)
I. Stimulating labor demand	
Additional public spending on infrastructure	87.0
• With employment criteria	33.3
• With green criteria	29.6
Public employment	24.1
New/expanded targeted employment programmes	51.9
Access to credit for SMEs	74.1
Access to public tenders for SMEs	9.3
Subsidies and tax reductions for SMEs	77.8
II. Expanding social protection and food security	
Social security tax reductions	29.6
Additional cash transfers	53.7
Increased access to health benefits	37.0
Increases in amount and coverage of old-age pensions	44.4
Changes in minimum wages	33.3
New protection measures for migrant workers	14.8
Introduction/expansion of food subsidies	16.7
Additional support for agriculture	22.2
III. Supporting jobs, job seekers, and unemployed	
Additional training measures	63.0
Increased capacity of public employment services	46.3
New measures for migrant workers	27.8
Working time reductions	27.8
Partial unemployment with training and part-time work	27.8
Wage reductions	14.8
Extension of unemployment benefits	31.5
Additional social assistance and protection measures	33.3
IV. Social dialogue and rights and work	
Consultations on crisis responses	59.3
Agreements at national level	35.2
Agreements at sectoral levels	11.1
Additional measures to fight labor trafficking	3.7
Additional measures to fight child labor	3.7
Changes in labor legislation	22.2
Increased capacity of labor administration and inspection	13.0

Source: ILO (2009).

worth noting that only a minority (and sometimes a small minority) of countries adopted such measures. In addition, not all such measures, when adopted, were necessarily sensitive to the requirements and conditions of women, and some even required more unpaid labor from women even though they were intended to alleviate their circumstances. (One obvious example is the expansion of Conditional Cash Transfer programs that require women/mothers to attend meetings and provide community labor.) Nevertheless, the countries that did adopt such measures often witnessed an improvement in overall labor market conditions as well as in the specific conditions of women workers.

As noted earlier, many of these crisis responses were relatively short-lived, being withdrawn or reduced as soon as output levels recovered somewhat, and most of them were adversely affected by the emphasis on fiscal austerity that became the international norm in early 2010. Table 2.6 indicates the incidence of fiscal austerity measures since 2010.

These are all measures that will reduce the quantity and quality of decent jobs, as well as the extent, coverage, and possibly the quality of social protection. When to these are added reforming moves in the labor market toward greater flexibilization, these measures are likely to add to the burden of the crisis by generating more precarious and vulnerable employment and putting further downward pressure on wages. Women workers (both paid and unpaid) are particularly hard hit by such measures.

4 Some positive examples of crisis responses that have been sensitive to women's employment conditions

Two countries that have shown how crisis responses can be gender-sensitive in terms of protecting or improving women's labor market conditions as well as the conditions of unpaid work are discussed below. These examples have been chosen not just for the gender-specific initiatives that were undertaken in the wake of a crisis, but also – and most importantly – because these responses were interwoven with and crucially integrated within a broader macroeconomic strategy for economic recovery. In other words, gender-based measures were not afterthoughts or additional measures that could even run counter to the broader

Table 2.6 Austerity measures in 158 countries, 2010–12

Austerity measure	Number of countries	Percentage of countries
Contracting public expenditure in 2012	133	74.3
Cutting or capping public sector wage bill	73	46.2
Reducing or removing food and fuel subsidies	73	46.2
Targeting or rationalizing social safety nets	55	34.8
Reforming (reducing) pensions	52	32.9

Source: Ortiz and Cummins (2012, p. 150).

economic policy paradigm, but integral parts of the overall response. The ability of both of these countries to exhibit relatively rapid recovery of GDP and employment was obviously affected by external forces, but was also very much related to the employment and wage-oriented development patterns that were sought to be pursued. This is important in providing feasible alternatives for economic strategy in other countries, which can integrate the work and well-being of women with the broader economic development strategy.

4.1 Sweden in the 1990s

Sweden provides an example of a country in which the response to a financial crisis involved explicit recognition of the pressures on women and included measures to maintain or ensure conditions of women's work and life that were incorporated into the broader strategy for economic recovery.

In the early 1990s, Sweden experienced a dual financial and real economic crisis that bears many similarities to both the subprime crisis in the United States and the current difficulties faced by some eurozone countries. Financial deregulation in the 1980s generated significant capital inflows and sparked a lending boom, which was then associated with rapidly increasing consumption and investment and asset price bubbles as well as heightened activity in the domestic non-tradable sector, particularly real estate and construction. The Swedish krona was pegged to the US dollar, and so the real exchange appreciated – but this was not the only problem since the capital inflows may have driven the nominal exchange up even higher, even with flexible exchange rates. Around 1990, the bubble burst and the boom turned into slump, with capital outflows, widespread bankruptcies, falling employment, declining investment, negative GDP growth, systemic banking crises driven by deterioration in banks' balance sheets, currency crises, and depression (Jonung 2009).

As a result, Sweden experienced a severe depression in the early 1990s. GDP fell by 5 percent, employment rates fell by nearly 10 percent, and there was a massive increase in unemployment, almost 500 percent in absolute numbers of people (Freeman *et al.* 2010). However, the policy response was swift and positive, addressing not just the financial imbalances, but also the real economic downswing and the impact on the labor market, including especially the conditions facing women workers.

In terms of financial policies, consolidation of struggling financial institutions was accompanied by an unlimited government guarantee against loss for all depositors and counterparties. This enabled credit lines to be re-established with foreign banks while maintaining the confidence of private retail depositors. The bailouts provided to banks were limited by the requirement that recipient banks had to fully disclose all their financial positions and open up their books to official scrutiny, so that only those banks that were deemed worth rescuing received government funds. Banks' shareholders were not protected by any guarantees. Some banks were taken over and nationalized, with zero compensation to shareholders because they were deemed to be worthless. These measures not only prevented a credit crunch from creating a more severe downturn, but also limited moral hazard and reduced the cost of the financial rescue, making it more politically acceptable as well.

In terms of macroeconomic strategy, an immediate measure was the devaluation of the exchange rate, which dramatically improved the export competitiveness of the economy and led to a long period of rapidly growing exports. However, the crucial point is that export-led growth was *not* seen as the only means of economic expansion, and measures were taken almost immediately to provide countercyclical fiscal policies that would generate internal demand to bring the economy out of the recession. This included labor markets and "social welfare" measures that affect women, which provided important countercyclical buffers. Thus, instead of forcing reductions in fiscal deficits through austerity and contraction of public spending, the Swedish government let fiscal deficits increase during the crisis. This took the form of maintaining some earlier expenditure and also expanding other spending to respond to the crisis and its employment effects. The famous welfare system – that simultaneously provided direct public employment for women and helped to reduce unpaid work in the care economy and household reproduction, which has been an essential element of the Swedish model – was not allowed to deteriorate. Instead, it was actually expanded because of renewed emphasis on employment programs and active labor market policies. This served to protect women from the worst effects of the financial crisis and economic downswing, and provided the demand cushion that assisted faster recovery of the real economy.

One important element of this strategy that has direct contemporary relevance was the creation of a personalized youth employment guarantee program (ILO 2012). This is a scheme in which all young people (18–24 years) in Sweden are offered employment in youth specific activities, following a period (90 days) of unsuccessful job search. The idea is to provide special measures and activities for the participant to enable him/her to get a job or return to education as soon as possible. In the initial period, the program includes assessment, educational and vocational guidance, and job search activities with coaching. Thereafter, these activities are combined with work experience, education and training, grants to business start-ups, and employability rehabilitation efforts. So the emphasis is on rapid integration with the labor market. A young person can participate in the job guarantee for up to 15 months. The program is estimated to have been quite successful (with nearly half of the young jobseeker participants getting successful outcomes as a result of the scheme) at relatively low cost. Female participation in such programs has been high, at around half. Given the high rates of youth unemployment that prevail currently not just in Europe, but also in many other parts of the world, such a program could have positive effects in other contexts as well.

The Swedish recovery program also focused on avoiding labor market exclusion, particularly for women. Two cornerstones of Swedish family policy – paid parental leave and subsidies to day care for children – that were both maintained during the crisis and even expanded to some extent have been recognized as being particularly beneficial to women workers, even by researchers who have otherwise queried the fiscal costs of such programs (Freeman *et al.* 2010). The welfare state provisions continued to provide strong social protection and safety nets to those at the bottom of the income and wage pyramid. Government benefits supplemented the incomes of the lower-paid and non-working population. These measures prevented the emergence of poverty, reduced tendencies to enhance inequality in the wake of the crisis, and also operated as countercyclical buffers cushioning domestic demand from further declines.

Another important element of the Swedish success was the continued maintenance of social dialogue, particularly in wage bargaining. This was made possible by the developed institutional structure in which trade unions and employer associations were active participants in tripartite dialogues with government in the Nordic model well before the crisis. The financial crisis did not lead to the abandonment of such dialogue, and its continuation allowed wage increases that protected workers to some extent but also secured the benefits of exchange rate devaluation in the form of greater competitiveness of the domestic manufacturing industry.

The result of this combination of measures was a relatively quick recovery from the financial crisis, in terms of both output and employment. Further, it was achieved at relatively small cost to the public exchequer, with recent estimates putting the cost of the financial rescue package at only 3 percent of GDP (Jonung 2009). In addition, it was achieved with relatively little increase in inequality or social disruption. As ILO (2012a) notes,

> Inequality increased modestly (as it did in many countries), but Sweden remained among the lowest inequality countries in the world. Swedish income inequality remains far lower than in the United States and rose by less in the 1990s. The collective-bargaining system proved flexible to the needs of the economy in wage settlements, and the market-oriented reforms that raised inequality provided incentives that seem to have helped the recovery. Swedish workers and young people responded to the new market realities with sizable mobility and investments in education. Educational earnings differentials that were modestly higher than in the past (but far below those in the United States) made university education more economically attractive.

4.2 Argentina

The Latin American region stands out in its ability to withstand the global crisis most particularly in terms of employment, including employment conditions for women workers. For the region as a whole (largely driven by large economies such as those of Brazil and Argentina but also along with a number of smaller economies such as Ecuador and Bolivia), while GDP fell by nearly 2 percent in 2009, it recovered quite rapidly in 2010. Further, while unemployment rates increased on average in 2009 after a decade of decline, they also fell again in 2010.

This rather positive response to the crisis in the region has been attributed (Marinakis 2011) to a combination of factors: sound pre-crisis macroeconomic conditions, including the relatively prudent macroeconomic policies that had generated a reasonable amount of fiscal space in the form of low government deficits and low public debt-to-GDP ratios; several favorable external factors, including most of all positive terms of trade effects and continuing relatively buoyant demand for some of the main exports, particularly for primary commodity exporters, as well as tourism earnings and remittances; and the implementation of proactive policies to sustain economic activity, employment, and wages. Here, the focus is on the last set of factors, and particularly on the labor market policies that played an active role in partly generating and then extending and enhancing the recovery. Throughout various countries of Latin America, several important policies were employed, including: countercyclical policies such as public investment, emergency job creation, subsidized work-sharing; automatic stabilizers such as unemployment insurance; social protection schemes including various types of cash transfer programs and non-contributory pension programs; and active minimum wage policies.

In what follows, the specific case of Argentina is examined because it also shows how these strategies can play an important role in recovery from a major financial crisis even before the outbreak of the Great Recession in 2008. Argentina suffered one of the most severe financial crises ever experienced by any developing country in 2001–02, after it was finally forced to abandon the currency peg that had linked the Argentine peso to the US dollar. Output dropped by nearly 20 percent over the course of the crisis, while employment collapsed and the incidence of poverty doubled. The period of instability continued until the middle years of the decade, but by 2003 the government had already embarked on a different macroeconomic strategy that was based more fundamentally on employment generation, which had fundamental results in terms of recovery from crisis.

Thereafter, the recovery was remarkable. Real GDP has grown at an annual rate of around 9 percent. This has been sustained not just by increasing exports fed by the global commodity boom (which is the point generally harped upon by most external commentators), but also by sustained expansion of the domestic market, strengthening of production, and increase in investment, which reached historically high rates of 23 percent in the period 2003–09. This was not all or only about public investment – there were nearly 130,000 new private enterprises registered between 2003 and 2009. This investment, in turn, powered a substantial increase in labor productivity, which had languished throughout the earlier two decades.

The increase in the domestic market was, in turn, led by labor market dynamics and the expansion of social protection systems – precisely in the manner advocated by proponents of wage-led growth. Total employment increased substantially, much of it in better-quality jobs. There was a significant increase in formal employment, which increased by 70 percent between 2002 and 2009. The ratio of registered workers to total working age population (which had stagnated for the previous 25 years) increased by 30 percent in just these seven years. The aggregate unemployment rate had fallen from 21.5 percent in 2002 to 7.9 percent in 2010.

And even during the latest crisis, the economy has shown substantial resilience in growth and employment terms. The unemployment rate has not changed and real wages have not suffered (although partly as a result of this, it is true that new problems are emerging in the form of inflation and its consequences).

Figure 2.7 indicates the pattern of changes in registered employment in the organized sector in Argentina over the last three economic crises. It is evident, first of all, that the recovery from the 2001–03 crisis was remarkable in that it and the subsequent growth process generated levels of registered employment that were far above the totals achieved in the earlier decade. And in the most recent crisis, the decline in employment was relatively small and the recovery was rapid.

This is due to a combination of macroeconomic and active labor market policies. Most importantly, in 2003 the government sought to change the economic policy model quite drastically to move away from dynamics of exclusion and marginalization in labor markets, which had become the norm in the economy since the mid-1970s. The promotion of quality, productive, and fairly remunerated employment, together with the expansion and redefinition of social

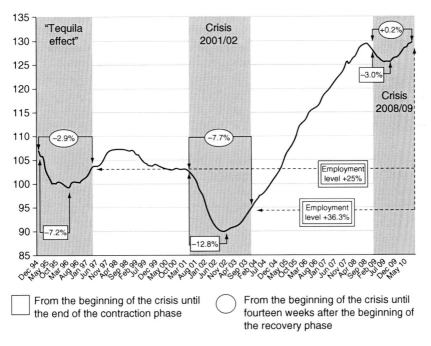

Figure 2.7 Changes in registered employment in organized activities in Argentina (source: Ministry of Labor, Argentina (2010, p. 70)).

protection focused on protecting a greater part of the population, were the main tools through which the model sought to improve the living conditions of the people. These turned out to have significant macroeconomic implications as well, providing a vibrant source of domestic effective demand that could encourage the proliferation of new productive employment.

Therefore, the economic advantage provided by a boom in primary commodity exports was not concentrated in the hands of a few privileged elite groups as had hitherto been the case, but spread much more widely among the population. The expansion of public employment and social protection provided opportunities for employment diversification within the economy and assisted the productivity improvements that have been witnessed in the recent past.

Some of the early changes were legislative or administrative in nature. In 2004, Law 25,877 for Labour Regulation was passed. The National Council for Employment, Productivity, and Minimum Salary was reactivated to decide upon and enforce minimum wage and salary rules. The National Plan for Work Regularization (PNRT) was set in motion, with the goal of expanding the government's ability to inspect and control compliance with labor laws and social security contributions of employers.

Importantly, collective bargaining – which had languished under the earlier regimes – was brought back to center stage with a dramatic (more than five-fold) increase in the number of agreements and negotiations approved each year. In addition, negotiation activity at the branch level was reintroduced so as to reach a greater number of workers and "collectivize" the benefits, as opposed to the "individualization" of employment relationships that had predominated in the 1990s. As a result, collectively agreed salaries accounted for 81 percent of the wage bills of enterprises in 2009, compared to less than 50 percent in 2001. As a result of these changes, the wage share of national income increased from 34.3 percent in 2002 to 43.6 percent in 2008 (Ministry of Labour 2010). While these changes were applicable to all workers, they were particularly beneficial to women workers who were earlier more likely to be excluded from the benefits of collective bargaining processes. Since more women workers received wages at the lower end of the wage spectrum, they have also directly benefited from increases in minimum wages.

Another major element was the doubling of social protection grants. There was an increase in the value of pensions and extension in coverage, including the introduction of social pensions for defined categories. Today, it is estimated that the pension system covers 84 percent of the elderly population. At the same time, social protection for children and adolescents was extended, from 37 percent coverage (in terms of monetary transfers) in 1997 to 86 percent in 2009. Some of this was the result of the expansion of registered employment, which allowed an extension of the coverage of family allowances. Those who were excluded from these worker-oriented family allowances benefited from the creation of a new non-contributory system: the Universal per Child Allowance for Social Protection, which currently reaches about 3.5 million children. These changes in social protection measures have also been important in providing a buffer for women predominantly engaged in the care economy and household work, whose contribution often goes unrecognized and unrewarded.

As a result of this emphasis on inclusion and social protection, social spending expenditures of the government increased significantly to amount to nearly a quarter of GDP in 2008. This and other measures outlined obviously had a direct effect on income distribution. Argentina was known as one of the more unequal countries in the world, and income inequality had been steadily increasing since the mid-1970s. In the past decade, this was finally reversed, as the Gini coefficient for income distribution improved by 16 percent between 2002 and 2009.

In the current crisis, these measures have been sought to be maintained and even expanded. There has been a focus on countercyclical macroeconomic policies, including public works, housing plans, incentives for stimulation of productive sectors, exports, pre-financing loans, and loans for small enterprises. In all policies implemented, an employment preservation clause was included as a requirement to access and maintain the benefits and subsidies. In addition, the reach of the Productive Recovery Program (REPRO), through which the state subsidizes part of the workers' salaries in enterprises in a critical situation, was extended. Fiscal incentives were provided for formal hiring and regularization of non-registered employment. There was also a strengthening of the active training and employment policies targeted to people that needed to further develop their skills in order to enhance their occupational insertion opportunities. Active income policies were maintained, so that as of the last quarter of 2008, the raises in retirement and pension transfers were guaranteed by law. Collective labor bargaining was sustained. There was a reduction in income taxes for salaried workers, and the amounts of the family allowances were increased. Also, there were monetary transfer programs for vulnerable or impoverished groups.

Obviously, these policies make severe fiscal demands, and the current inflationary pressures in Argentina do suggest that further increases will have to be moderated. However, this very different approach to social and economic distribution and the positive macroeconomic effects that it has generated thus far show that there are other viable economic trajectories that can deliver both growth and economic justice.

However, it has been noted that Argentina's economic recovery, while impressive, has been less favorable to women workers than to their male counterparts. Unemployment has been reduced less among women than men, women's salaries have grown less than men's, and the process of increasing feminization of the work force that occurred during the 1990s has not been evident in the past decade, probably because of the more rapid growth of economic sectors that have been traditionally male-dominated (Castillo *et al.* 2008). A study on gender wage gaps (Rojo Brizuela and Tumini 2011) found that the firm's branch of activity is the aspect that accounts most for gender wage differences. (The average gender gap is 20 percent for all workers.) This is why the type of growth that Argentina's economy underwent between 2002 and 2009, with numerous new firms entering into production and dynamism of industrial sectors that have traditionally had low numbers of female employees, has also led to an intensification of gender wage gaps within firms.

It is worth noting that within the economically active population of Argentina, women have spent more years in formal education than men. Nevertheless, women workers tend to be concentrated in positions with low-skill requirements, with direct effects on wage gaps. It was also noted that in addition, women receive substantially lower salaries at all skill levels (with the exception of those employed in the hotel industry). However, Rojo Brizuela and Tumini's (2011) study also found that the intensity of collective bargaining and the increase in the number of workers covered by collective labor agreements have had a compensatory role and have tended to equalize salaries between the sexes. Therefore, there is a strong case in countries such as Argentina for emphasizing labor institutions such as the minimum living wage and the base salaries that are established by collective labor agreements to function as an equalizing base between the salaries men and women, particularly, earn in low-income areas.

Finally, the positive role of social protection measures in Argentina should be noted. As mentioned earlier, these played a significant cushioning role in maintaining effective demand, of course. But we must be mindful because they also had major implications for women – not just in adding to household incomes and therefore necessary consumption, but also in relation to unpaid labor. This is important, because the method of providing social protection can have contrary effects, particularly in conditional cash transfer programs that require women to fulfill various conditions that are time- and labor-intensive.

In conclusion, we want to emphasize that government countercyclical policies matter greatly in periods of crisis. Nonetheless, to ensure that women benefit equitably, the particular allocation of public funds and specific types of active intervention in labor markets must be gender-sensitive.

Note

1 The link between the food and financial crises is elaborated in Ghosh (2009a).

References

Castillo, V., Esquivel, V., Rojo Brizuela, S., Tumini L., and Yoguel, G. (2008) "Changes in the gender composition of formal employment 2002–2006: effects of the new growth pattern on female employment," Serie Trabajo, Ocupación y Empleo No. 7, Buenos Aires, SSPTyEL, MTEySS.
Chandrasekhar, C.P. and Ghosh, J. (2011) "Public works and wages in rural India," Macro Scan.
Chen, M., Vanek, J., and Heintz, J. (2006) "Informality, gender and poverty: a global picture," *Economic and Political Weekly*, 41: 2131–9.
Chhibber, A., Ghosh, J., and Palanivel, T. (2009) *Asia Recovers but Sustained Growth Needs a New Paradigm*, Colombo: UNDP.
Elson, D. (1993) *Male Bias in the Development Process*, Manchester: Manchester University Press.

Ghosh, J. (2006) "The social and economic effects of financial liberalisaiton: a primer for developing countries," in K.S. Jomo (ed.), *Policy Matters*, London: Zed Books.

Ghosh, J. (2009a) "The unnatural coupling: food and global finance," *Journal of Agrarian Change*, 10: 72–86.

Ghosh, J. (2009b) "Adjustment, recovery, and growth after financial crisis: a consideration of five 'crisis' countries of east and southeast Asia," in C.P. Chandrasekhar and J. Ghosh (eds.), *After Crisis: adjustment, recovery and fragility in East Asia*, New Delhi: Tulika Press.

Ghosh, J. and Chandrasekhar, C.P. (2001) *Crisis as Conquest: learning from East Asia*, New Delhi: Orient Longman.

Ghosh, J. and Chandrasekhar, C.P. (eds.) (2009) *After Crisis: adjustment, recovery and fragility in East Asia*, New Delhi: Tulika Press.

Green, D., King, R., and Miller-Dawkins, M. (2010) *The Global Economic Crisis and Developing Countries*, Oxford: Oxfam.

Freeman, R.B., Swedenborg, B., and Topel, R. (eds.) (2010) *Reforming the Welfare State: recovery and beyond in Sweden*, Chicago: University of Chicago Press.

Futagami, S. (2010) "Non-standard employment in Japan: the gender dimensions," International Institute of Labour Studies Discussion Paper, DP/200/2010, Geneva.

ILO (2009) *Recovering from the Crisis: a global jobs pact*, Geneva: International Labour Office.

ILO (2011) *Key Indicators of Labour Markets*, Geneva: International Labour Office. Online: www.ilo.org/empelm/what/WCMS_114240/lang-en/index.htm (accessed May 20, 2013).

ILO (2012a) *Eurozone Jobs Crisis: trends and policy responses*, Geneva: International Institute of Labour Studies.

ILO (2012b) *Global Employment Trends 2012*, Geneva: International Labour Office. Online: http://public.eblib.com/EBLPublic/PublicView.do?ptiID=863032 (accessed May 20, 2013).

Jomo, K.S. (1998) *Tigers in Trouble: financial governance, liberalisation and crisis in East Asia*, London: Zed Books.

Jonung, L. (2009) "Lessons from the Nordic financial crises," in L. Jonung, J. Kiander, and P. Vartia (eds.), *The Great Financial Crisis in Finland and Sweden: the Nordic experience of financial liberalization*, London: Edward Elgar.

Kang, J. and Wei, L. (2010) "China's fiscal policies during the post-crisis era," mimeo, Research Institute for Fiscal Science, Ministry of Finance, PR China, Beijing.

Kabeer, N. (1994) *Reversed Realities: gender hierarchies in development thought*, London: Verso.

Kyrili, K. and Martin, M. (2010) *The Impact of the Global Economic Crisis on the Budgets of Low-Income Countries*, Research Report for Oxfam. Oxford: Oxfam. Online: www.oxfam.org/sites/www.oxfam.org/files/impact-global-economic-crisis-lic-budgets-0710.pdf (accessed on May 21, 2013).

Marinakis, A. (2011) "Explaining Latin America's robust recovery from the crisis," in ILO (ed.), *The Global Crisis: causes, responses and challenges*, Geneva: International Labour Office.

Ministry of Labor, Employment and Social Security of the Government of Argentina (2010) "Work and employment in the bicentenary: changes in employment and social protection dynamics for an extended inclusion, 2003–10," Buenos Aires, Argentina.

OECD (2012) *Gender Data Browser*. Online: www.oecd.org/els/family/oecdgenderinitiative.htm#Browser (accessed May 20, 2013).

Olafsdottir, K. (2009) "Gender effects of the economic crisis," Defentsoria Working Paper. Online: www.emakunde.euskadi.net/u72-10010/es/contenidos/informacion/publicaciones_seminarios_flash/es_2009/uploads/ponencias/katrin-olafsdottir.pdf(accessed May 21, 2013).

Ortiz, I., Vergara, G., and Chai, J. (2010) "Prioritizing expenditures for a recovery with a human face: results from a rapid desk review of 86 recent IMF country reports," *Social and Economic Policy Working Briefs*, UNICEF Policy and Practice, New York: UNICEF, April.

Ortiz, I., Chai, J., and Cummins, M. (2011) "Austerity measures threaten children and poor households: recent evidence in public expenditures from 128 developing countries," UNICEF Social and Economic Policy Working Paper, New York: UNICEF.

Ortiz, I., and Cummins, M. (eds.) (2012) *A Recovery for All: rethinking socio-economic policies for children and poor households*, New York: UNICEF.

Reinhart, C.M. and Rogoff, K.S. (2008) "This time is different: a panoramic view of eight centuries of financial crises," NBER Working Paper No. 13882, Cambridge, MA: National Bureau of Economic Research.

Rojo Brizuela, S. and Tumini, L. (2011) "Gender wage gaps in Argentina and how collective agreements could reduce them," Serie Trabajo, Ocupación y Empleo, Buenos Aires, SSPTyEL, MTEySS.

Seguino, S. (2009) "The global economic crisis, its gender implications and policy responses," paper prepared for *Gender Perspectives on the Financial Crisis* panel at the Fifty-Third Session of the Commission on the Status of Women, New York: United Nations, March 5.

Singh, A. and Zammit, A. (2000) "International capital flows: identifying the gender dimension," *World Development*, 28: 1249–68.

UNICEF (2010) "Protecting salaries of frontline teachers and health workers," *Social and Economic Policy Working Briefs*, New York: UNICEF, April.

Vaughan-Whitehead, D. (ed.) (2012) *Work Inequalities in the Crisis: evidence from Europe*, Geneva: International Labour Office.

3 Investing in care in the midst of a crisis

A strategy for effective and equitable job creation in the United States

Rania Antonopoulos, Kijong Kim, Tom Masterson, and Ajit Zacharias

1 Introduction

What began as a subprime mortgage debacle in the United States at the end of 2007 and early months of 2008 became the worst global financial and economic crisis since the Great Depression. The initial policy reaction was focused, first and foremost, on the reduction of financial sector (and credit market) instability and, second, on prevention of a total collapse in demand via some combination of fiscal and monetary expansion. This was the case for developed and developing countries. But following this first phase of countercyclical engagement, in the post-2010 period, sovereign debt concerns took center stage on both sides of the Atlantic. Despite still being in the midst of a crisis (or slowly emerging from it) government spending was perceived as profligate and the fight to curtail it at any cost began. While rising unemployment and anemic growth were in evidence, fiscal concerns ruled the day, overshadowing the much-needed public debate on how to better regulate financial markets and address other systemic global imbalances.

In the United States, the political stalemate regarding the "fiscal cliff" and the fear of downgrading the AAA status of US bonds – by the same rating agencies that failed to sound the alarm back in 2007 – is, so far, dominating the political debate. In Europe, the situation is even bleaker: a misguided mix of austerity and tax increases in the hopes of calming capital markets via fast-tracking Greece, Ireland, Portugal, Spain, and Italy into a primary surplus position is firmly in place. That these economies now face even higher debt-to-GDP ratios while austerity-driven unemployment and economic slowdown are decimating these countries and the living standards of their citizens does not seem to be shifting mindsets as yet.

By October 2012, almost five years since the onset of the "Great Recession," the world economy was still below recovery trends observed in previous crisis episodes. The latest International Labour Organization (ILO) figures show that an additional 27 million persons have joined the ranks of the jobless due to the crisis and lackluster recovery, and the International Monetary Fund (IMF) stated that "growth is now too low to make a substantial dent in unemployment in advanced economies" (IMF 2012). In this climate, it is rather unreasonable to expect that capacity utilization and new investment will accelerate sufficiently to bridge the job deficit.

What can be done when private sector investment is unable to generate work opportunities and what – if any – lessons does the recent past hold? To address the specter of massive and protracted (long-term) joblessness, in fact, some countries deployed a crisis containment policy commonly known as "public works programs" at the onset of the recent upheaval. Public Works (PW) and Employment Guarantee (EG) programs, at the most basic level, are government-funded initiatives that offer jobs to those who wish to work, but cannot find work. The best-known experience among developed countries is the New Deal program introduced by the Roosevelt Administration during the Great Depression. The New Deal's *Works Progress Administration* was a nationwide initiative that essentially made the federal government the largest single employer in the nation. When such programs are introduced, the state becomes the "employer of last resort,"[1] a term coined by Hyman Minsky, in that it provides direct job creation; namely, the state guarantees the security of a paid work option when all else fails. Whether common sense will return soon and space for reintroducing strong countercyclical policy, including direct job creation, opens up again is not clear. Given that a total of 200 million unemployed (ILO 2012) are looking *actively* for a job but are unable to find one, there is a need for public policy dialogue on this topic, as worldwide unemployment rates remind us.

From the case of the United States, the subject matter of this chapter, much can be learned, especially in the context of painfully high unemployment in some European countries, by exploring the American Recovery and Reinvestment Act of 2009 (ARRA). ARRA was one of the first policy actions that the Obama Administration undertook early in its tenure in February 2009. Essentially, it was a stimulus package roughly representing an injection of US$780 billion whose primary objective was to expand aggregate demand, but to do so in a targeted way that would contribute to saving and/or creating an estimated three million jobs.

As of June 2010, when we undertook this study, the official unemployment rate in the United States was 9.5 percent, or 14.6 million people. An alternative measure of labor underutilization, U-6,[2] revealed even more disheartening figures: those working part-time but needing and wanting a full-time job were 8.6 million persons; another 2.6 million persons were marginally attached, including discouraged workers. Thus, a total of 25.8 million people were without jobs or working only part-time jobs against their wishes, meaning that a stunning 16.5 percent of the total labor force was unemployed or underemployed.

At the same time, the employment-to-population ratio had declined to 58.5 percent, the lowest it had been over the last 25 years. Figure 3.1 shows the trends of the duration and severity of employment losses of the seven recessions since 1969. For each spell of recession, a seasonally adjusted nonfarm payroll employment level is indexed to be 100 at the start of the downturn and plotted to a period ranging 10 months before the onset to 30 months afterwards. The current

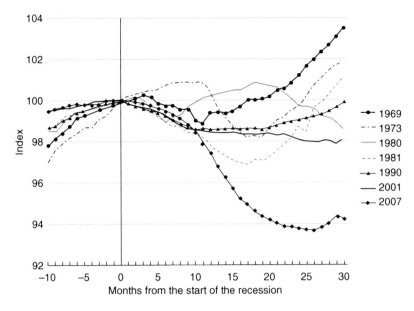

Figure 3.1 Nonfarm payroll extended job loss trend from the last seven recessions (1969–current) (source: BLS 2010a).

recession – the line with diamonds on the graph – started with a moderate impact on employment for the first 12 months, but unleashed its full destructive force thereafter. A painful further deterioration eased in the December 2008–June 2010 period, but recovery to the pre-recession level seemed as remote as ever.

Another issue of concern was the duration of unemployment. Figure 3.2 shows the historical trend of the shares of unemployed persons looking for a job for more than 27 weeks since 1970. The share reached 45.5 percent (6.8 million), again a worrisome figure as compared to previous harsh economic times. Long spells of unemployment degrade workers' skills and may send negative signals to potential employers, making a return to work more difficult (Heckman and Borjas 1980; Acemoglu 1995). But also, a grim labor market outlook leads workers to accept jobs below their skills, discourages job searches, forces people into inactivity, and lowers their future wages. Such large-scale failure of the private labor market requires public sector action to restore efficiency and equity (Acemoglu 1995).

In addition to income loss, unemployment entails other less recognized costs, and Amartya Sen summarized them aptly some time ago in *Development as Freedom*:

There is plenty of evidence that unemployment has many far-reaching effects other than loss of income, including psychological harm, loss of

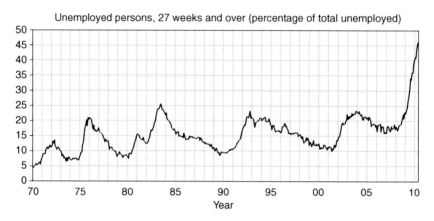

Figure 3.2 Historical trend of long-term unemployment (January 1970–May 2010) (source: BLS 2010b).

> work motivation, skill and self-confidence, increase in ailments and morbidity (and even mortality rates), disruption of family relations and social life, hardening of social exclusion, and accentuation of racial tensions and gender asymmetries.
>
> (Sen 1999)[3]

Temporary programs of direct job creation have traditionally tried to meet three objectives: first, that they create the maximum number of jobs for a given amount of public expenditure; second, that the projects undertaken are socially meaningful; and third, that wages are received by those most in need, namely, low-income households that are in danger of being pushed into poverty by joblessness. The ARRA contained provisions to create jobs in infrastructure and the green economy sector, but it also included budgetary allocations for job creation in the provisioning of care. In what follows, we present our proposal for direct investment in localized community-based *social care services*, in particular, home-based health care and early childhood development. Investment in care is a more cost-effective and equitable way to create jobs than investing in infrastructure construction or green energy development, as it generates more jobs per dollar spent than any other investment. The job creation potential of social care investment in the short run has been analyzed in several studies (Simonazzi 2009; Antonopoulos and Kim 2008; Warner and Liu 2006). Lessons learned from the Japanese experience with fiscal stimulus in the 1990s indicate that social care investment can be an effective means for employment generation as well as a strategy for sustainable growth (Fackler 2009).

In fact, as we mentioned above, the federal government did increase investment in care in ARRA, but it allotted a rather small amount of US$3 billion to Head

Start and Early Head Start programs (early childhood development programs for low-income families), and the intent was not job creation. State fiscal stabilization funds in the Act have helped to maintain coverage in the midst of state budget cuts, but these temporary measures were hardly enough to have resulted in meaningful job creation or to have met the growing demand for services.

Our objective is to understand the potential of the social care sector for effective and equitable job creation. To that end, we employ a modeling framework that combines input–output (I–O) analysis and microsimulation (Zacharias *et al.* 2009). First, we evaluate the job creation potential of social care vis-à-vis infrastructure investment by occupation and industry. Then, we assess the distributive impacts by examining the growth in earnings of workers in different socioeconomic groups. We find that social care spending generates twice as many jobs as infrastructure spending, and 50 percent more jobs than green energy development. Social care investment also yields more equitable outcomes: care investment creates twice as many jobs for low-income households as infrastructure construction does and care investment improves the earnings of poor workers more than infrastructure spending. We believe our findings continue to be important in the present climate and hope they can inform the policy debate in the context of many other countries that face intractable unemployment problems.

This chapter is organized as follows. The next section provides an overview of the social care sector, followed by an elaboration on the current employment conditions within the sector. We discuss our simulation methodology in Section 3. Our findings on job creation and distributive effects are reported in Section 4. Our conclusion follows in Section 5.

2 Social care sector: overview and employment

2.1 Social care overview

Social care – public provisioning of caring for others – consists of a range of activities to nurture and assist children, the disabled, and the elderly. For the purpose of this chapter, we will concentrate on early childhood development – preschool and formal child care – and home-based care for disabled and chronically ill patients. As is well known, in the absence of public sector provisioning, it is unpaid household production, primarily by women, that provides care – often in insufficient quantity and quality. A wide range of studies and articles in the popular press suggest that there is certainly room for additional federal contributions to care services in the United States.

Hidden demand for early childhood development services is larger than officially recognized. One way to estimate this demand is through counting the number of child care providers other than formal paid child care workers, including unpaid care by relatives: there are 1.9 non-parental, paid and unpaid caregivers for every paid care worker captured in the official survey (Burton *et al.* 2002; Warner 2009a). According to the National Household Education Surveys

Program of 2005, 60 percent of children under age five had at least one weekly non-parental care arrangement. Among those who had the arrangements, 60 percent participated in center-based care, 35 percent in relative care, and 22 percent in nonrelative care (Iruka and Carver 2006).[4] A mere 21 percent of children from families below the federal poverty line participated in Head Start or Early Head Start programs (Iruka and Carver 2006). The financial burden of care is also distributed unequally: an average family below the poverty level spent 29.2 percent of their income on child care, while a typical family above 200 percent of the poverty level spent only 8.3 percent (US Census Bureau 2010). Even with federal and state subsidies and grants, child care expenditure is a large financial burden to many families.

Demand for home-based care is increasing quickly as baby boomers age and advanced medical technologies extend the life expectancy of disabled and chronic patients. According to the National Home Health Aide Survey (NHHAS),[5] almost 1.5 million people were receiving care in 2007 and 7.2 million people had received care and had been discharged in 2000.[6] Over 14,000 agencies are in the business of recruiting and training caregivers and serving the patients.[7] Over US$58 billion – or 2.76 percent of national health expenditure – was spent on home health service in 2006.[8] Medicare and Medicaid cover the bulk of total home health care service payments – 37 and 19 percent, respectively, according to National Association for Home Care and Hospice (NAHC 2008). Home health care accounted for 3.9 percent of Medicare spending in 2006 and 16.3 percent of Medicaid expenditures in 2004.[9] Nonetheless, the bulk of the burden of care fell upon family, friends, and other volunteers. They covered 57 percent (36 percent by value of informal care and 21 percent by out-of-pocket payments) of long-term care responsibilities for the elderly (CBO 2004). Medicare and Medicaid picked up 38 percent of total costs, followed by private insurance (3 percent), and other undefined sources (2 percent).

Administration of investment in expanding social care does not require a parallel expansion of government size, nor a novel approach to channel the funds through the system. The delivery systems are already organized and administered by local and state governments through Head Start/Early Head Start and various home-based care organizations that qualify for reimbursement from Medicare and Medicaid. Scaling-up does not entail compromises on quality of care or skill mismatch of newly hired workers. Skill requirements and training time may not be as onerous as it can be for some construction-related jobs. A good deal of physical stamina and aptitude for care for others may be enough to begin with. Then, through on-the-job training with a current Child Development Associate (CDA) degree and/or home health aide certification, concerns for high-quality care could be addressed. With the expected budget shortfalls of about US$350 billion for 2010 and 2011 (McNichol and Johnson 2009), state governments are already in dire need of federal transfers to fill the gap of immediate social care demand just to provide the inadequate pre-recession level of social care. Scaling-up service delivery would not overwhelm the system or require extra federal scrutiny. Concerns about fraud and abuse of funds for

Medicaid and Medicare have already attracted the government's due diligence with successful enforcement under the newly enacted Affordable Care Act.

Aside from jobs and income growth, other economic and social benefits also justify the expansion of social care services. Children who get early childhood development care tend to become more productive members of society when they grow up.[10] Home-based care is more cost effective than care at a hospital or nursing home for chronic illness. For instance, caring for a low-birth-weight infant costs a minimum of US$873 per day in a hospital setting, whereas home-based care, including homemaking services, costs US$626 per day (Casiro *et al.* 1993). An oxygen-dependent child may need over US$12,000 per month for medical care in a hospital, but she can receive the same level of care at home for only 44 percent of the cost – US$5,333 (Fields *et al.* 1991).[11] Employees' care responsibilities cost more than US$33 billion a year to employers due to lost productivity (MetLife 2006). Scaling-up of home-based care could save much of the cost. Any sensible cost–benefit analysis would favor social care expansion.

2.2 Employment in social care

The child care and early childhood development providers in the industry are mainly preschool teachers (35 percent of total wage and salary jobs in the industry during 2008), child care workers (30 percent), and preschool teacher assistants (14 percent) (BLS 2009a).[12] The median age of the providers was 38 years and 19 percent of them were 24 years or younger, whereas the median age of all workers in the economy was 45 years and only 13 percent of them were 24 or younger. The age composition of the care providers suggests that the occupation may serve as one of the entry jobs for the young and low-skilled population. Education requirements vary, from a high school diploma with a CDA degree to a college degree in early childhood education, by states and sources of funding for programs. Family child care providers in small-scale and informal settings are not under state or federal regulation. The average hourly earning in the industry was US$11.32, lower than the overall private industry average of US$18.08. Median annual wages ranged from US$17,440 for child care workers, to US$22,120 for preschool teachers, and up to US$37,270 for preschool directors (BLS 2009b). The lower-than-average weekly earnings of US$345, compared to US$608 in overall private industry, imply that many providers work on a part-time basis. Overall, 25 percent of the workers in 2008 (15 percent for preschool teachers and 30 percent for child care workers) are from families with total income that fell below 150 percent of the official poverty line and 9.5 percent of them had received food stamps in 2008.[13]

Low-skilled women have dominated the work force – 88 percent of total workers – in home health care provision. The average age of workers in the sector was 41 years. Most were minority (52 percent), especially African American women (30 percent), while recent immigrants amounted to 21 percent of the work force, and 43 percent of workers were employed part-time in 2008 (PHI 2009). No education requirements exist for these jobs, although those who work for an agency receiving Medicare and Medicaid reimbursements are required to pass competency tests or state certification programs with a minimum of 75 hours of training. In fact, 58 percent of workers in 2008 had an educational attainment of high school diploma or less. The average hourly wage of home health aides was US\$10.31 in May 2008 and US\$21,440. Over 25 percent of the workers had family incomes below 150 percent of the official poverty line and almost 16 percent of them received food stamps in 2008 (King *et al.* 2009). Low wage rates may contribute in part to the poor economic status of the workers, but it is also true that many workers come from poor households. Thus, it is hard to establish a causal relationship between the low wages of individual workers and the poverty status of the households in which they live.

The expansion of services would directly create demand for more teachers and care providers as the programs cover more children. In addition, the increased demand for material and services to expand early childhood education programs means more job opportunities indirectly in the rest of the economy. This short-term employment impact has been scrutinized by a research team at Cornell University, led by Mildred Warner. She and her collaborators analyze the economic linkages of the child care sector to the rest of the economy, through which job multiplier effects take place (Warner *et al.* 2004; Warner and Liu 2006; Warner 2007; Warner 2009a; Warner 2009b). They demonstrate that child care sector expansion generates more jobs – direct and indirect combined – than the expansion of most of the other sectors in the economy on a jobs-per-dollar basis. As a regional development strategy, the expansion of child care is effective, according to their studies. To the best of our knowledge, expansion of home-based health care has not been viewed in the context of employment generation. This chapter attempts to fill the void.

Previous studies, assessing both long-term and short-term benefits of expanding social care, have not taken into account distributional impacts: who would receive jobs from the expansion and how much income they would receive from the jobs. Employment opportunities created directly and indirectly from the expansion may or may not reach the disadvantaged groups in the labor market (i.e., women, less-educated, and poor households) depending on the occupations and industries in which these jobs are created. A job as an administrator in the health care industry is likely to be held by a highly educated male worker from an affluent household, while a less-educated woman from a middle-class household would be more likely to take a job as a child care provider or preschool teacher. The individual characteristics of workers determine their likelihood of employment and earnings across occupations and industries. We use a microsimulation approach to analyze the distributional issues.

3 Methodology

To analyze the employment impact of our proposed intervention, we combine two different quantitative methods: at the macro level we make use of I–O analysis, and at the micro level we employ a microsimulation model. I–O analysis allows for the calculation of changes in total employment by industry, while the microsimulation model distributes these jobs by matching them to individuals who are most likely to take them based on nationally representative survey data.

The method we utilize captures multiplier effects through linkages of output growth between industries: as one sector of the economy experiences an increase in demand for its own output, it ends up demanding more goods and services from several other industries, which results in turn in direct, but also indirect, job creation downstream. To estimate the employment creation through industry linkages, we use the 2006 I–O table. The I–O table is constructed by the Bureau for Economic Analysis (BEA), using various data sources, i.e., the Economic Census by the Census Bureau, administrative data from the Internal Revenue Services, Social Security Administration, and other federal authorities. It presents a full accounting of transactions – production and consumption – in the economy. The I–O table used in our analysis is the version that was recompiled by the Bureau of Labor Statistics (BLS) for their employment projection. It depicts the inter-industry linkages of 201 industries, from which one can calculate employment multipliers. The most recent (2006) annual I–O table from the BEA available at the time of our study was at a higher-level of industrial aggregation than the BLS table, especially for the service and government sectors. Ideally, we would have preferred to use a benchmark I–O table, which contains a very high level of disaggregation (over 400 industries). However, the most current (2002) benchmark table available is based on the Economic Census of 1997, and we felt that this may not sufficiently reflect the current economic structure. Consideration of the trade-off between the detail and timeliness of data led us to use the 2006 BLS I–O table.

The employment matrix is a product of total requirement table (direct and indirect input requirements necessary to produce a unit of final output) and a vector of employment intensity by industry (a ratio of total number of workers to final output). The total requirement table is the Leontief inverse matrix, computed as $(I-A)^{-1}$ from the matrix of direct requirements table (A), which shows only the direct input requirements, or the technical coefficients of an industry. In I–O terminology, commodity output is given by $x=(I-A)^{-1} * y$, where x is the vector of industry output by commodity, I is the identity matrix, and y is the vector of final commodity demand. The total requirement table $(I-A)^{-1}$ has a layout of industry-by-commodity to construct the employment multipliers by industry. The employment multiplier matrix (E) is written as $E=w^* (I-A)^{-1}$, where w^* is a diagonal matrix with jobs-to-output ratios by industry along its principal diagonal. Therefore, the employment multipliers are computed by industry, and thus interpreted as the number of jobs created in each industry, directly and indirectly, to produce one additional unit of commodity output. We multiply the matrix by a vector of final expenditures on commodities to compute the number of direct and indirect jobs created by the spending.

The employment multiplier matrix captures the employment generation via inter-industry input supply and demand. We believe that I–O analysis is an appropriate tool to assess employment effects of industry-specific, *ex ante* policy studies. We believe that the benefits of using the multiplier analysis framework outweigh the shortcomings implicit in a comparative static analysis for the task at hand. With the estimates of new jobs by industry in hand we move on to the next step.

In this stage, all of the new jobs in each industry, direct and indirect, are classified by occupation, i.e., as preschool teachers and assistants, home health aides, and administrative staff, all of which would be considered direct jobs; in addition, it provides similar information in all other industries (sectors) that produce the needed intermediate inputs. To do so, we include the occupational classification of employment and its distribution across industries by using the National Industry-Occupation Employment Matrix created by the BLS. The rationale for considering the occupational mix is that it plays a key role in determining the distributive effects – occupation is a major determinant of earnings. The industry-occupation table of new jobs is subsequently made use of in the microsimulation.

Our microsimulation is based on the public-use file of the 2009 *Annual Social and Economic Supplement of the Current Population Survey*, produced by the Census Bureau. We assume that the additional demand for labor created by each alternative scenario considered in this study would be met by an increased supply of labor from the pool of "employable" individuals. The employable pool of potential workers consists of individuals (16 years and older) who are currently not working. We exclude individuals who did not work at all in 2008 and gave the reason for not working as being retired, disabled, taking care of family, or, for those less than 20 years of age, in school.

To assign jobs, we create a ranking of occupations and industries for each individual by estimating the likelihood of being employed in each job category.[14] The method was to estimate a multinomial probit regression for industry and occupation and then predict probabilities for each.[15] For each individual, industries and occupations were ranked based on highest propensity score. Then we estimated likelihood of being employed for each individual, using a probit regression and propensity score.[16] With these three sets of information for each individual, we assigned employment status to those in the employable pool using an iterative procedure, stepping through industry and occupation pairs, selecting those individuals most likely to be employed in that industry-occupation pair, in order of their likelihood to be employed, until all the available jobs were assigned. Once we assigned jobs, we imputed earnings to those individuals who received a new job. The method was imputation by hot-decking.[17]

Our simulation assumes an investment of US$50 billion in projects that increase social care provisioning. Divided equally between home-based health care and early childhood development for children under the age of five, this amount is equivalent to one-half of the total gross output of the two industries combined in 2006. In I–O analysis, the spending is interpreted as the increase in final demand of commodities by the amount. The increased final demand for child day care (North American Industry Classification System, NAICS 6244) and home health care services (NAICS 6216) leads to increasing labor demand in both industries directly as well as in other industries that supply intermediate inputs to them.

A recent national survey by the Department of Education on child care indicates that 40 percent of children under age five do not have any non-parental day care arrangements (Iruka and Carver 2006; USDE/NCES 2006). Even for non-parental care cases,[18] the true work burden of child care is probably seriously underestimated as a half of child care workers are unpaid, unaccounted for in data gathering, and thus dropped from policy consideration. In addition, a report from the Congressional Budget Office (2004) on long-term care for the elderly indicates that over a third of the care burden falls onto informal care by family and other volunteers. The BLS[19] predicts that home-based direct care will be one of the fastest-growing occupations in the period 2010–20, as the population grows older and lives longer. Given the large, hidden current and future need for social care, we feel that US$50 billion is not an exaggerated estimate to cover, at least partially, the need for care services in the United States.

The policy framework – as well as the scale of the intervention – for our job creation proposal is that of the ARRA outlays and tax cuts, which was passed by the Obama Administration.[20] We find this framework to be compelling for the following reason. Although the employment impact of the ARRA is still unfolding, the Act has influenced and will continue to influence labor markets. This is the case because the ARRA introduces a variety of employment options that would not have existed in its absence. For instance, a recent college graduate who would not have originally chosen to work in the construction industry may do so now, since the Act has raised demand for this sector's output and, hence, employment. Or the Act may help an experienced worker who had been forced into an unskilled part-time job to move into a full-time skilled job, leaving her/his previously held position to a less experienced person, who had not participated in the labor market for a while due to the grim outlook of the economy. Hence, in assigning jobs to individuals who are most likely to want them, the template we use to represent the economy must incorporate the labor supply responses that the ARRA is likely to elicit but have not been reflected in our microdata. The results reported in this chapter, however, net out the ARRA impacts in order to highlight the impacts of social care investment.[21]

We do not construct a baseline to which our simulation results may be compared. The purpose of the study is primarily to demonstrate the job creation potential and to identify beneficiaries of a social care sector expansion relative to infrastructure construction. Thus, the results in this chapter should not be translated into a dynamic framework in which one would discuss changes in labor market condition over time as a result of such investments. Furthermore, it is not valid to use the framework for forecast purposes, since there are many macro variables to take into account that this study does not.

We assume that social care services are delivered through a mix of: (1) direct purchases by consumers and (2) government subsidies to private sector service providers. We make use of the private care industry assumption because it reflects the current mechanism of the bulk of service delivery. In other words, although centers that act as service providers must meet certain state-level criteria, these entities do not act as government contractors whose activities otherwise would have fallen into the government production category.[22]

4 Findings

This section starts with the description of the size and types of jobs created from our simulations. Then we identify the beneficiaries of job creation in terms of the types of households that receive the jobs and the changes in household income due to job creation.

4.1 Direct and indirect employment generation by industry and occupation

We compare the employment distribution by industry in Table 3.1. US$50 billion in social care investment generates almost 1.2 million jobs, as opposed to 556,000 jobs in the case of a similar investment in infrastructure construction. Most jobs are concentrated within the respective industries in both cases, especially for social care. The relatively large within-sector employment multiplier of the social care sector is mainly due to the high jobs-to-output ratio in that sector. The results in Table 3.1 confirm the pattern: eight out of ten new jobs are created in social care, whereas infrastructure construction creates more indirect employment – four out of ten new jobs – in other industries, as the sector

Table 3.1 Total employment distribution across industries

Industry	Social care	Infrastructure
Agriculture	2,928	1,969
Mining	520	2,463
Utilities	773	1,808
Construction	4,489	*345,955*
Manufacturing	16,797	46,402
Wholesale	7,139	11,421
Retail	4,432	36,628
Transportation and warehousing	7,020	12,715
Information	4,989	4,312
Financial and real estate services	13,621	11,474
Professional and business services	57,672	55,675
Education	688	719
Health care and social assistance	21,046	675
Social care	*956,082*	107
Leisure and hospitality	15,650	6,509
Other services	3,113	5,009
Government	69,384	12,099
Total	1,186,342	555,942

Source: Authors' calculations.

requires more diverse inputs than social care does. On that basis alone, one might come to the conclusion that infrastructure construction is preferable. However, the effectiveness of infrastructure construction spending is lower because it creates less than half the number of jobs for the same amount of spending as social care expansion.

The occupational composition of jobs in social care (see Table 3.2) shows that 76 percent of total job creation takes place in the high-end and low-end service occupations, i.e., teachers, child care providers, and home health aides. These are the jobs in which women have better chances of gaining employment. On the other hand, 61 percent of the jobs generated by infrastructure construction are in production occupations – factory and construction workers, farmers, and truck drivers – that are traditionally more male-oriented. Although current public sentiment may favor reviving the American manufacturing sector – and indeed this may be slowly happening already – and creating construction jobs for the workers hit hardest by the Great Recession, expanding investment in social care is in fact a more effective way to create jobs than investment in physical infrastructure alone.

4.2 Distribution of jobs: who benefits?

In this subsection, we present the results from the microsimulation assignment of jobs to individuals with different characteristics and analyze the distributional impacts of the simulated investments on social care versus infrastructure construction.

Table 3.2 Occupational composition of social care and infrastructure construction, number of jobs and shares (in percent)

Occupation	Social care		Infrastructure	
Manager	69,256	(5.8)	47,685	(8.6)
Professional	159,307	(13.4)	27,748	(5.0)
High-end service	448,077	(37.8)	7,273	(1.3)
Low-end service	450,660	(38.0)	133,462	(24.0)
Production	59,043	(5.0)	339,774	(61.1)
Total	1,186,342 (100.0)		555,942 (100.0)	

Source: Authors' calculations.

Note
"Managers" include management, business, and financial occupations. "Professionals" include computer and mathematical science; architecture and engineering; life, physical, and social science; legal; and healthcare practitioner and technical occupations. "High-end services" include community and social service; education, training, and library; arts, design, and entertainment; and health care support occupations. "Low-end services" include protective service; food preparation and serving; building and grounds cleaning and maintenance; personal care and service; sales and related; and office and administrative support occupations. "Production" include farming, fishing, and forestry; construction and extraction; installation, maintenance, and repair; production; and transportation and material moving occupations.

4.2.1 Job distribution

To compare the employment-generation potential of the two types of investment, we normalize the number of jobs per US$1 million of spending on social care and infrastructure investment. In addition, we use findings from Pollin *et al.* (2009) to analyze the job impacts of "green energy" investment for workers with various levels of educational attainment. This study provides analysis on the new types of infrastructure investment that the current administration is promoting with regards to carbon emission reduction and future economic growth.

Figure 3.3 depicts our estimates of job creation for workers with different levels of educational attainment for the two scenarios that we simulated, plus Pollin *et al.*'s (2009) estimates for green energy investment. As we have indicated above, social care expansion is well suited to creating jobs for groups with lower levels of educational attainment. In particular, expansion in social care spending would benefit a very vulnerable part of the work force – those with high school diplomas or less – creating 16.2 jobs for this group per US$1 million of spending, as compared to 8.5 in infrastructure. In absolute terms, the social sector also creates more jobs for the educated group than infrastructure construction: 7.3 jobs (3.4+3.9) per US$1 million of spending are created from social care expansion whereas infrastructure generates a mere 2.6 jobs (1.7+0.9) for those with at least some college education. Early childhood development workers are, in some cases, required to have at least an associate degree in early childhood education. This regulation, in part, explains why the more-educated group also receives more jobs than in the case of infrastructure. Green energy investment produces eight jobs for the less-educated work force, indicative of employment generation for home retrofitters, solar panel installers, and other construction-related field workers, as discussed in Pollin *et al.* (2009). Green

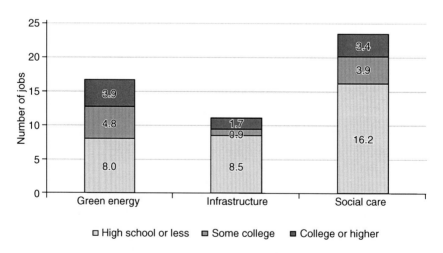

Figure 3.3 Jobs by education per million dollars of spending (source: For green energy estimates, see Pollin *et al.* 2009; other estimates are from authors' calculations).

investment benefits the more-educated group slightly more than the less-educated one, creating 8.7 jobs versus 8.0 jobs for each group respectively. A significant number of the jobs created by green energy investment are for engineers and technicians who generally have higher education credentials.

Figure 3.4 shows the number of jobs assigned by our microsimulation model to workers from different levels of annual (pre-simulation) household income by deciles, grouped into three categories.[23] Social care expansion outperforms infrastructure in terms of job creation for lower-income households. For the bottom 40 percent of households in the income distribution, social care investment generates 10.6 jobs per US$1 million of spending, compared to 3.9 jobs from infrastructure construction. This result is consistent with the previous finding on job assignment by education, for income levels are highly correlated to the level of educational attainment of workers. Home health aides, one of the major occupation groups in social care, mainly consists of women from low-income households: 88 percent of the workers are women, 58 percent have high school diploma or less, and 45 percent of the workers are from households under 200 percent of the federal poverty line.[24] The social care expansion thus aids those workers specifically.

What is equally important to notice in these figures is that the care expansion also generates more jobs for the middle-income and top-income groups – 5 and 7.9 jobs each – compared to infrastructure. This is in part because many care workers, in particular early education workers, are likely to come from dual-earner households whose combined incomes place them in higher-income groups. Still, for each US$1 million of spending, the social care scenario provides more jobs to the low-income workers relative to the higher-income groups than infrastructure does.

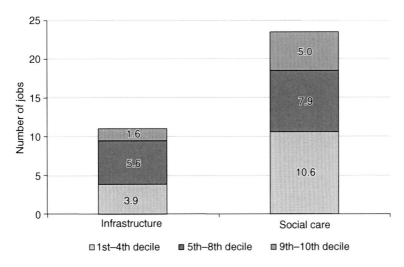

Figure 3.4 Jobs by household income per million dollars of spending (source: Authors' calculations).

Tables 3.3a and 3.3b depict the job distribution in absolute numbers and shares by various characteristics of workers hired in the two sectors. They show the net counts, excluding jobs created by the ARRA.[25] It should be noted that total number of jobs from both cases are slightly smaller than the number of jobs generated from the I–O framework, due to a small amount of non-assignment in the simulation.[26]

The gender composition of job assignment shows almost exactly inverse ratios between social care and construction. Over 90 percent of jobs go to women in social sector investment, as more than 80 percent of jobs are created within the sector. On the other hand, infrastructure construction generates over 88 percent of jobs for men as most jobs (almost 71 percent) are created in male-dominated industries – construction and manufacturing. The racial composition shows more or less even distribution in the social care case, whereas infrastructure construction favors whites heavily. The higher proportion of whites in the employable pool and their slightly higher employability (as measured by our model) explain their dominance in the job assignment for the infrastructure scenario. The even distribution of jobs in the case of social care is attributable to the fact that 52 percent of home-based care workers are nonwhite.

The decomposition of job assignment by educational attainment highlights the greater inclusiveness of social care investment. Over 42 percent of jobs

Table 3.3a Job assignment: social care

Social care	Jobs assigned	
	Number	%
Gender		
Male	116,525	9.9
Female	1,059,401	90.1
Race		
White	459,368	39.1
Black	310,370	26.4
Hispanic	286,484	24.4
Other	119,704	10.2
Education		
Less than HS	500,959	42.6
HS grad	308,810	26.3
Some college	196,407	16.7
College grad	169,750	14.4
HH Income		
1st–4th decile	530,763	45.1
5th–8th decile	395,846	33.7
9th–10th decile	249,330	21.2
Total	1,175,939	100.0

Source: Authors' calculations.

Table 3.3b Job assignment: infrastructure

Infrastructure	Jobs assigned	
	Number	%
Gender		
Male	489,814	88.6
Female	63,051	11.4
Race		
White	409,708	74.1
Black	47,497	8.6
Hispanic	78,984	14.3
Other	16,675	3.0
Education		
Less than HS	77,482	14.0
HS grad	345,897	62.6
Some college	46,609	8.4
College grad	82,877	15.0
HH income		
1st–4th decile	194,915	35.3
5th–8th decile	279,438	50.5
9th–10th decile	78,516	14.2
Total	552,869	100.0

Source: Authors' calculations.

generated by the latter go to people with less than a high school diploma, compared to only 14 percent of jobs created by the infrastructure investment. For the infrastructure scenario, the majority of jobs (62.6 percent) are assigned to workers with high school diplomas. This is largely driven by the fact that the construction-related jobs are typically held by men with high school diplomas. Although social care investment more highly favors the group with less than a high school diploma, it also provides more opportunities than infrastructure investment to people with at least some higher education (31.1 to 23.4 percent, respectively). This reflects the certificate requirement for preschool teachers and certain child care providers that are under state or federal regulations for reimbursement purposes. Infrastructure investment raises the demand for engineers and architects whose jobs are categorized in the professional and business services industry (architectural, engineering, and related services, NAICS 5413) and professional occupation (architecture and engineering occupations, SOC 17), and typically require a completed college education for qualification. These requirements seem to explain the job assignment to higher-education groups.

4.2.2 Changes in earnings

First, we look at the changes in earnings of the workers assigned jobs by the microsimulation in the social care and construction industries. These two industries account for the majority of the jobs created by the simulations. The overwhelming majority of workers – 93 to 97 percent of hired workers in social care and construction, respectively – had jobs with earnings some time during 2008. This allows us to make a comparison of their earnings before and after the simulated investment, excluding individuals with zero earnings from the following impact analysis. One should note a certain selection bias. Many of these newly "hired" workers were unemployed and/or may have had incomplete jobs during the survey period – full-year/part-time, part-year/full-time, and precarious jobs with very short-term contracts – which will push down their reported annual earnings during the survey period. Thus, the results should be interpreted with caution and analyses be confined to the selected sample.

Tables 3.4a and 3.4b show the changes in individual median and mean earnings of those who are assigned jobs in social care and infrastructure construction. The comparison highlights the disparate distributional impacts of the two investments. It is noteworthy to mention that the mean-to-median earnings ratio decreases as the level of educational attainment increases among workers. It is more so for workers in social care than in infrastructure construction, which is indicative of the stronger equalizing effect of social care investment.

Workers with less than a high school diploma tend to benefit the most in relative terms from both of the simulated investments compared to workers with higher levels of educational attainment. Their median and mean earnings increase the most (in percentage terms) among all the groups, partly because their "before" earnings are quite low. Infrastructure construction turns out to raise earnings of the least-educated workers more than social care investment

Table 3.4a Changes in median earnings by individual

Education	Social care			Infrastructure		
	Before	After	Change (%)	Before	After	Change (%)
Less than HS	3,120	7,000	124.4	7,000	17,000	142.9
HS grad	15,000	26,500	76.7	18,000	30,000	66.7
Some college	14,000	30,000	114.3	15,000	30,002	100
College grad	26,000	55,000	111.5	28,000	52,000	85.7
Income						
1st–4th decile	7,000	22,029	214.7	8,060	27,500	241.2
5th–8th decile	20,000	30,000	50.0	22,000	33,000	50
9th–10th decile	30,000	34,002	13.3	35,000	38,000	8.6

Source: Authors' calculations.

Table 3.4b Changes in mean earnings by individual

Education	Social care			Infrastructure		
	Before	After	Change (%)	Before	After	Change (%)
Less than HS	7,641	12,893	68.7	11,583	21,900	89.1
HS grad	21,654	31,382	44.9	23,163	35,304	52.4
Some college	22,950	33,169	44.5	23,994	33,960	41.5
College grad	44,475	67,694	52.2	45,693	69,284	51.6
Income						
1st–4th decile	9,940	29,862	200.4	10,863	33,787	211
5th–8th decile	23,503	40,183	71.0	25,227	43,875	73.9
9th–10th decile	50,810	46,903	(7.7)	55,879	51,569	(7.7)

Source: Authors' calculations.

does. The result is attributable to the much higher average hourly wage rates of construction workers, US$21.87 (BLS 2009a). Even unskilled construction laborers earn an average hourly wage over US$14.30, which is significantly more than the US$11.30 that a preschool teacher earns, on average.

For workers with higher educational attainment (some college or more), social care investment appears to raise median earnings relatively more than infrastructure investment does. The occupational composition of the jobs created by social care investment may explain the difference: the sector hires more managers and professionals than infrastructure, and these jobs, unlike the lower-skilled occupations, usually offer wages comparable to similar jobs in the construction sector. Thus, social care investment appears to be more beneficial for highly educated workers than for those with the least education in terms of earnings growth. But one should note that social care investment generates many more jobs for workers with less than a high school diploma (500,959) than infrastructure construction (77,482).

Workers from the poorest households (first–fourth) definitely receive the largest jump in their earnings: a more than 200 percent increase in all measures from both types of investments. Very low initial earnings of the group attributes to the jump. Earnings for workers from the middle-income households (fifth–eighth) increase more than 50 percent and the infrastructure investment seems to yield a greater increase for that group. Workers from the high-income households (ninth and tenth) show a moderate gain in median earnings, but a moderate loss in mean earnings. This result implies that earnings from the new jobs are below the earnings from their previous jobs. It may be indicative of the downward transition of some of the newly hired workers from the high-income groups. Again, the infrastructure investment raises the earnings of all groups more than the social care, simply due to relatively higher wage rates in construction industries.

5 Conclusion

Unusual times call for innovative approaches; the hands-on approach of the current administration toward job creation – the ARRA and the American Jobs Act, for instance – has renewed interest in direct job creation through expansionary fiscal policies. Most of the direct job creation measures in the bills focus on infrastructure investment on road, railways, and green energy initiatives. The male-biased job losses, in particular, have implicitly justified physical infrastructure investment as a just scheme to provide employment opportunities. Expansion of social services and in-kind benefits is unfortunately not considered a valid job creation measure. Expansion of early childhood development programs is rather regarded as a part of the administration's education reform efforts and increasing in-kind benefits is considered merely as a stop-gap measure to prevent beneficiaries from falling into poverty.

In this study, we assess social care investment – expansion of early childhood development and home-based health care – as a job creation measure for its effectiveness and equity. We find that investment in social care provision can generate twice as many jobs as infrastructure construction. At the same time, the jobs created by social care investments are more beneficial for the less-educated and the poor than those created by infrastructure investment: more jobs are likely to be taken by people from disadvantaged groups and the marginal impacts on earnings are highest for them as well. According to our estimates, more than 42 percent of the jobs created by social care investment are likely to be taken by people with less than a high school diploma, whereas only 14 percent of jobs in infrastructure construction go to these workers; workers from poorer households receive 45 percent of the jobs in the social care sector as compared to 35 percent in the case of infrastructure construction. Even within the poor households, the care sector is more likely to hire workers from the lower end of the income scale than the construction sector is, based on the *ex ante* median and mean earnings data for the workers.

Thus, we show that social care sector investment is both an effective (more jobs per dollar of spending) and equitable (more for the low-skilled and poor) strategy of job creation. Social care investment would also be an effective policy to address the expected increase in household poverty through long-term unemployment and forced premature retirement from the Great Recession.

We acknowledge that the low wage rates and high labor intensity characteristic of the care sector account at least partly for its superior performance in job creation per se and its inclusiveness toward the low-skilled and poor workers. But it is this very fact that ensures that the investment is an effective and equitable job creation measure. Without these measures, would-be workers may be left marginalized by the labor market, which will certainly negatively influence both their current earnings and their chances of future employment.

Implementing increased social care investment can be done on very short notice. Governments – federal, state, and local – all have their organizational and administrative systems in place through Medicare, Medicaid, Head Start and Early Head Start, and the Child Care and Development Fund. Scaling-up the federal funding to these programs would suffice to generate immediate employment opportunities to disadvantaged workers. These workers will be able to provide care for the ever-increasing demand from demographic changes as well as from people who can no longer afford such services because the Great Recession has eliminated their jobs and undermined their financial security.

Notes

1 For a full exposition see Papadimitriou (1998), Kaboub (2007), and Antonopoulos (2007).
2 The measure includes people who are not currently in the labor force but are available and want to work. See Table A-15 of the Bureau of Labor Statistics' Employment Situation Report. Online: www.bls.gov/news.release/empsit.t15.htm (accessed November 5, 2012).
3 Quoted in Wray and Forstater (2004).
4 The sum is greater than 100 percent because some children have multiple care arrangements.
5 The 2007 survey collected data on only current care recipients. The previous surveys from 1996, 1998, and 2000 showed 7.2 to 7.7 million discharges. Given this trend, it is reasonable to assume 7 million discharges in 2007. Trend tables from the survey are available from the National Center for Health Statistics at: www.cdc.gov/nchs/nhhcs/nhhcs_patient_trends.htm (accessed November 5, 2012).
6 According to the 1996, 1998, and 2000 surveys, the annualized discharge numbers were between 7.2 and 7.7 million. It seems reasonable to assume that the discharge number in 2007 was around 7 million.
7 The number includes hospice care agencies that may or may not provide home health care in addition.
8 In 2008, expenditure on home health care exceeded US$65 billion, according to Centers for Medicare and Medicaid Services.
9 See NAHC (2008) for more information.
10 See Dickens *et al.* (2006) and Heckman and Masterov (2007) for macroeconomic impacts of early education through productivity growth. Golin *et al.* (2004) provide a concise summary of the literature on a series of research on estimating benefits of high-quality, intensive pilot projects, including the Abecedarian project in North Carolina, the HighScope Perry Preschool study, and Title I Chicago Child–Parent Centers. Additional references include Barnett *et al.* (2004, 2005).

11 Recognizing these benefits of home-based long-term care, the Centers for Medicare and Medicaid at the Department of Health and Human Services awarded US$1.7 billion for a five-year demonstration project, called "Money Follows the Person," which assists states in transitioning about 34,000 individuals from institutional settings to home- and community-based care services.

12 The reference year for the information in this section is 2008, unless otherwise noted.

13 The estimates are based on a preliminary analysis of 2009 Annual Social and Economic Supplement of the Current Population Survey (ASEC), compiled and harmonized by King *et al.* (2009) at the Minnesota Population Center.

14 There are 22 industries and 22 occupations used in the simulation that generate 484 job categories.

15 Independent variables for the industry and occupation multinomial logits were census division, metropolitan status, age, marital status, sex, educational attainment, and race.

16 Independent variables for the employment probit were census division, metropolitan status, age, age squared, marital status, sex, educational attainment, and race.

17 A three-stage Heckit model is used to predict imputed wage and usual hours for each individual in the pool, within age–sex cells. These, together with census division, metropolitan status, marital status, spouse's labor force status, industry, and occupation of assigned job, dummies for age category of youngest child, and the number of children were used in the imputation procedure.

18 See Burton *et al.* (2002).

19 See www.bls.gov/news.release/ecopro.t06.htm for the complete table of the 30 fastest-growing occupations, 2006–2016 (accessed November 6, 2012).

20 See Zacharias *et al.* (2009) for detailed information.

21 See Zacharias *et al.* (2009) for detailed analysis on the impacts of ARRA.

22 A small exception to this convention is pre-K facilities under local school systems, which are counted as government activities under the current industry account convention, and thus may not suit the industry assumption. However, the dominance of private providers allows us to use the "private" assumption in the study, even if care comes from "social" provisioning.

23 The green energy investment scenario is not included, since the original data was not available for microsimulation analysis.

24 The federal poverty line for a family of four was US$20,650 in the 48 contiguous states and Washington, DC in 2007.

25 See Zacharias *et al.* (2009).

26 Of the total jobs, 0.7 percent is not assigned. Most of the missed jobs are a relatively small number of manager and professional positions in various industries. There may be too many of the employable workers in these categories in the data for our current ranking system to discern precisely the most likely workers out of the pool.

References

Antonopoulos, R. (2007) "The *right* to a job, the *right* types of projects: employment guarantee policies from a gender perspective," Working Paper No. 516, Annandale-on-Hudson, NY: Levy Economics Institute of Bard College.

Antonopoulos, R. and Kim, K. (2008) "Impact of employment guarantee program on gender equality and pro-poor economic development in South Africa: scaling up the expanded public works program," Research Project No. 34, Annandale-on-Hudson, NY and New York, NY: Levy Economics Institute of Bard College and the United Nations Development Programme. Online: www.levy.org/pubs/UNDP-Levy/EGS.html (accessed November 6, 2012).

70   *R. Antonopoulos* et al.

Acemoglu, D. (1995) "Public policy in a model of long-term unemployment," *Economica* 62: 161–78.

Barnett, W.S., Hustedt, J.T., Robin, K.B., and Schulman, K.L. (2004) *The State of Preschool: 2004 state preschool yearbook*, New Brunswick, NJ: National Institute for Early Education Research.

Barnett, W.S., Lamy, C., and Jung, K. (2005) *The Effects of State Prekindergarten Programs on Young Children's School Readiness in Five States*, New Brunswick, NJ: National Institute for Early Education Research.

BLS (Bureau of Labor Statistics) (2009a) *Career Guide to Industries, 2010–2011 Edition*, Washington, DC: U.S. Bureau of Labor Statistics Office of Occupational Statistics and Employment Projections.

BLS (2009b) *Occupational Employment and Wages*, May 2008. Washington, DC: U.S. Bureau of Labor Statistics Office of Occupational Statistics and Employment Projections. Online: www.bls.gov/oes/2008/may/oes_nat.htm (accessed November 6, 2012).

BLS (2010a) *Current Employment Statistics*, Washington, DC, via Federal Reserve Economic Data (FRED2) by the Federal Reserve Bank of St. Louis.

BLS (2010b) "Labor force statistics," in *Current Population Survey*, Washington, DC: U.S. Bureau of Labor Statistics Office of Occupational Statistics and Employment Projections.

Burton, A., Whitebook, M., Young, M., Bellm, D., and Wayne, C. (2002) *Estimating the Size and Components of the U.S. Child Care Workforce and Care giving Population: key findings from the child care workforce estimate (preliminary report)*, Washington, DC and Seattle, WA: Center for the Child Care Workforce and Human Services Policy Center at the University of Washington, Seattle.

Casiro, O.G., McKenzie, M.E., McFayden, L., Shapiro, C., Seshia, M.M.K., MacDonald, N., Moffat, M., and Cheang, M.S. (1993) "Earlier discharge with community-based intervention for low birth weight infants: a randomized trial," *Pediatrics* 92: 128–34.

CBO (Congressional Budget Office) (2004) "Financing long-term care for the elderly," CBO Paper, Washington, DC: Congressional Budget Office.

Dickens, W., Sawhill, I., and Tebbs, J. (2006) "The effects of investing in early education on economic growth," Policy Brief 153, Washington DC: The Brookings Institution.

Fackler, M. (2009) "Japan's big-works stimulus is lesson for U.S.," *New York Times*, February 5. Online: www.nytimes.com/2009/02/06/world/asia/06japan.html?pagewanted=all&_r=0 (accessed November 6, 2012).

Fields, A.I., Rosenblatt, A., Pollack, M., and Kaufman, J. (1991) "Home care cost-effectiveness for respiratory technology-dependent children," *American Journal of Diseases of Children* 145: 729–33.

Golin, Stacie C., Mitchell A.W., and Gault B. (2004) *The Price of School Readiness: a tool for estimating the cost of universal preschool in the states*, Washington. DC: Institute for Women's Policy Institute.

Heckman, J.J. and Borjas, G.J. (1980) "Does unemployment cause future unemployment? Definitions, questions and answers from a continuous time model of heterogeneity and state dependence," *Economica* 47, New Series (August): 247–83.

Heckman, J.J. and Masterov, D.V. (2007) "The productivity argument for investing in young children," *Review of Agricultural Economics* 29: 446–93.

ILO (International Labour Organization) (2012) *Global Employment Trends 2012: preventing a deeper job crisis*. Geneva. Online: www.ilo.org/jobspact/WCMS_171700/lang-en/index.htm.

International Monetary Fund (IMF) (2012) *World Economic Outlook, October 2012: coping with high debt and sluggish growth*, Washington, DC: International Monetary Fund. Online: www.imf.org/external/pubs/ft/weo/2012/02/pdf/text.pdf (accessed November 5, 2012).

Iruka, I.U. and Carver, P.R. (2006) *Initial Results from the 2005 NHES Early Childhood Program Participation Survey* (NCES 2006-075), Washington, DC: US Department of Education, National Center for Education Statistics.

Kaboub, F. (2007) "Employment guarantee programs: a survey of theories and policy experiences," Working Paper No. 498, Annandale-on-Hudson, NY: Levy Economics Institute of Bard College.

King, M., Ruggles, S., Alexander, T., Leicach, D., and Sobek, M. (2009) *Integrated Public Use Microdata Series, Current Population Survey: version 2.0* [Machine-readable database], Minneapolis, MN: Minnesota Population Center.

McNichol, E. and Johnson, N. (2009) "Recession continues to batter state budgets; state responses could slow recovery," Washington, DC: Center on Budget and Policy Priorities. Online: www.hapnetwork.org/assets/pdfs/hen/cbpp-recession-report.pdf (accessed November 6, 2012).

MetLife (2006) "The MetLife caregiving cost study: productivity losses to U.S. business," Metropolitan Life Insurance Company and National Alliance for Caregiving. Online: www.caregiving.org/data/Caregiver%20Cost%20Study.pdf (accessed November 6, 2012).

National Association for Home Care and Hospice (NAHC) (2008) *The Basic Statistics about Home Care: updated 2008*, Washington, DC: National Association for Home Care and Hospice. Online: www.nahc.org/facts/08HC_STATS.pdf (accessed November 6, 2012).

Papadimitriou, D.B. (1998) "(Full) employment policy: theory and practice," Working Paper No. 258, Annandale-on-Hudson, NY: Levy Economics Institute of Bard College. Online: www.levyinstitute.org/pubs/wp258.pdf (accessed November 6, 2012).

PHI (2009) "Who are direct-care workers?" PHI Facts No. 3, New York: Paraprofessional Healthcare Institute. Online: http://phinational.org/sites/phinational.org/files/clearing-house/PHI%20Facts%203.pdf (accessed November 8, 2012).

Pollin, R., Heintz, J., and Garrett-Peltier, H. (2009) "The economic benefits of investing in clean energy: how the economic stimulus program and new legislation can boost U.S. economic growth and employment," Amherst, MA: Department of Economics and Political Economy Research Institute (PERI), University of Massachusetts, Amherst. Online: www.americanprogress.org/issues/2009/06/pdf/peri_report.pdf (accessed November 6, 2012).

Sen, A. (1999) *Development as Freedom*, New York: Knopf; Oxford and Delhi: Oxford University Press.

Simonazzi, A. (2009) "Care regimes and national employment models," *Cambridge Journal of Economics* 33: 211–32.

U.S. Census Bureau (2010) "Table 6: average weekly child care expenditures of families with employed mothers that make payments, by age groups and selected characteristics," in *Who's Minding the Kids? Child Care Arrangements: summer 2006 – detailed tables*, Online: www.census.gov/hhes/childcare/data/sipp/2006/tables.html (accessed November 6, 2012).

U.S. Department of Education, National Center for Education Statistics (USDE/NCES) (2006) *National Household Education Survey, 2005*, ICPSR04599-v1, Washington, DC: U.S. Department of Education, Institute of Education Sciences [producer], Ann

Arbor, MI: Inter-university Consortium for Political and Social Research [distributor], Online: www.icpsr.umich.edu/icpsrweb/ICPSR/studies/4599 (accessed November 6, 2012).

Warner, M.E. (2007) "Child care and economic development: markets, households and public policy," *International Journal of Economic Development* 9: 111–21.

Warner, M.E. (2009a) *Recession, Stimulus and the Child Care Sector: understanding economic dynamics, calculating impact*, manuscript, Ithaca, NY: Cornell University.

Warner, M.E. (2009b) *Child Care Multipliers: stimulus for the states*, manuscript, Ithaca, NY: Cornell University.

Warner, M., Adriance, S., Barai, N., Hallas, J., Markeson, B., Morrissey, T., and Soref, W. (2004) *Economic Development Strategies to Promote Quality Child Care*, Ithaca, NY: Cornell University.

Warner, M.E. and Liu, Z. (2006) "The importance of child care in economic development: a comparative analysis of regional economic linkage," *Economic Development Quarterly* 20: 97–103.

Zacharias, A., Masterson, T., and Kim, K. (2009) "Distributional impact of the American Recovery and Reinvestment Act: a microsimulation approach," Working Paper No. 568, Annandale-on-Hudson, NY: Levy Economics Institute of Bard College. Online: www.levyinstitute.org/publications/?docid=1158 (accessed November 6, 2012).

4 Macroeconomic policies and gender equality in Latin America

Assessing the gender impact of the global economic crisis

*Valeria Esquivel and Corina Rodríguez Enríquez**

1 Introduction

This chapter discusses the impact of the global economic crisis in Latin America, with particular emphasis on its gender implications. The negative impacts of the crisis, which began in late 2008 in United States and quickly spread worldwide, were heavily felt in Latin America, a region characterized by its external vulnerability, the limited diversification of its productive structures, and a large amount of social and economic inequality – among which gender inequalities are quite significant.

This chapter follows a feminist economics approach to macroeconomics, by tying the analysis of the crisis's country-specific impacts and the public policy responses implemented with their social and gender implications. With such an analytical approach, this chapter aims not only to disentangle the gender effects of the current crises (and suggest policy paths that counterbalance them) but also to confront the so-called "gender neutrality" of orthodox approaches.

Indeed, Latin America has had a long history of economic crises.[1] Some have been home-grown (such as the Mexican crisis of 1996, or the one that hit Argentina in 2001), while others have been triggered by external shocks.[2] When the latter was the case, transmission mechanisms have been many, and sometimes concurrent. The first transmission mechanism – which emerged in its full force at the end of the 1970s – is the financial system. Sudden capital outflows in search of "safety" can cause abrupt domestic and external imbalances, putting pressure on money supply and the exchange rate. Depending on specific economic dynamics, external financial shocks might trigger the acceleration of prices and (high or hyper) inflation, the rationing of foreign credit, and, in its more acute forms, full-fledged debt crises.

* A previous version of this chapter, which included Central America as a case study, was published in Spanish. See Esquivel, V., A. Espino and C. Rodríguez Enríquez (2012) "Crisis, regímenes económicos e impactos de género en América Latina," in V. Esquivel (ed.) *La Economía Feminista desde América Latina*, ONU MUJERES/GEM LAC, Santo Domingo. The authors gratefully acknowledge the support of ONU MUJERES, as well as that of ECOSOC, which funded their initial research at the beginning of 2010.

Alternatively, crises can be transmitted by channels associated with the real economy. This seems to be the case in the current crisis. There are three "real" mechanisms at stake. First, the slowdown of world trade may have an impact on the price and volume of countries' exports. The relevance of this transmission mechanism is logically dependent on the degree of country openness to foreign trade, the exporting profile, and the relevance of exports as a source of foreign exchange. It also depends on trade partners, and whether these are more or less affected by the crisis. For example, in the current crisis, countries whose exports are mainly directed to the US market have faced impacts more severe than those experienced by countries more dependent on China's demand.

Second, the crisis may lead to a reduction of foreign direct investment (FDI), as uncertainty (and recession) discourages production capacity building. Again, the impact of a slowdown in FDI will depend on the relevance it has as a mechanism for financing infrastructure investment.

Third, the crisis in developed countries may lead to a reduction of the remittances that Latin American migrants send from these countries (the United States and European Mediterranean countries in particular). This is due to the deterioration of income and employment opportunities in recipient countries, which affect migrants' ability to save and remit. Remittances have played an increasingly significant role in the Balance of Payments, and their reversal can be heavily felt by countries lacking in alternative sources of foreign exchange.

All of the above have (or could have) had impacts in the region's real economies, affecting activity levels and, in time, employment and earnings. The deterioration of living conditions, in turn, can lead to household survival strategies that combine an increase in labor force participation rates (as having more household members in the labor market increases the chances of getting some income), longer or more intense working times, and/or the replacement of subsistence consumption of goods and services for market production.

Such critical context can certainly have differential consequences on women and men. The experience of previous crises provides some clues of what might happen this time (Montaño and Milosavljevic 2010). History teaches that crises can promote women's labor force participation as a response to the deterioration of their partners' employment and earnings. In addition, men's employment may worsen more than women's, if productive sectors affected by the decline in foreign trade, consumption, and overall activity are those where men are overrepresented. This can result in a reduction in gender employment gaps, despite the fact that women's employment opportunities remain scarce. Conversely, the deterioration of earnings can result in increasing pressures on women's unpaid care work in order to meet households' needs.

This chapter focuses on three national cases: Mexico, Argentina, and Ecuador, countries that represent well the effects that the global economic crisis has had in Latin America and the array of policies that were implemented (or not) to counterbalance its deleterious impacts.

These countries are quite different regarding their pre-crisis situation and the objective "policy space" they enjoyed. Also, these countries have followed different approaches to their macroeconomic policies, which shaped their pre-crisis economic paths and the responses to the crisis they envisioned and were able to implement. Mexico, whose government has adopted orthodox economic policies over the last two decades, was the most severely hit economy in the region due to the combined effect of its oil and manufacturing export orientation and its links to the United States. Argentina is among the countries that have experienced only mild impacts, and it has a heterodox approach to economic issues. Finally, Ecuador is a country highly dependent upon remittances, whose heterodox government has to deal with a dollarized economy – the most "orthodox" monetary framework.

There are, however, common aspects. In particular, and irrespective of the strength of their official gender policy mechanisms (strong in Mexico, very weak in Argentina, and somewhat in between in Ecuador), gender equality has been relegated in all three countries as a tool to face the crisis. But clearly, neither the crisis itself nor the countercyclical policies implemented were gender-neutral, as gender issues were heavily present in the policies implemented.

The authors believe that an in-depth review of the selected national cases allows us to derive fairly "general" conclusions about the main drivers behind the impacts that the current economic crisis has had in the region and their gender effects.

2 The global crisis and its impact on Latin American economies from a gender perspective

Latin America experienced tough times in 2009. After five years of uninterrupted growth of approximately 3 percent, Latin America and the Caribbean's GDP contracted by 1.9 percent (–2.8 percent in per capita terms) in 2009 (UN 2011a, p. 93).[3]

These figures reflect the impact of the global financial crisis, which hit Latin American economies hard since the last quarter of 2008. During the second half of 2009, when there was some evidence suggesting that the first phase of the global financial crisis might have passed[4] – most possibly because of the active government interventions undertaken by developed economies – Latin American economies showed some positive signs of recovery, which extended over 2010.

As the crisis unfolded, it became clear that Latin American economies would not be immune to the negative developments in the global economy, i.e., would not "decouple" as some had expected based on the countries' "sound" macroeconomic and fiscal conditions. True, the global financial shock did not become full-fledged domestic financial crises, and most countries were able to contain the capital outflows or cope with them without major disruptions in their foreign exchange markets thanks to the improved macroeconomic context. However, the crisis hit Latin American economies through the contraction of international trade, the collapse of commodity prices, and the lower remittances, all *real* "channels of transmission" from which export-oriented Latin American economies could not be "shielded."

Indeed, Latin America's growth in the period 2004–07 had been driven by an exceptionally favorable external context in commodity prices (particularly minerals), booming international trade, abundant foreign financing, and high levels of remittances (Ocampo 2007).[5] All these factors had made it possible for most Latin American economies to sustain current account surpluses, improve their public sector balance sheets, reduce their foreign debt burdens, and accumulate foreign assets (reserves).[6,7]

Trade conditions had started deteriorating before September 2008, and its effects were already visible in that year, though they greatly worsened since then (Ocampo 2009). The drastic drop in the external demand for oil, and to a lesser extent for foodstuffs, affected commodity prices negatively, hurting oil exporters and South American food-exporter countries. The deep contraction of trade volumes, in turn, hit Latin American export-oriented countries that specialize in manufactures and services, like Mexico. The Economic Commission for Latin America and the Caribbean (ECLAC) has estimated that during 2009, Latin American exports shrank by 9.6 percent in real terms, and by almost *a quarter* (23.4 percent) in value terms, reflecting the severe deterioration of the regions' terms of trade (UN 2010a, p. 15).

Also, the deterioration of real incomes and employment in the United States and Europe (notably Spain) forced migrants to lower their remittances. Countries highly dependent on remittances have experienced strong contractions, like Colombia (–17.9 percent), Mexico (–16.1 percent), and Ecuador (–12.6 percent, all figures in dollar terms).[8] It should be noted that in Colombia and Mexico, the depreciation of their currencies against the dollar might well have *increased* the purchasing power of recipient families even if they received fewer dollars. For Ecuador, instead, the use of the exchange rate policy was out of the question, being that Ecuador is a dollarized economy, and the contraction of remittances was heavily felt (Ocampo 2009, p. 706).

In this grim context, Latin American countries experienced the crisis with differing intensity. Some went through acute recessions, the extreme case being Mexico, whose GDP plummeted 6.7 percent in 2009. Other countries saw their growth rates come to a halt, like Ecuador (–0.4 percent), and yet others (in particular, those in the Southern Cone and the Andean region) greatly decelerated their growth rates (for example, Argentina, 0.7 percent, and Bolivia, 3.5 percent) (UN 2010a).

This mixed picture is the result of the ways in which the external "channels of transmission" operated during the crisis, depending on countries' links to the US economy, their openness to external financial flows, their pre-crisis real exchange rate, and their dependency on remittances (Puyana 2010). But also, countries fared quite differently depending on whether they were able to implement countercyclical policies and, if implemented, on the approach, magnitude, and timeliness of these policies. The fiscal and monetary policy space that countries might have enjoyed not only depended on past savings, foreign reserves, and debt burdens (Fanelli and Jiménez 2009), but were also shaped by countries' ideological approach to macroeconomic policy, the way priorities were established, and the capacity of local bureaucracies to put these policies into place.

With their countercyclical policies, the countries sought to maintain aggregate demand – privileging public expenditure and social programs over tax cuts and employment programs. Latin American countries' low tax base and the indirect effect of tax cuts on consumption made governments generally opt for expansionary policies associated directly with the expenditure side. Targeted programs – mostly in the form of conditional cash transfers – had been in place for over a decade in Latin America, their bureaucracies able to timely implement anti-crisis strategies of this sort.[9] Countries where these institutional bases were absent privileged consumption subsidies (Kacef 2009).

Recession brought about high social costs. According to ECLAC, the unemployment rate rose to 8.1 percent in 2009, i.e., almost 1 percentage point over the figure a year before (UN 2012, p. 114). This figure was less pessimistic than early 2009 forecasts owing to the combined effect of a lower labor force participation rate – the discouraged worker effect, which operated mainly among the young – the positive signs economies showed during the second half of the year, and possibly the countercyclical policies that countries managed to implement (ILO/UN 2009). As in previous crises in Latin America, the rise in unemployment was greater among men, who are concentrated in the most dynamic economic sectors, and are therefore more prone to be affected by the downturn. In countries with available information, the manufacturing industry was the most affected by the decline in employment in the first half of 2009. Contractions in manufacturing industry employment ranged from –0.9 percent in Colombia to –7 percent in Mexico (although there was timid trend reversal in 2010). Construction, traditionally male, also saw its employment plummet by –2.4 percent in Mexico and –5.3 percent in Venezuela (ILO/UN 2009, 2010).

Although it is difficult to gauge the effects of the many public policies implemented beyond sustaining aggregate demand, it should be noted that the adopted countercyclical policies were not always chosen with their potential for directly creating employment in mind, and definitely not for creating women's employment. Only the bigger Latin American economies were able to channel resources to public investment during the crisis, whose job creation potential is greater than that of transfers of any kind, although the employment created is typically male employment. (Whether governments were able to execute this public investment in a timely fashion is another matter.) Emergency employment programs are more labor-intensive, and could reach women, but the Latin American experience is scattered and concentrated in Central American countries (ILO/UN 2009, p. 13).

As a result of the worsening labor market conditions, men's labor force participation decreased, while that of women remained constant or even increased in some countries (for example, in Mexico). These figures simultaneously show a continuation of the long-term trend of a narrowing gap between male and female labor force participation, and the "secondary worker" effect, as women tend to enter the labor market precisely in its worse conjunctures to increase the chances of getting at least some income for their households.

However, women averages in labor force participation and unemployment incidence are the result of different dynamics, depending on household income. In the last decade, labor force participation decreased and unemployment increased for women in the lower income strata, while the opposite trend was evident among women in the uppermost income strata (UN 2011c). Differences were even greater among mothers since 2005 and during the crisis years (UN 2011b, p. 30), which meant that *labor force participation and unemployment gaps have risen* among them. Moreover, while mothers in the uppermost quintile of the income distribution present roughly the same unemployment figures irrespective of the age of their children, those who are among the poorest and have children below school age suffer even higher unemployment than their fellow disadvantaged mothers, a fact that underscores the links between disadvantageous labor market insertions and the pressures of providing care.

The quality of employment also appeared to worsen at the onset of the crisis, although data on this issue is still insufficient. Self-employment increased and the numbers of registered wage workers came to a halt in 2009 (ILO/UN 2009, 2010). Being overrepresented in these jobs, women are relatively more affected than men in the deterioration of quality of employment.

Recently published information on the impacts of the crisis on poverty and income distribution shows that poverty remained the same, at 33 percent, but extreme poverty increased in the region by approximately half of a percentage point during 2009, reaching 13.1 percent (UN 2011b, p. 11). Although these figures are high, they did not reverse the gains brought about by positive growth records in the period 2004–08. However, the 2009 crisis might have pushed back below the poverty line one of the 41 million people who had made their way out of poverty over the previous years.[10] The same picture arises from trends in income distribution. In a region that stands out for its high levels of income inequality, the fact that Gini coefficients did not deteriorate during the crisis is also indicative that pre-crisis gains did not fade away for most of the countries (UN 2011b, p. 14).

In Latin America, women are overrepresented among the poor households, either because they have lower income-generating opportunities, or because their income is low.[11] The abovementioned poverty figures might therefore affect women more heavily, and increase their unpaid care work burdens.

The reduction in tax revenues has important gender implications if governments opt to redirect (or cut) some social public spending (education, social protection, basic infrastructure) as a result of the crisis. However, social programs, whose beneficiaries are overwhelmingly women, did not change in most countries – a welcome change from past practices. Indeed, it should be noted that, in the past, the combination of decreasing households' income and restricted state-provided social services resulted in an increase in unpaid care work burdens. Although there is no fresh evidence to investigate whether this is currently the case, the effects on unpaid care work burdens should be borne in mind when analyzing changes in employment and state-provided social services as a result of the crisis.

3 National responses to global crisis in Latin America

3.1 The case of Mexico

Mexico is the Latin American country that saw its economy most severely hit by the international crisis. Mexican GDP plummeted 6.7 percent in 2009, after a record drop of –10.1 percent between the second quarters of 2008 and 2009 (INEGI 2009). During the same period, manufacturing output dropped 9.9 percent and FDI *halved*. These dynamics followed the path of the US economy, as the Mexican economy – highly integrated with its bordering North American Free Trade Agreement (NAFTA) partner as an oil and industrial commodity exporter – did not "decouple" from the adverse external shock.

In the last two decades, the Mexican economy has consistently followed a liberalization and market-oriented policy path, opening up its current and capital accounts and diminishing the economic role of the state. Thus, Mexico became a very open economy, where international trade (exports and imports) represent as much as 60 percent of GDP – a high proportion for a medium-sized economy. On average, Mexico received FDI for US$20 billion a year during the last decade.[12]

Macroeconomic policy has adopted an orthodox stance. Price stability became the overriding objective of monetary policy, and an independent central bank embraced the "inflation targeting" paradigm. The exchange rate was allowed to float, with little intervention from the monetary authority. The fiscal front was characterized by a strong fiscal discipline, as fiscal deficits were blamed for past inflationary pressures and public debt would "crowd out" private savings and investment. In 2006, a cap on fiscal deficits of 1 percent GDP was established by law. As a result, Mexico ran primary public sector surpluses of around 2 percent in the period 2005–08, its foreign debt was among the lowest in Latin America relative to GDP in 2008 (6 percent),[13] and inflation has been curbed to around 5 percent in the past decade (UN 2010a).

Although other economies in Latin America certainly followed a similar path during the 1990s, many (notably, Argentina, Bolivia, Brazil, Ecuador, and Venezuela) reverted from the neoliberal paradigm in the current decade, and both in discourse and action, reshaped their economic policies along heterodox lines.[14] This was not the case in Mexico. On the contrary, the path that Mexico followed before the crisis made it particularly vulnerable to negative external shocks. At the same time, the pro-market policy orientation (and the lack of pragmatism of its authorities) made it ill-equipped to face the crisis and implement sound and far-reaching countercyclical policies.

Indeed, in the years before the crisis, the Mexican economy made itself increasingly vulnerable to the reversal of trade and financial flows. The emphasis on price stability prevented the monetization of the capital inflows and the use of the exchange rate as a tool to promote local production. The nominal exchange rate was invariant between 2005 and August 2008, and the real exchange rate appreciated.

Also, the much sought export-led growth failed to materialize. Growth has been sluggish as compared to Latin America, particularly during the period 2004–07, when Mexico grew at approximately 4 percent, two percentage points below Latin America's average GDP growth. Imports grew *pari passu* with exports, leading to an increase in the import content of GDP, and worse, trade deficits of 2.2 percent of GDP, on average, during the period 2001–08 (Moreno-Brid 2009, p. 10). Oil exports accounted for over 10 percent of the value of total exports before the crisis, making Mexico particularly vulnerable to the reversal of the oil boom. In turn, FDI crowded out national investment, had low linkages with the rest of the economy, and generated relatively low employment (Puyana 2010).

Mexico's fiscal discipline and the state's minimal intervention in the economy were coupled with low levels of tax revenues as compared with other Latin American countries, of only 14 percent of GDP. Moreover, oil revenues represent 40 percent of total fiscal revenue. As a result, Mexican families and firms face the *lowest* tax burdens in Latin American (9 percent of GDP).

The international crisis hit the Mexican economy through the financial, trade, and remittances channels. The reduction of external financing drastically rationed the Mexican government and firms' access to capital markets. This was particularly acute for big conglomerates that faced problems meeting their financial obligations (Moreno-Brid 2009). The credit crunch transmitted to the local banking system, dominated by American banks. Total bank credit shrank by 5 percent, and consumer credit by 22 percent, thus contributing to the contraction of consumer demand (11 percent). In this context, FDI shrank to approximately US$13 billion (–40 percent) and total investment (gross capital formation) contracted 6.5 percent.

Short-term capital outflows led to an active intervention in the exchange market, particularly acute in the first months of the year. After a depreciation of 18 percent in October 2008, Mexico continued to devalue its currency up to March 2009. On average, the Mexican peso lost 19 percent against the dollar during 2009. After losing almost a quarter of its reserves, Mexico received a credit line US$47 billion from the International Monetary Fund (IMF). Even though these funds were not used, the credit line helped to reverse negative expectations of further devaluations, and therefore contributed to the stabilization of the exchange rate.[15]

The high ratio of exports to GDP (between 30 and 35 percent) meant that the contraction of exports transmitted rapidly to the rest of the economy. Thus, the main impact in the Mexican economy has been the contraction of oil prices and the reduction of international demand for industrial parts and components, particularly those related to the automobile industry, highly integrated to the United States. Exports contracted 23.3 percent in 2009, with oil exports plummeting 43 percent. Although imports also shrank 25 percent as a result of the recession, the trade deficit was approximately US$13 billion in 2009. But remittances (net transfers), though down by 20 percent in 2009, were enough to finance most of the abovementioned deficit. The current account deficit is estimated to have been around US$6 billion in 2009, approximately half of that experienced in 2008.

Among the industries most severely hit by the external shock were those most oriented to exports and highly integrated with the United States. ECLAC has estimated that the contraction of automobile exports (–33 percent) might be *directly* responsible for the 1.1 percentage point drop in Mexican GDP (UN 2009a, p. 3). Tourism was also hit by the combination of the H1N1 human influenza outbreak and low demand in Northern countries – the number of tourists dropped by as much as 30 percent compared to the previous year in May 2009, though the situation was normalizing at the end of the year.

Fiscal revenue contracted 8.7 percent in real terms (24.4 percent reduction in oil revenues, and 12.8 percent reduction in non-oil revenues). Public expenditure increased 4.2 percent in real terms between January and September 2009, led by capital expenditure. It is therefore estimated that the fiscal deficit reached 2.3 percent in 2009 (calculated including capital expenditures in the oil industry; see below).

3.1.1 Social and gender implications of the crisis

Such serious economic downturn had immediate social costs. At the beginning of 2009, unemployment rose to 5 percent – a level unknown for a decade – from 4.47 percent at the outset of the crisis, and remained high over the year, reaching 6.8 percent in September 2009 (national data) (ILO/UN 2010).[16] From November 2008 to July 2009, women's and men's unemployment rates increased more than 2 percentage points. During the pre-crisis years, women's unemployment had been consistently higher than men's, showing an "anti-cyclical" pattern.[17] Women's labor force participation increased when the labor market started deteriorating. In 2007, women's labor force participation was approximately 40 percent, while in the third quarter of 2009, it remained over 43 percent, a feature that might explain women's high unemployment rate in those months.[18]

Mexican employed women are concentrated in the services sector (almost 80 percent are employed in services and commerce), and are therefore highly dependent upon the dynamics of domestic demand. On the contrary, approximately 30 percent of employed men work in the manufacturing industry and construction sectors, and 20 percent in the primary sector.

Table 4.1 shows the absolute variations in employment between the third quarters of 2007, 2008, and 2009, making clear the impact of the external shock on employment. The contraction in the manufacturing industry rapidly produced a downward adjustment of 136,000 jobs. Women in the manufacturing industry lost more jobs than men did, relative to their participation in industrial employment (2 percent vis-à-vis 0.9 percent). The primary sector also shed women's jobs, so 116,000 jobs were lost by women, in both the primary and secondary sectors. Job losses were compensated by the services and commerce sectors, which created jobs. Between 2008 and 2009, another half-a-million jobs were lost in the manufacturing industry, three-quarters of which were male jobs. Indeed, men lost jobs *in absolute terms* during this last period, while women gained 460,000 jobs (although the job creation in services and commerce was lower than the previous year).

Table 4.1 Absolute differences in employed population by industry and sex, 2007–09, Mexico

Industry	Absolute differences III 07–III 08			Absolute differences III 08–III 09		
	Total	Men	Women	Total	Men	Women
Total	709,169	525,873	183,296	291,465	−169,264	460,729
Primary sector	15,627	73,189	−57,562	80,498	70,422	10,076
Manufacturing industry and construction	−136,282	−76,769	−59,513	−541,203	−388,489	−152,714
Services and commerce	808,986	523,495	285,491	796,942	181,137	615,805
Other	20,838	5,958	14,880	−44,772	−32,334	−12,438

Source: Authors' calculations, based on BIE, Banco de Información Económica (INEGI: www.inegi.org.mx/sistemas/bie).

In this context, the quality of jobs also deteriorated. From October 2008 to October 2009, the number of formal workers (affiliated with the Mexican Institute of Social Security) decreased by over half-a-million, or 4.3 percentage points. While total employment shrank, the already large informal sector expanded. Women increasingly found informal job opportunities, making the informal sector responsible for 29.5 percent of female employment and partially compensating losses in formal employment. Absolute loses in men's jobs have also led to an expansion in the proportion of men working in the informal sector. From the lowest participation in 2006 (26 percent), men's employment in the formal sector went up in 1.5 percentage points in the third quarter of 2009.[19]

Gender wage discrimination is pervasive and sustained over time. For the years 2008–10, approximately 40 percent of women employed earn up to two minimum wages, while 30 percent of employed men are in this situation. Or, as Puyana (2010, p. 41) puts it, the average wage of female workers was equal to three times the poverty line, well below wages for male workers, which was 5.3 times the poverty line in the same period.

In all, the Mexican labor market showed the impact of the strong downturn of macroeconomic variables in the period 2008–09. Men lost jobs in absolute terms, given that they are concentrated in the sectors most severely hit by the external shock (manufacturing industry, primary sector). Women increasingly entered the labor market to counteract the job losses of other family members, and found job opportunities in the service sectors, and in particular in the informal sector.

It should be borne in mind that behind these figures lies the "escape valve" of the Mexican labor market – a constant flow of migration to the United States. Migration flows have slowed down considerably since their peak in the period 2006–07 (over half-a-million migrants) to the period 2008–09 (200m). The continuous reversal of migration flows can put more pressure on Mexican labor force participation, and increase unemployment.

Lastly, just before the crisis, in 2008, 34.8 percent of Mexicans lived below the poverty line, and 11.2 percent below the extreme poverty line. As poverty incidence is calculated every other year in Mexico, there has been no information on poverty incidence for the year 2009. The figure for 2010, very recently published, sets poverty incidence at 36.3 percent in 2010 (UN 2011b, p. 13). Therefore, one can safely speculate that poverty incidence must have been even higher the previous year.

3.1.2 Policy responses to the crisis

Policy responses to the crisis were slow, initially guided by the belief that the Mexican economy was "shielded" from the external shock by its "sound" fiscal and external position. However, initial estimations of the impact of the crisis (a contraction of GDP of –2 to –4 percent) proved to be too optimistic.[20] As the crisis unfolded and revealed the magnitude of its negative effects on the Mexican economy, an array of measures – not always consistent with each other – were announced.[21]

Along with monetary policy (lowering of interests rates and the creation of new credit lines) and exchange rate policy (efforts to curb capital outflows, devaluation, and a *swap* guaranteed by the US Federal Reserve), fiscal policies were of varied nature and extent, and those are the ones that interest us in terms of their gender implications.

Main fiscal measures included the National Infrastructure Fund (FONADIN), introduced in February 2008, whose goal is to expand infrastructure for a period of five years; and the Program to Promote Growth and Employment (PICE), introduced in October 2008. The program aimed at channeling public expenditures to capital formation in an amount of 0.7 percent of GDP ($6.4 billion), along with funds directly channeled to development banks ($11.7 billion). But, at the same time, current public expenditure contracted by US$6 billion in 2009 due to the drop in fiscal revenues. However, this contraction did not affect social policy programs (UN 2009a).

A third major initiative was launched in 2009. The National Agreement in Favour of Employment and Family Economy was composed of an array of actions aimed at improving families' income (reductions of 10 percent in liquid gas prices and 75 percent in diesel prices, freeze in electricity costs), support dwellings' acquisitions, and give new credit to small and medium-sized enterprises (SMEs). It also included several labor market measures, most notably the Temporary Employment Program, which grants temporary income to men and woman aged 16 or older through the participation in family and community projects for a maximum of 132 working days a year, and which covered 722,000 unemployed people in 2009 (ILO 2010).[22] Also implemented were measures to sustain employment in severely strained firms, an ease of the requirements to receive unemployment benefits, and a new emergency employment program aimed at covering 60,000 extra workers. Support was channeled to the tourism industry, and remedial funds were deployed to firms affected by the H1N1 outbreak.

According to several sources, Moreno-Brid (2010) estimated that the countercyclical measures amounted around 1.5 percent of GDP in 2009 – a timid response as compared to the losses in employment and output.[23] Mexico shows *in extremis* the contradiction between the so-called "fiscal policy space" and the need to implement countercyclical policies. In the Mexican case, fiscal policy space was not built during the pre-crisis years,[24] and the orthodox approach to economic policy meant that an alternative to increasing public sector debt in order to fund further countercyclical measures was left out of the question (UN 2009a). Only in 2009, the Law of Fiscal Responsibility, which mandated a zero fiscal balance, was amended in order to exclude the investment carried out by Pemex (Mexico's national oil monopoly). Such an amendment freed up resources of 78.3 billion pesos in 2009, which compares to the total costs of fiscal stimulus programs of 190.4 billion pesos that year (ILO 2010). Fiscal spending was also made possible by the increased domestic value of oil revenues due to depreciation and central bank surpluses (Ros 2010, cited by Moreno-Brid 2010).

Regarding social policies, the Mexican government received a US$1.5 billion loan from the World Bank in order to extend Oportunidades, the Mexican conditional cash transfer program. Oportunidades, the older and the second most extensive conditional cash transfer (CCT) plan in Latin America, has been widely criticized from a gender perspective, in particular regarding the reinforcement of a maternal model of care and the little impact on women's empowerment (see, for example, Molyneux 2006, 2009). It should be noted that beyond its objectives, the loan in itself has a strong macroeconomic effect, helping to sustain foreign reserves and support the monetary expansion implied by the expanded CCT program.

A last point to note is that even though Mexico has a strong gender mechanism (INMUJERES, the National Institute for Women), none of these measures have had an explicit gender perspective. Funds explicitly targeted to finance initiatives that would support women (*fondos etiquetados*) were not reduced in the fiscal year of 2009, but were not increased either. They amount to US$600 million, 0.05 percent of GDP (García Gaytán 2009).

3.1.3 Gender implications of the public policy measures taken by the Mexican government to face the crisis

First, the dynamics of the Mexican crisis are not new. The exchange rate appreciation prior to the crisis, the vulnerabilities in the production sectors, the low local linkages of manufacturing exports, and the emphasis on orthodox macroeconomic recipes all have been there before. To be sure, the flexible exchange rate was better than the fixed exchange rate, and fiscal balances were better than fiscal imbalances. But the delays in recognizing the magnitude of the crisis led to timid responses – the long list of measures and the huge peso (and dollar) figures should not distract from the fact that they account for 1.5 percent of GDP – that have not been enough to counteract the high social costs incurred by the recession and might have exacerbated existing gender inequalities.

As the economic crisis was understood as only a "temporary" and "external" disturbance by Mexican economic authorities, the measures to counteract the crisis become "compensatory" in nature, designed in order *not to* "jeopardize future growth" by deviating from the correct functioning of markets.[25] By definition, such a pro-market state response is weak (and possibly inaccurate), a fact that might be harmful for women as the costs of the crisis are neither recognized nor sufficiently counteracted in a timely fashion.

Mexico's excessive dependence on oil exports, the low linkages of FDI to the rest of the economy, and the extremely low tax revenues all point to the need of long-term economic and social development policies that *re-shape* the functioning of markets and give the Mexican government more room for maneuver. However, the Mexican government opted for an ambitious (and yet to be implemented) investment plan linked to oil production (a new refinery), which creates few employment opportunities and emphasizes the government's commitment to the existing male-biased productive structure.

None of the policies that would have given the Mexican government more fiscal policy space were implemented in 2009. Among those are a much-needed fiscal reform that increases tax revenue while making it more progressive and less dependent upon export revenues, a change of the central bank's mandate so that full employment becomes one of its goals, and a fundamental change in the "fiscal responsibility law" beyond mere amendments. In short, the "transformation of the role of the State and the market in the Mexican economy, essentially a change in the scope and forms of regulation and public sector intervention in the allocation of resources towards a long-term growth of the Mexican economy" has been left off the menu of policy transformation (Moreno-Brid 2009, p. 23).

As was the case in the past, there is a complete absence of considerations of gender equality in policy design and implementation. No quotas were established for women's beneficiaries of employment-generating initiatives like the national employment plan. According to the information provided by *Portal de Empleo* (PET),[26] employment was given to 14,115 women and 23,704 men in 2009. All employment-generating programs, in turn, generated or sustained 896,402 jobs, of which 282,814 went to women, 378,680 went to men, and in 234,908 cases there is no information of the beneficiary's sex. These gender differences might be related to the fact that lay-offs were greater among men than among women, although the array of programs and situations, as well as the enormous regional dispersion, does not allow for a more nuanced analysis.

Finally, no policy responses were designed to specifically handle women's issues. It seems that INMUJERES – a strong gender mechanism – was happy to maintain budgeted resources, but has had no saying in shaping policy responses to the crisis, or even evaluating them *ex post facto*. Giving voice and technical tools to INMUJERES for their partaking in economic debates and policy design is a challenge that needs to be addressed urgently for INMUJERES to effectively gain recognition as a partner in development, trade, and macroeconomic policy design.

3.2 The case of Argentina

The history of Argentina's economy has been marked by recurring crises. In fact, the process of the country's economic growth can be characterized by its instability. From 1975 to 2007, GDP per capita grew at an annual rate of 0.6 percent; there were 19 years of growth in terms of economic activity and 14 years of negative growth. These facts are proof of the stagnation and volatility that has marked the economy, both of which have led to growing heterogeneity and social exclusion (Anlló *et al*. 2007). For this very reason, the repercussions that the global crisis can have at the national level are nothing new. What could appear as novel or different are, perhaps, some of the features of the macroeconomic context in which the crisis occurs.

Between 2002 and 2007, the economy grew at an average annual rate of 8 percent. The rise in the levels of economic activity, in addition to a certain renewal of local production, permitted several improvements: jobs were created, the unemployment rate dropped, and the real salary level gradually rose. Though less notable, the levels of poverty also improved, as did – though to a far lower extent – inequality in terms of income distribution. When the global crisis began, Argentina had a "sound" macroeconomy. The current account of the balance of payments and the trade balance both presented surpluses. The affluence in the country's foreign accounts as well as in the fiscal sphere were two of Argentina's distinguishing features in comparison to previous crises.

In spite of the fact that the country was in a better position, the crisis had an impact on the Argentinean economy. The negative variation of the GDP during the second (–0.85 percent) and third (–0.3 percent) quarter of 2009 ended the economic growth that had started in 2003. In the same period, private consumption also dropped by 1.8 percent, while public consumption remained stable. Manufacture production decreased (–2.3 percent in the first quarter of 2009 and –0.8 percent in the second). The investment also showed a negative variation from the last quarter of 2008 up to mid-2009. Both exports and imports decreased. Exports declined –6.5 percent between 2008 and 2009, due to the simultaneous drop in volume and values (especially in commodity prices).

As a consequence of all of the above, the fiscal situation also deteriorated. By the end of the second quarter of 2009, the fiscal balance turned negative at –0.2 percent of GDP. While primary surplus was still positive, it had been declining since the end of 2008.

3.2.1 Social and gender implications of the crisis

The impact of the negative evolution of the real economy in the labor market was clear. By the end of 2008, the positive trends of all indicators of the labor market turned negative. Between 2008 and 2009, the employment rate decreased by 2 percent, and the unemployment rate increased, to reach 9.2 percent at the end of 2009.

The differential impact of the crisis for women and men mimics the experience of past crises. Available data shows that: (1) women in the formal and informal work force show "countercyclical" behavior, with increased participation rates during recessions and decreased rates during periods of recovery; (2) some of the features corresponding to women's employment get worse during recessions, such as a rise in job mobility, greater precariousness, and lower incomes; (3) the job situation of men deteriorates more quickly than that of women during periods of recession, but it also improves more rapidly during times of economic expansion; and (4) the deterioration of the work status of men during periods of crisis also has an impact on women, in which the increased pressure on reduced family income leads to an increased intensity of women's work and on women's time use, both on paid and unpaid work.

Data for the crisis years shows that women's labor force participation remained stable, while that of men decreased. Simultaneously, the male unemployment rate decreased faster than that of women, although the last one remained higher. Rotation between jobs increased, more sharply for women. Losses of formal employment occurred more heavily for men than for women.

Unfortunately, there is no reliable data on labor earnings, household income, and poverty incidence, though it is assumed that these indicators worsened during the period of economic slowdown.

3.2.2 Policy responses to the crisis

In terms of its discourse, the general position adopted by the national government can be summarized as follows:[27] (1) the national economy was strengthened by the policies implemented since 2003, and thus the impact of the crisis would be lessened along with the effort needed to confront the crisis;[28] (2) the government's priority in this scenario is to conserve the level of employment and defend the quality of jobs as much as possible; and (3) public spending in social areas such as education, health, and social security must be preserved from the negative impacts that the crisis may have on public financing.

Along these lines, policy responses to the crisis focused on sustaining the level of public spending as well as supporting the level of private consumption, while promoting investment. The implicit logic of these interventions involves preserving real demand as a determining factor in employment. On top of this, explicit interventions to avoid firing were implemented through tax credit systems.

The first group of actions was based on the financing of subsidized loans and in continuing tax benefits to promote private investment. While there is no available data to assess the success of this action, it seems it has been pretty ineffective. The second major group of actions was implemented by the Ministry of Labor, and its main goal was to prevent employment losses and a drop in wages. An indirect consequence of these measures was sustaining domestic demand as a countercyclical measure.

The labor-related measures adopted were not strictly new, but rather a follow-up or in some cases a redeployment or extension of existing actions. These policy interventions included the following:

- Enacting Law 26476, which entails a System for the Promotion and Protection of Formal Employment. This law encourages employers to declare informal workers by offering tax write-offs on withholdings and contributions, and any fines or penalties may be paid in installments. The law does not establish any preference for enforcement in terms of economic sector or the gender of workers that occupy newly created or newly declared jobs. Passing this law served three purposes: (1) to promote formal employment, (2) to sustain tax revenue, and (3) to promote capital influx that could turn into productive investment.
- The second action was the Productive Recovery Program (REPRO). This program was created in 2002, as part of the Occupational Economic Emergency. Its aim is to sustain and promote employment, helping the recovery of the private sector and geographical areas in crisis. To access this benefit, companies must provide evidence that their operations are in serious trouble,

outline a recovery plan, and commit to maintaining their current staff level for a 12-month period. The program grants a fixed monthly subsidy that has to be used to complete workers' salary. The number of beneficiaries represents approximately 10 percent of the unemployment benefits paid monthly.[29] Although there is no official data about the gender of beneficiaries, officials from the Ministry of Labor admit that they are mostly men. The program does not establish any specific coverage goals in terms of gender, total number of beneficiaries, or sectors.

- Another instrument currently being implemented is the Crisis Prevention Process. This instrument was created by the 1991 Employment Act, and it was conceived to prevent early dismissals in crisis periods. Companies that make significant staff reductions[30] are required to provide evidence of being in serious trouble. The Ministry of Labor acts as a mediator between companies and workers.

In order to sustain workers' real income, the Ministry of Labor also applied adjustments to the nominal value of the minimum wage.[31]

The Ministry of Labor (along with the Ministry of Social Development) also adopted measures to increase the wages of lower-income workers and monetary welfare benefits. In December 2008, an additional payment was allocated to workers who earned the minimum wage and beneficiaries of: (1) Non-taxable Pensions, (2) The *Familias* Plan, and (3) The Unemployed Head of Household Plan.[32]

While not considered by the government as part of the anti-crisis package, other relevant policy measures were implemented during recent months. These policy interventions included the following:

Creation of the Argentine Integrated Retirement System (SIPA): By creating the SIPA, the state resumed control of the pension system by eliminating the component previously managed by the private pension funds. This was a relevant measure in a context of global crisis and economic slowdown because it enabled the government to gain access to resources and, thus, actively intervene with actions that may have countercyclical effects. Evidence shows that most of these resources were used to finance the public sector, including the financial support to the anti-crisis package.

The Universal Child Allowance: This is the most recent public policy initiative on the complex map of social-security-related monetary-transfer programs. Implemented at the end of 2009, it was geared toward supporting income and had great potential in a crisis context, given the drop in earnings and household income.

The program is targeted to children under 18 and disabled people irrespective of their ages, and makes provisions for a monetary benefit per child or disabled to all unemployed individuals or individuals at informal jobs that yield less than the monthly minimum wage. It is a non-taxable monetary benefit, paid monthly per child under 18 or disabled, up to a maximum of five children per family. In addition, children younger than four must comply with all public health care requirements and all children must provide proof of attendance at a public school. Women are the ones responsible for guaranteeing these requirements are met. The program reached almost three million beneficiaries. Its timely implementation in the context of the crisis was a key countercyclical policy, with women their most relevant actors.

3.2.3   Gender implications of the public policy measures taken by the Argentinean government to face the crisis

Two general considerations are in order. First, there is a substantive difference in the way the crisis was tackled in comparison with previous crises. This is related to the disbelief of the market self-regulation paradigm and recognition of the need for and advisability of an active role for the state. In this sense, a response to crisis that does not entrust recovery solely to free market forces but is rather brought about by active politics is more likely to favor gender equality.

Second, and as general comment applicable to all the public policy measures adopted, the absence of explicit consideration of gender equality in policy design and implementation is remarkable. Argentina must strive to bring to the forefront gender issues in decision-making on public policy. This constitutes a challenge to women's organizations, and to all sectors committed to gender equality. Despite this absence of a consideration of gender in public policies, it is evident that these issues affect both men and women in different ways.

Policy measures adopted to sustain the level of demand through promoting consumption and investment proved to be quite ineffective by themselves. Those targeted to support employment level were also of little significance in budget terms. Furthermore, gender issues were not taken into account, nor did they specifically address the problems of women in situations of severe labor employment vulnerability.

Policies aimed at supporting income were more actively implemented. In this sense, it should be noted that any action seeking to increase individual and household income is positive, especially the income of those with fewer economic resources. Given the unequal share of men and women in income distribution, these measures should favor gender equality. This is especially true because the majority of the beneficiaries of social welfare programs are women.

Indeed, the measures adopted during the crisis that did not specifically target the core employment problem may have favored women to a greater extent. This is particularly the case of the enforcement of the Universal Child Allowance. Several issues should be highlighted regarding this program and its implications for women.

First, given the overrepresentation of women among unemployed and informal workers, a measure like this, which extends family allowance benefits to these population segments, has a positive impact on women. Second, the fact that this benefit is not specifically allocated to mothers, but rather to mothers *or* fathers, may be interpreted as a way of not considering child care a female responsibility.[33] However, this mechanism may allow fathers to "misappropriate" these resources (fathers who may not even live with their children). In fact, in the case of formal workers, the child benefit is mostly granted to men. Third, child tax allowance does not revert, but rather consolidates, the fragmentation of social welfare system. Finally, none of the aforementioned policies addresses the roots of discrimination against female workers in the labor market. The government missed the chance to set up policies that while addressing the emergency also established the foundations for a long-run transformation.

3.3 The case of Ecuador

Ecuador is a very interesting national case, given its actual stage of transformation. The government of President Correa is leading a change, shifting away from neoliberalism toward an economic system shaped by social and solidarity considerations. While real changes are still to be seen, the strength of this discourse, the openness to greater political participation of citizens, as well as the faith of people in the possibility of real changes points out a different context for policy-making.

This perspective has been fortified by the new National Constitution, as well as by the "Plan of Good Living," the Ecuadorian national plan of development. This plan represents a good synthesis of the ideological commitment of the current government in Ecuador.[34]

The latest development plan, which runs for the period 2009–13, was built by the National Secretary of Planning and Development (Senplandes), after consulting with national and local authorities, public and private institutions, social movements, and representatives of different sectors of civil society. This process is understood as the first step toward building the National Decentralized System of Participatory Planning (Sistema Nacional Descentralizado de Planificación Participativa). The aim of this system is to decentralize power and to build the Plurinational and Intercultural State.

Within this context, equity becomes a core element of the new economic and social model. Equity is understood as closing inequality while respecting diversity. While it is stated that gender equity (together with indigenous rights), in particular, is at the forefront of this perspective, the translation of this into concrete policy is not yet evident. The features of the Ecuadorian macroeconomy seem to have played a role in this regard.

The macroeconomics of Ecuador is characterized by the following features: (1) it is a dollarized economy, which means that the space for monetary policy is narrow; (2) oil exports are very significant both for total exports as well as in GDP terms;[35] (3) commodities are also important for Ecuadorian exports;[36] and (4) remittances are an important source of dollars, reaching 7 percent of GDP.

In this context, whatever happens to the external sector will affect directly the money supply in the domestic economy. As exports of oil are also a prevalent source of public sector revenues, the decrease in its sales will directly affect public spending.

Therefore, Ecuador is facing the following contradiction: while in the middle of a transformation that gives priority to social goals and the role of the state in the economy, the degree of freedom for this "new state" to act is small. This is due to the fact that, given the Ecuadorian economy's features, the economic crisis *endogenously* leads to a typical structural adjustment, like those promoted by the IMF and the World Bank. This happens because two basic things happen: the contraction of the money supply and the contraction of public spending.

The concurrence of the decrease in the price of oil, the decrease of international commodities prices, as well of the global credit crisis affected the Ecuadorian economy. GDP went down 1.5 percent between 2008 and 2009.

Two sectors showed a permanent decrease from the beginning of 2008 to the end of 2009: mining and domestic service. Among manufactures, the sectors that showed major decreases between 2008 and 2009 are: processed sugar, coffee and tea, electric machinery, and textiles.

As stated by the Central Bank of Ecuador, during the first quarter of 2009, household consumption decreased 3.03 percent vis-à-vis the same period of 2008. During the second quarter, it further decreased 1.42 percent.

Between the last quarter of 2007 and same period of 2009, the real median labor income decreased 3.8 percent.[37] This was due both to the increase in the price of goods (mostly of food) as well as the deterioration of the conditions in the labor market.

Ecuadorian international trade was heavily affected both by the global crisis and the specific decline in the international price of oil. Between the first three quarters of 2009, imports decreased by 18 percent, vis-à-vis the same period of 2008. Exports decreased by 39 percent. As a consequence, the foreign trade balance showed a deficit result of US$507 million.

All of the above implied a decrease on fiscal revenue. As informed by the Ministry of Finance, total revenue of the central government declined 23 percent between 2008 and 2009, with a significant reduction of oil revenues (–71.8 percent), which accounted for 15 percent of total revenue in 2009.

3.3.1 Social and gender implications of the crisis

The decrease in economic activity provoked by the global crisis has a direct implication on the labor market. Both unemployment and underemployment showed an increase since the third quarter of 2008, reaching 9.1 percent for the first and 51.7 percent for the second by September 2009.[38]

The situation worsened both for men and women, though it seems to have hit the latter more heavily. While labor force participation remained almost unchanged, unemployment grew more for women, who historically present a higher unemployment rate than men. By the end of 2009, the unemployment rate for males was at 7 percent and for females it was at 10.4 percent.

However, it is interesting to note that the labor force composition of the formal and informal sectors, both for male and female, does not change substantively between the third quarter of 2008 and September 2009. In fact, for both women and men, the share of formal employment in the labor force was greater at the end of 2009 than at the beginning of the crisis (44 percent for men, 36 percent for women).

The increase of unemployment as well as the decrease in labor income reduced household income. This situation was deepened by the significant decrease in remittances. As shown in Figure 4.1, remittances declined from the second quarter of 2008, though the decrease seems to have decelerated by the second quarter of 2009.

As a consequence of all of the above, the Ecuadorian poverty rate increased, reaching 25 percent of the population by the end of 2009.

3.3.2 Policy responses to the crisis

Policy responses in Ecuador were tailored by the concurrence of three factors. First, there were the macroeconomic restrictions imposed by a dollarized economy. Second, there was the ideological orientation of a government that prioritizes goals of "good living" (*buen vivir*) and therefore keeps social objectives on top. Third, there was a weak policy-making capacity that made it difficult to change the core structure of inequality and poverty in Ecuador, despite its good intentions.

As stated above, the space for macroeconomic policy space in Ecuador is narrow. In monetary terms, the dollarization of the economy leaves little room to act. The government does not have the option to increase money supply with monetary policy instruments in order to act countercyclically. The only way to stimulate the economy by monetary policy is thus to administer interest rates, in order to decrease the cost of credit, thus promoting productive investment. In this case, however, the situation is dictated by two factors: the nominal interest rate that is administered by the state, and inflation. Given the fixed nominal interest rate established by the monetary authority, and the fact that inflation decelerated during 2009, the real interest rate increased. This, in

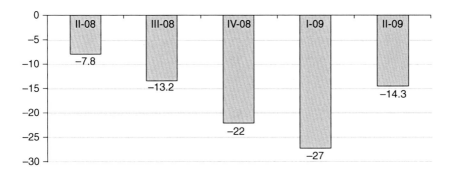

Figure 4.1 Ecuador – Remittances – Quarterly variation same period year before (%) (source: Central Bank of Ecuador 2009).

turn, made access to credit more expensive and funding of productive activities more difficult.

As a consequence of lower public revenues, public spending was not expanded in real terms (after adjusting for inflation). However, a positive feature of the Ecuadorian government response to the crisis was to prioritize social spending (which includes social investment). This was a feature of the government prior to the crisis, and it was sustained during and after the crisis. Therefore, the composition of social spending shifted toward social investment. As stated by the Ministry of Finance, the share of social investment in social spending grew up to 32 percent in 2009 (from 23.3 percent in 2007).

Besides this general orientation, specific responses were assumed by the Ecuadorian government to face the economic crisis.[39] These responses included three elements. The first was to promote SMEs as a way to sustain employment. The policy tool used for this is the National System of Public Buying.

The second was to foster some specific tools in terms of public investment, in order to sustain both employment as well as production. As declared by the Ministry of Finance, priority was given to: (1) credit for housing, (2) subsidies to agriculture production, and (3) basic infrastructure. All three policies might be considered positive from a gender perspective. First, both housing and basic infrastructure can be considered helpful for care organization, and therefore might reduce the pressure on women's unpaid care work. Second, women play an important role in agricultural production; therefore, whatever incentive is given to this sector might benefit women.

The third policy response had to do with sustaining the benefits distributed by the Ecuadorian CCT program. This is the Bono de Desarrollo Social (BDS), a monthly transfer of US$35 to households whose income is below the poverty line. The benefit is received by mothers and they have to fulfill some requirements in terms of children's education and health. In 2009, there were 1.2 million beneficiaries of the BDS.

The BDS suffers from the same ambiguous implications in gender terms that apply to other CCTs in the region. While they guarantee some income for women, the level of the benefit is low. While it is sometimes stated as a monetary recognition of women's unpaid care work, it might imply the consolidation of an unequal distribution of care responsibilities between women and men. It might prevent households from suffering extreme poverty, but it also prevents women from entering the labor market and gaining an independent income.

Finally, the government also shifted more public spending toward labor programs during the crisis, and it also increased the spending on microcredit programs. Unfortunately, there is no available information on the sex composition of beneficiaries of these programs. Other experiences in the region proved that both training programs and microcredit programs are usually focused on women. While they might have positive effects on specific cases, overall they do not change structural discrimination against women in the labor market as well as in their access to economic resources.

3.3.3 Gender implications of the public policy measures taken by the Ecuadorian government to face the crisis

Despite the restrictions imposed by the global crisis, the Ecuadorian government renovated its desire of prioritizing social goals and of promoting the "good living" of the entire population. This is a good starting point, particularly when compared with the tendency to adjustment that has prevailed in previous crises. When social goals are to the fore, no matter how fast or concrete the possibility of reaching these goals might be, the situation will definitely be friendly to women.

However, the policy responses adopted by the Ecuadorian government missed making specific gender considerations. There are neither specific programs aimed at women, nor are there women "quotas" among existing ones, and there are no policy responses that specifically handle women's issues. The weakness of the Ecuadorian gender mechanism might partially explain this feature.

Still, there are some positive aspects. First, there was the decision to sustain the level of social investment even when total public spending is not increasing. The priority given to basic infrastructure, for example, is good for women as it is expected to somehow facilitate women's unpaid care work.

Second, there was the decision to sustain the level of beneficiaries of the CCT program. While this is positive in terms of guaranteeing women's access to income, it has the already-mentioned ambiguous implications that are characteristic of this type of program. They provide income to women, but consolidate their main responsibility for child care.

Third, there was the decision to foster different spaces for citizens' participation in policy decision-making, which is also good for women as it has been proven that they are the ones who take the lead on this type of process.

In terms of gender implications, the main lack of policy responses is that they are not handling two of the most severe consequences that the crisis imposes on women: the increase in unemployment and the lack of employment opportunities in domestic service. Regarding the former, it should be important that the Ecuadorian government implement some policy instruments that allow women facing unemployment to sustain their income while not creating disincentives for them to search for new jobs. Regarding the latter, and given that this is the main source of labor demand for women, the implementation of a specific interventions on this population group should be considered – such as improving working conditions and social security guarantees.

4 Conclusions and policy recommendations

Clearly, the global financial crisis did not affect Latin American economies in a vacuum. The structural features of these economies, their past economic and institutional trajectory, and the nature of the existing gender inequalities are all at stake and shape the ways in which the crisis affected, molded, or counterbalanced gender inequalities.

Beyond the average experience of Latin America as a whole, the country cases studied show that there are heterogeneities both in the intensity with which the crisis has affected growth, employment, and incomes, and on the policy responses to it.

Mexico represents a sort of continuity with the 1990s neoliberal paradigm with an overarching emphasis on stability over growth. The emphasis on "fiscal responsibility" (and the belief in the market) prevented the Mexican government from intervening in a timely manner and more forcefully in the economy – even when it had the resources and bureaucracy to do so. The results in terms of growth and employment (worse than the worst scenario forecast at the beginning of 2009) have proven that the policy responses to the crisis have been weak and transitory relative to the shock.

Argentina has explicitly departed from neoliberal policy since 2002, changing its exchange rate and fiscal policies and having a greater involvement of the state in the economy. The fiscal and external space gained in previous years allowed the government to implement countercyclical policies and sustain already existing social and labor market policies without much external support. Strong institutions made it possible for the government to implement the initiatives in a timely fashion.

Ecuador, in turn, is paradoxical in its mix of political transformation, its weak institutional fabric, and its inherited dollarized economy, which shows the tensions between political discourse and effective fiscal and monetary space in a small and open economy.

The review of these experiences shows that in the cases where governments were able to implement policy initiatives that do not entrust recovery to market forces and explicitly establish employment generation and sustaining families' incomes as their priorities, there is a *potential* to favor gender equality in macroeconomic policy and for a structural economic transformation that simultaneously mitigates gender inequality.

For this potential to be realized, however, it is required that gender considerations are explicitly introduced in the policy agenda. A striking result of the above review is that the countercyclical policy packages in all three countries under study have had *no explicit consideration of the gender dimensions involved.* No assessment has been made of the effects of recession on women and men, their differential vulnerability to the shocks that the global crisis has brought about, and the visible and invisible costs borne by women and men from different socioeconomic strata and from different household types as a consequence of the deteriorated economic conditions.

Clearly, the countercyclical policy packages analyzed do have a gender dimension in their design and impacts. Programs to support employment in the productive sectors that have been most severely hit by the crisis have helped sustain male employment, as men are overrepresented in these sectors' labor force. The increase in public investment is also concentrated in a type of public works that demands mostly male labor. While this is to be expected, the expansion of female-dominated sectors might well have equivalent aggregate demand and employment impacts, plus gender equality impacts.

Regarding gender effects of the countercyclical policies, it is good news that the three countries under analysis recognize the importance of not slashing social policies. It is, however, a far cry from a social protection framework that departs from the emphasis on most vulnerable groups to warrant universal access to social security, health, education, a decent job, and sufficient incomes. Such policies would contribute to change structural gender inequalities in the access of economic resources and to income-generating opportunities.

Lastly, the absence of consideration of the many gender dimensions implied in the design and implementation of countercyclical policies vividly reveals the state of gender mainstreaming in the region, and the low power of local gender policy mechanisms (Argentina's Secretaría Nacional de la Mujer, Mexico's INMUJERES, and Ecuador's Comisión de Transición hacia el Consejo Nacional de las Mujeres y la Igualdad de Género (ex-CONAMU)). So far, local and national gender policy mechanisms have failed to take advantage of the current crisis to strengthen their voice in economic policy design and action taking.

4.1 Policy recommendations

The previous review has shown that structural features of the Latin American economies and their approach to economic policy *matter* to macroeconomic performance *and* advancing toward achieving gender equality. Therefore, it should be stressed at this juncture that crises not only call for "emergency" countercyclical measures but also provide an opportunity to implement policies that could attend short-term policy objectives – sustain employment and incomes – and initiate structural transformations that prevent (or mitigate) future crises.

In particular, gender equality must not be relegated as a policy objective that is considered to be only appropriate for good economic times. Not addressing gender inequality during crises might jeopardize achievements made in the gender Millennium Development Goals and generate drawbacks that will be costly and hard to revert. The case in point is labor market functioning, as shown in this chapter. The fact that men have been losing jobs faster than women does not deactivate the processes that lie behind gender discrimination and segregation in the labor market – something that becomes quite evident when crises end and men's employment reacts faster than women's. Labor market policies that contribute to women's employment and to lowering gender wage gaps by *increasing* women's opportunities and access to income-generating activities can make a contribution in this sense.

Therefore, policy actions should *foster women's employment and monitor the quality of the jobs created.* To do so, it might be good to consider a specific women's target in employment programs. For example, in cases where state subsidies are provided to firms that commit themselves to keep jobs, it could be established that a specific share of the "guaranteed jobs" should be for women.

Given that women are overrepresented in informal work, they are also over-represented among those who are unable to apply for unemployment benefits. Actions that extend unemployment benefits as well as other income support policies would be positive for women and will have a clear expansionary effect.

Public investment programs should have a proper balance between infrastructure and social investment. This would be positive not only to balance the demand for male and female labor, but could guarantee that state-provided social services, which are a key element influencing equality in the provision of care, are not weakened as a response to fiscal constraint (UN 2010b; Antonopoulos 2009).

Gender mechanisms should take an active role in monitoring countercyclical policies. Every policy response should be evaluated for its implications for women's economic positions and for gender equality. These offices should develop clear criteria for this assessment and should supervise that they are applied at different stages of policy design and implementation. The fact that this has not happened shows the current weakness of gender mechanisms and the low priority of women's agendas in public policy.

A particular case in point is the proposal of countercyclical policies with a special emphasis on reverting gender inequalities. These might include as a relevant component the promotion of employment in care services. Even though the public provision of new care services (or strengthening of existing ones) implies fiscal costs, these should be compared to the costs of *not having them* – costs that women, children, and other dependants have to bear in their absence. Moreover, public provision of care services – a very labor-intensive service – can become a genuine tool to increase women's employment. At the same time, when these services are provided without fees, they contribute to free families from some of their care responsibilities, boosting women's labor force participation, employment, and incomes, and thus contributing to mitigate poverty.

Finally, CCTs – a central element of social policy in countries that can afford their bureaucracies, like Mexico and Argentina – should be revised to foster their strengths and moderate their weaknesses. CCTs' coverage should be enlarged, aiming at universal coverage, and funds should be derived from stable sources. CCTs should not discourage women's labor force participation, nor should they emphasize care as women's responsibility. On the contrary, their design should contribute to social and gender *shared* responsibilities in the provision of care.

4.2 Postscript

In the year 2010, and the first half of 2011, the region continued to experience recovery. In 2010, the region grew at a rate of 5.9 percent (4.8 percent in per capita terms), while it is estimated that growth decelerated to 4.3 percent (3.2 percent in per capita terms) in 2011. The stronger growth performance was reflected in the labor market; the regional unemployment rate went down to around 7.3 percent in 2010, and a further half a percentage point in 2011 (UN 2012).

Such a recovery translated into continuing improvements in social indicators, as absolute poverty went down to 31.4 percent (or 177 million people) in 2010, and it is estimated that it was 30.4 percent (or 174 million people) in 2011 – a full three percentage points less (or 10 million less) when compared to 2009 (UN 2011b, p. 11). Whether these gains remain in the future will depend on labor market performance and continuing food inflation, which might hit those in extreme poverty (12.3 percent in 2010 and an estimated 12.8 percent in 2011).

Growth was sustained by the abovementioned countercyclical policies, as well as by the expansion of external markets up to the first half of 2011. Behind this positive performance lie the same risks and contradictions that were present before the crisis: the reappearance of a commodity price boom, with its negative effects on food and fuel-importing countries and its middle-term re-primarization effect on food and fuel-exporting countries; booming international trade, which benefits export-led growth countries but leaves them vulnerable to sudden changes in external conditions; and an upsurge in international liquidity (capital inflows) in times when it became increasingly difficult or costly to shield economies from them, leaving a trail of exchange rate appreciation and high interest rates, particularly in the larger Latin American economies (Mexico and Brazil). Such trends put pressure on domestic prices, and gave more strength to stabilization policies oriented at curbing inflation at the expense of penalizing GDP growth, in spite of its still fragile foundations. There were also concerns that exchange rate appreciation coupled with high interest rates might induce a new wave of debt-led growth in the region.

However, during the second half of 2011, the region experienced the impact of the grim world economic outlook, as the European crisis unfolded and Asian economies slowed down. As a result, an "endogenous" adjustment process took place as capital flew out, economic activity slowed down, and depreciation pressures re-emerged. Prospects are also grim, depending on how severe the slowdown of international demand becomes during 2012.

The ups and downs of the Latin American economies during the last four years emphasize the region's vulnerability to external shocks – be they real or financial; the differential effects that these shocks have on countries' economies, depending on their external specialization and their dependence on external financing (including the size of their foreign debt and their stocks of foreign reserves); and the macroeconomic space different economies have to fence themselves from such shocks. Paradoxically, even though the 2011–12 external shock appears to be less severe than that of 2008–09, the fiscal and monetary space some Latin American economies enjoy seems to be more restricted than before.

Neither the recovery of growth nor the deceleration experienced at the time of finalizing this chapter (December 2011) alter this chapter's main messages: the need to prioritize growth and employment generation over stabilization; an active role for the state in shaping fiscal, monetary, and exchange rate policies in order to produce sustained and inclusive growth; and the need to give explicit consideration to the gender dimensions involved in macroeconomic policy design.

Notes

1 For a historical review, see Ffrench-Davis *et al.* (1994).
2 Of course, reality tends to be not so clear-cut. Pre-crisis domestic paths are not independent of the international context, and external shocks usually exacerbate pre-
  existing domestic disequilibria.
3 The picture is grimmer for the Caribbean, which contracted by 2.1 percent in 2009.
  The Caribbean economies, quite different from those of Latin America, are not
  covered in this chapter.
4 At the time, there was talk of whether the financial crisis would become "L-shaped"
  or "V-shaped." With the benefit of hindsight, it seems clear that the crisis as such is
  still unfolding, and might become "double-dip" for the United States, as a result of the
  combination of sluggish international demand and ceilings to public debt.
5 It should be noted that energy-importer countries, like those in Central America,
  experienced deterioration in their terms of trade during the period due to the price
  boom in oil and minerals.
6 Not without tensions on the exchange rate, as these factors generate appreciation pressures. For example, Chile, Argentina, and Brazil saw their real exchange rates appre-
  ciate during the booming years.
7 It is still a matter of some debate whether it is the better than before macroeconomic
  "fundamentals" (UN 2010a; BID 2009) or the extraordinarily good external conditions (Ocampo 2009) that allowed Latin American economies to be better equipped
  to face the crisis. Policy recommendations differ depending on which diagnosis is
  favored. The authors are inclined to follow the second hypothesis.
8 Data from Colombia and Ecuador for the period 2008–09; data from Mexico, January–September 2009. Remittances were the first to worsen, as the crisis hit in the
  North, and there are indications that they started to increase again in 2009 (UN 2010a,
  p. 16). Although the contraction in remittances had a huge impact in recipient countries, the overall regional impact was weaker than the trade and financial impacts
  (Ocampo 2009, p. 706).
9 With this, the authors mean that there might be path-dependency in social policy, not
  that the CCTs are necessarily more "efficient" (the view of UN 2010a, p. 21). Universal transfers and workfare programs were less extensive, making it harder for these
  proposals to make progress in the current situation. There are exceptions, however.
  See the discussion in this chapter on Argentina's Universal Child Allowance, and on
  Mexico for the Temporary Employment Program.
10 These estimates are more benign than those published at the end of 2009, which set
  poverty incidence at 34 percent of population, and extreme poverty at 14 percent for
  that year (UN 2010b).
11 Although they are overrepresented among female-headed households, female head-
  ship is not automatically equated to poverty. See Chant (2003).
12 All nominal figures in dollar terms, unless otherwise stated.
13 Total public debt (including peso-nominated debt) was 27 percent of GDP in 2008.
14 These paths were far from "revolutionary," though. See Cornia (2009) for a review of
  the changes in economic policy that left-to-centre governments have implemented in
  Latin America.
15 A US Federal Reserve *swap* of US$30 billion also contributed to this.
16 The authors have emphasized the *change* in the unemployment rate, from relatively
  low levels as compared to those of other Latin American countries. As it is developed
  in this chapter, this is the result of a constant migration outflow that operates as an
  "escape valve" for the Mexican labor market.
17 This effect is less noticeable in observed data.
18 Information from "Portal de Empleo." Online: www.empleo.gob.mx.
19 The informal sector shrank as a proportion of total employment after 2009.

20 The outbreak of the H1N1 human influenza also contributed to the downturn. ECLAC (UN 2009b, p. 3) has estimated its impact in 0.7 percent of GDP.

21 Data on measures based on UN (2009b) and ILO (2010).

22 The figure seems to correspond to all employment programs and not only with PET. According to the information provided by the "Portal del Empleo," during 2009 PET provided employment for 37,819 persons, while all employment programs gave jobs to 896,402 persons.

23 However, there is no information on the timely implementation of the above-mentioned plans.

24 For a definition of the "fiscal space," see Fanelli and Jiménez (2009).

25 For a description of this view, see BID (2009).

26 www.empleo.gob.mx (accessed November 12, 2012).

27 This summary is based on the systematized public statements made by the president, her ministers, and public officials from different departments between October 2008 and June 2009.

28 This line of thought follows that of the Message of the Budget 2009, which reads: "The importance of sustaining positive results in terms of taxes and foreign trade grants the government greater tax and currency autonomy to defend the process of growth with social insertion to confront exogenous shocks" (p. 11). "The perspectives for 2008 and 2009 suggest that the expansion of the previous years will continue, though at a slower rhythm than that observed in the previous two year period (2006–2007)" (p. 15).

29 According to data provided by the Social Security Department, the total unemployment benefit paid in December 2008 was AR$126,040; 72 percent of beneficiaries were male and 28 percent were female. The historical rate of people to receive unemployment benefits has never exceeded 10 percent of the unemployed population.

30 When affecting more than 15 percent of workers in companies that have less than 400 workers; more than 10 percent in companies that have between 400 and 1,000 workers; and more than 5 percent in companies that have more than 1,000 workers.

31 The minimum wage increased to AR$1200 in August 2008, AR$1,240 in December 2008, AR$1,400 in August 2009, AR$1,440 in October 2009, and AR$1,500 in January 2010, which is to say US$390.

32 The income compensation amounts to US$200 for workers who earn the minimum wage (AR$1,240); AR$150 for beneficiaries of the *Familias* Plan (the amount of this benefit varies from AR$155 to AR$305); AR$100 for beneficiaries of non-taxable pensions (the average benefit is under AR$500), and beneficiaries of the Unemployed Head of Household Plan (the benefit is AR$150). In all cases the additional income is paid only once.

33 This is a positive difference with the existing CCTs.

34 See Ramirez Gallegos and Mintegviaga (2007).

35 It is evident that oil exports are very dependent upon the international oil price. Oil exports represented 65 percent of total exports in 2008, 48 percent in 2009 and 55 percent in 2010.

36 Bananas are the main non-oil export product in Ecuador, sharing 15 percent of total exports.

37 As informed by the Central Bank of Ecuador, Informe Trimestral del Mercado Laboral (2009).

38 Underemployment is defined as visible and other forms of underemployment. The five main cities are: Quito, Guayaquil, Cuenca, Machala, and Ambato. The reason for the "dip" in underemployment in December 2008 is unclear.

39 Unfortunately, there is little information regarding characteristics of the specific policy tools. Therefore, the authors are only able to make a general description, which, regardless, allows us to come to some relevant conclusions for our gender analysis.

References

Anlló, G., B. Kosacoff, and A. Ramos. (2007) "Crisis, recuperación y nuevos dilemas," in B. Kosacoff (ed.), *Crisis, Recuperación y Nuevos Dilemas: la economía argentina 2002–2007*, Santiago: CEPAL.

Antonopoulos, R. (2009) "The current economic and financial crisis: a gender perspective," Working Paper No. 562, Annandale-on-Hudson, NY: Levy Economics Institute of Bard College.

BID (2009) *Políticas Sociales y Laborales para Tiempos Tumultuosos: cómo enfrentar la crisis global en América Latina y el Caribe*, Washington.

Central Bank of Ecuador (2009) *Informe Trimestral de Mercado Laboral*, Quito: Banco Central de Ecuador.

Chant, S. (2003) "Nuevas contribuciones al análisis de la pobreza: desafíos metodológicos y conceptuales para entender la pobreza desde una perspectiva de género," Serie Mujer y Desarrollo No. 47, Unidad Mujer y Desarrollo, Santiago: CEPAL (LC/L.1955-P).

Cornia, G.A. (2009) "Democratic change and income inequality in Latin America during the last decade," draft.

Fanelli, J.M. and J.P. Jiménez. (2009) "Crisis, volatilidad y política fiscal en América Latina," in O. Kacef and J.P. Jiménez (eds.), *Políticas Macroeconómicas en Tiempos de Crisis: opciones y perspectivas*, Colección Documentos de proyectos, ECLAC: Santiago (LC/W.275).

Ffrench Davis, R., Muñoz, Ó. and Palma, J.G. (1994) "Latin American Economies 1950–1990," in L. Betell (ed.), *The Cambridge History of Latin America*, Vol. VI: *Latin America since 1930 – economy, society and politics*, Part I, Cambridge: Cambridge University Press.

García Gaytán, M. (2009) "Palabras de María del Rocío García Gaytán, Presidenta del Instituto Nacional de las Mujeres, durante la reunión de especialistas: Análisis de la crisis económica y financiera desde la perspectiva de género: entendiendo su impacto sobre la pobreza y el trabajo de las mujeres," INMUJERES, Mexico DF, July 23, 2009.

ILO (2010) Mexico's Response to the Crisis, G20 Country Briefs, G20 Meeting of Labour and Employment Ministers, April 20–21, 2010, Washington DC.

ILO/UN (2009) *ECLAC/ILO Bulletin: the employment situation in Latin America and the Caribbean*, Lima: ECLAC/ILO.

ILO/UN (2010) *ECLAC/ILO Bulletin: the employment situation in Latin America and the Caribbean*, Lima: ECLAC/ILO.

INEGI, Instituto Nacional de Estadística, Geografía e Informática (2009) "Producto Interno Bruto en México durante el tercer trimestre de 2009," Comunicado Núm. 312/09, 20 de noviembre, Aguascalientes.

Kacef, O. (2009) "Crisis y políticas públicas en América Latina y el Caribe," in O. Kacef and J.P. Jiménez (eds.), *Políticas Macroeconómicas en Tiempos de Crisis: opciones y perspectivas*, Colección Documentos de proyectos, CEPAL: Santiago (LC/W.275).

Molyneux, M. (2006) "Mothers at the service of the New Poverty Agenda: Progresa/ Oportunidades, Mexico's conditional transfer programme," *Social Policy and Administration*, 40: 425–49.

Molyneux, M. (2009) "Conditional cash transfers: pathways to women's empowerment?" Research Paper, IDS Series on Social Policy in Developing Countries.

Montaño, S. and Milosavljevic, V. (2010) "La crisis económica y financiera: su impacto sobre la pobreza, el trabajo y el tiempo de las mujeres," Santiago: Cepal, *Serie Mujer y Desarrollo* 98.

Moreno-Brid, J. (2009) "Mexican economy facing the international crisis," paper presented at IDEAS Conference on re-regulating global finance in the light of the global crisis, Tsinghua University, Beijing, China, April 9–12.

Moreno-Brid, J. (2010) "The Mexican economy and the international crisis," paper presented at the WIEGO Conference on Research on the Informal Economy, Cape Town, South Africa, March 25–26.

Ocampo, J.A. (2009) "Latin America and the global financial crisis," *Cambridge Journal of Economics*, 33: 703–24.

Ocampo, J.A. (2007) "The macroeconomics of the Latin American economic boom," *CEPAL Review*, 93: 7–28.

Puyana, A. (2010) *The Impact of Trade Liberalization and the Global Economic Crisis on the Productive Sectors, Employment and Incomes in Mexico*, International Centre for Trade and Sustainable Development (ICTSD) Programme on Competitiveness and Sustainable Development, Issues Paper No. 15, December.

Ramirez Gallegos, F. and A. Mintegviaga (2007) "El nuevo tiempo del Estado: la política posneoliberal del correísmo," CLACSO: *OSAL*, 22.

UN (United Nations) (2009a) "México," in *Balance preliminar de las economías de América Latina y el Caribe*, Santiago.

UN (2009b) *La reacción de los gobiernos de las Américas frente a la crisis internacional: una presentación sintética de las medidas de política anunciadas hasta el 30 de septiembre de 2009*, Santiago.

UN (2010a) *Preliminary Overview of the Economies of Latin America and the Caribbean, 2009*, New York: United Nations ECLAC.

UN (2010b) *Social Panorama of Latin America, 2009*, New York: United Nations ECLAC.

UN (2011a) *Preliminary Overview of the Economies of Latin America and the Caribbean, 2010*, New York: United Nations ECLAC.

UN (2011b) *Social Panorama of Latin America, 2011*, New York: United Nations ECLAC.

UN (2011c) *Panorama social de América Latina 2011*, New York: United Nations ECLAC (preliminary version, not edited).

UN (2012) *Preliminary Overview of the Economies of Latin America and the Caribbean, 2011*, New York: United Nations ECLAC.

5 Trade contraction in India and South Africa during the global crisis

Examining gender and skill biases in job loss

*David Kucera, Leanne Roncolato, and Erik von Uexkull**

> *"For most nations in the world ... this is not a financial crisis – it is a trade crisis."*
> Richard Baldwin (2009)

1 Introduction

The role that trade played as a transmission channel in the global crisis was unprecedented, and was a result of what has been referred to as the "Great Trade Collapse" (Baldwin 2009). That global trade would have fallen alongside global output is unremarkable. Yet real global output is estimated to have declined by 2.2 percent in 2009 and real global trade by 12.2 percent (World Bank 2010; WTO 2010). That global trade declined over five times more than global output is remarkable and unforeseen not just by the governments of India and South Africa, but also by economists.

The *ex post facto* efforts of a number of economists to come to terms with the causes of the "Great Trade Collapse" resulted in an edited volume of the same name (Baldwin 2009). Baldwin's introductory chapter argues that there is an emerging consensus on the importance of the "compositional effect" and the "synchronicity effect." The "compositional effect" describes how the demand shock associated with the crisis focused on "postponeable" consumer durable and investment goods, including electrical and non-electrical machinery, transport equipment, chemicals, steel and other metal products, and raw materials. Since these goods make up a much larger share of traded goods than GDP, a

* The authors are very grateful to Marion Jansen for suggesting this research, to Frederic Lapeyre, Eddy Lee, Sher Verick, three anonymous referees, the participants of the DPRU-EPP-TIPS Conference in Johannesburg in October 2010, and the participants of the ILO Research Conference in Geneva in February 2011 for providing helpful comments, and to Julia Urhausen for providing EU trade data. The views expressed in this chapter are those of the authors and should not be attributed to their affiliated organizations. This chapter is reprinted from *World Development*, 40 (6): 1191–210 (2012).

given change in the demand for them would have a much larger effect on trade than on GDP. The "synchronicity effect" describes how the expansion of global production networks – characterized by just-in-time supply of intermediate inputs – caused the effects of falling export demand to be rapidly transmitted across borders.

World trade began to recover in late 2009, and the World Trade Organization projected that it would grow by 9.5 percent in 2010 (WTO 2010). It might be thought, in this regard, that studying the effects of trade contraction in the crisis is of only passing concern, since employment losses may be temporary and quickly recouped. At the same time, even short-lived shocks may have long-lasting consequences, so-called "scarring effects." This is all the more so in countries like India and South Africa, where large numbers of people have limited means to cope with temporary losses of work and income. More generally, studying the effects of the trade shock can provide a fuller appreciation of the potential costs associated with greater trade openness, which policy-makers can set against the gains from trade.

This chapter estimates the effects of trade contraction in the global crisis on employment in India and South Africa, using social accounting matrices (SAMs) in a Leontief multiplier model in which the change in demand is represented by the change in exports from India and South Africa to the European Union and United States. To be explicit, this chapter does not endeavor to estimate changes in employment during the crisis, which would be of limited value in the face of actual employment data. Regarding gender differentiated effects, this analysis does not explore the biased responses of employers during economic crisis, i.e., the buffer versus substitution hypotheses (Rubery 1988). Rather, this analysis addresses the extent to which patterns of job segregation among industries may lead to disproportionate employment losses for men or women as a result of the trade collapse. More broadly, the chapter may usefully inform policy discussions in three ways.

First, this modeling approach provides a *ceteris paribus* result, for which the effects of trade contraction are to a large extent isolated from other simultaneous events, both potentially negative (e.g., a decline in foreign investment) and positive (e.g., government crisis responses). This can facilitate a clearer sense of the relative importance of the various transmission channels of the global crisis. Second, the multiplier analysis enables the distinction among direct, indirect, and income-induced effects, providing an explanation of the strong spillover effects from tradable to non-tradable sectors resulting from trade contraction. Third, different industries and types of workers may have been differently affected by trade contraction, and such distinctions can usefully inform governments' crisis responses. As such, this chapter evaluates employment impacts at aggregate and industry levels, with breakdowns by gender and skills.

In our view, a SAMs-based Leontief multiplier model is a valuable means to estimate the employment effects of a short-term trade shock. Because of its relative simplicity combined with detailed results, the method can help design timely policy responses in an environment of great uncertainty, such as one created by the global crisis. Due to this simplicity and the transparency of underlying assumptions, results are well suited for informing non-specialist audiences and policy-makers. Despite its limitations, the model may be as appropriate for analyzing short-term shocks as more complex computable general equilibrium (CGE) models that are typically designed to simulate dynamic adjustment processes to longer-run changes in the structure of trade.

Our main findings are that India and South Africa experienced substantial employment declines as a result of the "Great Trade Collapse." A large share of these declines occurred in the non-tradable sector and resulted from income-induced effects, illustrating how a shock originating in the tradable goods sector had wide-ranging effects. For South Africa, we find that industries with higher shares of unskilled and male workers are disproportionately affected by employment declines, while no such evidence of skills or gender bias is found for India. These findings are discussed in the context of actual changes in employment in the two countries during the crisis along with aspects of the governments' crisis responses.

2 Trade patterns before and during the crisis

Both India and South Africa are noteworthy for their rapid pace of trade liberalization and because they figure importantly in debates on the role of trade liberalization in economic development.[1] Shown in Figure 5.1 for the two countries is total trade (exports plus imports) of goods and services as a percentage of GDP – that is, de facto trade openness. By this measure, India has been much less open than South Africa, yet there was convergence between the countries up to the early 1990s, after which openness increased in both

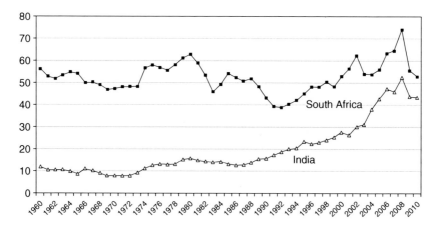

Figure 5.1 Total trade as a percentage of GDP, 1960–2010 (X+M/GDP%) (source: World Bank 2011).

countries, from about 20 to 45 percent in India and 40 to 65 percent in South Africa up until 2008. That is, both countries saw a 25 percentage point increase in de facto trade openness in just a decade-and-a-half, indicating a dramatic increase in their engagement with the world economy. Between 2008 and 2009, this measure declined by 9 and 18 percentage points in India and South Africa, respectively, with no rebound for either country in 2010.

Kucera and Roncolato (2011) analyze the impact of trade expansion in South Africa from 1993 to 2006 and estimate that South Africa gained employment from trade with developed countries and lost employment from trade with developing countries. Due to the disproportionate concentration of women in labor-intensive industries, they estimate the overall employment effects of trade expansion to be biased against women. They similarly analyzed trade expansion in India from 1993 to 2004, but found little evidence of gender bias.

Because of the limited availability of recent export data at a detailed industry level for India and South Africa, our study is based on mirror data on imports from the two countries reported by the EU and US. Yet these are important markets for Indian and South African exports and so provide a useful if partial account of the effects of the crisis through trade contraction.[2]

Shown in Figures 5.2 and 5.3 are exports (in constant prices) from India and South Africa to the EU and US from January 2003 to April 2009. For India, there was a substantial decline in exports from early 2008 on, driven more by trade with the US; for South Africa, the decline was even sharper, driven more by trade with the EU. These differences in export patterns with respect to the EU and US are reflected, we will see, in our employment results.

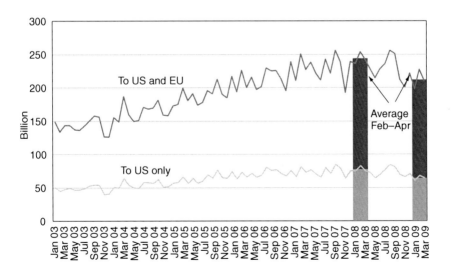

Figure 5.2 Indian exports to the EU and US, in 2003 rupees (bn.) (source: Authors' calculation based on data from European Commission 2010 and US 2010).

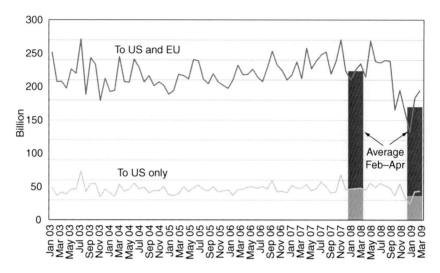

Figure 5.3 South African exports to the EU and US, in 2000 rand (bn.) (source: Authors'
calculation based on data from European Commission 2010 and US 2010).

3 Method

A social accounting matrix (SAM) is a representation of national accounts
showing the two-way flows of economic transactions in a country. SAMs for
India and South Africa – for 2003–04 and 2000, respectively – are used in a
Leontief multiplier model to estimate the effects of the 2008–09 trade contraction. The analysis was conducted using both Type I and Type II multipliers,
though the presentation focuses more on results using Type II multipliers. Type I
multipliers address the direct effects of trade contraction on employment as well
as indirect effects through forwards and backwards production (input–output)
linkages. In addition to these direct and indirect effects, Type II multipliers
address income-induced effects resulting from changes in household
expenditures.

For employment, the Leontief multiplier model is defined as:

$$L = \hat{E}[(I - A)^{-1}T],$$

where L = the vector of changes in industry-level employment associated with
the changes in trade, expressed as full-time equivalent (FTE) jobs lasting one
year; $\hat{E}$ = the diagonal matrix of industry-level labor coefficients employment
per unit of output); I = the identity matrix; A = the average propensity to spend
matrix; and T = the industry-level export demand vector. Because the SAMs for
India and South Africa provide separate commodity accounts (including
imports) and production accounts (excluding imports), T enters the model

through the commodity account and impacts the domestic economy through the production account.

T is constructed in two ways. T1 is defined for each industry as the difference in exports between early 2008 and early 2009, coinciding with the "Great Trade Collapse." More specifically, T1 represents the annualized difference in exports between the three-month period from February to April of these years, shown by the shaded bars in Figures 5.2 and 5.3. Because industry values for T1 are mainly negative, using T1 in the Leontief multiplier model yields estimates of what we define as "jobs lost" during the crisis as a result of trade contraction. T2 is constructed by assuming that, were it not for the crisis, exports would have continued to grow at the same rate to February–April 2009 as they had in previous years. We base this on industry-level export growth for the years 2004–06 and exclude the years 2007–08 to filter out possible effects of commodity and food price shocks during this latter period. T2 is then defined for each industry as the annualized difference between this hypothetical level of endpoint exports and actual exports in February–April 2008. As with T1, industry values for T2 are for the most part negative, resulting from most industries' favorable export growth prior to the crisis, particularly in India. In this sense, using T2 in the model yields estimates of what we define as "jobs not created" during the crisis as a result of trade contraction.[3]

Results are presented according to two scenarios based on T1 and T2:

- *Scenario A* refers to estimated "jobs lost" (based on T1 by itself).
- *Scenario B* refers to the estimated sum of "jobs lost" and "jobs not created" (based on T1 plus T2).

Studies using similar methods to estimate the effects of trade on employment generally construct a trade demand vector based not on changes in exports but rather on changes in net exports (exports minus imports) relative to domestic production or domestic production for final demand plus imports (or plus net imports) (e.g., Sachs and Shatz 1994; Kucera and Milberg 2003). In other words, these studies estimate the effects of a changing *structure* of trade. It might be argued, on these grounds, that we overestimate the effects of the crisis, since imports into India and South Africa also declined during the period we evaluate.

We do not expect this to be a concern for Scenario A, since these earlier studies were evaluating the employment impact of trend changes in the structure of trade. Trend changes in the structure of imports could be expected to have predictable effects on domestic employment because of substitutions between imported and domestically produced goods. But this would not hold for an import shock, given the associated instability and uncertainty and the fact that import declines were driven by a reduction in total demand rather than substitutions between imports and domestically produced goods. Unlike Scenario A, however, Scenario B is based on extrapolating a trend from a period in which *net* exports declined markedly in both India and South Africa, and where export growth is consistent with job loss resulting from trade expansion (Kucera and Roncolato 2011). In this sense, results based on T2 could be regarded as *gross* jobs not created rather than *net* jobs not created. On these grounds, we regard Scenario A results as more definitive and rely more on them in our presentation.

In addition to the breakdowns between Scenarios A and B and between exports to the EU and the US, employment results are further broken down between male and female workers and between more- and less-educated workers. We use data on less-educated workers as a proxy for less-skilled workers, with less-educated workers defined as those having no more than lower secondary education, equivalent to eight years of education in India and nine years in South Africa.

Though the Leontief multiplier model has been widely used in the literature on trade and employment, it nonetheless has well-known limitations, in particular that it is linear and non-dynamic. This study does not, for example, address dynamic effects through economic growth or trade-induced labor-displacing technical change. Yet we do not regard these as serious limitations on our estimates, given the short time frame considered and the contractionary effects of the crisis more generally. In both India and South Africa during the crisis, there were concerns about exchange rate volatility and appreciation, which in normal circumstances would be expected to result in a substitution of domestic for imported inputs (Kumar and Alex 2009; Marais 2009). As noted in our discussion of Scenarios A and B above, though, we would not expect this to hold in a predictable manner given the exceptional nature of the crisis, during which producers faced great uncertainty and imports declined as a result of plummeting demand rather than a substitution of domestic inputs. Note, also, that $\hat{E}$ is based on employment and output data for SAMs base years, which precede the crisis by several years. Given trends toward labor-displacing technical change (more output with less employment), this suggests that our employment estimates are somewhat overestimated in this regard.

The scope of the study is necessarily limited by the databases used in the analysis. The SAMs and labor force surveys used cover both formal and informal establishments and workers, and in this sense are comprehensive. But our trade data for the EU (European Commission 2010) and the US (US 2010) do not include trade in services. From 1990 to 2006, trade in services increased as a percentage of GDP from 3 to 15 percent in India and 5 to 10 percent in South Africa (World Bank 2009). While global trade in services during the crisis has been referred to as "the collapse that wasn't," service exports did decline substantially for India, though not as much as merchandise exports (Borchert and Mattoo 2009; Kumar and Alex 2009). In this sense, our study underestimates the effects of trade contraction in the crisis. Our study does, however, address the indirect and income-induced effects of trade contraction on service industries, which turn out to be substantial. For the sake of expediency, we define tradable goods industries as those for which we have trade data and define all other industries as non-tradable, including service industries. These are delineated below in industry-level results.[4]

Finally, the gender analysis of this methodology is limited by the structure of the SAMs for India and South Africa. Engendered SAMs such as those used by Fontana (2003) should be considered as a possible way of enriching this analysis in the future. Fontana's Zambia and Bangladesh SAMs disaggregate male and female labor within the factors of production accounts and categorize households by gender type. Both SAMs also include activity and commodity accounts for "Social Reproduction" and "Leisure." These engendered SAMs enable a much more thorough analysis of the ways in which men and women are differently affected by changes in trade (Fontana 2003).

4 Results

4.1 Country-level results

In developing countries with extensive informal employment and underemployment, the estimation of changes in employment via changes in production is not straightforward. This holds particularly for India where, as of 1999–2000, the vast majority of workers were in the "unorganized" sector – 77 percent in urban areas and 95 percent in rural areas (Sakthivel and Joddar 2006). In this sense, what we refer to as employment declines represented in terms of FTE jobs may in many cases translate into movements from formal into informal employment or increases in underemployment. In any case, our results provide a measure of the negative impact for workers, on average, through some combination of job loss and income loss.

Country-level employment results based on Type II multipliers are presented in absolute and relative terms in Table 5.1 for Scenarios A and B, respectively. That is, this table shows the number of FTE jobs and the number of such jobs as a percentage of the SAMs base year employment, broken down between trade with the EU and US and between what we define as tradable goods and non-tradable industries.

For India, taking trade with the EU and US together, employment declines are estimated to be 3.9 million FTE jobs for all industries based on Scenario A and 10.1 million based on Scenario B – equivalent to 1.1 and 3.2 percent of base year employment. That is, trade contraction during the crisis is estimated to have resulted in 3.9 million "jobs lost" and an additional 6.2 million "jobs not created," as we have defined these. The large estimate for "jobs not created" reflects the rapid growth of exports from India prior to the crisis. Employment declines are driven more by trade with the US than the EU. Estimated employment declines for non-tradable industries are substantial, even though these do not include direct trade effects for these industries. These are equivalent to 17.6 and 19.1 percent of estimated employment losses for all industries based on Scenarios A and B, respectively.

For South Africa, taking trade with the EU and US together, employment declines for all industries are estimated to be 886,000 FTE jobs based on Scenario A and 963,000 based on Scenario B. That is, trade contraction is estimated to have

Table 5.1 Country-level employment effects from trade (Type II multiplier)

Scenario A

	India			South Africa		
	EU	US	EU and US	EU	US	EU and US
Number of jobs (FTE)						
Tradable goods industries	−1,163,804	−2,088,266	−3,252,070	−354,302	−166,124	−520,426
Non-tradable industries	−195,327	−496,734	−692,061	−266,992	−99,068	−366,060
All industries	−1,359,131	−2,585,000	−3,944,131	−621,294	−265,192	−886,486
Number of jobs as a % of SAMs base year employment						
Tradable goods industries	−0.46	−0.82	−1.28	−8.30	−3.89	−12.19
Non-tradable industries	−0.19	−0.48	−0.66	−3.32	−1.23	−4.56
All industries	−0.38	−0.72	−1.10	−5.05	−2.16	−7.21

Scenario B

	India			South Africa		
Number of jobs (FTE)						
	EU	*US*	*EU and US*	*EU*	*US*	*EU and US*
Tradable goods industries	−3,741,618	−4,400,303	−8,141,920	−369,835	−183,822	−553,657
Non-tradable industries	−845,412	−1,076,805	−1,922,217	−298,954	−110,290	−409,245
All industries	−4,587,030	−5,477,108	−10,064,137	−668,789	−294,113	−962,902
Number of jobs as a % of SAMs base year employment						
Tradable goods industries	−1.47	−1.73	−3.20	−8.66	−4.31	−12.97
Non-tradable industries	−0.81	−1.03	−1.84	−3.72	−1.37	−5.09
All industries	−1.28	−1.53	−2.81	−5.44	−2.39	−7.83

Source: Authors' calculations.

resulted in 886,000 "jobs lost" and an additional 77,000 "jobs not created." Though absolute employment declines are much lower for South Africa than India, relative declines are much higher, equivalent to 7.2 and 7.8 percent of base year employment based on scenarios A and B respectively. In contrast with India, employment declines are driven more by trade with the EU than the US. Estimated employment declines for non-tradable industries are also relatively higher for South Africa, equivalent to 41.3 and 42.5 percent of estimated employment declines for all industries based Scenarios A and B, respectively.

How important were income-induced effects versus direct and indirect effects in accounting for these findings? For India, taking EU and US trade together, the share of total employment effects resulting from income-induced effects is about one-half for tradable goods industries, two-thirds for non-tradable industries, and one-half for all industries; for South Africa, the comparable shares are about one-third for tradable goods industries, two-thirds for non-tradable industries (essentially the same as for India), and just over 40 percent for all industries.[5]

In sum, we estimate that India and South Africa experienced sizeable employment declines as a result of trade contraction with the EU and US during the global crisis, even based on our more conservative Scenario A. In India and especially South Africa, a large share of these employment declines occurred in non-tradable industries through indirect and income-induced effects originating from tradable goods industries. Income-induced effects also accounted for sizeable shares of estimated employment losses in tradable goods industries.

4.2 Industry-level results

Country studies evaluating the industry-level effects of trade liberalization on employment commonly find patterns of winning and losing industries. Such patterns are consistent with the playing out of differences – within and among countries – in industry competitiveness in the face of market opening. Yet the "Great Trade Collapse" is a fundamentally different phenomenon than trade liberalization, and there is less of a foundation for developing theoretical priors about industry-level effects. The "compositional effect" can provide useful guidance in this regard, however, describing as it does particularly rapid trade declines for "postponeable" consumer durable and investment goods.

Trade patterns for India and South Africa provide some support for the "compositional effect." For example, the three industries with the greatest drop in exports to the EU and US (taken together) can be classified as "postponeable" consumer durable and investment goods. Indeed, these are the same three industries in both countries: iron, steel, and non-ferrous metals; non-electrical machinery; and miscellaneous manufacturing (the last including jewellery and precision instruments).[6] Yet not all industries fit neatly into this pattern, for there were increases in exports of chemicals for both India and South Africa, and large declines in exports of agriculture and manufactured food products for India. Moreover, the effect of industry-level changes in exports on industry-level changes in employment is somewhat roundabout, mediated as it is by indirect and income-induced effects as well as by differences in the labor intensity of production across industries.

Industry-level results based on Type II multipliers are shown for India and South Africa in Tables 5.2 and 5.3, respectively, expressed in absolute terms for trade with the EU and US separately, and together and in relative terms for the EU and US together. Also shown are percentages of female and less-educated workers and labor coefficients (relative to aggregate labor coefficients) for SAMs base years. The upper panel of these tables show tradable goods industries, with manufacturing industries shaded, and the lower panel shows non-tradable industries. For the sake of brevity, we focus on Scenario A results.[7]

For India, looking at trade with the EU and US together, only 2 of 37 industries (23 of these tradable goods industries) are estimated to gain employment: fishing and rail equipment and other transport equipment, with estimated increases of about 18,000 and 12,000 jobs, respectively – small in comparison to overall estimated employment declines.

In absolute terms, agriculture had far and away the largest estimated employment declines, accounting for 2.2 million of the estimated 3.9 million jobs lost economy-wide. As noted above, given extensive informal employment and also subsistence agriculture in India, these estimated job losses would be made manifest in a combination of job loss and income loss. Because the agricultural sector in India is so large, however, estimated employment declines from trade contraction relative to 2003–04 employment are actually somewhat smaller than for the economy as a whole (1.07 versus 1.10 percent).

In relative terms, the industries with the largest estimated employment declines in India are miscellaneous manufacturing, which includes gems and jewelry (7.8 percent of 2003–04 employment); jute, hemp, and mesta textiles (4.3 percent, though with small absolute declines); iron, steel, and non-ferrous metals (3.9 percent); non-electrical machinery (3.2 percent); furniture and wood products (3.2 percent); and metal products (3.1 percent). Some of these industries are of a similar type, such as iron, steel, and non-ferrous metals, metal products and non-electrical machinery – all metal-based heavy industries. But these industries vary in other respects. For example, while furniture and wood products is labor-intensive and reliant on less-educated workers, non-electrical machinery is capital-intensive and skills-intensive (Table 5.2).[8]

For South Africa, only construction had estimated employment gains, with a small increase of 4,000 jobs. As with India, agriculture (grouped together with hunting, forestry, and fishing) had the largest absolute employment declines, with an estimated 241,000 jobs lost, equivalent to 11.6 percent of 2000 employment. In contrast with India, however, there was an increase in agriculture exports to the EU and US, taken together. There was also an increase in exports from the food processing and beverages and tobacco product industries to the EU and US, taken together, which relied heavily on inputs from agriculture. These positive trade effects were more than offset by negative trade effects from the textiles, rubber and plastic products, and furniture industries, which also relied heavily on inputs from agriculture.[9]

Table 5.2 Industry-level employment effects from trade for India: Scenario A (Type II multiplier)

	Number of jobs (FTE)			No. jobs as % of 2003–04 employed	% of 2003–04 employed		Labor coefficient (2003–04, rel. to avg.)
	EU	US	EU and US	EU and US	Female	Less educated	
Tradable goods industries							
1 Agriculture	−910,021	−1,290,224	−2,200,245	−1.07	35.0	95.6	5.60
2 Forestry and logging	−5,797	−8,066	−13,864	−1.40	37.5	95.8	0.61
3 Fishing	9,540	8,281	17,821	1.39	12.6	97.3	0.75
4 Coal and lignite, crude petroleum, and natural gas	2,539	−11,420	−8,881	−1.15	5.3	72.0	0.22
5 Iron ore and other minerals	−21,201	−14,865	−36,065	−2.38	21.3	96.5	1.90
6 Manufacture of food products	−32,047	−27,014	−59,061	−1.47	23.1	85.7	0.35
7 Beverages and tobacco products	−9,434	−18,245	−27,679	−0.74	70.6	97.5	1.12
8 Cotton textiles	−18,712	−42,312	−61,024	−2.43	31.1	90.3	0.67
9 Wool, synthetic fiber, and silk fiber textiles	−15,392	−23,242	−38,634	−2.01	27.7	94.2	0.95
10 Jute, hemp, and mesta textiles	−2,629	−5,113	−7,742	−4.30	21.2	92.4	0.66
11 Textile products	45,891	−197,926	−152,035	−2.75	33.1	91.2	1.63
12 Furniture and wood products	−71,170	−98,209	−169,379	−3.16	20.3	95.5	6.10
13 Paper, paper products, printing, and publishing	−2,607	−8,786	−11,392	−0.90	10.7	64.6	0.50
14 Leather products	−1,044	−18,962	−20,006	−1.35	15.6	86.8	1.63
15 Rubber and plastic products, petroleum products, and coal tar products	4,888	−11,276	−6,388	−0.81	10.5	70.9	0.06
16 Chemicals	−8,298	−600	−8,897	−0.52	37.3	68.6	0.14

17 Other non-metallic mineral products and cement	-18,837	-23,463	-42,300	-1.11	24.1	93.9	1.19
18 Iron, steel, and non-ferrous metals	-18,329	-45,459	-63,788	-3.91	2.6	76.4	0.16
19 Metal products	-17,620	-29,763	-47,383	-3.06	5.2	83.7	0.70
20 Non-electrical machinery	-21,575	-14,483	-36,058	-3.18	4.2	60.2	0.25
21 Electrical machinery	-15,131	-16,980	-32,111	-1.70	3.7	67.6	0.39
22 Rail equipment and other transport equipment	53,046	-41,247	11,799	0.36	1.5	80.6	0.59
23 Misc. manufacturing	-89,864	-148,894	-238,758	-7.82	15.3	87.2	0.68
Non-tradable industries							
24 Construction	-5,907	-14,341	-20,248	-0.09	9.9	94.3	1.07
25 Electricity and gas	-3,361	-8,781	-12,142	-1.35	4.5	58.1	0.12
26 Water supply	-177	-622	-799	-0.43	4.6	83.4	0.36
27 Railway transport services	-3,400	-8,587	-11,986	-1.26	3.4	60.9	0.41
28 Other transport services	-30,754	-76,045	-106,799	-0.83	1.3	88.1	0.70
29 Storage and warehousing	-221	-552	-773	-0.93	0.0	75.6	0.60
30 Communication	-4,430	-9,545	-13,975	-0.86	12.4	52.5	0.51
31 Trade	-84,773	-211,284	-296,058	-0.94	11.5	78.9	1.35
32 Hotels and restaurants	-10,160	-24,824	-34,984	-0.71	17.9	90.1	1.14
33 Banking	-6,310	-16,319	-22,629	-1.15	13.5	29.8	0.20
34 Insurance	-1,290	-3,364	-4,654	-0.90	14.1	16.2	0.25
35 Education and research	-13,321	-32,292	-45,613	-0.46	39.2	23.1	1.29
36 Medical and health	-5,913	-14,379	-20,292	-0.66	36.9	43.6	0.57
37 Other services	-25,310	-75,800	-101,109	-0.74	31.5	82.1	1.59
38 **All industries**	-1,359,131	-2,585,000	-3,944,131	-1.10	27.5	87.9	

Source: Authors' calculations.

Table 5.3 Industry-level employment effects from trade for South Africa: Scenario A (Type II multiplier)

	Number of jobs (FTE)			No. jobs as % of 2000 employed	% of 2000 employed		Labor coefficient (2000, rel. to avg.)
	EU	US	EU and US	EU and US	Female	Less educated	
Tradable goods industries							
1 Agriculture, hunting, forestry, and fishing	−155,049	−85,990	−241,038	−11.62	44.7	74.9	5.06
2 Coal mining	−2,230	−775	−3,004	−4.03	2.1	60.0	0.48
3 Gold mining and other mining	−6,214	−1,678	−7,893	−1.49	3.0	52.1	0.84
4 Food processing	−10,215	−3,873	−14,088	−6.38	32.1	38.1	0.42
5 Beverages and tobacco products	−3,397	−1,367	−4,764	−6.50	36.8	43.0	0.34
6 Textiles	−1,635	−2,182	−3,817	−4.22	64.5	36.6	0.94
7 Clothing	−7,969	−2,477	−10,447	−4.60	82.9	45.0	3.37
8 Leather products	−80	−194	−273	−1.80	37.7	25.0	0.82
9 Footwear	−1,552	−541	−2,093	−6.29	52.1	46.1	1.55
10 Wood products	−72,933	−55,986	−128,919	−141.45	16.2	49.8	1.14
11 Paper products	−3,254	−848	−4,102	−13.07	30.6	31.0	0.16
12 Printing and publishing	−21,087	−2,039	−23,126	−35.46	30.0	17.3	0.64
13 Petroleum products	−926	−324	−1,249	−5.19	12.3	10.1	0.09
14 Chemicals	−2,445	−922	−3,367	−5.79	28.1	15.8	0.12
15 Rubber and plastic products	−2,260	−922	−3,181	−5.31	33.3	24.2	0.48
16 Glass products	−16,333	5,992	−10,342	−60.93	22.1	40.7	0.88
17 Non-metal minerals	−648	−849	−1,497	−1.90	23.6	58.9	0.82
18 Iron, steel, and non-ferrous metals	−6,211	−1,419	−7,630	−8.05	11.0	35.9	0.21

19	Metal products	−33,584	−7,819	−41,403	−29.59	8.9	37.3	0.68
20	Non-electrical machinery	−1,417	−410	−1,827	−3.12	18.9	29.5	0.33
21	Electrical machinery	−710	−261	−971	−2.15	21.7	13.8	0.41
22	Communications equipment	−106	−33	−140	−1.60	51.5	15.3	0.22
23	Scientific equipment	−125	−46	−171	−2.94	45.6	19.4	0.44
24	Vehicles	−1,964	−378	−2,342	−3.13	19.0	24.1	0.17
25	Transport equipment	−52	−16	−68	−1.51	4.8	43.5	0.15
26	Furniture	−936	−390	−1,326	−3.85	21.3	36.6	0.65
27	Misc. manufacturing	−970	−377	−1,348	−3.51	39.3	44.5	0.76
	Non-tradable industries							
28	Electricity, gas, and water	−2,430	−1,527	−3,958	−4.21	15.6	34.3	0.30
29	Construction	5,387	−1,267	4,121	0.60	7.3	58.5	1.19
30	Trade services, hotels, and catering	−129,280	−47,090	−176,370	−7.42	47.8	34.6	1.65
31	Transport and communication services	−17,994	−4,340	−22,334	−3.82	14.9	34.0	0.53
32	Financial and business services	−28,124	−11,607	−39,730	−4.02	39.9	10.9	0.52
33	Human health, veterinary, and social work	−18,417	−7,320	−25,738	−4.49	75.9	25.7	2.39
34	Education, other services, and other activities n.e.c.	−75,743	−25,689	−101,433	−4.65	69.2	44.7	5.85
35	Government services	−391	−227	−618	−0.11	30.5	18.4	0.39
36	**All industries**	−621,294	−265,192	−886,486	−7.21	43.1	42.6	0.39

Source: Authors' calculations.

In relative terms, the industries with the largest estimated employment declines are wood products (an impossibly high 141.5 percent of 2000 employment[10]), glass products (60.9 percent), printing and publishing (35.5 percent), and metal products (29.6 percent). As with India, these industries vary widely in terms of their labor intensity and skills intensity. For example, wood products is labor-intensive and reliant on less-educated workers, whereas metal products is capital-intensive and skills-intensive (Table 5.3).

4.3 Gender and skills bias results

There are large literatures on skills and gender biases of trade liberalization (e.g., WTO 2008; van Staveren *et al.*, 2007). Much of the skills bias literature is motivated by the Heckscher-Ohlin theorem regarding relative factor endowments as determinants of comparative advantage. According to this theorem, developing countries are posited to generally have a comparative advantage in unskilled labor-intensive goods with respect to developed country trading partners. The question of gender bias too can be motivated along these lines, for women are commonly overrepresented among less-educated workers as well as in such export-oriented labor-intensive industries as clothing and footwear.[11]

In India and South Africa, women and less-educated workers are indeed disproportionately concentrated in labor-intensive industries. More specifically, there are positive correlations between labor coefficients and the percentages of female and less-educated workers, though with generally weaker relationships for India than South Africa.[12] In the context of the crisis, the "compositional effect" may also come into play, depending on the representation of women and less-educated workers in "postponeable" consumer durable and investment goods industries. For example, the percentage of female and less-educated workers is lower than average in the non-electrical machinery and iron, steel, and non-ferrous metal industries in both India and South Africa (Tables 5.2 and 5.3).

We evaluate the extent of gender and skills bias by comparing the percentages of female and less-educated workers in the SAMs base years with the percentages of female and less-educated workers estimated to have lost jobs as a result of trade contraction in the crisis. Breakdowns between male and female and more- and less-educated workers are based on the assumption that employment changes are proportionate to actual shares of employment in the SAMs base years.[13] Regarding employees, for example, we assume that employers do not make distinctions by gender or education in the face of employment changes, maintaining the same proportions of men and women and more and less-educated workers. This is, of course, a rather strong assumption, and there is literature on how firms' hiring and firing patterns may differ for men and women and more- and less-skilled workers over economic fluctuations (e.g., Rubery 1988; Leung *et al.* 2009). In this sense, a precise interpretation of our results on gender and skills bias is that they illustrate whether *industries* in which women and less-educated workers are disproportionately represented are particularly affected by job loss as a result of trade contraction in the crisis.

Results are shown in Figure 5.4 regarding gender bias and Figure 5.5 regarding skills bias. We present results based on Scenario A for all industries and for EU and US trade together. Regarding gender bias for India, an identical percentage of women workers, 27.9 percent, is estimated to have lost jobs as the actual percentage of women workers in 2003–04. That is, the effects of the crisis through the channel of trade contraction are estimated to be gender neutral in a technical sense. The degree to which women may compensate for income losses during a financial crisis with increased unpaid labor time is not measured by this analysis, given the limitations of the SAM structure noted above.

For South Africa, a somewhat lower percentage of women workers is estimated to have lost jobs than the actual percentage of women workers in 2000, 40.7 to 43.1 percent. For the economy as a whole, then, there is a gender bias in favor of women workers as a result of trade contraction in the crisis. That is, industries in which women were disproportionately concentrated were less affected by the decline in exports to the EU and US. Though the difference of 2.4 percentage points is not large, it is consistent with the results of two prior studies assessing the overall effect of the crisis on employment in South Africa using labor force survey data (Leung *et al.* 2009; Verick 2010).

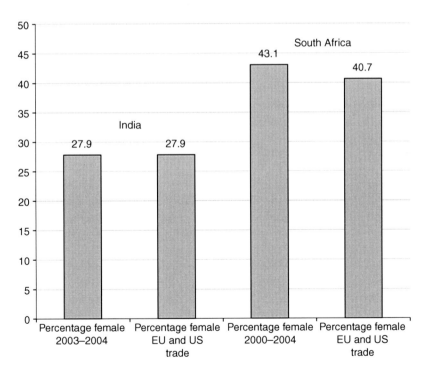

Figure 5.4 Gender bias from trade contraction, all industries: Scenario A (source: Authors' calculations).

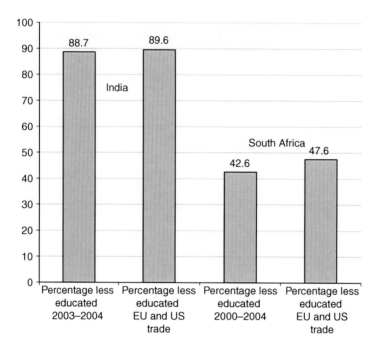

Figure 5.5 Skills bias from trade contraction, all industries: Scenario A (source: Authors' calculations).

Regarding skills bias for India, a slightly higher percentage of less-educated workers is estimated to have lost jobs than the actual percentage of less-educated workers in 2003–04, 89.6 to 88.7 percent. This might indicate a small bias against less-educated workers as a result of trade contraction in the crisis, but we regard this finding as inconclusive, given the magnitude of the gap and the absence of corroborating studies.

For South Africa, a higher percentage of less-educated workers is estimated to have lost jobs than the actual percentage of less-skilled workers in 2000 in these industries, 47.6 to 42.6 percent. That is, industries in which less-educated workers were disproportionately concentrated were hit harder by trade contraction in the crisis. As with the finding on gender bias, this is consistent with the results of two other studies (Leung *et al.* 2009; Verick 2010).

In sum, for India, we estimate that there was no gender or skills bias in employment resulting from trade contraction in the crisis. In South Africa, there was somewhat of a gender bias in favor of women workers and a stronger bias against less-educated workers. The result on gender bias in favor of women workers during the crisis is usefully set against a prior study's findings of gender bias against women workers during the period of trade liberalization from 1993 to 2006 (Kucera and Roncolato 2011). An important determinant of the gender bias against women workers prior to the crisis was the large numbers of jobs lost in the clothing industry as a result of trade expansion with developing countries, combined with the high share of women workers in the industry. This same study also found no skills bias against less-educated workers during the period of trade liberalization prior to the crisis. In this sense, both the gender and skills biases observed in South Africa as a result of the 2008–09 trade contraction represent breaks from previous trends.

5 Comparison with actual changes in employment and governments' crisis responses

The "Great Trade Collapse" may have been the most important transmission channel through which India and South Africa were affected by the crisis, but it was not the only channel, and the negative effects of all transmission channels were offset to an extent by the governments' crisis responses. Our employment estimates are based on the effects of trade contraction only, further limited to trade with the EU and the US. We have also noted that our estimates of employment declines represented as FTE jobs may actually mean income declines or increases in underemployment, such as informal or part-time employment, which would not be reflected in data on actual changes in employment.

For all these reasons, comparing our estimated changes in employment with actual changes in employment is necessarily an incomplete exercise. It can be useful, nonetheless, in providing context for our results. Already noted, in this regard, is the consistency between our results for South Africa on gender and skills bias and the findings of other studies on the impact of the crisis on employment (Leung *et al.* 2009; Verick 2010).

The Indian government carried out establishment surveys in eight industries that reportedly account for 60 percent of India's GDP, though these were "quick" small-sample surveys addressing mainly formal employment (Government of India 2010). Notably, the surveys did not include agriculture, which accounted for 57 percent of employment in India as of 2005 (NSSO 2006). Based on these surveys, there were employment declines of 131,000 workers in the second quarter of 2009 for the eight industries taken together. Yet employment increased, overall, in these industries by 1,060,000 workers between the first quarters of 2009 and 2010.

Industry-level survey results for India are shown in Table 5.4 as cumulative percentage changes since the last quarter of 2008 alongside estimated percentage changes in employment from trade contraction, taken from Table 5.2. The two sources were matched by industry to the extent possible, though this remains highly imperfect because of different definitions used, and there is also a difference in base periods. The two shaded columns indicate the first two quarters of 2009, which overlap with the period of the trade shock as captured by our export demand vectors. Industries marked by an asterisk are those having received government crisis support, as described below.

Table 5.4 Comparing actual employment changes with estimated employment changes resulting from trade contraction, India

Sectors in survey	Actual employment changes as cumulative quarterly % changes (Base = 2008 Q4)					Sectors in SAM	Estimated employment changes from trade contraction as % changes from SAM year (Base = 2003/04)
	2009 Q1	2009 Q2	2009 Q3	2009 Q4	2010 Q1		
Textiles and apparel*	1.0	0.3	1.6	1.7	0.9	Cotton textiles	-2.4
						Wool synthetic and silk fiber textiles	-2.0
						Jute, hemp, and mesta textiles	-4.3
						Textile products	-2.7
						Total textile products	-2.6
Leather*	-2.8	-2.2	-2.8	-1.9	-1.9	Leather products	-1.3
Metals	-0.6	-0.6	0.6	1.1	1.1	Metal products	-3.1
Automobiles*	0.1	1.3	2.6	2.9	4.3	Rail and other transport equipment	0.4
Gems and jewelry*	3.1	1.4	6.5	7.3	10.2	Misc. manufacturing	-7.8
						Railway transport services	-1.3
						Other transport services	-0.8
Transport	-0.4	-0.4	-0.4	-0.6	-0.8	Total transport services	-0.9
IT/BPO*	0.8	0.5	0.7	4.9	6.1	Other services	-0.7
Handloom/powerloom*	0.3	2.6	3.3	4.0	3.6	Total textile products	-2.6
Total for surveyed industries	0.6	0.3	1.3	3.1	3.2		

Source: Government of India (2010); authors' estimates (as shown in Table 5.2)

Note
Asterisks indicate industries receiving governmental crisis support, as described in text; shaded areas indicate periods overlapping with the trade shock.

For the first two quarters of 2009, survey results are broadly consistent with our employment estimates for leather, metals, and transport, with employment declines in both the government surveys and our estimates, and for automobiles (grouped with rail and other transport equipment in our estimates), with employment gains in both the government surveys and our estimates. The remaining four industries show employment gains in the government surveys and employment declines in our estimates, matching with the most closely corresponding industries (e.g., gems and jewelry are a component of miscellaneous manufacturing). This discrepancy could be partially accounted for by our finding for India that "jobs not created" as a result of the global crisis was a more important factor than "jobs lost" (Table 5.1). In other words, even though employment grew in these sectors, it may have grown by less than it would have had there been no global crisis.

The Indian government initiated three fiscal stimulus packages between December 2008 and February 2009, but these were relatively small, totaling less than 1 percent of the country's GDP (ILO 2010a). In addition to public works, specifically transport and electrical power infrastructure, policies included tax reductions and measures to ease credit constraints. Industries targeted for support included banking and finance, information technology, automobiles, food processing, textiles, handloom, carpets, handicrafts, leather, jewelry, and seafood products (ILO 2009, 2010a). These industries overlapped to a large extent with those in the government's "quick" establishment survey. An important complement to the government's crisis response was the National Rural Employment Guarantee Act (NREGA), adopted in 2005, which guaranteed to poor rural households a minimum of 100 days of paid employment.

One potential problem with industry-level crisis responses is that they may focus unduly on industries more directly affected by the crisis, and in general, the Indian government's industry-level policies did indeed focus on such industries. As we have observed, though, some of the largest estimated employment declines as a result of trade contraction occurred in non-tradable industries that were not targets of government support. These include wholesale and retail trade, transport services, and other services (Table 5.2).

The South Africa government undertakes quarterly labor force surveys, which show economy-wide year-on-year employment declines of 770,000, 833,000 and 870,000 for the periods ending with the third and fourth quarters of 2009 and first quarter of 2010, respectively (Statistics South Africa 2010). These figures are similar to our estimated employment declines of 886,000 based on Scenario A and 963,000 based on Scenario B. Our estimation's result of a gender bias against men is also confirmed by the actual employment numbers. Between the fourth quarter of 2008 and the fourth quarter of 2009, total female employment decreased by 5.2 percent while total male employment decreased by 7.2 percent (Statistics South Africa 2010). Because of the qualifications noted in the beginning of this section, there is an element of happenstance in this similarity, but it nevertheless suggests that our estimates are of a reasonable order of magnitude.

Industry-level survey results for South Africa are shown in Table 5.5, following the same conventions as Table 5.4 for India, with cumulative percentage

Table 5.5 Comparing actual employment changes with estimated employment changes resulting from trade contraction, South Africa

Sectors in survey	Actual employment changes as cumulative quarterly % changes (Base = 2008 Q4)					Estimated employment changes from trade contraction as % changes from SAM year (Base = 2000)	
	2009 Q1	2009 Q2	2009 Q3	2009 Q4	2010 Q1	Sectors in SAM	
Agriculture	-3.4	-7.1	-14.5	-19.5	-14.9	Agriculture, hunting, forestry, and fishing	-11.6
						Coal mining	-4.0
						Gold mining and other mining	-1.5
Mining*	3.7	-0.7	-6.9	-7.8	-7.8	Total mining	-1.8
Manufacturing*	-3.2	-3.7	-11.4	-10.4	-12.1	Total manufacturing	-16.9
Utilities	16.3	8.2	-5.8	14.0	-18.6	Electricity, gas, and water	-4.2
Construction*	-5.5	-6.3	-11.3	-9.0	-14.4	Construction	0.6
Trade	-4.5	-6.4	-9.9	-9.2	-10.8	Trade services, hotels, and catering	-7.4
Transport*	-2.2	-6.1	-4.8	-4.5	-0.9	Transport and communication services	-3.8
Finance*	5.4	4.5	2.8	7.5	-0.2	Financial and business services	-4.0
Community and social services	-0.4	0.1	-1.3	-1.3	-0.2	Government services	-0.1
Total for surveyed industries	-1.5	-3.5	-6.9	-6.3	-7.5		

Source: Statistics South Africa (2010); authors' estimates (as shown in Table 5.3)

Note

Asterisks indicate industries receiving government crisis support, as described in text; shaded areas indicate periods overlapping with the trade shock.

changes since the last quarter of 2008 alongside estimated percentage changes in employment from trade contraction, taken from Table 5.3. As for India, only a rough match is possible between the two sources. In particular, most of our industry breakdowns are within manufacturing, which is treated as one industry in the published labor force survey.

Consistent with our findings are employment declines in agriculture, mining, manufacturing, trade, and transport, with agriculture being particularly hard hit. At odds with our findings are employment declines in construction, for which we estimate essentially no change in employment. For finance, the story is ambiguous. We estimate employment declines, while the survey shows essentially no cumulative change up to the first quarter of 2010 following four quarters of employment gains.

The automobile and mining industries in South Africa merit additional discussion, as they are reported to have been particularly hard hit by the crisis, and yet our estimates show that relative employment losses are lower than average (–1.5 percent for gold mining and other mining and –3.1 percent for vehicles, compared to –7.2 percent for all industries, as shown in Table 5.3) (Gabru 2009; SARW 2009). For the automobile industry, much of this discrepancy can be accounted for by the fact that half of the industry's exports (as of 2003) were to Japan (35 percent) and Australia (15 percent), which are not included in our analysis (ECDC 2005). Similarly for the mining industry, two of the largest export markets are China and Japan, also not included in our analysis (SARW 2009). These two industry examples illustrate that our estimates of employment losses must be read as referring exclusively to trade with the EU and US and that the effects of global trade contraction would seem to be much more severe.

The South African government's crisis response has been referred to as a "mega-stimulus package," equivalent to about one-fourth of the country's GDP with the largest share spent on public works (Kumar and Vashisht 2009, p. 4; ILO 2010b). Though some of these policies were initiated prior to the crisis, they were embodied in the *Framework for South Africa's Response to the International Crisis* of February 2009, as well as the *Progress Report* of December 2009 (NEDLAC 2009a, 2009b). The *Framework* addresses transport and electrical power infrastructure, macroeconomic, trade and industrial policies, job training and policies to avoid job cuts, social policies, and global coordination.

Worth noting is that the *Framework* aims to not only provide support to such tradable good industries as "clothing, textiles and footwear, mining and the auto and capital equipment sectors," but also to "retail, housing construction and private services" (NEDLAC 2009a, p. 9). In this sense, the government's crisis response is broadly consistent with the results of our analysis as well as with the South African Quarterly Labour Force Survey. Though agriculture is absent from the *Framework*, a "Comprehensive Rural Development Programme" was approved by the government in August 2009 (SA 2010). In addition, the government extended social transfer programs and implemented an emergency food relief program (Hirsch 2010). Given the importance of income-induced employment effects, such programs not only address the social impacts of the crisis but can mitigate job losses by stabilizing household incomes.

The crisis responses of the governments of India and South Africa differed in scale and scope, partly reflecting the different challenges these countries faced. For example, real GDP in India grew by 5.7 percent in 2009, down from 9.4 percent in 2007 and 7.3 percent in 2008, but was still respectable nonetheless. In contrast, real GDP shrank in South Africa by −1.8 percent in 2009, compared to growth rates of 5.5 percent in 2007 and 3.7 percent in 2008 (IMF 2010).

The two countries faced more similar challenges, though, when it came to employment, suggested by the considerably less favorable employment growth rates for the first quarter of 2010 than the fourth quarter of 2009 for both countries. For India, the average monthly growth rate of employment was 1.7 percent in the fourth quarter of 2009, but only 0.2 percent in the first quarter of 2010 for the eight industries surveyed (Government of India 2010). For South Africa, the quarter-to-quarter growth rate of employment was 0.7 percent in the fourth quarter of 2009 after three quarters of negative growth, but was −1.3 percent in the first quarter of 2010 (Statistics South Africa 2010). With respect to employment, the governments of both India and South Africa faced pressing challenges well after the initial impact of the crisis.

6 Concluding remarks

This study finds that declining exports to the EU and US during the "Great Trade Collapse" had a substantial negative effect on employment in India and South Africa. We estimate that the decline in exports to the EU and US between early 2008 and early 2009 (the more conservative of our two scenarios) resulted in the loss of nearly four million jobs in India and about 900,000 jobs in South Africa, equivalent to about 1 percent of base year employment in India and 7 percent in South Africa.

The effects of trade contraction swept widely across these countries. The vast majority of industries are estimated to have experienced employment declines as a result of trade contraction, in both tradable and non-tradable sectors. Even though the shock originated in the tradable goods sector, a large share of total estimated employment declines resulted from ripple effects in non-tradable industries (about 18 and 40 percent in India and South Africa, respectively). A large share of estimated employment declines is income-induced (about 50 and 40 percent in India and South Africa, respectively), which has an important policy implication: stabilizing household incomes, in addition to its social benefits, can be an effective means of reducing job loss.

Regarding the differential impact of trade contraction on male and female and skilled and unskilled workers, we find no evidence for India of gender or skill bias. For South Africa, however, we find that industries with higher shares of unskilled and male workers are disproportionately affected by employment declines, consistent with two prior studies (Leung *et al.* 2009; Verick 2010).

The importance of trade as a transmission channel has particular bearing on countries like India and South Africa that have rapidly opened up to international trade in recent years. International trade is arguably a necessity for developing countries aiming to narrow the technology gap with developed countries, for it enables them to earn foreign currency and purchase foreign technology. Yet the global crisis reveals how greater trade openness can be a source of vulnerability in a volatile global economy. This presents a significant challenge to policy-makers and emphasizes the importance of governments' ability to deliver timely and effective responses to external shocks in open economies.

Notes

1 See, for example, Rodrik and Subramanian (2005), Rodrik (2008), and Krueger (2008) for competing views on the role of trade liberalization in economic development in India and South Africa.
2 Regarding South Africa, the point is made by Marais (2009) as follows: "Ultimately, a recovery depends primarily on developments in South Africa's main trading partners in Europe and North America" (p. 3).
3 Note that our method differs from that of a United Nations Conference on Trade and Development (UNCTAD) study for India also using input–output analysis (UNCTAD 2009). The UNCTAD study uses export data for 2006–07 and 2007–08 to estimate employment projections for 2008–09, 2009–10, and 2010–11.
4 Notes on data-cleaning procedures for the construction of T1 and T2 are available from the authors upon request. Further notes on data sources are provided in an appendix.
5 Detailed results are available from the authors upon request.
6 Export demand vectors are available from the authors upon request.
7 Scenario B results are available from the authors upon request.
8 With respect to the labor intensity of production, one way of addressing this is by looking at the correlation between export demand vectors and labor coefficients, that is, between T and the diagonal elements of $\hat{E}$. For India, there is effectively no correlation between these variables, with a Pearson correlation coefficient of 0.07, based on Scenario A for exports to the EU and US together. For South Africa, there is also effectively no correlation, with a comparable Pearson correlation coefficient of 0.16.
9 Further details are available from the authors upon request.
10 Such a result can arise from the heterogeneous nature of the wood products industry and a subsequent mismatch between the labor intensity of production for export to the EU and US compared with the average labor intensity of production in the industry. In addition, the number of workers in the industry may have increased between 2000 (the year of the South Africa SAM) and the crisis.
11 In India, 94 percent of women have no more than lower secondary education, compared with 87 percent of men as of 2003–04; in South Africa, the figures for women and men are nearly equal, with 43 percent of women and 42 percent of men having no more than lower secondary education as of 2000.
12 Results are available from the authors upon request.
13 For example, if trade contraction is estimated to have resulted in a loss of 500 jobs in an industry in which one-fourth of workers are female, these 500 jobs are broken down into 375 male and 125 female jobs.

References

Baldwin, R. (2009) *The Great Trade Collapse: causes, consequences and prospects*, London: Centre for Economic Policy Research.

Borchert, I. and Mattoo, A. (2009) "Services trade: the collapse that wasn't," in R. Baldwin (ed.), *The Great Trade Collapse: causes, consequences and prospects*, London: Centre for Economic Policy Research.

ECDC (2005) *An Overview of the Eastern Cape Automotive Industry and Its Opportunities in the South African Context*, London: Eastern Cape Development Corporation.

European Commission (2010) *Eurostat*, Brussels: European Commission. Online: http://epp.eurostat.ec.europa.eu/portal/page/portal/international_trade/introduction (accessed October 23, 2012).

Fontana, M. (2003) "Modeling the effects of trade on women, at work and at home: a comparative perspective," TMD Discussion Paper No. 110, Washington, DC: International Food Policy Research Institute.

Gabru, F. (2009) "Financial crisis batters SA's automotive industry," *Creamer Media's Engineering News Online*, February 6. Online: www.engineeringnews.co.za/article/financial-crisis-batters-sas-automotive-industry-2009-02-06 (accessed October 22, 2012).

Government of India (2010) *October–December 2008 to January–March 2010: report on effect of economic slowdown on employment in India*, Chandigarh: Ministry of Labour and Employment, Labour Bureau.

Hirsch, A. (2010) "South Africa's response to the Global Economic Crisis: some reflections," presentation given at the Development Policy Research Unit, the Employment Promotion Programme and Trade & Industrial Policy Strategies Conference, Johannesburg, October 27–29.

ILO (2009) *Review of Sector-Specific Stimulus Packages and Policy Responses to the Global Economic Crisis*, Geneva: International Labour Organization, Sectoral Activities Programme.

ILO (2010a) *India's Response to the Crisis*, Geneva: International Labour Organization.

ILO (2010b) *South Africa's Response to the Crisis*, Geneva: International Labour Organization.

IMF (2010) *World Economic Outlook, April 2010: rebalancing growth*, Washington, DC: International Monetary Fund.

Krueger, A. (2008) "The role of international economic policy in Indian economic performance," *Asian Economic Policy Review*, 3: 266–85.

Kucera, D. and Milberg, W. (2003) "Deindustrialization and changes in manufacturing trade: factor content calculations for 1978–1995," *Review of World Economics*, 139: 601–24.

Kucera, D. and Roncolato, L. (2011) "Trade liberalization, employment and inequality in India and South Africa," *International Labour Review*, 150: 1–41.

Kumar, R. and Alex, D. (2009) "The great recession and India's trade collapse," in R. Baldwin (ed.), *The Great Trade Collapse: causes, consequences and prospects*, London: Centre for Economic Policy Research.

Kumar, R. and Vashisht, P. (2009) "The global economic crisis: impact on India and policy responses," ADBI Working Paper No. 164, Tokyo: Asian Development Bank Institute.

Leung, R., Stampini, M., and Vencatachellum, D. (2009) "Does human capital protect workers against exogenous shocks? South Africa in the 2008–2009 crisis," IZA Discussion Paper No. 4608, Bonn: The Institute for the Study of Labor.

Marais, H. (2009) "The impact of the global recession on South Africa," ARI Paper No. 114, Madrid: Real Instituto Elcano.

NEDLAC (2009a) *Framework for South Africa's Response to the International Economic Crisis*, Johannesburg: South Africa National Economic Development and Labour Council.

NEDLAC (2009b) *Progress Report to the President of the Republic of South Africa on the Implementation of the Framework for South Africa's Response to the International Economic Crisis*, Johannesburg: South Africa National Economic Development and Labour Council.

National Sample Survey Organisation (NSSO) (2006) *National Sample Survey: employment–unemployment NSS 61st round, July 2004–June 2005*, New Delhi, Government of India National Sample Survey Organisation.

Rodrik, D. (2008) "Understanding South Africa's economic puzzles," *Economics of Transition*, 16: 769–97.

Rodrik, D. and Subramanian, A. (2005) "From 'Hindu growth' to productivity surge: the mystery of the Indian growth transition," *IMF Staff Papers*, 52: 193–228.

Rubery, J. (1988) *Women and Recession*, London and New York: Routledge & Kegan Paul.

Sachs, J. and Shatz, H. (1994) "Trade and jobs in US manufacturing," *Brookings Papers in Economic Activity*, 1: 1–84.

SA (Government of South Africa) (2010) *Department of Rural Development & Land Reform Strategic Plan, 2010–2013*.

SARW (2009) "Impact of the global financial crisis on mining in Southern Africa," Southern Africa Resource Watch.

Statistics South Africa (2003) *Revised Estimates, Labour Force Survey September 2000*, Pretoria: Statistics South Africa.

Statistics South Africa (2010) *Quarterly Labour Force Survey* (Quarter 1, 2009 to Quarter 1, 2010), Pretoria: Statistics South Africa.

Sakthivel, S. and Joddar, P. (2006) "Unorganized sector workforce in India: trends, patterns and social security coverage," *Economic and Political Weekly*, 41: 2107–14.

Saluja, M.R. and Yadav, B. (2006) *Social Accounting Matrix for India 2003–04*, Haryan: India Development Foundation.

Thurlow, J. (2005) *South African Social Accounting Matrices for 1993 and 2000*, Washington, DC: International Food Policy Research Institute.

UNCTAD (2009) "Impact of global slowdown on India's exports and employment," draft for comments, New Delhi: United Nations Conference on Trade and Development India Team.

US (2010) *United States International Trade Commission*, Washington, DC: United States Government. Online: www.usitc.gov (accessed October 24, 2012).

Van Staveren, I., Elson, D., Grown C., and Cagatay, N. (2007) *The Feminist Economics of Trade*, London: Routledge.

Verick, S. (2010) "Unravelling the impact of the global financial crisis on the South African labour market," ILO Employment Sector Working Paper No. 48, Geneva: International Labour Organization.

World Bank (2009) *World Development Indicators*, Washington, DC: World Bank.

World Bank (2010) *Global Economic Prospects 2010: crisis, finance, and growth*, Washington, DC: World Bank.

World Bank (2011) *World Development Indicators*, Washington, DC: World Bank.

WTO (2008) *World Trade Report 2008: trade in a globalizing world*, Geneva: World Trade Organization.

WTO (2010) "Trade to expand by 9.5% in 2010 after a dismal 2009, WTO reports," press release, WTO PRESS/598, Geneva: World Trade Organization. Online: www.wto.org/english/news_e/pres10_e/pr598_e.htm (accessed October 22, 2012).

6 Impacts of financial crisis and post-crisis policies on China

A gendered analysis

*Yan Liang and Sara Hsu**

1 Introduction

The 2007 global financial crisis originated in the US but rapidly engulfed the rest of the world. Emerging economies, China included, were inevitably affected by the crisis due to disruptions in global trade and financial flows. Such negative impacts were inflicted on both men and women; however, there is some evidence that on a global scale, pre-existing gender gaps were increased by the crisis,[1] reinforcing women's disadvantages, and in those cases in which gaps were reduced it was mostly due to deteriorating labor market conditions for males (see ILO 2012). As Floro *et al.* (2010, p. 13) point out,

> In general, compared to men, women have poorer command over productive resources such as education, land, technology, and financial assets. This translates into lower earnings, weak bargaining power, and fewer livelihood options, placing women at greater risk than men during economic crises.

In China, the direct impacts of the financial crisis fell heavily on women due to their specific social status and employment patterns. Policy responses to the crisis adopted by the Chinese government – in particular, the US$586 billion stimulus package enacted in November 2008 – helped to stall the economic free-fall. These policies also have had complex gendered impacts. Due to differing impacts of crisis and policy responses on different social groups, it seems appropriate to adopt a gendered perspective for an effective impact assessment and for sensible policy recommendations.

As Antonopoulos (2009, p. 14) states

> [T]he vulnerability individual men and women are now facing depends on the country's position within the global economy prior to the crisis and on the particular location individuals occupied in the world of work prior to the crisis, as well as the degree to which prior commitments will be honored.

* This chapter has benefited from the comments of two anonymous referees, and from the comments of Rania Antonopoulos.

In other words, both the role of a country in the global division of labor and the individuals' positions within the national economy would shape the impacts of crisis, making some individuals more vulnerable than others. With this understanding, we will start with a general overview of the impacts of the financial crisis in Asian economies and highlight some studies that examine the experience of other Asian countries that share similar economic openness and development with China. We will then show the general social status and employment patterns of women in China prior to the crisis, then proceed to highlight China's role in global trade and production as well as the impacts of the global financial crisis on its export production. This will then allow us to investigate the impacts of the crisis on female workers who are overrepresented in the export production. Following the impact analysis, we will look into the policies adopted by the Chinese government and analyze the gendered impacts of these short- and longer-term policies. The former policies include mainly the stimulus package launched at the end of 2008 while the latter policies are featured in the 12th Five-Year Plan that was proposed at the fifth plenary session of the 17th Central Committee of the Communist Party of China and passed by the National People's Congress at the beginning of 2011. The Five-Year Plan is to govern the development goals between 2011 and 2015.

To be sure, the impacts of the financial crisis on Chinese women are overarching and we will focus only on the world of work. Moreover, due to a data shortage, we will confine ourselves to paid work, leaving out unpaid work, although we will briefly discuss a time-use survey conducted in 2008, which may shed light on the disproportionate share of unpaid work undertaken by women and infer the heightened burden of unpaid work due to the crisis.

2 Financial crisis and gendered impacts on Asian countries

The 2007 global financial crisis has taken a notable toll on the Asia and Pacific region, where GDP fell by 5–6 percent in the six months following the crisis. In particular, countries like the Republic of Korea, Singapore, Taiwan Province of China, Malaysia, and Hong Kong had the most significant slowdown due to their tight integration into the world economy through trade and capital flows. Floro *et al.* (2010) give a comprehensive review of the crisis's impact on women's well-being and empowerment, and they identify eight areas of impacts, including deteriorating employment, shrinking access to credit, reduced consumption, increased burden of unpaid work, depletion of assets, increasing food insecurity, hunger, and rising gender-based violence.[2] Much of the research on Asia finds varying degrees of impacts in these areas.

Given that many of the Asian economies are export-oriented, the crisis (which significantly reduced world trade) had a severe impact on employment. Because women generally are less educated and less skilled than their male counterparts, they often concentrate on low-skilled and labor-intensive manufacturing, which is the major industry in an export-oriented economy. So the decline in exports and export manufacturing has a significant impact on women workers. Moreover, because the male "breadwinner" bias still persists and because women are often considered as the "flexible" work force, they are the first to be let go when employment opportunities shrink (Sirimanne 2009). As the ILO report, *Global Employment Trend for Women* (2012), states, between 2002 and 2007 there was a 0.5 percentage point gender gap in unemployment and the global financial crisis raised the gender gap to 0.7 percent, which amounts to 13 million job losses for women. In Cambodia, 70,000 workers lost their jobs in the garment industry, most of whom were young women. Many of the laid-off female workers sought work in the entertainment industry, putting themselves in danger of exploitation and abuse. In Indonesia, women workers in the furniture export production industry have usually been involved in the "less critical" parts of the production process in the past, and so they often have been the first to be discarded when export sales dwindle (Édes 2009; see also Miller-Dawkins and Abimanyu 2010). Other studies also corroborate with the discernible gender bias in unemployment. Emmett (2009) reports that as export manufacturing declined in East Asia, women's jobs were the first to go. In India, 700,000 clothing and textile workers lost their jobs in 2008; more than half of the 40,000 jobs lost in the Philippines were from the export-processing zone, where 80 percent of workers were women (see also Gaerlan *et al.* 2010). Sri Lanka and Cambodia lost 30,000 mostly female garment industry jobs (Dasgupta and Williams 2009). In Vietnam, women workers in several export industries reported a fall in income of 24 percent, compared to 21 percent for men (Hung 2009; see also Nguanbanchong 2010). Not only did women lose jobs more readily during the crisis, but they also suffered the most from deteriorating working conditions, such as freezes on the minimum wage or reductions in working days or hours (King and Sweetman 2010).

In addition to deterioration of formal employment, women also faced heightened unpaid work, as shrinking household income and declining public services forced them to spend more time caring for the sick and the elderly and carrying out household activities. Coping strategies of cutting food consumption (partly due to the rising staple-food price) and health spending and withdrawing children from schools also affected women and girls more than their male counterparts (Sirimanne 2009). Evidence of reductions in health care and education after the crisis as well as increases in bodily atrophy among girls and women in Bangladesh and India underscore the enhanced gender-biased impact of the crisis (Jones *et al.* 2010).

Further, tension between husbands and wives has increased in Bangladesh and Indonesia over the need to increase food allocations to children (Jones *et al.* 2010). The same occurred in Lao and Cambodia – tuk-tuk drivers in Lao faced arguments if they returned with less money than usual or spent their time socializing, while garment workers in Cambodia noted that wives may face domestic abuse due to lower incomes and resulting mounting tensions (Turk and Mason 2010).

One of the reasons women were hit hard by the crisis seems to stem from the fact that gender inequality has been prevalent in some of these Asian countries before the crisis, and many of the countries provide limited social protections for women. As an Asian Development Bank official put it, "In developing Asia, rising overall prosperity over the years has been accompanied by growing inequality, poor social service delivery and lingering real risk of impoverishment in the case of calamity." Governments of Asia's developing countries only dedicate about 4.3 percent of their GDP to social protection (Édes 2009, p. 20).

Policy responses after the crisis were immediate and largely effective in stemming the freefall of the economies. Government coffers were much "more full" this time compared to during the Asian financial crisis. However, even though many of the fiscal stimulus programs were pro-poor, they had notable gender biases and were not likely to close the gender gap that prevailed before the crisis. King and Sweetman's sobering reflections on policy responses are worth quoting at length (2010, p. 11):

> Often policy responses fail to consider adequately either the needs of people living in poverty or how they might begin to address the gender inequality in power, workload, and opportunities that exacerbate women's experience of the world's multiple crises. Nor are policy responses sufficiently attuned to providing holistic solutions that challenge the status quo, rather than simply providing temporary respite from the symptoms of just one crisis.

Corner (2009) provides a comprehensive review of gender differential impacts of fiscal responses in five Asian countries, including Cambodia, China, Indonesia, Lao PDR, and Vietnam. For example, public investment in infrastructure that took place in China, Indonesia, and Vietnam tended to create "masculine" jobs taken by men.[3] These jobs may require men to work far from their families and the income generated was often "leaked" in the location of the employment rather than remitted back home for the families. Personal taxation relief in Indonesia again tended to benefit men because they were more likely to pay income tax and were in a higher tax bracket than women. Enterprise taxation relief in Indonesia and China and producer goods subsidies benefited men the most because they tended to own businesses, their businesses were likely to be bigger, and they had better access to information about these relief and subsidies. And finally, even social protection programs may benefit men more because the eligibility may be tied to employment and earnings or require formal employment status (e.g., in Vietnam) but women are more likely to be employed on an informal and casual basis. Indeed, according to the ILO (2009b), social protection measures that cover informal sector workers and the self-employed exist in only a third of all developing countries. Moreover, according to Édes (2009, p. 20),

> many of the social spending packages have been one-off measures or simply topped-up existing programmes, regardless of their efficiency or impact. Recent spending has generally failed to address the more fundamental weaknesses of social protection programmes, such as patchy coverage and poor targeting.

3 Social standing and employment patterns of women in China

Before the crisis hit, China's gender gaps were already worsening. As Figure 6.1 indicates, two worrying trends emerged since the 1990s. First, employment-to-population ratios for both men and women have been declining since the mid-1990s; and second, female employment-to-population ratios have been consistently lower than those of males. Some 67.5 percent of Chinese women over the age of 15 were employed in 2008, down from 2000 when 71.52 percent of women were employed, compared with 82.47 percent of men. In addition, women earn 63.5 percent of men's salaries, a drop from 64.8 in 2000 (Tatlow 2010).

Not only is female labor participation lower and decreases more than male, but female workers also take on more precarious jobs than their male counterparts. During China's market reform and industrialization era, many rural residents became redundant in the agriculture sector and had to leave their rural homes to seek employment in the industrial and service sectors in the urban areas. These workers are dubbed "migrant workers" or "floating population." These workers do not hold urban "hukou" (a type of household registration) but have only temporary residence permits that are conditional upon employment. An urban hukou entitles residents to many benefits, including better job opportunities. Migrant workers possess rural hukous, which entitle them to relatively fewer benefits. They therefore have very limited access to social services in urban areas due to their hukou status.[4] The lack of social protection and assistance to fall back on seriously undercuts migrant workers' bargaining power in the labor market; they are to some extent forced to take any jobs they can find. Rural women account for a majority of the migrant workers. According to the National Bureau of Statistics of China (2009), there were 132 million migrant

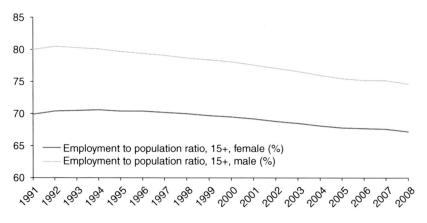

Figure 6.1 Employment to population ratio by gender, 1991–2008 (source: World Bank 2010).

workers, of whom 40 percent were female as of 2006. This share is much higher than the share of female workers in the state-owned enterprises (SOEs) or joint-stock enterprises, which stood at 34.9 percent in 2006. SOEs and joint-stock enterprises provide far more stable employment than migrant work. Women have also faced a higher probability of layoffs from SOEs and a loss thereafter of coordinated social security.

Much of the social protection and assistance in China depends on one's employment status. Those with formal, urban jobs are protected in terms of pension, health care, and unemployment insurance, while those without are largely unprotected. Because women are more likely to work in the informal sector or as migrant workers, they generally have less access to social protection than men. During economic decline, spending on social protection and assistance falls in step and women's access to these services falls even further. But women are in greater need of social protection during downturns. For example, domestic violence due to financial stress within households is normally exacerbated during downturns. Although there is very little written about domestic violence in China, one study performed after the crisis hit indicated that domestic violence was a rising problem in rural areas due to economic hardship (Hsu 2009). Women have been protected only recently by laws against domestic violence (Palmer 2007), but most of it goes unreported.

China's social protection includes a social insurance system, a social assistance system, and a social welfare system (Zhang 2010). The Ministry of Human Resources and Social Security is responsible for basic pension, unemployment, injury, and maternity insurance for urban workers, basic medical insurance for urban workers and residents, and new rural pension insurance. The Ministry of Health is in charge of rural medical insurance, and the Ministry of Civil Affairs is responsible for social welfare programs, including a minimum livelihood guarantee for urban and rural residents.

For pension schemes, urban workers must pay into pension schemes along with employers.[5] In addition to the compulsory pension scheme, businesses may establish an "enterprise annuity" for their employees as a supplementary pension insurance program. Currently, enterprise annuities are provided mainly to SOE employees and 90 percent of the funds are raised by big SOEs (Zhang 2010). Social insurance for rural residents was absent for a long time in the past, and the rural pension insurance was piloted in 2009 as one of the coping measures to the financial crisis. The scheme combines individual contributions, collective assistance, and government subsidies. The basic rural pension was 55 yuan per person per month in 2009 (or US$8.70 at the current exchange rate). The minimum age for retirement is 60 for male employees, 55 for female cadres, and 50 for female workers.

Unemployment insurance covers most urban workers in the formal sector and is paid into by employees and employers (Zhang 2010). The level of benefits and the income replacement rate are quite low, however (Vodopivec and Tong 2008). Provinces determine the level of benefits and duration of unemployment insurance. Unemployment insurance is not income related and has a flat benefit level, although the duration of benefits does depend on number of years of contribution. To be eligible for benefits, one must: (1) have contributed to unemployment insurance for at least one year, (2) have been separated from the employer involuntarily, and (3) be registered as unemployed and willing to work. The unemployment insurance issued is currently insufficient, not only because benefit levels are low, but also because of its very limited coverage. Rural–urban migrants, rural surplus laborers and informal sector workers make up a large part of the work force, but are not counted as part of the official unemployment rate (Li 2011). This presents a higher degree of insecurity for individuals working in these precarious sectors.

Finally, three different types of medical insurance are established, including a basic medical insurance for urban workers and residents, respectively, and a cooperative medical insurance for rural residents. Urban employees and their employers contribute 2 and 6 percent of wages, respectively, to both pooled funds and individual accounts. In terms of disbursement, when medical spending is below the bottom-line payment, it is paid out of the individual account; if spending is above the bottom line of payment and below a cap, it will come out from the pooled funds with a 20 percent co-pay. In addition, a maternity insurance system covers women in urban enterprises, providing them with a childbirth allowance for 98 days (gov.cn 2012).

Women must be in compliance with family planning regulations, including the one-child policy (Khan 2011). Insurance funds for urban residents (who are not employed) come from individual contributions and governmental subsidies, and are mainly used for in-hospital and serious illness expenses with a reimbursement rate of 60 percent of the total expense. The rural cooperative medical scheme was introduced in 2003, which aims to cover all peasants. Funding comes from a variety of sources, including individual contribution, collective support, and government subsidies. The current average reimbursement rate is around 60 percent of the total expenses.

Overall, China's social protection and welfare system is still highly unequally developed. Urban residents enjoy much better benefits than rural residents and rural migrant workers. As of 2010, 50.32 percent of the population still live in rural areas and have fewer protections than under the command economy, even taking into account more recent social protection policies. In rural areas, most people still have not been covered by any pension plans, despite the higher degree of aging than in the urban areas. Decollectivization at the outset of market reform weakened the rural community-based social welfare system. In spite of the establishment of an institutional framework to assist the rural poor, including the central Poor Area Development Office and programs within other ministries, rural social welfare programs currently provide only a minimum level of assistance (Wang *et al.* 2006).

Rural migrants are particularly excluded from the social protection and welfare system largely because they fall into the urban and rural divide. As Zhang (2010, pp. 388–9) puts it,

Without urban Hukou, the migrants can hardly participate in the urban social security scheme and even despite their accession to it, they will not only face the problem of dealing with the issue of rural land income but also the risk that on returning to the rural areas, they will be unable to receive off-site social security benefits. Meanwhile, though these migrants have rural Hukou and land, in fact, they have become "urban people" and many are not likely to return to rural life in the future, so joining a rural social insurance system is not particularly meaningful to them.

Given that females make up 49.3 percent of the migrant population and have only a 65.5 percent employment rate (as compared to males, who make up 50.7 percent of the migrant population, but have a 92.5 percent employment rate), as of 2009, it is alarming that the most vulnerable population – female migrant workers – are the least protected (NPFPC 2010). This is an important situational factor to be included in the analysis of gendered crisis impacts, to which we now turn.

4 Gendered impacts on employment

In this section, we will start with a general overview of China's role in the global division of labor. We will then provide descriptive statistics that show nation-wide impacts of the crisis on male and female employment. Following this, we will proceed to a regional survey by the International Labour Organization (ILO) that provides more details of the crisis impacts.

4.1 Export production in China

It has been well noted that China's economic growth depends heavily on exports and investment. The impacts of the crisis on China were channeled mainly through exports and foreign direct investment (FDI).[6] Exports are an important component of China's economy. Since 2007, China overtook the United States to become the world's second largest merchandise exporter after the European Union (Morrison 2009). The success of China in global trade rests mainly on the unskilled, low-cost manufacturing that in turn relies on the large supply of cheap labor. Although some commentators have argued that China has progressively moved up the technological ladder and no longer relies on cheap labor to maintain its comparative advantage, evidence abounds that China still maintains its status as a low-tech, labor-intensive manufacturing power house. The so-called high-tech export production is mainly undertaken by foreign-invested enterprises that import technological-intensive components, conduct processing, and assembly production in China, then export these high-tech products (Liang 2007, 2008). As of the late 2000s, processing exports still accounted for around half of China's total exports, and processing trade only generated around 40 percent of value-added within China. This suggests that China still occupies the low end of the global division of labor and relies on cheap labor as its main comparative advantage. Rural migrants, especially female workers, are most desired for the export production industry. As mentioned above, these workers are not only demanding lower wages and are less militant and more hard-working than their urban counterparts for the lack of choices, but they are also more nimble and efficient in processing and assembly production (Harney 2009).

Although export production is a far less-than-ideal source of employment, it does provide an employable opportunity for rural migrants. But as developed country demand slowed just after the global crisis hit in 2007, export production declined in step, as indicated in Figure 6.2. Exports declined for 12 consecutive months between November 2008 and November 2009; the average rate of growth was –16 percent on a year-to-year basis. The decline of exports was accompanied by the decline in inward FDI flows, as depicted in Figure 6.3. The reduction in FDI was a response to the declining export demand, and it in turn reduced exports because foreign-invested enterprises were the main contributors to China's exports.

As a result of falling exports, employment fell dramatically at the end of 2008. Although many workers were affected, the impact was particularly adverse for informal and migrant workers as opposed to formally employed workers (Zhang and Lin 2010). By February 2009, job losses had deteriorated to the extent that 20 million rural migrant workers were sent home (Anderlini and Dye 2009). Many of the employment losses were in the manufacturing sector that produces for exports, while small enterprises also experienced sharp contractions. The employment impacts of the crisis fell differently on workers who held urban hukou and those who were migrant workers with permits to temporarily live and work in the urban areas. This is not only because migrant workers are more than proportionately represented in the export production sector, but also because they are the first to be let go since they are less protected by formal employment contracts than urban workers. Based on estimates, unemployment among rural migrants was greater than unemployment among nonmigrants, about four times more (Cai and Chan 2009). As mentioned above, most migrant workers did not receive unemployment insurance, and without a job, they were not able to stay in urban areas. So unemployment hit these migrant workers

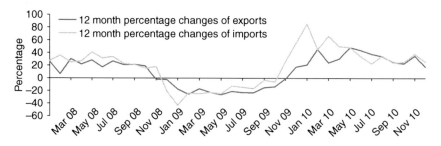

Figure 6.2 China's exports and imports (12-month percentage changes), January 2008–
October 2010 (source: China Customs 2010).

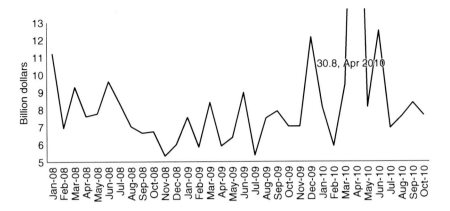

Figure 6.3 Inward FDI flows to China, January 2008–October 2010 (source: Ministry of Commerce 2010).

much harder than their urban counterparts (Zhang and Lin 2010). We will examine more specifically the national employment data below to provide evidence of the hardship women workers encountered due to the disproportionately large job losses.

4.2 Gendered impacts of employment due to falling exports: evidence from national official data

When examining the national statistics regarding working hours of male and female urban and rural workers, there are several interesting features to notice. As Table 6.1 indicates, first, the category of "normal" working hours range (41–48 hours per week) shows a clear urban–rural divide. While urban male and female workers saw a 1 percent and 0.7 percent increase in this category, rural male and female workers experienced a –0.3 percent and –0.8 percent change during 2008–09. Second, for the overtime category (48 hours+), all four working groups experienced a decline in 2007–08 when the crisis hit and export orders dried up, but the decline among rural male and female workers was much larger than among urban workers. By 2008–09, while urban workers were still experiencing a decline in the overtime category, rural workers had a slight increase in this category. It is difficult to decipher the reasons for such a change; it is possible that wage and benefit cuts made overtime work a lot less attractive and only rural workers were willing to take the jobs. And it is also possible that rural workers remained more "flexible" in the sense that they were more capable of coming back to work on short notice.

Another noticeable change from the national statistics is the decline in the percentage of female workers in the manufacturing industry. Other than that, the crisis continued to produce a declining trend in working hours for all age groups

Table 6.1 Change in urban working hours by registration type and sex (in % change)

	1–8 hours	9–19 hours	20–39 hours	40 hours	41–48 hours	48 hours+
Urban hukou, male						
2005–06	0.0	0.0	0.1	−3.9	4.3	−0.5
2006–07	0.0	0.0	0.0	0.0	0.0	0.0
2007–08	0.0	0.1	0.8	1.6	2.1	−4.6
2008–09	0.1	−0.1	0.5	1.0	1.0	−2.6
Urban hukou, female						
2005–06	0.1	0.1	0.0	−3.9	4.0	−0.2
2006–07	0.0	0.0	0.0	0.0	0.0	0.0
2007–08	0.0	0.2	1.6	0.9	1.9	−4.6
2008–09	0.1	0.0	0.3	1.8	0.7	−3.0
Rural hukou, male						
2005–06	0.2	0.6	2.1	−3.0	6.1	−5.9
2006–07	0.0	0.0	0.0	0.0	0.0	0.0
2007–08	0.2	0.7	5.2	3.8	3.1	−12.9
2008–09	−0.1	−0.3	−2.0	1.3	−0.3	1.4
Rural hukou, female						
2005–06	0.4	1.3	2.8	−2.3	4.3	−6.4
2006–07	0.0	0.0	0.0	0.0	0.0	0.0
2007–08	0.3	1.2	6.4	2.9	1.7	−12.5
2008–09	0.0	−0.3	−1.7	1.4	−0.8	1.4

Source: National Bureau of Statistics (2011).

and both sexes since 2007, with no real change in overall female employment rates due to the crisis.

Examining employment trends by sector also yields noteworthy features. As shown in Figure 6.4, finance and insurance; wholesale and retail and catering services; manufacturing; farming, forestry, animal husbandry, and fishery; and real estate trade were the top five sectors for female employment. From 2000 to 2009, the share of female employment in the finance and insurance sector had a significant increase and that in other sectors stayed relatively stable, but the share of female employment in the manufacturing sector has declined quite noticeably since 2007. Given that the manufacturing sector remained the third largest sector

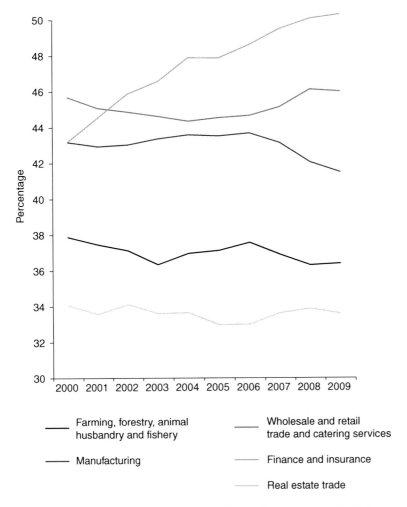

Figure 6.4 Percentage female employment in top five sectors, 2001–09 (source: *China Labour Statistical Yearbook* 2010).

for female employment, the decline at the onset of the global financial crisis seemed to suggest that the impact of the crisis on female employment was far from negligible.

Overall, official employment data shows that the global crisis had quite a significant impact on female workers who were disproportionally concentrated in the export production sector as migrant workers. Even if migrant workers kept their jobs, many faced pay cuts, benefits cuts, delayed wage payments, and general deterioration of working conditions. A salient example was the closing of toy factories in Dongguan, a small city in Guangdong province known for the large-scale export production of toys, shoes, and electronics. In October 2008, the manager of the Hong Kong-listed toy company, Smart Union Group Holdings, fled after Smart Union filed for bankruptcy, leaving 7,000 workers at the company's two factories in Dongguan without jobs and pay (deferred wage payments totaled more than 24 million yuan) (Chao and Battson 2009).

The inability of official national data to capture the full extent to which rural migrant workers, especially female, were affected by the crisis led us to look for more in-depth and focused survey data.[7] An ILO survey of two southern provinces provides some good insights into the gendered impacts of the crisis on employment, to which we now turn.

4.3 Gendered impacts of employment due to falling exports: evidence from an ILO survey

To get a good glimpse of the impacts of the global financial crisis on migrant workers, the ILO conducted a survey in early 2009 in Hunan and Fujian provinces.[8] The survey found that worsening conditions for migrant workers were quite common and women's situations were much worse than men's. As indicated by the survey results, depicted in Table 6.2, both male and female migrant workers were faced with layoffs, wage delays and wage cuts, prolonged working hours, worsening work conditions, and increasing precariousness of jobs; but the share of women who encountered these hardships was significantly higher than that of men. The survey also found the lack of positive outlook of many migrant

Table 6.2 Survey results of migrant workers in Hunan and Fujian provinces, January/February 2009 (%)

	Laid off	Delayed wage	Wages cut	Benefits cut	Prolonged working hours	Worsening work conditions	Precarious job
Female	9.4	10.1	31.6	28.7	12.1	5.3	24.6
Male	5.9	11.8	30.3	27.7	5.9	3.4	24.4
Total	8.6	10.5	31.3	28.5	10.7	4.9	24.6

Source: ILO (2009a).

workers. A survey in Fujian province showed that 30 percent of migrant workers feared losing their jobs and 37.2 percent believed jobs were difficult to find. In Hunan province, 17.6 percent said it was "very difficult" to find a job, 77.8 percent said "somewhat difficult," and only 4.6 percent said it was "not at all difficult." In addition, 46.7 percent of the interviewees indicated their willingness to accept low wages (primarily within a 10 percent margin).

Besides the hukou system that weakens migrant workers' bargaining power and renders them vulnerable, the lack of skills is also a major factor that makes migrant workers, especially female workers, subject to greater risks and hardships. Female migrant workers are particularly low skilled and low paid as compared to male migrant workers. The survey by the ILO in Fujian province (Table 6.3) suggests that more than half of the female migrant workers had no skills, as compared to 37.6 percent of males, and the share of female workers who earn over 1,600 yuan a month was a meager 25.8 percent, as compared to 46.6 percent for men. Meanwhile, the survey in Hunan indicates that lack of education and skills was still considered one of the biggest obstacles for female workers to find a job (see Table 6.4).

Due to data limitations and informality of rural migrant employment, a full disclosure of the crisis impacts along the gender line is hard to come by. However, the more in-depth localized survey corroborates national data, which suggests that migrant workers, especially female migrant workers, were hit hard

Table 6.3 Survey results in Fujian province on migrant workers' skill and pay levels

	Female	*Male*
University education	4.1	8.4
No skills	57.7	37.6
Entry-level skill	17.8	18.8
Mid-level skill	18.5	32.5
High-level skill	1.9	7.1
Wage income over 1,600 yuan	25.8	46.6

Source: ILO (2009a).

Table 6.4 Survey results in Hunan province regarding major challenges in finding a job

	Female (%)	*Male (%)*
Low educational attainment	37.7	27.7
Lack of skills	61.6	41.2
Lack of information	31.2	31.1
Lack of social network	41.1	31.9
Lack of opportunities	20.5	21.8

Source: ILO (2009a)

Note
Shares do not sum to 100 percent due to multiple choices.

during the crisis. They faced job losses, income reductions, worsening work conditions, and increasing instability. Because female migrant workers are heavily concentrated in the export production sector and because they often lack skills and education, the crisis exerted particularly harsh impacts on these workers. The government's efforts in providing training would help to relieve the hardships faced by these workers,[9] but more institutional reforms (e.g., the eradication of the hukou system and strong enforcement of labor laws) are still required to fundamentally improve the social and economic status of migrant workers – especially female workers.

The negative impacts of the crisis on the economy have provoked the Chinese government to take action. In addition to the specific training and educational programs launched by national and local governments, macroeconomic policies, especially fiscal policies, have generated significant gendered impacts as well. We will now turn to an analysis of the policy impacts.

5 Gendered impacts of the stimulus package on employment and social services

The Chinese government responded swiftly to the crisis and instituted a series of policies trying to revive the economy. One of the most significant policies was the 4 trillion yuan (around US$568 billion) fiscal stimulus plan announced in September 2008. As indicated by the composition of the package (Table 6.5), 909 billion RMB out of the 4 trillion RMB stimulus package are expected to be used for improving the quality of people's lives in areas such as housing, health care, and education. In addition, the government pledged that 850 billion RMB (US$120 billion) will be spent over three years to establish a basic health care system. The government also launched a new type of rural social pension pilot scheme in 320 counties to increase the coverage to 130 million rural residents for the first time (Qian 2010).

The 2008 fiscal stimulus package had a profound effect on ameliorating China's sudden spike in unemployment due to the global crisis. The Chinese

Table 6.5 Sectoral composition of the fiscal stimulus package

Percentage allocated	Areas/projects
37.5	Transport and power infrastructure (railroad, road, airport, electricity grid)
9.3	Rural village infrastructure
5.3	Environmental investment
10	Affordable housing
9.3	Technological innovation and structural adjustment
3.8	Health and education
25	Post-earthquake reconstruction

Source: NDRC (2013).

economy continued its growth trajectory because the stimulus package was large and implemented in a timely manner. National spending on infrastructure was the key component of the package, while local spending acted as a complement by implementing infrastructure projects that crowded in private investment (Fardoust *et al.* 2012). According to the official tally, these spending projects have created 22 million job opportunities over the past two years. And the government helped 1.6 million troubled enterprises to stabilize 60 million job posts in 2009 by postponing the collection of social security contributions, lowering social insurance premium rates, and offering social security, post, and training subsidies (Qian 2010). However, there were discussions over the fact that the package targeted employment in male-dominated industries and did not address farmers and agriculture, whose work force is predominantly female (Chen 2009). And these concerns are not groundless. Ten industries that received most of the support through the stimulus package include auto, steel, shipbuilding, textile, machine-manufacturing, electronics and information industries, light industry, petrochemicals, non-ferrous metals, and logistics. Most of these industries are male-dominated. Therefore, it is likely that the job creation benefits are mainly enjoyed by male workers.

However, expansion of social benefits was in effect pro-female. Women, especially elderly women, were largely not covered by health insurance, as indicated by the third survey of health care services in China. With the pledged investment in a universal basic health care system, the coverage of health care will increase to 90 percent of the urban residents. This investment will also help build 29,000 rural medical centers, 5,000 rural clinics, 2,000 rural hospitals, and 2,400 urban clinics. Furthermore, it will help increase government's subsidies to each person's health care coverage each year from 100 RMB in 2009 to 120 RMB in 2011 (Chen 2009; Wong 2009).[10]

All of these not only directly improve women's health benefits, but also help relieve the burden of women as care givers and major providers of other unpaid services. As Seguino (2009, p. 5) points out, "directing funding to activities that help women with their care burden – e.g., child care services, contraception, and school feeding programs – can attenuate some of the negative effects of the crisis on them and the children they care for." Finally, the increase in investment in care services would create more jobs for women, as they typically take on these kinds of service jobs.

Table 6.6 illustrates significant gender differences in performing unpaid but socially necessary activities, based on a survey of time use by urban and rural male and female residents.[11] This is the first national-level time-use survey ever conducted in China. Because the survey took place during 2008 when the crisis had already taken a toll on the economy and there was no comparable survey done before, it is difficult to analyze how the crisis affected individuals' time use. However, it does allow us to infer the gender gap in performing unpaid care and other social services, and hence to assess impacts of fiscal spending on health care, consumption subsidies, transportation, and other public goods and services.

It is clear that men spend more time on gainful employment and businesses. On average, men spend 37 percent more time on these than women, whereas women devote 1.5 times more time to unpaid activities. In rural areas, women spend twice as much time on unpaid activities, such as household duties, caring for family members, and community services than men. Women also enjoy less free time than their male counterparts. This shows not only that women are insufficiently and unjustly remunerated for their work, but also that without sufficient public goods and services (such as health care and child care) or if access to these public services were to decline due to income constraints, women and girls would have to take on even more unpaid work. This is especially the case during an economic downturn when both government revenues and public spending fall. As Antonopoulos (2009, p. 23) puts it, "Income-poor households will also witness a rise in women's time poverty." By contrast, the increase in investment in care services and education by the Chinese government as part of the response to the crisis would help to relieve the burden of unpaid work that women disproportionately shoulder. In this sense, the increase in public spending on social services is positive in reducing gender gaps.

Furthermore, to stimulate demand, the central government also expanded the pilot program to subsidize electronics purchases for farmers in February 2009.[12]

Table 6.6 Results of National Survey of Daily Time Uses by Urban and Rural Residents, 2008

	Total		Urban		Rural	
	Male	*Female*	*Male*	*Female*	*Male*	*Female*
Total	1,440	1,440	1,440	1,440	1,440	1,440
Paid activities	360	263	283	214	443	320
Employment	179	120	223	169	132	64
Family business	129	109	11	10	257	222
Transportation	52	35	49	36	55	34
Unpaid activities	91	234	111	237	69	230
Household work	62	180	76	178	47	182
Caring family members	13	33	15	30	10	35
Offer help outside family	2	2	1	1	2	2
Community services	1	1	1	1	1	1
Transportation	12	18	16	25	8	10
Personal activities	989	943	1,046	989	927	890
Studying and training	30	28	35	32	25	25
Free time	242	207	290	240	190	169
Sleeping, dining and other personal activities	698	692	697	697	699	686
Undefined activities	1	1	0	0	1	1

Source: National Bureau of Statistics (2009).

Based on the program, which runs until 2012, the government pays 13 percent of the retail price for designated models of refrigerators, washing machines, color television sets, mobile phones, and personal computers. According to official data, rural electronics purchases surged by 70 percent from February to March (Liu 2009). The subsidy was also extended to farmers' purchases of automobiles. As of June 2010, the government has dispensed 30.7 billion yuan of subsidies to rural purchasers of home appliances, cars, and motorcycles (Yu 2010). This program helped to increase the purchasing power of rural residents, improved domestic demand, and facilitated manufacturing growth. More importantly, many of the household appliances helped to relieve the burden of women's household duties. As indicated in Table 6.6, women, in general, spend twice as much time as men on household work, which includes cleaning and preparing food; house cleaning; laundry; shopping for food, clothing, and other items; and many other activities. In rural areas, where modern household appliances are in short supply, women spend as much as 182 minutes a day on household work, as compared to the 47 minutes spent by men. Therefore, subsidies for home appliance purchases could potentially help to relieve rural residents, especially women, from the burden of household work.

In short, the Chinese government's fiscal stimulus policies are likely to produce mixed results as far as gender impacts are concerned.[13] Some policies, such as employment creation, may disproportionately benefit male-dominant industries, such as construction; but its labor training and consumption subsidy programs would produce large benefits for women. To effectively provide income subsidy and stimulate job creation, a stimulus program must make sure that women enjoy an equal share of the benefits. This is not only the key to minimizing welfare losses due to the economic downtown, but it is also an indispensable condition of boosting demand. As many feminist economists have demonstrated, women are overrepresented in the low-income group, which has a higher propensity to consume, and women have a higher tendency to spend money on necessities for the household instead of luxury goods like cigarettes and alcohol. Therefore, women's consumption would help to generate a higher level of demand through multiplier effects.

6 Economic restructuring, the 12th Five-Year Plan and potential gendered impacts

Although China recovered quickly from the economic downturn, it is still too early to claim victory. The structural imbalance in the Chinese economy is accentuated by the crisis. The heavy reliance on export and external demand puts China at a vulnerable position because it does not have full control over imports by other countries; and when external demand falls, its economy slows down. Furthermore, rising Chinese exports have invited attacks from countries with trade deficits. It will become increasingly difficult for China to expand its exports as its trade partners adopt policies to reduce their imports and pressure China to revalue its currency.

Under this circumstance, China has two options: one is to continue its export-oriented growth path. Given the growing upward pressure on the currency value, producers must try other ways to cut down production costs and remain competitive. Provided that China's exports are still mainly labor-intensive, maintaining export competitiveness would require reductions in labor costs. Indeed, the deferment of the new Labor Contract Law, which was passed in 2008 and considered to be pro-labor, was an indication that the protection to women and other vulnerable workers could be sacrificed in exchange for low production costs. The fact that the Chinese government raised the export tax rebate three times in 2008 clearly suggests that the government will continue encouraging export growth, including labor-intensive growth, through policies.[14] Some of the policies may help to reduce labor costs, or seen from the other side, repress workers' wages.

However, without a fundamental revamping of China's export-led, labor-intensive growth, unemployment, with its gender-specific pattern and impacts, is unlikely to improve in a sustainable manner even if it got a temporary boost through fiscal stimulus. A recent survey of 8,000 households suggests that urban unemployment rose sharply to 8.1 percent in 2012, nearly twice the official rate of 4.1 percent. The unemployment rate of the 160 million migrant workers rose sharply to 6 percent in mid-2012, up from 3.4 percent in August 2011. Unemployment rose as a result of the lackluster exports as Western countries still experienced stagnant growth and due to the slowdown of real estate construction. A loss of around 4.5 million jobs for migrants in 2012 has taken the total unemployment migrant workers to ten million, and although this was much less than the 23 million out of work in 2009, it was still significant (Orlik 2012). In addition, the labor-intensive export-led growth model requires wage repression. A survey by Xin Meng of the Australian National University shows annual wage growth for migrant workers slowed significantly to only 1.7 percent percent in 2012, compared to 23 percent in 2011 (China Real Time Report 2013). Therefore, it seems that although the crisis-provoked stimulus helped to temporarily relieve unemployment and wage repression for migrant workers, without a fundamental change in the growth model (see below) and institutional reform, including the removal of the hukou system and establishment of a universal pension, unemployment, and welfare system, it is unlikely that employment and worker conditions can be sustainably improved. An alternative growth path is more internal demand driven. That is, China will reduce its dependence on exports but boost its consumption demand. Indeed, there are emerging challenges associated with external demand-driven growth. Externally, tensions between China and its trade partners, in particular, the United States, have been heightened. With growing trade deficits, the United States has been pushing China to revaluate its currency and stop export subsidies. Moreover, given the slowing economic growth worldwide, it is difficult for China to continue producing large trade surpluses like before. Internally, the emphasis on investment and exports has generated uneven, unbalanced, and unsustainable growth. One of the most significant problems is rising inequality, indicating that the past decades' high growth has not benefited different regions and social groups evenly. The Gini coefficient reached 0.47 in 2009, up from 0.21–0.27 three decades ago. The income ratio of urban and rural residents stood at 2.56 in 1978 and increased to 3.33 in 2009. Rising inequality not only aggravates social conflicts but also undermines the capacity of spending. These problems have prompted the Chinese government to take measures to accelerate structural transformation and demand shift.

There is evidence that the government has been making rebalancing efforts. As mentioned above, the government has been investing in a social safety net, increasing the coverage of health care and pension schemes. In addition, a total of 27 provinces and municipalities have raised minimum wage levels, and 20 have increased them by 20 percent since February 2010 (China.org 2010). More systematically, the 12th Five-Year Plan (2011–15), just passed in the Fifth Plenary Session of the 17th Central Committee of the Communist Party of China, proposes the strategy of "inclusive growth," that is, to balance economic growth and social progress through sustainable development. The 12th Five-Year Plan will focus on increasing domestic demand and reducing economic inequality while changing the structure of the economy from a focus on manufacturing to a focus on services (Hsiao *et al.* 2010). Among the proposed reform agendas, two are especially interesting as far as gendered impacts are concerned. The first is to reduce income disparity between urban and rural areas and between different regions and different industries through tax policies. Although this does not relieve inequality due to primary distribution, it may help to reduce inequality through secondary distribution. Given the low skill level and subordinate status of women, a general improvement in secondary distribution would help to reduce income disparity between men and women.

A second reform area concerns the dual structure between urban and rural areas. One of the ways to eliminate this is to substantially loosen the standards of giving urban hukou to migrant workers. This would help tremendously to enhance the conditions of migrant workers, especially female workers, by giving them more bargaining power and institutional protection. In short, should China put these policies in effect and move toward an internal demand-led growth path, it would help to improve equality, enhance welfare for the general populace, and make growth more sustainable.

In the final analysis, although the proposed long-term development agenda seems promising, there is mixed evidence as to whether the government really has the will and capacity to restructure China's growth and enhance the general well-being of the population, especially that of the poor and the vulnerable. To improve gender equality and better women's conditions, macro-level policies must be oriented toward promoting wage income growth, more equitable income distribution, and hence consumption growth. In the meantime, more gender-equitable social spending on health, education, social safety net, and welfare is also necessary to close the current gender gap.

7 Conclusion

The 2007 global financial crisis has exerted short-lived but nevertheless significantly negative impacts on China. Declining exports and FDI has caused millions of job losses in the export sector. Migrant workers, especially female
workers, were particularly affected by job and income losses. The Chinese government's stimulus policies have generated mixed benefits for men and women.
It is likely that job creation mainly occurs in male-dominant sectors, but women
benefit from job training, consumption subsidies, and social welfare programs.
Moving forward, China is facing the option of continuing old, external demand-
driven growth or transitioning to internal demand-led growth. The former may
perpetuate the urban–rural duality and fail to fundamentally improve migrant
workers' and rural residents' conditions. On the other hand, should China carry
out pragmatic policies and shift to an internal demand-led growth path, it would
help to promote more balanced and equal growth, thus making economic benefits more fairly shared by men and women.

Notes

1 In 2000, on a world scale, women's unemployment rate was 0.5 percentage points
   higher than that of men; the difference remained around the same in 2007–09, but it
   increased to 0.6, 0.7, and 0.6 in 2010 and 2011. In Asia, the trend is mixed, e.g., in
   East Asia, women have had lower unemployment rates than men, while in South Asia,
   the reverse is true.
2 Elson (2010) also provides a sound general framework to analyze the impacts of crisis
   by focusing on three spheres of the economy: finance, production, and reproduction.
   She argues for the importance of paying attention to "gender numbers" and "gender
   norms."
3 One oft-cited example is that of the Philippines; after the loss of 42,000 jobs in the
   female-dominated garments, semi-conductor, and electronics industries, the government announced the creation of 41,000 new jobs through government infrastructure
   projects. Even though women were disproportionately suffering from job losses, the
   government projects will most likely exclusively benefit men (Emmett 2009).
4 For the history and impacts of the hukou system, see Wang (2005).
5 Total contribution rate is 28 percent of payroll, of which 20 percent comes from the
   employer and goes into the social pooling account and 8 percent comes from the
   employee and enters the individual account.
6 Given that FDI does not contribute significantly to fixed investment, the impacts of
   FDI are mainly felt through export production because foreign-invested enterprises
   engage mainly in export-oriented production. For example, as of 2008, foreign-
   invested enterprises accounted for 55.3 percent and 54.7 percent of China's total
   exports and imports, respectively.
7 Some studies, such as Huang *et al.* (2010), find that rural off-farm employment,
   including that of rural migrants, decreased by 6.8 percent by April 2009, as did wages,
   but increased thereafter.
8 Studies were conducted during the Spring Festival period (January–February 2009) in
   sending and receiving areas and 533 and 686 questionnaires were collected in Hunan
   and Fujian, respectively.
9 To cushion the hardships faced by migrant workers due to job losses, central and local
   governments made efforts to provide training to workers. This not only helped to
   reduce the risk of disorderly forced return to rural hometowns by migrant workers,

but it also buttressed their confidence and improved their employability. According to the Ministry of Human Resources and Social Security, about four million laid-off workers in China attended vocational training for reemployment in 2008, and another 400,000 received education to start self-employed businesses (*China Daily* 2009). During a recent trip to Dongguan, one of the authors was told by a government official that the local government provided vocational training and financial support to migrant workers who were laid off by several large toy factories. The government believed that by retaining workers, it helped to stabilize the local economy and to provide employable workers once economic recovery resumes.

10 Although the increase in government's medical subsidies is a step in the right direction, it has still been criticized for doing relatively little to provide rural residents with access to quality medical care (Public Radio International 2011). The plan also requires that patients pay out-of-pocket fees and large deductibles. Facilities and equipment are in the process of being improved, but medicine is still costly and is used as a major source of income for hospitals and other medical centers (PBS 2011).

11 The survey was conducted in May 2008, surveying residents between the ages of 15 and 74. It collected time-use data from 16,661 households or 37,142 individuals, among whom 19,621 were urban residents and 17,521 were rural residents. The number of males is 18,215 and females 18,927. The survey included Beijing, Hebei, Henlongjiang, and seven other provinces.

12 The pilot program was first initiated to subsidize farmers' purchases of 197 types of appliances in three agricultural provinces of Shandong, Henan, and Sichuan, as well as Qingdao City from December 2007 through May 2008 (*People's Daily* 2009). The consumption subsidies, along with the rural cooperative medical care project introduced in 2003 and the removal of the agricultural tax in 2006, have helped to boost farmers' income and spending.

13 China's monetary policy was not as beneficial as its fiscal policy. China loosened its monetary policy as well in late 2008, requiring that banks lend more money. Rather than being invested into productive endeavors, much of the money was invested in the real estate market, driving up real estate prices and creating an asset price bubble in eight major cities (Deng *et al.* 2011). This has resulted in a large misallocation of assets and created potentially large economic risks.

14 In November 2008, the Ministry of Finance announced an increase in export tax rebate of a list of 3,770 items. This is the third time export tax rebates were raised in order to stimulate exports. The items that received increased rebates included labor-intensive, mechanical, and electrical products (Ministry of Commerce 2008).

References

Anderlini, J. and Dye, G. (2009) "Downturn causes 20m job losses in China," *Financial Times*, February 3. Online: www.ft.com/cms/s/0/19c25aea-f0f5-11dd-8790-0000779fd2ac. html#axzz2TOEEkSFj (accessed May 15, 2013).

Antonopoulos, R. (2009) "The current economic and financial crisis: a gender perspective," UNDP. Online: http://content.undp.org/go/cms-service/stream/asset/?asset_id=3231031 (accessed May 15, 2013). Also published as Working Paper No. 562, Annandale-on-Hudson, New York, Levy Institute of Bard College. Online: www.levyinstitute.org/pubs/wp_562.pdf (accessed May 15, 2013).

Cai, F. and Chan, K.W. (2009) "The global economic crisis and unemployment in China," *Eurasian Geography and Economics* 50: 513–31.

Chao, L. and Battson, A. (2009) "China's small factories struggle," *Wall Street Journal*, February 2. Online: http://online.wsj.com/article/SB123335472433734877.html (accessed May 15, 2013).

Chen, L. (2009) "Gender and the financial crisis: Chinese aspiring equitable response," presentation at an event co-sponsored by the Heinrich Böll Foundation North America, the Center of Concern, and the Institute for Women's Policy Research (IWPR), April 22.

China Customs (2010) *Statistics*. Online: http://english.customs.gov.cn/tabid/47819/Default.aspx (accessed May 20, 2013).

China Daily (2009) "China advances vocational training to help laid-off workers," January 27. Online: www.chinadaily.com.cn/bizchina/2009-01/27/content_7429584.htm (accessed May 15, 2013).

China Real Time Report (2013) "What worker shortage? The real story of China's migrants," January 4. Online: http://blogs.wsj.com/chinarealtime/2013/01/04/what-worker-shortage-the-real-story-of-chinas-migrants (accessed May 20, 2013).

China.org (2010) "Hu advocates inclusive growth," September 29. Online: www.china.org.cn/business/2010-09/29/content_21032034.htm (accessed May 15, 2013).

Corner, L. (2009) "The differential impact on women, men and children of fiscal responses to the global economic crisis," UNICEF Report, Washington, DC: UNICEF.

Dasgupta, S. and Williams, D. (2009) "Women facing the economic crisis," in A. Bauer and M. Thant (eds.), *Poverty and Sustainable Development in Asia: impacts and responses to the global economic crisis*, Manila: ADB.

Deng, Y., Morck, R., Wu, J., and Yeung, B. (2011) "Monetary and fiscal stimuli, ownership structure, and China's housing market," NBER Working Paper No. 16871, Cambridge, MA: National Bureau of Economic Research.

Édes, B.W. (2009) "Asia after the crisis: social protection and inclusive growth," *OECD Observer*, 276/277: 19–20.

Elson, D. (2010) "Gender and the global economic crisis in developing countries: a framework for analysis," *Gender and Development*, 18: 201–12.

Emmett, B. (2009) "Paying the price for the economic crisis," Oxford: Oxfam International.

Fardoust, S., Lin, J.Y., and Luo, X. (2012) "Demystifying China's fiscal stimulus," World Bank Policy Research Working Paper 6221, Washington, DC: World Bank.

Floro, M., Tas, E., and Törnqvist, A. (2010) *The Impact of the Global Economic Crisis on Women's Well-being and Empowerment*, Stockholm: Swedish International Development Agency (SIDA).

Gaerlan, K., Cabrera, M., and Samia, P. (2010) "Feminised recession: impact of the global financial crisis on women workers in the Philippines," *Gender & Development*, 18: 229–40.

gov.cn (2012) *China's Social Security and Its Policy*. Online: http://english.gov.cn/official/2005-07/28/content_18024.htm (accessed May 15, 2013).

Harney, A. (2008) *The China Price: the true cost of Chinese competitive advantage*, New York: Penguin Press.

Hsiao, F., Lee, S., Koo, S., and Chiang, B. (2010) "Decoding China's new five-year plan," *Common Wealth Magazine*, 456. Online: http://english.cw.com.tw/article.do?action=show&id=12283&offset=0 (accessed May 13, 2013).

Hsu, S. (2009) *Personal Interviews in Sichuan Province*, unpublished surveys.

Huang, J., Zhi, H., Huang, Z., Rozelle, S., and Giles, J. (2010) "The impact of the global financial crisis on off-farm employment and earnings in rural China," Policy Research Working Paper Series No. 5439, Washington, DC: World Bank.

Hung, S. (2009) "Lessons not learned? Gender, employment and social protection in Asia's crisis-affected export sectors," paper presented at conference on Impact of the Global Economic Slowdown on Poverty and Sustainable Development in Asia and the Pacific, Hanoi, September 28–30.

ILO (2009a) *The Impact of the Economic Crisis on China's Young Female Migrants*, Bangkok: ILO Regional Office for Asia and the Pacific.

ILO (2009b) *World of Work Report 2009*, Geneva: International Labour Office.

ILO (2012) *Global Employment Trend for Women*, Geneva: International Labour Office.

Jones, N., Holmes, R., Marsden, H., Mitra, S., and Walker, D. (2010) "Gender and social protection in Asia: what does the crisis change?" in A. Bauer and M. Thant (eds.), *Poverty and Sustainable Development in Asia: impacts and responses to the global economic crisis*, Philippines: Asian Development Bank.

Khan, N. (2011) "Longer maternity leave in China signals more women's rights," *Bloomberg*, November 22. Online: www.bloomberg.com/news/2011-11-22/longer-maternity-leave-in-china-signals-more-women-s-rights-1-.html (accessed May 16, 2013).

King, R. and Sweetman, C. (2010) *Gender Perspectives on the Global Economic Crisis*, Oxford: Oxfam International.

Li, S. (2011) "Issues and options for social security reform in China," *China: An International Journal*, 9: 72–109.

Liang, Y. (2007) "China's technological emergence and the loss of skilled jobs in the United States: missing link found?" *Journal of Economic Issues*, 41: 399–408.

Liang, Y. (2008) "Why are China's exports special: the role of FDI, regional trade, and government policies," *The Chinese Economy*, 41: 99–118.

Liu, J. (2009) "Chinese subsidies boost rural consumption," *BBC News*, April 30. Online: http://news.bbc.co.uk/2/hi/business/8025227.stm (accessed May 16, 2013).

Miller-Dawkins, M. and Abimanyu, R. (2010) *The Real Story behind the Numbers the Impacts of the Global Economic Crisis 2008–2009 on Indonesia's Women Workers*, Oxfam Research Report, Oxford: Oxfam.

Ministry of Commerce (2008) "China announces 3,770 items involved in 3rd export tax rebate rise," November 17. Online: http://news.xinhuanet.com/english/2008-11/17/content_10372861.htm (accessed May 16, 2013).

Ministry of Commerce (2010) *Statistics*. Online: http://english.mofcom.gov.cn/article/statistic (accessed May 20, 2013.

Morrison, W. (2009) "China and the global financial crisis: implications for the United States," CRS Report for Congress RS22984, Washington, DC: Congressional Research Services.

National Bureau of Statistics (2011) *China Labour Statistical Yearbook 2010*. Beijing: China Statistics Press.

National Bureau of Statistics (2009) "Compilation of reports on 2008 time-use survey," Online: www.stats.gov.cn/tjsj/qtsj/2008sjlydczlhb/index.htm (accessed May 16, 2013).

NPFPC (National Population and Family Planning Commission of China) (2009) "Report on living and development conditions of China's floating population: results based on study of floating population in five cities." Online: www.chinapop.gov.cn/stjzz/ldrk-fwgls/gzdt/201004/t20100402_199844.html (accessed May 16, 2013).

Nguanbanchong, A. (2010) *Beyond the Crisis: the impact of the financial crisis on women in Vietnam*, Oxfam Research Report, Oxford: Oxfam.

Orlik, T. (2012) "Chinese survey shows a higher jobless rate," *Wall Street Journal*, December 8. Online: http://online.wsj.com/article/SB10001424127887323316804578164784240097900.html (accessed May 16, 2013).

PBS (Public Broadcasting Service) (2011) "China struggles with healthcare reform amid growing demand," *Newshour*, April 14. Online: www.pbs.org/newshour/bb/health/jan-june11/china_04-14.html (accessed May 16, 2013).

Palmer, M. (2007) "On China's slow boat to women's rights: revisions to the women's protection law, 2005," *International Journal of Human Rights*, 11: 151–77.

People's Daily (2009) "China boosts rural consumption with household appliance subsidy program," February 2. Online: http://english.people.com.cn/90001/90778/90857/90862/6583290.html (accessed May 20, 2013).

Public Radio International (2011) "China's far-from universal healthcare," *Here and Now*, January 25. Online: www.pri.org/stories/health/global-health/china-s-far-from-universal-health-care2579.html (accessed May 16, 2013).

Qian, Z. (2010) "China's 4 trillion yuan stimulus package creates 22 million jobs," *People's Daily*, September 17. Online: http://english.peopledaily.com.cn/90001/90776/90882/7143609.html (accessed May 16, 2013).

Seguino, S. (2009) "The global economic crisis, its gender implications, and policy responses," paper prepared for Gender Perspectives on the Financial Crisis Panel at the 53rd Session of the Commission on the Status of Women, New York: United Nations, March 5.

Sirimanne, S. (2009) "Emerging issue: the gender perspectives of the financial crisis," UN Commission on the Status of Women 53rd Session, New York, March 2–13.

Tatlow, D. (2010) "For China's women, more opportunities, more pitfalls," *New York Times*, November 25. Online: www.nytimes.com/2010/11/26/world/asia/26iht-china.html?pagewanted=all&_r=0 (accessed May 16, 2013).

Turk, C. and Mason, A. (2010) "Impacts of the economic crisis in East Asia: findings from qualitative monitoring in five countries," in A. Bauer and M. Thant (eds.), *Poverty and Sustainable Development in Asia: impacts and responses to the global economic crisis*, Philippines: Asian Development Bank.

Vodopivec, M. and Tong, M.H. (2008) "China: improving unemployment insurance," Social Protection and Labor Discussion Paper 820, Washington DC: World Bank.

Wang, F. (2005) "Brewing tension while maintaining stabilities: the dual role of the hukou system in contemporary China," *Asian Perspective*, 29: 85–124.

Wang, L., Bales, S., and Zhang, Z. (2006) "China's social protection schemes and access to health services: a critical review," World Bank Working Paper. Washington, DC: World Bank.

Wang, M. (2010) "Impact of the global economic crisis on China's migrant workers: a survey of 2,700 in 2009," *Eurasian Geography and Economics*, 51: 218–35.

Wong, E. (2009) "China announces subsidies for healthcare," *New York Times*, January 21. Online: www.nytimes.com/2009/01/22/world/asia/22beijing.html (accessed May 16, 2013).

World Bank (2010) *World Development Indicators*, Washington DC: World Bank.

Yu, H. (2010) "Subsidies to rural consumers top 30m yuan," *China Daily*, June 30. Online: www.chinadaily.com.cn/business/2010-06/30/content_10041670.htm (accessed May 16, 2013).

Zhang, J. (2010) "Social protection in China: current status and challenges," in M.G. Asher, S. Oum, and F. Parulian (eds.), *Social Protection in East Asia: current state and challenges*, ERIA Research Project Report No. 9. Online: www.eria.org/pdf/research/y2009/no9/CH-13_China_pp. 371-398.pdf (accessed May 16, 2013).

Zhang, X. and Lin, S. (2010) "The impact of the global slowdown on the People's Republic of China's rural migrants: empirical evidence from a 12-city survey," in A. Bauer and M. Thant (eds.), *Poverty and Sustainable Development in Asia: impacts and responses to the global economic crisis*, Philippines: Asian Development Bank.

7 Has India learned any lessons from the global crisis?

The case of a less well-known but most globalized industry from a gender perspective

*Indira Hirway**

1 Introduction

Contrary to the initial thinking in 2008–09 that developing countries would be "decoupled" from the global crisis, the global crisis did impact developing countries. The magnitude of the impact depended on both the nature and extent of globalization of the economy as well as on the features of the development policy framework of the country, which could or could not provide social protection to its workers. While the nature and extent of globalization determined the strength of the channels through which the global crisis was transmitted to the economy, the domestic policy framework shaped the vulnerability of the population to the global crisis. Several studies on the impact of the global crisis on developing countries have sharply highlighted the structural weaknesses in many countries, while revealing the shortcomings of the development paradigm being followed.

However, such studies usually do not examine the impact on small producers and informal workers, in general, or on informal and self-employed women workers, in particular, as data on these subjects are not readily available. Furthermore, few studies have examined whether the affected countries have learned any lessons from the crisis, modified policies, or designed any special programs to ensure that such a crisis does not adversely affect the vulnerable sections and sectors of the economy again. This chapter intends to examine the impact of the global crisis (2008–09) on small producers and informal workers, including women workers. In addition, this chapter studies whether any lessons have been learned by the affected countries. The sector selected for the study is the diamond cutting and polishing industry, one of the most globalized industries in India.

The impact of the crisis is likely to be different on men than it is on women, for several reasons. First of all, men and women are placed differently in the labor market, with women having inferior and unstable status in almost all

* The author is thankful to UNDP New Delhi for funding her first study on the impact of the global crisis.

dimensions of employment. Because of their supply-side constraints and lower human capital, women have a lower work force participation rate, and they are usually overcrowded in low-productivity, low-wage activities. Additionally, they are, as compared to male workers, predominant as temporary and casual workers, largely employed in informal work, including home-based work that is usually scattered and unstable. Female workers also earn lower wages than male workers, due to occupational segregation and discrimination in the labor market. In short, with temporary and unstable work, women workers are likely to be laid off first in the event of crisis. Furthermore, due to poor access to regular jobs, women workers tend to take up self-employment, which offers several disadvantages. They have less access than men to credit (as they do not usually own assets), and in a severe credit crunch and crisis, their access to credit is almost nonexistent. Self-employed women also have poor access to skills, marketing, and other infrastructure support – and during crises, this access declines even further.

Second, women are likely to suffer as homemakers or as unpaid domestic workers. This is primarily due to the fact that when employment and incomes fall, a major coping strategy of cash-poor households is likely to be substituting market goods and services for homemade goods and services. For example, women who are likely to take care of the sick at home buy less food from outside the home, or produce goods at home when possible, rather than buying them from the market. This impact, however, tends to remain invisible, as no data are collected on this. No data are available, either, on women's taking up of work that is casual, scattered, or part-time.

This chapter presents the findings of a study on the impact of the global crisis on one of the most globalized sectors of the Indian economy, the diamond cutting and polishing industry. In order to gain a better understanding of the gender dimension of the impact, this chapter focuses on its effects on small producers and informal workers, as well as those on women workers and homemakers. The chapter also examines the status of the sector and its workers two years after the crisis to determine whether any lessons have been learned from the crisis. The chapter observes that policy-makers, who seem to focus on maximizing the rate of economic growth, tend to neglect the well-being of workers and, particularly, the well-being of women workers. As a result, if such a crisis occurs again, the same painful story may be repeated.

The chapter is divided into three sections: Section 2 presents the overall impact of the crisis on the Indian economy; Section 3 examines the impact of the crisis on the workers, small producers, and women in the diamond industry; and Section 4 studies the situation two years after the crisis, drawing some policy inferences.

2 The Indian economy and the crisis

The Indian economy has been on a high-growth path since the introduction of the economic reforms in 1991, and particularly since the mid-1990s. From 2002 to 2008, the period just before the global crisis, the economy grew at more than 8 percent per year. The Indian economy has also increasingly globalized since 1991. The total value of exports increased twenty-fold between 1991 and 2008. The export-to-GDP ratio also increased from 5.72 percent in 1990–91 to 13.58 percent in 2007–08. Although the capital account has not been opened up in India, over the same period, gross capital inflows and outflows exhibited a sharp rise (from 12 percent of GDP in 1990–91 to around 64 percent in 2007–08). In other words, the Indian economy grew rapidly, with the growth becoming increasingly dependent upon the globalization of the economy (Banerjee and Piketty 2003).

The rapid growth, however, has not been accompanied by a corresponding rise in employment. Additionally, about 92 percent of the work force is informal, almost entirely without any social protection.[1] Likewise, economic achievements in the field of poverty and social indicators have not been very impressive. According to official figures, the headcount ratio of poverty is 37.2 percent – 41.8 percent in rural areas and 25.7 percent in urban areas, and the rate of decline in poverty has not kept up with the high rate of growth in the economy, either (UNDP 2009a). Again, despite continuous efforts in the health and education sectors, India lags behind many other developing countries like Sri Lanka, Malaysia, and Bangladesh in human development. India's ranking on the Human Development Index (HDI), at 134, is much lower than that of several other Asian countries (UNDP 2009b). In short, the high proportion of the population below the poverty line, the slow growth of employment, and the high vulnerability of the majority of workers due to the informal nature of their employment have all resulted in relatively small increases in income for the majority of the poor, limiting the size of the domestic market. This has encouraged further globalization and increasing dependence on external markets.

Against this background of increasing dependence on the global market for economic growth coupled with high levels of vulnerability of the majority of the population, the 9 percent decline in world trade that followed the global financial turmoil (the biggest since World War II) had a highly adverse impact on globalized sectors of the Indian economy. The crisis led to the collapse in exports of major industries like textiles and garments, engineering goods, and diamond cutting and polishing, among others. This led to a crash in employment and workers' wages in these sectors, and adversely affected industrial growth as well as the overall growth of GDP. Indian exports declined by more than 14 percent between June 2008 and June 2009 (CMIE 2009).

Capital outflows from India, mainly of portfolio investment, made the Indian equity markets plunge by more than 50 percent in 2008, and they remained volatile for a very long period (Chhibber and Palanivel 2009; Kumar *et al.* 2009). These developments led to a severe liquidity crunch in the economy, with the small and informal sector suffering the most. The pressure on the exchange rate, coming from capital outflows, declining reserves of foreign exchange, and a decline in export earnings reduced the value of the Indian rupee. This depreciation of the Indian rupee raised the cost of imported raw materials and intermediary goods, which in turn increased the cost of production in the industries concerned. Although the prices of export goods declined in the global market, there was also an overall decline in global demand. In addition, the decline in the demand for tradable services, such as tourism, information technology services, and so on, led to a further decline in the growth rates of GDP and employment. As per the quarterly studies by the Labor Bureau (Ministry of Labor, Government of India), the Indian economy lost about 500,000 jobs between October and November 2008. Another 100,000 jobs were lost in January 2009 (Government of India 2009a, 2009b, 2009c).

The other channels through which the crisis was transmitted to India were the decline in public revenue (caused by a decline in export revenues, a decline in foreign direct investment and official development assistance, and an overall decline in the economy) and the fall in remittances. The overall growth rate was adversely affected for a relatively short period (between August 2008 and March 2009), which caused a decline in public expenditure on health and education, an increase in unemployment, and an increase in the number of poor people in the country (Gangopadhyay 2009; Government of India 2009a, 2009b).

3 Crisis in the diamond industry

Since the broad-brush picture revealed by the macroeconomic data did not acknowledge ground realities related to the impact of the crisis on small producers and informal workers who dominate the Indian economy, the United Nations Development Programme (UNDP) supported a quick survey (April–June 2009) in the major affected sectors in selected states in India (Hirway 2009a, 2009b). The sectors selected were the diamond industry, engineering, the auto-part industry, agriculture, the textile industry (Chikan craft[2]), and the home-based garment industry. This chapter discusses the diamond industry because it is the most globalized sector in the Indian economy.

3.1 The diamond industry in Gujarat

Diamond cutting and polishing started as a small industry in Surat in the 1960s, when some entrepreneurs belonging to the Patel community imported rough diamonds for polishing. The industry expanded gradually from the 1960s to the 1980s. However, after the introduction of the economic reforms in 1991, the industry took a great leap by taking advantage of the new environment.

The structure of the diamond industry is like a pyramid: at the top are a small number of large modern factories, each employing up to 4,000–5,000 workers; below them there are medium units employing up to 500 workers; and at the bottom are a large number of small units employing up to 50 workers. The large units are registered under the Factories Act, as they cannot export or import directly without the De Beers Trading Company Certificate, which is only accessible to registered units. The large units use the latest technologies, cut and polish top-end quality diamonds, and have sophisticated factory environments with full security arrangements. However, 60–70 percent of the workers in large units are temporary or contract workers. Large units also subcontract job work to smaller units, including units located in distant towns and villages. Small units, mostly unregistered, are usually engaged in job work, or sell their products to local traders, who in turn sell these to exporters. They do not normally use bank credit. These are normally family units that cut and polish low-quality diamonds and employ young men from their family, caste, or village, located in Saurashtra or North Gujarat. The medium-sized units are somewhere in between, and are primarily engaged in job work of a slightly higher quality.

There are no reliable data on the number of units and workers in the industry, as many of the units are unregistered and a large number of workers even in large units are not on any official records. Though the Gujarat High Court passed an order in 1998 asking all diamond units to register under the Factories Act (as even the smallest diamond units use power and employ ten or more workers), most units are not registered. The state government started a survey of the units before the crisis, but the units did not cooperate since they were unwilling to bear the burden of the obligations underlying the Factories Act (such as enforcement of labor laws and payment of taxes). Officially, there were 532 diamond factories in Gujarat in 2008, which employed 128,000 workers. The task force set up by the Reserve Bank of India (RBI, the Indian Central Bank), however, estimated that there were approximately 6,547 diamond units in the state employing 710,000 workers (RBI 2009). This was an underestimate because the survey did not cover all the regions. According to the Industry Associations, there were about 8,000 diamond units in the state, employing 800,000 to 1,000,000 workers (SDA 2010). Most of these workers are informal workers – employed in unregistered units or working as contract or casual workers in registered units.

Before the crisis, there were 2,500 diamond units in Surat according to the RBI task force (RBI 2009), while there were about 4,000 diamond units employing about 400,000 workers[3] according to industry leaders (Mehta 2010). Apart from providing direct employment, the industry supported a large number of workers indirectly in trading, hotels and restaurants, lodging and boarding, etc.[4]

3.2 Exports of polished diamonds and the crisis

Globally, the diamond industry is organized into a value chain, which includes a range of activities, such as exploration and mining, sorting, cutting and polishing, jewelry manufacturing, and retail. Exploration and mining of diamonds are done mainly in Africa, Australia, Canada, and Russia; diamonds are sorted by size, shape, color, and quality and sent for cutting and polishing through the certified Kimberly Process.[5] Cutting and polishing are labor-intensive processes, performed in countries where labor is cheap. India is thus a major destination for cutting and polishing activities. Jewelry manufacturing and retail, two high-value added processes accounting for more than 70 percent of the total value added, are performed in developed countries. Cutting and polishing, the lowest activities in the value chain, account for around 8 percent of the value added. India is at the low end of this value chain of the industry, which is dominated by large firms like De Beers, Al Rosa, Rio Tinto, Aber, etc. India is highly dependent on the global market, both for raw materials as well as for final sales.

Though India is no longer a major producer of diamonds, it is responsible for about 80 percent of the diamond cutting and polishing in the world. India imports raw diamonds and exports cut and polished diamonds. The average annual production of the diamond industry in India is around 78,000 carats (2005–07). Of this, about 80 to 85 percent is exported and between 15 and 20 percent is consumed at home (CMIE 2008). The export of finished diamonds increased dramatically after the adoption of the economic reforms in 1991, from US$7,511 million in 1999–2000 to US$19,667 million in 2007–08, indicating a CARG of 13 percent.

The share of diamonds in total commodity exports from India was 12.36 percent in 2007–08. About 25 percent of the diamonds were exported directly to the United States, 25 percent were exported to Hong Kong, 10 percent to Belgium, and the rest to Israel, Japan, and Thailand. Since many of these countries manufacture diamond jewelry that is then exported to the United States, the United States is a major buyer of diamonds, both directly and indirectly. The crisis in the United States therefore had a severe impact on the diamond industry.

Of the total cutting and polishing of diamonds in India, 80 percent is done in Gujarat, while diamond trading is done largely in Mumbai (Maharashtra), followed by Gujarat (Surat). Surat is the main center for diamond cutting and polishing, with about 80 percent of the cutting and polishing done in Gujarat. However, this work is also carried out in a number of towns and villages in Gujarat. This study, conducted in April and May 2009, was undertaken in Surat.

The global financial crisis impacted the diamond industry largely through declining demand in the US market and then in EU markets. This decline resulted in large-scale closure of diamond units. The second channel of transmission of the crisis was capital outflow from India, which resulted in a liquidity crisis and created a huge shortage of funds, particularly for the small units in the industry. The third channel was the depreciation of the rupee that raised the price of imported raw diamonds.

The crisis in the industry started in October and November 2008 with the fall in the demand for diamonds in the US market, which received – directly and indirectly – about 50 percent of India's exports. The crisis reduced demand by 75 percent, as many traders preferred to use up existing stocks. In December, about 20 percent, and by January 2009, 60 percent of factories closed down. Thereafter, imports of rough diamonds stopped, as stocks piled up. Furthermore, the depreciation of the Indian rupee made import of raw diamonds more expensive. The industry felt a severe liquidity crunch because the capital outflow had created a general shortage of credit, and banks were not enthusiastic about lending to the losing industry.

3.3 Approach of the study

This quick survey started with an analysis of the available secondary data and literature to understand the impact of the global crisis on the diamond industry. This also involved in-depth discussions with concerned industry leaders, producers, and exporters; concerned policy-makers and government officials; and prominent labor leaders. Surat, the most prominent diamond industry center with about 4,000 diamond units employing more than 400,000 workers was selected for an in-depth study.

Along with using participatory methods (such as focus group discussions), a sample survey was planned covering 127 workers and 34 small producers in Surat. Since almost half of the diamond workers from Surat had gone back to the villages in Saurashtra, a small sample of 34 workers was selected from the Bhavnagar district, the destination of many workers from Surat. The total sample, which covered 195 workers from Surat and Bhavnagar, was selected purposively on the basis of the typologies of workers and location of workers, with the result that it did provide a good understanding of the impact of the global crisis on the ground, particularly on workers and small producers. Two questionnaires were designed for the field survey: one for workers, and the other for producers or employers. Finally, a few case studies were done to understand the dynamics of the household-level impact of the crisis.

A quick review of the industry and workers in Surat was done two years after this survey (2011) when the crisis was long over. This was done (1) by analyzing the secondary data on the industry and labor, (2) through discussions with industry leaders from the Surat Diamond Association (SDA) and concerned government officers, and (3) by interviewing and holding focus group discussions in Surat with workers and producers who have resumed their work in the industry.

3.4 Major findings of the study

3.4.1 Profile of workers

About 80 workers in the industry are Patels and Jains, the two enterprising high castes, who are primarily responsible for setting up and developing the industry in Surat and in Gujarat. Many of them have migrated from Saurashtra[6] and North Gujarat.[7] The rest are also migrant workers from Gujarat and outside Gujarat, belonging to lower castes. The workers are relatively young, with an average age of 34, and most of them are school drop-outs after studying up to 4–9 standards. Some 62 percent of workers live in their own houses ("pucca" houses), while the rest live in rented houses, with an average rent of Rs 1,179 per month.

Female workers constitute less than 5 percent of the total workers in this male-dominated industry. This is because (1) most of the workers are migrant workers (from Saurashtra and other parts of Gujarat), who migrate all the way to Surat without family; (2) they live in groups in rented rooms and work long hours – which girls and women are not expected to do; and (3) diamond cutting and polishing is a skilled job that women are not expected to do. However, women are employed in groups in large-scale factories where there is a separate room for them, or in small villages where local girls are employed.

3.4.2 *Impact of the crisis on employment, wages, and incomes*

About 45 percent of workers lost their jobs immediately, although half of them managed to get some work in the industry at much lower wages. Of the rest, 30 percent remained unemployed, while the others managed to get some work outside the industry in the embroidery industry, casual unskilled work, petty trade, or petty services. Women workers, who constitute about 5 percent of the total diamond workers and have been largely employed in low-paid polishing activities, were the first to exit, as men were seen as "breadwinners" and therefore more important employees. About 80 percent of female workers lost their jobs.

On average, the monthly income of workers declined from Rs 5,896 before the crisis to Rs 3,135 after the crisis (excluding the unemployed), indicating a huge 48 percent decline. Almost half the workers earned less than Rs 3,000 a month. The workers who remained in the diamond industry also experienced a decline of about 48 percent in their daily wages, from Rs 195 before the crisis to Rs 102 after the crisis. Their monthly income declined by 40 percent, from Rs 5,846 to Rs 3,588 per month. This decline was due to the decline in the wage rates as well as the decline in employment. As against 95 percent of workers earning more than Rs 100 in daily wages before the crisis, only 62 percent of workers earned more than Rs 100 after the crisis. Again, about half the workers experienced a significant decline in their monthly employment and in hours of work, from 9.5 a day before the crisis to 5.2 hours a day after

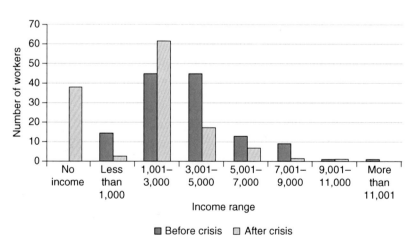

Figure 7.1 Monthly income of workers, before and after the crisis (source: Field survey, 2009).

the crisis. Before the crisis, 88 percent of workers worked for eight hours or more, while after the crisis only one-fourth of the workers were able to find work for eight hours a day.

3.4.3 Working conditions and employment status

Affected diamond workers also experienced poorer working conditions and lower employment status. Before the crisis, all workers enjoyed provisions such as clean drinking water and toilets, a weekly holiday, and an annual Diwali vacation. A few regular workers also received an annual bonus or provident fund. None received social security like the old age pension, gratuity, medical allowance, or maternity benefits.[8] After the crisis, however, the meager facilities at work also declined: weekly holidays and paid leave almost disappeared, and the other facilities were not available to the workers who shifted to smaller units or to petty services and small trading. With regard to employment status, there was an overall decline even within informal employment. The share of regular workers in total workers declined from 80 percent before the crisis to 14 percent after the crisis. That is, employment security declined significantly. Again, the share of casual workers increased from a mere 1 percent to 24 percent after the crisis, while the share of temporary workers increased from 12 to 20 percent. In short, the instability and uncertainty of employment increased after the crisis.

3.4.4 From skilled to unskilled work

All diamond workers are skilled in diamond cutting or polishing. They all acquired this skill on the job. However, when they lost their job, one-third of the skilled workers were forced to take up unskilled work. This was a loss to the economy, as the skills and experience acquired over the years could not be used.

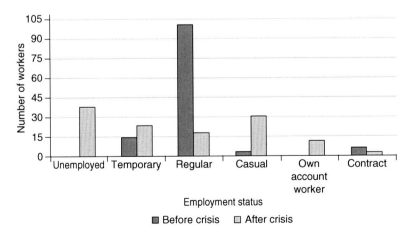

Figure 7.2 Employment statuses of workers, before and after the crisis.

3.5 How did diamond workers manage?

In the absence of any kind of social protection, workers expected support from the government, employers, industry associations, or nongovernmental organizations (NGOs) in protecting their level of consumption and in searching for alternative employment. However, only 25 percent of workers received some cash support, which was "far from adequate" (as reported by workers during the investigation). The governments, SDA, and some employers provided some support in cash, food grains, and education expenditure. Assistance in searching for alternative work was much lower. The government's support in training[9] was not suitable, and the support from NGOs was almost nonexistent. Only a few employers provided help in obtaining alternative work, mostly in the diamond industry, for about 11 percent of workers. In short, about 67 percent of workers were left to fend for themselves in protecting their levels of living, and 88 percent of workers had no support in searching for alternative employment. The affected diamond workers therefore used various strategies to manage.

3.5.1 Reduction in remittances

Reduction in remittances was one such strategy. Sending remittances to families back home is a very common practice in this industry. Before the crisis, about 38 percent of households sent an average monthly remittance of about Rs 1,585. After the crisis, however, only 16 percent of households could send remittances home, and the average amount of the remittance declined to Rs 842. This drastic reduction in remittances had a severe impact on the living standards of the households back home and on the local economies of the villages where the remittances were sent. We shall examine this while discussing the impact of the crisis in terms of return migration.

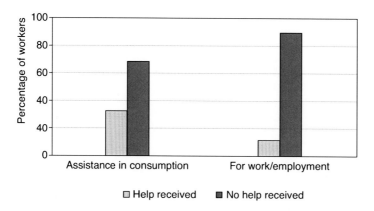

Figure 7.3 Help received from different sources (source: Field survey, 2009).

3.5.2 Dis-saving, mortgaging, and selling of assets

Dis-saving, mortgaging, and selling of assets was another strategy. Since diamond workers earn relatively good wages, many of them had savings of their own. More than half of the households used their savings to survive during the crisis – at least in the initial months. However, as the crisis continued, households started mortgaging (12 percent of households) and selling assets like gold, silver, houses, appliances, etc. (11 percent).

3.5.3 Borrowing

Borrowing from friends and relatives, from money lenders, and from banks (if possible) was another important coping strategy of some workers. The number of households borrowing for consumption more than doubled, from 20.01 percent before the crisis (used mainly for social functions or for major health problems) to 51.15 percent after the crisis. The main reasons for borrowing after the crisis were to meet day-to-day consumption needs (87.7 percent of households) and to meet health expenditures (13 percent of households), followed by education and social functions.

3.5.4 Reduction in consumption expenditure

Reduction in consumption expenditure, however, turned out to be a major coping strategy: in the absence of any adequate support coming from the government and other agencies, and due to the inadequacy of the other strategies, like mortgage and sale of assets and borrowing, the main option for the workers was to reduce their own consumption in different ways. All except 12 percent of households reduced their consumption, many of them as a precautionary measure against the uncertain future. The most important area of reduction was in food, with 88.18 percent households adopting this strategy. About half of the households stopped or reduced eating out, about 38 percent of households reduced or

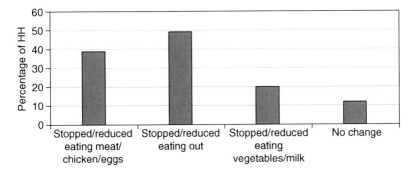

Figure 7.4 Reduction in food consumption (source: Field survey, 2009).

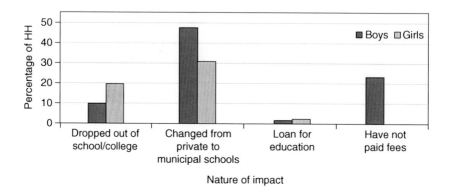

Figure 7.5 Reduction in expenditure on education (% of households) (source: Field survey, 2009).

stopped consuming expensive food items (such as meat, chicken, and eggs), and 20 percent of households reduced or stopped eating fruits and vegetables.

Another major reduction was seen in education expenditure by (1) withdrawing children from school or college, (2) not paying school fees (as long as the schools tolerated nonpayment), (3) shifting children to municipal schools from private schools, and (4) cutting down on expenditure on books and other school items. About one-fifth of the households withdrew children, particularly girls, from school. More than half of the households shifted their children to cheaper municipal schools to avoid paying fees, and about one-fifth of the households did not pay the fees in the hope that the government would provide some financial support to them. In all of about 84 percent of cases, households chose to reduce their expenditure on education to make ends meet. This is indeed a matter of concern, as it would affect the future generation of the workers.

In the case of expenditure on health, households went for medical help only in the case of emergency, and tried to manage with home-based treatments as much as possible. About 66 percent of households reported reduction in health-related expenditures. With regard to other expenditures, a major reduction was in house rent: more than two-thirds of households could not pay rent on time.

3.5.5 Increased participation in the labor market

Another major strategy was to increase participation in the labor market. Several non-workers entered the labor market: 7.22 percent of students, 12.22 percent of non-working housewives, and 10.56 percent of retired persons joined the work force to help their households. Many of them took up low-paying jobs or self-employment in small and petty trade and services. Some of the working persons (from 17 percent of households) started putting in longer hours in the labor market.

I need credit!

Rajesh Singh (aged 32), born and brought up in the Motihari village of Bihar, had migrated to Surat in 2001 after the earthquake. He is staying in Surat with his wife (aged 30) and three children, who are studying in an English-medium school. Earlier, Rajesh was settled in Mumbai, where he used to work as a sweet-maker. He was inspired by his brother who works in a diamond unit in Surat and decided to move out from Mumbai. He received training from his brother, but the stipend was not sufficient to support his family. So he shared one house with his brother. Before the crisis, Rajesh used to earn Rs 8,000–9,000 per month, which has fallen to Rs 5,000–6,000 per month after the crisis. Due to his low income, he took a loan of Rs 25,000 from his friend for the education of his children. Before the crisis, he sent a fixed amount of Rs 2,000 to his parents, but now he cannot, and that pains him. He does not want to compromise on food even during the crisis. He prefers to cut down his other expenses: for example, he comes to the unit by bicycle instead of by auto rickshaw. He will never allow his wife to work outside the home.

3.6 Women as shock absorbers

Women were the worst affected and the main shock absorbers: they increased their participation in the labor market in several ways. About 17 percent of households reported that "non-working" housewives entered the labor market to take up whatever work was available. Another 17 percent of households reported more labor market work for women, i.e., longer working hours. Most of these workers took up low-productivity, low-wage work such as construction work, vegetable vending, embroidery, and tailoring. The average monthly earning in these activities was less than Rs 2,000 and the work involved 8–10 hours a day.

More than one-fourth of the households reported increased domestic unpaid work of women. This was because (1) eating out as well as buying food from outside the home declined or stopped in many households, (2) hired domestic help was removed in many cases, (3) women took care of the sick in the family, (4) unemployed men spent more time at home and needed more looking after by women, and (5) women tried to replace market goods, such as clothing and food, with homemade goods. It has been reported by the households with increased domestic work that the average hours of housework increased by 2–3 hours per day.

In addition, women also suffered from increased tension, conflicts, and domestic violence. Several women in focus group discussions reported increased tension and violence. Reduced income at home, uncertainty about the future, and reduced prospects for children gave rise to conflicts and tensions. Men's increasing expenditure on addictions, particularly on liquor, added to the level of conflict and violence. One-fourth of the households reported increased domestic tension and violence and almost half of the households reported increases in drinking and smoking, mainly by men.

The inability to access any reliable support and the struggle to make ends meet in an uncertain environment adversely impacted the family life of the workers, increasing tension, conflicts, and violence. More than 50 cases of suicides of diamond workers were reported in Surat city during the six months immediately after the crisis. Some 20 percent of households from our sample reported suicides of diamond workers around them. Overall, more than half of the households reported increased tension and conflicts.

Too much work!

Revaben was a housewife before the crisis. Her husband, Dalpatbhai, was working in a diamond factory, earning Rs 9,000 per month. After the crisis, however, he earned only Rs 4,000. The family came to Surat from a village in the Bhavnagar district about nine years ago. They have three children, two boys (aged 12 and 10) and one daughter (aged 5). Revaben started vegetable vending after the crisis. Dalpatbhai goes to the wholesale market at 5 a.m. to buy vegetables and then goes to work at 10 a.m. for four hours. Revaben also gets up at 5 a.m. and after finishing all household work (cooking, cleaning, washing, and sending children to school), she goes to sell vegetables at about 8:30 a.m. and comes back by 3:30 p.m. After this she does the remaining household work, she cooks for the evening and gets to sleep after 11 p.m. She earns between Rs 2,500 to 3,000 per month. Her day is very long and she sleeps for only about six hours! She hopes that soon these days will pass. However, she does not want to leave her vegetable vending – though it is a tough job – even after the crisis is over, as the family has borrowed Rs 50,000 from a relative to meet the crisis.

3.7 Return migration of workers

As seen earlier, a large number of youths, most of them school drop-outs from towns and villages in Saurashtra and North Gujarat, go to Surat and to other cities for diamond cutting and polishing. As was estimated by industry leaders, about half of the workers who lost jobs (about 200,000 workers) went back to their native places after the crisis. This is because Surat is expensive, while workers' native villages were cheap. We traced these workers back to their villages (in the Bhavnagar district, which received a large number of returned migrants) in order to study their status.

We selected Piprola village (Umrala block), Tarsara village (Talaka block), and Tarsaniya village (Talala block), as well as Gogha, a small town of Bhavnagar district, for an in-depth study. All of these villages and towns sent 35–40 percent of their youth to Surat for diamond cutting and polishing. Our study showed that half of them came back after the crisis in Surat.

3.8 Depression in the village and local economies

The RBI task force has estimated that about 60,000 diamond workers in Bhavnagar city were made unemployed after the crisis (RBI 2009). Many of them went back to their native villages in the district. In addition, about 30,000 workers from Surat also went back to their villages in Bhavnagar. These workers caused a severe depression in the local economies, particularly in the villages where out-migration was large. The huge decline in the remittances to these villages resulted in closure of local tea and paan shops, and reduced business of local shops. As a shopkeeper pointed out, "There are not enough customers now." This depression was also observed in the town of Ghogha, where a number of restaurants closed down in the affected pockets. The pressure of the diamond workers was also felt on the prevailing wage rates: it was noticed that the mason's wage rate declined from Rs 200–250 per day before the crisis to Rs 100–150 after the crisis; the agricultural wage rate declined from Rs 80–100 to Rs 60–80; the wage rate at the Alang Ship Breaking Yard also declined from Rs 200–250 to Rs 100–150; and the overall unskilled wage rate declined from Rs 80–100 to Rs 60 or so. In short, affected pockets with return migration were badly hit by the crisis.

These boys had left their village for Surat because there were limited employment opportunities in these villages where rain-fed agriculture was the main economic activity. That is, they left the villages to escape the lack of work and poverty that existed a few years before. However, after enjoying the good life for a few years, they had to come back to the same situation. Since they did not want to take up the unskilled manual work at low wages that was now available to them, they did not fit well into the labor market and were depressed and frustrated. One-third of them remained unemployed, waiting for better days. Of the rest, 9 percent worked in agriculture, 36 percent worked as manual workers in construction and related work around their village, and the rest took up petty services (such as a driving jobs). A few of them started their own petty businesses (selling vegetables, starting tea shops, etc.) and petty services (working as a helper to a driver, as an office boy, etc.). Except for the four workers in Ghogha who got work in a diamond factory, all the workers took up work outside the diamond sector. The wages and incomes of these workers declined drastically. The average wage rate of the returned migrants declined by 70 percent from Rs 244.70 per day to Rs 75 per day. The low wage rates accompanied by low employment reduced their incomes from Rs 5,642 to Rs 806 – a decline of 85 percent. Average working hours remained more or less constant for the workers after the crisis, as manual work in agriculture and outside agriculture requires long hours.

Overburdened with worries and frustration!

Mukhadbhai, living in Piprali Village in Bhavnagar, worked as a diamond polisher in Surat for the last nine years. He was a daily wager and was working almost ten hours a day. His monthly income was Rs 5,000. Having one child and a wife, he is the only earning member in his family.

In October 2008, he lost his job because of the recession. Since he did not get any suitable work in Surat due to his lack of skills in other fields, such as embroidery, he found it difficult to live in Surat. Ultimately, he decided to return to his home. He now works for about 15–16 days a month as a wood cutter and earns Rs 60 per day. The rest of the time, he just thinks of his uncertain future. He somehow manages Rs 1,000 from this work, but is unable to pay tuition fees and other education-related expenses for his son. He just does not know how to manage with this small income.

Having no alternatives, he has taken a loan of Rs 50,000 from a bank at an interest rate of 5 percent. Like other diamond workers, Mukhadbhai has not received any help from the government or from any other organization. His only hope is for the revival of the diamond industry.

As a coping strategy, these workers reduced their consumption levels drastically. They reduced food consumption, in spite of food being cheap in the villages. They stopped eating out and reduced consumption of milk and fruits as well as of eggs and chicken. A few households (11.76 percent) even reported a reduction in the number of meals from three to two per day, by skipping breakfast.

Another adverse impact was on the education of the workers' children. All children were put into free government schools, which are considered inferior schools in Surat. About 10 percent of households stopped sending their children to schools. They used fewer medical services and tried to manage with home-based medicines. Health expenditure declined, also, due to poor health infrastructures in the villages. The households of returned migrants increased their participation in the labor market: about 50 percent of housewives and 20 percent of students joined the labor market, mainly in unskilled farm work. Some women joined home-based work like embroidery, incense stick making, domestic help, and collection of free goods such as wood, leaves, and fruits for sale. In short, one observes a deterioration of employment in terms of employment status, skill level of work, and wages and incomes. Here women also bore the major brunt of the crisis.

Women earned Rs 25 a day making incense sticks, Rs 70 helping male masons, Rs 50 in domestic work, and Rs 50–60 in agriculture. The work involves hard labor and long hours. Men earned higher wages, mainly because women worked as their assistants. In masonry work, for example, men lay bricks and earn Rs 100–150 per day, while women, who invariably work as helpers, earn Rs 70–75 per day. Again, as in Surat, women's unpaid domestic work increased significantly. One-third of households reported such an increase. The shortage of cash to buy things from the market seems to be an important cause of this.

One expected these workers to take advantage of the National Rural Employment Guarantee Act (NREGA)[10] as an alternate form of employment. However, in all the villages we visited, there was evidence neither of diamond workers using NREGA nor of NREGA being implemented in these villages. Our discussions with the Village Panchayat and other officials revealed that there were no serious attempts made to implement this program in these villages. Our study has also shown that these workers have received hardly any assistance from the other government programs or other government departments. In fact, they are left to fend for themselves.

3.9 Small producers

As seen earlier, the diamond industry has a pyramid type of structure, where small producers predominate. They are usually engaged in job work, though some of them do sell their products to traders or exporters. Small units predominate mainly because it is easy to enter this industry than to undertake job work. Small units employ the labor of friends and relatives or young men from their villages who do not usually demand higher wages and higher benefits. Almost all small units are unregistered units, as they do not see any advantage in registering under the Factories Act.

As mentioned earlier, a sample consisting of 34 small producers was selected from four major centers of the city, namely, Varachha, Katargam, Punagam, and Mehdalpura. Smaller units have been the worst sufferers of the crisis for several reasons: (1) their survival depends on job work – and the moment it stops, they have no option but to close down; (2) they have limited access to credit for survival; (3) they deal with low-quality diamonds, the demand for which declined much more than the demand for high-quality diamonds; and (4) since they do not import raw diamonds directly or export finished diamonds directly, the burden of the crisis is frequently passed on to them by big traders and exporters. As the president of the SDA pointed out, more than 60 percent of the small units closed down under the crisis and the rest of the units reduced their business drastically. Those who continued with diamond cutting and polishing could not do so for long, due to the severe shortage of rough diamonds. Of the rest of the units, those who could start embroidery units (30 percent) did well. The rest of them either took up hired wage work outside the diamond industry or started self-employed ventures.

The non-viability of small entrepreneurs is frequently seen as a major problem in the Indian economy. The crisis reinforced their vulnerability within the diamond industry since small producers were the worst-affected group of producers. About 10 to 50 percent of small producers and self-employed individuals (those with a small number of hired workers) closed down after the crisis. The owners of the closed enterprises, on average, (1) took up petty trade or petty services (15 percent), (2) started a new enterprise in a new and similar sector (15 percent), or (3) started working as hired laborers for others. The majority of small enterprises (about 60 percent) experienced lower employment, lower incomes, and more insecurity. The crisis highlighted some of the structural weaknesses in this sector, as discussed below.

It is observed that although small enterprises contribute more than 30 percent of national exports and provide large-scale employment, their share of institutional credit is between 2 and 4.3 percent (Government of India 2008). The efforts made by the government to help them over the years have not been effective. In the case of small diamond units, the liquidity crunch under the crisis almost dried up their access to credit. Even after the recommendations made by the RBI task force to lend to this sector, and particularly to small units, access of the units to credit remained miserably poor (RBI 2009). High and fluctuating prices of raw materials were another major problem for these enterprises. Such prices reduced their regular access to these goods and made it difficult for them to survive. The depreciation of the rupee during the crisis raised the prices of imported raw materials and intermediary goods, making it more difficult for these units to manage. Low technology and low productivity were additional constraints for these units. In spite of the decline in the global demand for exports, there was still some demand for high-value-added quality products in the global market. However, this demand could not be met by small enterprises due to their low-value-added goods. And finally, small units did not receive the kind of infrastructural support that was accessible to medium and large units.

To sum up, small diamond units that did not close down were not confident about their future. They did not know how long they would survive. Those who could shift to embroidery were better off, as they also sell in the domestic market. However, those engaged in petty, low-productivity, low-earning activities, were not in a good shape.

3.10 Implications and inferences

This study has shown that the highly competitive, uncertain global market for polished diamonds can cause huge suffering to poorly protected workers and poorly supported small producers functioning at the lowest end of the global value chain. The global crisis impacted all dimensions of diamond workers' employment, reducing their incomes by almost half. Their coping strategies adversely affected not only their levels of living but also their children's education. The conditions for the returned migrants were even worse. Being thrown back to the place they had left to escape poverty and unemployment a few years before was both depressing and frustrating for them.

Women have emerged as the main shock absorbers of the crisis. Women have suffered as wage earners, as self-employed individuals, and as homemakers. However, no data are available on the impacts of the crisis, and no policy has been designed to bail women out of the crisis. The crisis has laid bare a number of weak points of our policies and efforts, particularly of the trade and industrial policy. One can say that the crisis gave the country an opportunity to make radical changes in these major policies. In light of the above, our study made the following recommendations.

3.10.1 Universal social protection for workers

There is an urgent need to design and institutionalize a package of universal social security consisting of some minimum critical social protection to all the workers in the economy. Such a package should include unemployment insurance, health insurance, old age pension, maternity benefits, and compensation against injury, disability, or death. Although the National Commission for Enterprises in the Unorganized Sector (NCEUS) had designed a comprehensive bill including such elements for India, only a highly watered-down version was accepted by the Indian government.[11]

3.10.2 Ensuring employment services for workers

The study has shown that there is a need to institutionalize assistance and support for skilled workers in the competitive market to facilitate their movement from one (skilled) job to another (skilled) job. This requires well-organized employment services that include labor market information services, counseling of workers on the availability of work, and training and retraining of workers.

3.10.3 Ensuring food, health, and education for all

The adverse impact of the crisis on the workers and small producers could have been avoided if critical gaps in social goods, including health, education, and skills, were closed for all. It is recommended that a special fund be created, preferably through welfare boards, to provide soft loans with subsidies to workers to take care of their educational and health-related needs.

3.10.4 Addressing problems of small producers and micro enterprises

In order to ensure access of small producers to credit, we recommend (1) including them in priority sector lending, (2) reducing the rate of interest on their credit, (3) relaxing the process of debt recovery from them, (4) providing export credit, (5) strengthening micro credit to help them to run their businesses, and (6) providing soft loans to tide them over through times of crisis as well as to help them to remain in business. It is highly desirable that special bailout packages are designed for these enterprises in times of crisis.

3.10.5 Improving the database on workers and producers

There is an urgent need to register all diamond factories and their workers, as this was one of the serious problems in estimating the need for support to small producers and workers in the industry. Strong action is needed from the government here.

3.10.6 Strengthening NREGA to help returned migrants

Effective implementation of NREGA could have helped returned migrants by providing them work at minimum wages (which is much higher than market wages). This would have prevented depression of the local wages, built productive assets, and raised effective demand in the local economy. An employment guarantee scheme deserves special focus in such a time of crisis. One can also recommend an urban employment guarantee program to prevent painful disloca- tion of workers in the event of a crisis.

3.10.7 Bailout package for women

This study has shown that women are the worst sufferers of the crisis. However, there is a clear male "breadwinner" bias on the part of the employers (since women are the first ones to lose jobs) as well as the government (which does not address women's employment specifically). And though women provide a "safety net" or become "shock absorbers" by taking on the burden of paid and unpaid work, there are no policies that address their concerns; there is no bailout package for women.

There is a need to address all three aspects of women's problems in a focused manner through designing a special package for female producers, female wage earners, and unpaid female workers. Focused efforts should be made to support female producers by addressing their specific needs, female wage earners (and also male wage earners) should be provided decent work conditions, and suitable infrastructure and services should be ensured to reduce their unpaid work. The crisis should be seen as an opportunity to take some important steps in promot- ing gender equality in the economy.

The study raises serious questions about the validity of the growth path the country has chosen, particularly with regard to treating exports as a major growth engine. This study questions the advantages of globalizing at the lowest end of the value chain, where the work is labor-intensive and the employment gain is positive but the quality of employment is very poor, and the control or the decision-making power is in the hands of global production networks located in developed countries. By treating exports as a goal in itself, rather than as a means to increase quality employment and well-being of workers, real develop- mental goals are kept outside the purview of globalization-related policies.

Expansion of decent employment with minimum wages and social protection is a macroeconomic strategy that can raise the purchasing power of labor and promote wage-led labor-intensive growth in the economy. It can also expand the domestic market, reducing the vulnerability of the economy to the volatility of the global market.

4 Two years after the crisis

4.1 Diamond industry sparkling after the crisis

An important development in the diamond industry after the crisis is that it has been on a high-growth path. After the crisis period of about ten months (September 2008–July 2009), the conditions started improving and the industry is now sparkling again.

The exports from the industry stagnated until the end of 2009, but they picked up rapidly thereafter. It showed an unprecedented growth of 60 percent in

2010–11, and higher growth thereafter (CMIE 2011). According to the secondary data and the industry leaders, there are several reasons for this reversal. The first reason is that the world markets have improved and the demand for diamonds in the main export destination countries (United States, EU member states, Canada, and Japan) has revived to a considerable extent. Second, this industry has accessed new markets in China, Indonesia, Thailand, Vietnam, and other East Asian countries. The share of these new markets has almost doubled for Indian diamond exports. Third, the prices of gold and silver have increased phenomenally in the global market, while the prices of diamonds have remained relatively stable. Diamonds have therefore become relatively cheap, expanding the global markets for diamonds. And finally, the domestic market for diamonds has expanded within India, as the rich and upper-middle classes have grown.

From the industry perspective, industry leaders have learned some lessons from the crisis and changed their strategy accordingly (Mehta 2010; SDA 2010): (1) to develop new markets outside the United States and the European Union to reduce risk (the industry has expanded markets in China and other East Asian countries); (2) to reduce the dependence on credit, and use cash as much as possible to maintain liquidity; (3) to not overproduce, creating a glut situation, but rather to regulate production; (4) to maintain high levels of liquidity, and remain cash-rich to fight any unforeseen conditions; and (5) to not become too pessimistic, as the industry is resilient. As the president of the SDA pointed out, "we over-reacted and panicked too much" and forgot that "diamonds are forever" (President, during the discussion in 2010).

In addition, two favorable developments have taken place in the industry. First, efforts have begun to move up the value chain by setting up Diamond Park and Diamond Borges for manufacturing high-value-added jewelry (Indian Diamond Institute 2009–10); and efforts have been made to tap the domestic market for diamonds. The Indian diamond industry is now trying to develop its jewelry industry. It has developed a few brands like "Ananta" and "Sparkle" to sell in the global and domestic markets. The state government in Gujarat has set up a Gems and Jewelry Park near Surat for promoting the manufacturing and export of jewelry. The diamond industry has also become more professional (mainly in the large units) and has started polishing big diamonds and producing high-value products. The leaders of the industry want to move away from the "family business" stamp and set up professional units. In short, the industry is growing and trying to make advancements. As pointed out by a senior officer of the Gems and Jewelry Export Promotion Council, "this is the golden period of the industry" (IDI 2009–10; Mehta 2010).

4.2 Workers, small producers, and women

An important question now is whether the bright performance in the post-crisis period has helped small producers and workers, including female workers and homemakers. Do they share the benefits of this unprecedented growth? Are they now secured against crisis or against fluctuations in the industry?

4.2.1 Registration under the factories act and enforcement of labor laws

One major problem during the crisis was that there were no proper records of workers to identify and assist them. It is important, therefore, to register all diamond units under the Factories Act as is legally required, and to record all workers as workers of these factories. However, the Department of Factories under the government of Gujarat has failed to register them under the Act. There were 532 diamond units registered under this Act before the crisis (2008); the number increased to 555 in 2010, an increase of only 23 units, whereas the total number of units in the state is estimated to be more than 8,000. In the case of Surat, the city worst affected by the crisis, the number increased from 453 in 2008 to 475 in 2010 (Government of Gujarat, Office of Factories 2010). Neither the units nor the workers are registered.

There are several reasons for this. The units as well as the industry associations are unwilling to get registered under the Act, as (1) they think that the Act puts too much responsibility (of ensuring basic working conditions and social protection) on them that they cannot bear, (2) they also feel that the regulations will bring with them harassment and corruption from government officers, and (3) they argue that since workers in the industry are mobile and do not stay in one unit for long, workers do not want any protection. The government is not much interested in enforcing the Act, as the industry is adding to the GDP in the state and also to the state revenue. There is no reason to disrupt the industry.

Again, the labor department is ill-equipped to enforce the Factories Act, as it has no staff to conduct inspections,[12] and the staff is not encouraged to impose fines or to fight cases against the violators of the Act. The powerful lobby of the industry frequently does not allow official inspections. In the Surat Division, there are only six officers (for all industries) against the sanctioned posts of 19 and the requirement of many more. In addition, as pointed out by a senior officer in Surat, there is political pressure that does not allow them to take any strict actions for registration. In short, registering diamond units under the Factories Act is not even a distant dream of the department.

However, the workers are now very keen to have unemployment insurance, pension or provident funds, and other social protections, as they do not want to go through the same "nightmare" again. The SDA has recently initiated a scheme under which identity cards are issued to diamond workers in Surat city so that in times of crisis workers can be contacted and helped. The state government has also initiated such a scheme. However, it is not progressing well, as employers do not want their workers to acquire the card because doing so will reveal that the workers are employed by them. There does not seem to be any solution to this problem and it seems to be difficult to bring diamond workers within the purview of labor laws and social protection. In short, there is a deadlock here, and there is no serious thinking about breaking this deadlock, as the status quo is good for the industry and good for the government.

4.2.2 Terms and conditions of employment in the post-crisis phase

It is argued by the industry as well as by the labor department that workers do not want social protections like provident funds, gratuities, bonuses, insurance, or others because they are mobile and move from unit to unit. It is also argued that these semiliterate workers do not understand their long-term interests in having social protections and welfare schemes. As we saw above, this is not the reality. However, the workers do not have the bargaining strength to demand these benefits. The prospects of receiving these benefits are poor. In large units also, except for a small core staff, no workers are entitled to social protections.

During our 12–15 focus group discussions in the different industrial centers of the city, we found that not all workers have returned to this industry because the experience has been too painful for some. These workers do not want to resume work in an industry that depends so much on the volatile global market. About one-fourth of the workers who lost their jobs in the industry have joined other industries, such as the embroidery or power loom industry. As a result, the thriving industry is suffering from a severe shortage of workers.

The wage rate in the industry has increased by 15 percent from the pre-crisis wage rate. However, the daily working hours have increased to 9–10 hours. Also, if one considers the price rise, there is a decline of about 10 percent in the real wage rate. It is interesting to note that workers as well as employers agree that if a crisis returns, workers will have to repeat the same painful experience. Employers argue, however, that a future crisis will be less severe, as they have diversified their markets to larger areas.

4.2.3 Conditions of small producers

Is the growth in the post-crisis period beneficial to small producers? The basic problem with small producers is that they work on cash and borrow funds from private sources, as they do not have a legal existence as production units. They do not go to banks for credit. They also cannot access benefits from the different government schemes or from District Industrial Centers, as they are not registered as factories. In other words, the basic problems of small producers more or less remain the same.

However, they have been able to expand their businesses, have taken up job work from thriving large producers, and when on their own, have sold their products to large traders. The diamond streets of Surat are now crowded and noisy with hundreds of units working overtime in the thriving industry.

To sum up, the industry is improving, but it contains the same structure. The future can change only if (1) the units are given a legal existence and (2) workers are recognized as workers in the industry. Both of these seem to be difficult to accomplish at this stage.

4.2.4 *Women workers and women of workers' households*

Have women workers and women of workers' households experienced any positive changes? Are they better protected if a crisis occurs again? Unfortunately, the answer is in the negative. No serious efforts have been made to change the terms and conditions of employment of women workers in this industry or in other industries. Although scattered social security schemes for informal workers are still implemented halfheartedly, no significant impact has been observed on the ground. Neither has any serious effort been made by the state government to address the burden of unpaid work on women, except for a few scattered schemes enforced in an indifferent manner. Policy-makers are happy that growth has picked up and the industry is thriving.

4.3 *Some serious concerns*

In concluding this chapter, it is important to note two aspects of growth in this industry. The first is the prevalence of massive black money and the second is the danger of blood diamonds entering the industry.

This industry is known for withholding its earnings from declarations of income in order to avoid taxation of it, in addition to avoiding customs and sales taxation. Poor record keeping of units and workers also aids the industry in doing so. According to a recent statement by the Director General of the Income Tax Department (Investigations), Mr. B.P. Gaur, the diamond industry contains the most corrupt economic activities in the country (as quoted in *Times of India* 2011). This is because, as he reported, the industry hides information at every stage – on the value of rough diamonds and other raw materials, on the cutting and polishing of diamonds, the value of output and exports, profits earned, workers hired, and wages paid. The Director General stated that there is a huge gap between what they report and the ground reality.

The second major concern is regarding "blood diamonds," or conflict diamonds, which refer to diamonds mined in a war zone and sold to finance insurgencies, war lords, and terrorism. India is one of the founding members of the Kimberly Process Certification Scheme (KPCS), which prevents the trading of blood diamonds. Since a huge rise in the demand for rough diamonds in the industry has made them more expensive, blood diamonds (which are 30 percent cheaper) are more attractive to buyers. Recently, two traders from Surat were caught dealing in blood diamonds worth Rs 101.7 million. According to De Beers, the share of blood diamonds is 4 percent in world trade, while according to some other experts, it is 15 percent (*Times of India* 2011). If not eradicated at its roots, this behavior can harm the future of this industry in India.

Finally, it is important to determine whether the Indian government has made any serious progress in ensuring social protections for informal workers who constitute 92 percent of the total work force, or whether it has at least covered export workers under social protections when these sectors are making huge profits by selling their products at global prices. The answers to these questions are not very encouraging. The NCEUS has drafted two important bills: the first is for comprehensive coverage of informal workers under a minimum level of social protection, and the second is to ensure decent working conditions for informal workers in the country. While the first bill has been watered down and includes only minimal health insurance, the other bill has been rejected by the government. The need to protect workers by appropriate social security measures has not yet been realized by policy-makers. Women, both workers and homemakers, also have not received adequate attention from policy-makers, either in terms of collection of relevant statistics or in terms of effectively addressing their constraints.

It appears that the policy-makers have not learned many lessons from the crisis as far as labor and women are concerned. If a crisis occurs again, workers will go through the same painful experiences.

Notes

1 According to the National Commission on Enterprises in Unorganized Sectors (NCEUS), about 46 percent of the workers in formal sectors are also employed in informal contracts (Government of India 2007).
2 Chikan craft, an important handicraft, is a fine art in which embroidery is done with white untwisted yarn on a fine cloth (viol, silk, cambric, georgette, terry cotton, and so on). This is mainly a home-based industrial activity, largely performed by female artisans and workers.
3 The Surat Diamond Association (SDA), the local industry association, had only 1,854 members in 2007–08.
4 The Patel community has acquired a high social and political status not only in Surat, but also in Gujarat. The industry associations and industry leaders of Surat have also contributed generously during various crises and disasters in the state.
5 The Kimberly Process was created by diamond exporting and importing countries in 2002, at Kimberly, to provide a global regulatory framework certifying that there has not been any human rights abuse in the process of mining the particular diamonds and that the diamonds do not come from a conflict zone.
6 Some 70 percent of workers are from Bhavnagar and Amreli districts, 13 percent from Juangadh, 6 percent from Rajkot, and the rest are from other districts of Gujarat.
7 It is claimed that there are no employer–employee conflicts in the industry because of this "family" environment. The wage rates are determined by the Diamond Associations in consultation with producers and employers. However, in July 2008, workers in the industry went on strike when the 20 percent increase in the salary, recommended by the SDA, was not implemented. Though the employers accepted the demand, not all of them implemented it. (There has been no increase in the salary of these workers for the past ten years).
8 It was argued by employers and industry leaders that workers do not want any provident fund and are happy with their relatively high salaries. The workers also reported that they do not want any provident fund because, as non-permanent workers, they find it difficult to claim it after they leave the job.
9 On the recommendation of the RBI Taskforce, the state government started a training program to train the diamond workers in other trades. However, as we will see later in the chapter, this did not work well.
10 The Government of India passed the NREGA in 2005, under which all rural households are guaranteed employment of 100 days at the legal minimum wage rate within 15 days of the demand.

11 The NCEUS has drafted two important bills: (1) for comprehensive coverage of informal workers under a minimum package of social protection and (2) for ensuring decent working conditions of informal workers in the country. While the first bill has been watered down and includes only health insurance, the other bill has been rejected by the government.
12 There are only 59 officers with the Factories Department in the state against the need for 232 labor officers.

References

Banerjee, Abhijit and T. Piketty (2003) "Top Indian incomes, 1956–2000," Working Paper 03-32, MIT Department of Economics, Boston, MA: Massachusetts Institute of Technology.

Chhibber, Ajay and Palanivel, T. (2009) "The impact of the global financial and economic crisis in India: challenges and policy responses," mimeo, New Delhi: United Nations Development Programme (UNDP).

CMIE (2011) *Foreign Trade Statistics for Monitoring Indian Economy*, report, Mumbai: Centre for Monitoring Indian Economy.

CMIE (2009) *Foreign Trade and Balance of Payments*, Mumbai: Centre for Monitoring Indian Economy.

CMIE (2008) *Monthly Reports, June 2008–July 2009*, Economic Intelligence Services, Mumbai: Centre for Monitoring Indian Economy.

Gangopadhyay, S. (2009) "Impact on slowdown on Indian economy," paper presented at Joint Panel Discussion on Impact of Global Crisis in South Asia, July 2, New Delhi: UNDP.

Government of Gujarat, Office of Factories (2010) *Annual Report*, Ahmedabad.

Government of India (2007) *Promotion of Livelihoods in the Unorganized Sector*, New Delhi: National Commission for Enterprises in the Unorganized Sector.

Government of India (2008) *Report on Definition and Statistical Issues Related to Informal Economy*, New Delhi: National Commission for Enterprises in the Unorganized Sector.

Government of India (2009a) *Economic Survey 2008–09*, New Delhi: Oxford University Press.

Government of India (2009b) *Labour Bureau Report on Effect of Economic Slowdown on Employment in India*, January–March, Shimla: Labour Bureau.

Government of India (2009c) *The Global Economic Crisis and the Informal Economy in India: need for urgent measures and fiscal stimulus to protect the informal economy*, New Delhi: National Commission for Enterprises in the Unorganized Sector.

Hirway I. (2009a) "Global economic crisis: impact on the poor in India: a synthesis of sector studies," in *Lasting Solutions for Development Challenges*, New Delhi: UNDP.

Hirway I. (2009b) "Losing the sparkle: impact of the global crisis on the diamond cutting and polishing industry, in India," in *Lasting Solutions for Development Challenges*, New Delhi: UNDP.

Indian Diamond Institute (2009–10) Ministry of Commerce, Government of India, New Delhi.

Kumar, R., Debroy, B., Ghosh, J., Mahajan, V., Prabhu, K.S. (2009) "Global financial crisis: impact on India's poor – some initial perspectives," in *Lasting Solutions for Development Challenges*, New Delhi: UNDP.

Mehta, R. (2010) "Lessons from the global crisis," *Quarterly Bulletin of Surat Diamond Association*, December.

RBI (2009) "Report of the task force for diamond sector," Ahmedabad: Reserve Bank of India.

SDA (2010) *Annual Report for 2007–08*, Surat: Surat Diamond Association.

UNDP (2009a) *Global Economic Crisis – Impact on the Poor in India: a synthesis of sector papers*, New Delhi: UNDP.

UNDP (2009b) "Global economic crisis: response of the international community," *India Quarterly: A Journal of International Affairs*, New Delhi.

8 The economic crisis of 2008 and the added worker effect in transition countries

*Tamar Khitarishvili**

1 Introduction

The recent financial crisis pushed the economies of Central and Eastern Europe and former Soviet Union (CEE/FSU) into a sudden recession, the worst region-wide experience since the "transitional recession" of the early 1990s.[1] The contraction in the economic activity was to a large extent an outcome of the export-led growth strategy and to a lesser degree an outcome of the dependence on foreign capital. These factors fueled the brisk regional output growth during the decade prior to 2008, which averaged 6.44 percent. These same factors, however, left the region highly susceptible to negative external shocks. The crisis resulted in regional output shrinking by 4.8 percent in 2009, excluding energy-exporting transition countries.[2] In comparison, the US economy shrank by 3.1 percent, whereas the EU economy shrank by 4.3 percent.

Despite this output contraction, the countries of the region were able to avert a full-scale financial collapse because of an overall sound financial system and strong fiscal positions. The subsequent domestic and international policy response contributed to the rebound in the region's macroeconomic indicators, with GDP growth reaching 4.6 percent in 2010. However, the prolonged euro-zone sovereign debt crisis stalled the recovery, slowing the output growth to just above 3 percent, according to the most recent forecasts by the European Bank for Reconstruction and Development (EBRD) and by the United Nations (UN) (EBRD 2013; UN 2013).

Underlying the vulnerability of the recovery are weak labor markets. According to the most recent estimates, the regional unemployment rate reached 14.19 percent, the highest rate in a decade (EBRD 2013). Past experience has demonstrated that the labor market impact of crises may differ by gender (Rubery 1988). During this crisis, men's unemployment rate in the transition region increased more sharply than women's. Furthermore, the decline in their employment rate was more pronounced than the corresponding drop for women. Finally, men's labor force participation rate declined, whereas women increased their

* The author thanks Rania Antonopoulos and the participants of the Economics Seminar at the Levy Economics Institute for helpful comments and suggestions. The chapter has appeared earlier as a Levy Economics Institute Working Paper.

involvement in the labor force. These developments prompted many to argue that, unlike previous crises, which disproportionately hurt the female labour force, this crisis has been particularly devastating to men (Cho and Newhouse 2013).

In this chapter, we critically evaluate this claim by assessing the extent to which the increase in the female labor force participation rate, in particular, may reflect a distress response to the crisis, as has been found to be the case during past crises in other regions (Cerrutti 2000; Sabarwal *et al.* 2011). We do so by investigating the presence of the added worker effect, broadly defined as an increase in labor supply in response to an income shock.

The analysis of the forces behind the gender differences in the movements of labor force participation rates is particularly salient for transition countries. This is the case in part because of their shared socialist legacy of gender equality and in part because of the post-socialist deterioration of the gender balance in the region. The regional evidence from past crises reveals that labor supply responses were commonly used to mitigate the impact of crises (Lokshin and Yemtsov 2004). The evidence from this crisis is limited and reveals no labor supply response to the crisis or very weak added worker effect among women (Cho and Newhouse 2013; Bhalotra and Umaña-Aponte 2010). However, these findings are either limited to middle- and high–middle-income transition countries or are based on employment outcomes. In this chapter, we address these limitations by including the data for 28 countries of the region and considering labor force participation outcomes.

The rest of the chapter is structured as follows. The next section presents some of the key features of the crisis in the transition region and establishes crisis-related gender dynamics in their labor markets. The subsequent sections include a literature review, discuss the methodology, and provide data summary. Empirical results and robustness checks follow. We conclude the chapter with a discussion of the results and their implications.

2 Background

The transition region includes a heterogeneous group of countries. Before the crisis in 2007, their per capita GDP ranged from US$217 in Tajikistan to US$13,378 in Slovenia.[3] Although the crisis, which began in the summer of 2007 in the US mortgage sector, quickly spilled over to the Western European financial markets, it didn't hit the region until late 2008 and early 2009. Its initial financial impact was in fact surprisingly mild. In 2008, transition countries maintained a moderate 5.83 percent average growth rate and the unemployment rate declined to 11.93 percent in 2008 from 12.49 percent in 2007. This was despite their relatively high exposure to international financial and output markets as evidenced by the higher than 40 percent share of exports in the GDP throughout the last decade. Indeed, financial capital continued to flow in during the first half of 2008 and, even when the signs of financial contagion became visible by the last quarter of 2008, capital inflows remained positive.

It was through the real side of the economy that the full-blown wave of the crisis finally hit the region in the last quarter of 2008 with a drop in exports reaching as high as 17 percent in Moldova. The slide continued in 2009 as exports shrank further in the majority of countries, with Ukraine experiencing a 22 percent drop. The subsequent contraction in output was almost universal: with the exception of Poland, all countries of the region experienced negative output growth in at least one quarter. On an annual basis, all but nine countries of the region observed a drop in GDP in 2009. Out of the nine that didn't contract, three were energy-exporting Kazakhstan, Turkmenistan, and Azerbaijan. Agriculture was the only sector that grew in 2009 at about 1 percent. The slowdown of industry and services, which started already in 2008, turned into negative digits by 2009, with industry shrinking the most at 7.84 percent and services at 1.45 percent.

The magnitude of the recession that each country experienced was tied to the initial output composition, the degree of export dependence, and the performance of the main trading partners, with open economies contracting more than closed economies. The recession was exacerbated by the eventual decline in foreign direct investment (FDI) that followed the export contraction, domestic credit contraction, and a drop in remittances (EBRD 2009).

By 2010, the region appeared to have bounced back, with output growth turning positive in all but three countries. By 2011, the GDP growth rate reached 4.6 percent (EBRD 2013). From today's vantage point, it can be argued that the buffers that prevented the crisis from entering the region with full force until 2009 and allowed it to start growing again only a year later were the overall strong fiscal positions, the relatively healthy financial sector, and the FDI-dominated financial flows, less prone to the sudden reversals that characterized the Asian financial crisis (EBRD 2009). A further contributing role was likely played by active international and domestic policy responses. The adopted domestic policy tools have differed, but overall the fiscal response was expansionary, with per capita government expenditures increasing from US$623 in 2007 to US$650 in 2010.

However, the robust turnaround has proven to be short-lived mainly due to the protracted nature of the eurozone sovereign debt crisis, which stalled the recovery of exports and domestic credit and dented the region's growth prospects. By 2012, the GDP growth rate had slowed down to 2.6 percent and in 2013 is forecast to rise to between 3.1 and 3.6 percent (EBRD 2013; UN 2013).

The vulnerability of the economic recovery in the region has been amplified by the weak state of the labor markets. Despite the turnaround in output in 2010, the unemployment rate continued to grow, reaching 14.19 percent, according to the most recent regional update (EBRD 2013). The youth unemployment rate, largely on the decline during the previous decade, spiked up from 19.96 percent in 2008, the lowest rate in the previous ten years, to 22.42 percent in 2009 and to 26 percent in 2010 (ILO 2012).

Crises-induced labor market outcomes have historically differed by gender. The socialist collapse resulted in the worsening of labor market conditions, evidenced by a spike in the unemployment rate and a decline in employment and labor force participation rates of both men and women. However, in its initial aftermath, women's position in the labor markets weakened more compared to men's, as their employment rate dropped more sharply. Women also withdrew from the labor force in proportionately greater numbers.

During this crisis, on the other hand, the worsening of the labor market indicators was accompanied by a very different gender picture. Both unemployment rates increased; however, in 2010 men's unemployment rate surpassed that of women for the first time since 2000. Moreover, although both employment rates decreased, women's employment rate contracted proportionately less, indicating that employment losses were more substantial among men than among women. Importantly, between 2008 and 2010, men's labor force participation rate slightly decreased from 73.89 to 73.71 percent; however, women's labor force participation rate slightly increased from 59.43 to 60.01 percent.

The literature has developed a conceptual framework for analyzing these patterns and has proposed a number of channels potentially responsible for the heterogeneous impact of crises on men and women's labor force participation rates (Rubery 1988). Broadly defined, these include gender differences in the occupational and sectoral distribution, and gender-dependent labor demand and labor supply responses. Occupational and sectoral segregation by gender has been shown to be a frequent conduit of the first-round effects of crises. Women worldwide are more likely to work in the service sector, whereas men are more likely to work in manufacturing (ILO 2010). During past crises, women working in export-oriented manufacturing sectors suffered disproportionately high losses (Antonopoulos 2009). However, because this crisis hit the male-dominated construction and manufacturing sector the hardest, men likely experienced greater job losses than women and possibly exhibited more active withdrawal from the labor force.

From the labor demand side, the second-round adjustments that firms make in response to crises, too, can translate into different labor market outcomes for men and women. For example, firms' perceptions regarding the productivity and attachment of workers are often an influential determinant of hiring and firing decisions. If women are viewed to be less attached to the labor market due to their reproductive role and cultural expectations of their household responsibilities, they will be more likely to be let go. In fact, some studies (Singh and Zammit 2000) argue that these perceptions explain why women suffered disproportionately higher job losses during the Asian financial crisis. This explanation can be viewed under the umbrella of the buffer hypothesis, according to which women are a flexible labor reserve that enters the work force during expansions and exits it during economic downturns in greater proportions than men, resulting in a pro-cyclical movement of the female employment rates (Rubery 1988). On the other hand, because women tend to receive lower pay, hiring women over men can be viewed as a cost-saving strategy by the crisis-hit firms, resulting in an increase in women's wage employment during crises at the expense of men. This possibility is known as the substitution hypothesis and results in a countercyclical behavior of the female employment rates (Rubery 1988). Using a sample of 17 middle-income countries, Cho and Newhouse (2013) find some evidence in support of this hypothesis during the most recent crisis. Whereas these hypotheses are directly applicable only to employment outcomes, they may also apply to shifts in the labor force participation rates.

3 Crises and labor supply responses: literature review

Our interest in this chapter lies in understanding the third mechanism linking crises and labor market outcomes of men and women – that of households' labor supply responses to income shocks induced by crises. Similar to the demand-side responses, this mechanism, too, can be viewed as a second-round impact of a crisis (Heltberg *et al.* 2012; Sabarwal *et al.* 2011).

Labor supply changes can take place in response to both household-specific income shocks and economy-wide shifts. Some examples of household-specific income shocks are employment loss, wage reductions, or a decrease in remittances. We study a particular type of a household-specific income shock, stemming from the loss of another household member's job. This shock can induce an increase or a decrease in the desired labor supply. The positive labor supply response of one household member in response to the loss of another household member's job is known in the literature as the added worker effect.[4] The added worker effect can be induced via at least two channels. First of all, the increase in labor supply can be a coping strategy aimed at compensating for the income reduction due to a household member's job loss, the channel known as the income effect (McKenzie 2003). At the same time, it can result from the reduction in the reservation wage of the formerly inactive household members and their entry into the labor force, now that the newly unemployed individuals can take over some of their household responsibilities. On both counts, women are the more likely drivers in the added worker effect. On the first count, they are the ones more likely to be outside the labor force to begin with and hence available to respond by joining the labor force. On the second count, given that women are the primary providers of household needs, such as care for children, adults, and the elderly, daily maintenance, cooking, shopping, etc., the reservation wages are likely to be more sensitive to others taking over some of their household responsibilities.

The loss of another household member's job can also cause a negative labor supply response. The income reduction due to the loss of a household member's job may induce a withdrawal from the labor force if households are forced to substitute market goods for household-produced goods. In such a case, some previously unemployed individuals may stop looking for paid work opportunities and exit the labor force altogether. Arguably, the unemployed women are the more likely candidates to do so due to their role as primary producers of household goods.

Beyond the household-specific shocks, economy-wide shocks, too, can induce changes in the labor supply even if households have not been directly affected by a household-specific shock. Some studies have, in fact, interpreted the evidence of an increase in labor supply in response to weaker macroeconomic conditions as a manifestation of the added worker effect (Congregado *et al.* 2011; Cunningham 2001). On the other hand, the crisis-induced reduction in overall wages may lower the labor force participation rate by reducing the opportunity cost of leisure, resulting in an increase in leisure and a drop in the labor supply (McKenzie 2003). For many individuals, this reduction may also pull the prevalent wage offers below their reservation wages, inducing them to exit the labor force. Finally, the lower odds of finding a job in a weak economic environment may raise perceived and actual job search costs, resulting in the discouraged worker effect. It is noteworthy that, although the literature has commonly contrasted the added worker effect and the discouraged worker effect (Congregado *et al.* 2011), the first is properly defined as a response to household-specific income shocks and the second as a response to the worsening of the macroeconomic environment.

Historical evidence of the added worker effect from developed countries is mixed, although recent literature argues against the presence of a considerable added worker effect. This, at least in part, has been attributed to the presence of strong unemployment insurance and financial systems in developed countries (e.g., Juhn and Potter 2007; Stephens 2002; Prieto-Rodriguez and Rodriguez-Gutierrez 2003).

Even in developing countries, however, despite weaker unemployment insurance mechanisms and higher barriers to accessing credit, the available evidence reveals a complex story and a range of experiences. Fernandes and de Felicio (2005) find that the added worker effect among wives in Brazil is between 7.35 and 12 percent, attributing it to the absence of unemployment insurance mechanisms. McKenzie (2004) reports the added worker effect of 11 percent in Argentina. Focusing on the case of Mexico before the 1994 peso crisis, Cunningham (2001) finds the presence of the added worker effect among wives in response to the husband's loss of a job as well as in response to higher unemployment rates. During the peso crisis, evidence once again indicates the presence of the added worker effect among wives with respect to the spousal job loss (Skoufias and Parker 2004). However, unlike the pre-crisis period, there is no evidence of the added worker effect in response to the worsening macroeconomic environment (McKenzie 2003). Evidence from Turkey reveals the presence of the added worker effect among wives in response to husband's loss of a job during the 1994 economic crisis (Başlevent and Onaran 2003) and during the last decade (İlkkaracan and Değirmenci 2013; Karaoglan and Okten 2012). In response to unemployment rates, on the other hand, Karaoglan and Okten (2012) find support for the discouraged worker effect. These findings underscore the heterogeneity in which households respond to idiosyncratic shocks as opposed to macroeconomic shocks.

The studies with weaker or complete lack of evidence of the added worker effect in developing countries provide a fruitful ground for investigating a range of coping strategies and the interplay among them. Posadas and Sinha (2010) report the added worker effect of 2.1–5.1 percent among wives in Indonesia, attributing the relatively low magnitude to the fact that the main transmission mechanism of the crisis in Indonesia was the change in the wages, rather than the loss of employment. Serneels (2002) finds no evidence of the added worker effect among women in response to other household member's loss of a job in Ethiopia, and points to the use of other strategies, such as tapping into savings to compensate for the loss of income. Similarly, McLaren (2012) finds no evidence of the added worker effect among men or women in response to another household member's loss of a job in South Africa, concluding that households depend on remittances as the buffer for the loss of employment income. In the case of South Africa, especially, extremely high unemployment rates largely preclude the use of labor supply as a coping strategy and indeed result in the dominance of the discouraged worker effect.[5] The findings of no added worker effect in Serneels (2002) and McLaren (2012) may be, in part, due to the use of another household member's job loss (rather than a spousal job loss). For example, Cunningham (2001) finds no evidence of the added worker effect with respect to another household member's job in Mexico. But her evidence with respect to the spousal job is conclusive in favor of the added worker effect. Nevertheless, the link connecting these studies is the emphasis that they place on the importance of other coping strategies.

Considering transition countries, the literature has evaluated the gender impact of crises in general terms (Unal *et al.* 2010; UN 2009). However, more work needs to be done to develop a better understanding of the gender patterns in the labor supply responses to crises in the region. This is the case, in part, due to the unavailability or poor quality of the data from the early transition period. Lokshin and Yemtsov (2004) evaluate different coping strategies used by households in Russia after the 1998 financial crisis and find that labor supply responses were used as an important strategy. However, they stop short of estimating the labor supply changes in response to household-specific shocks and do not provide a gender picture. The evidence from the recent crisis is limited, but appears to lean against the presence of the added worker effect (Cho and Newhouse 2013; Bhalotra and Umaña-Aponte 2010). Cho and Newhouse (2013) use data from six middle- to higher–middle-income transition countries to reach their conclusion of the weak added worker effect. However, because these countries also have stronger social safety nets and financial systems, the results might not be generalizable to the region as a whole.[6] Bhalotra and Umaña-Aponte (2010) do incorporate mostly lower-income transition countries and find no evidence of the added worker effect; however, their conclusions are based on the lack of a relationship between the employment status and per capita GDP, rather than between the labor force status and household-specific shocks. The latter relationship represents a more appropriate measure of the added worker effect because it reflects the desire to work,[7] whereas employment outcomes are a result of joint labor supply and labor demand decisions. This study attempts to address these limitations by evaluating a sample of 28 transition countries and considering the relationship between labor force status and household-specific shocks in order to assess the presence of the added worker effect.

4 Methodology and data

The individual and household variables in our dataset are based on the 2010 Life in Transition survey, conducted by the EBRD at the end of 2010. The survey includes questions covering demographic and socioeconomic characteristics as well as perceptions and attitudes about political, economic, and social issues. The survey covers all 29 countries of the transition region and includes the economic crisis module, which asks questions regarding the ways in which the recent crisis has affected the households.[8] The survey contains data on 32,084 households from the transition region, a little over 1,000 per country for each of the 28 countries used in the analysis. The survey followed a two-stage clustered stratified sampling design. In the first stage, local electoral territorial units were used as primary sampling units (PSUs) and in the case of most countries 50 PSUs were selected with the likelihood of selection being proportional to the PSU size. In the second stage, households were selected within each PSU with the goal of ensuring that each household in a given country had an equal probability of being selected. As such, the survey sample was designed to be representative at the country level.

We narrow down the sample to the individuals aged 18–64, exclude individuals out of the labor force who reported being retired or students, as well as observations with missing values, resulting in 22,067 observations. The construction of the variable representing the household-specific shock places additional constraints on the data. The question of interest is posed as "Has head of household lost job" or "Has other household member lost job" in the last two years. Hence, with the exception of the household head, the survey does not identify specifically which household members have lost a job. In order to identify with certainty that another household member has lost a job, we first look at the non-household head respondents and identify if the head has lost a job. Next, for household head respondents, we identify if another household member has lost a job. We drop the observations for which the household head respondents respond that they were the only ones in the household who have lost a job. In addition, we drop the observations for which non-household-head members state that only non-household-head members have lost a job, since we cannot identify with certainty that it was not the respondents themselves that have lost the job. These constraints bring the sample further down to 18,234 households.

Our choice of the loss of another household member's job rather than a spousal job loss as the preferred specification is determined by the extended household structure in the region and, more generally in developing countries (see also Bhalotra and Umaña-Aponte 2010; Serneels 2002). Indeed, 41.69 percent of the households in our sample have three or more adults, as compared to only 19.40 percent of the households in the United States that were shared households in 2010.[9] In order to place our results in the context of the studies that evaluate the added worker effect with respect to the spousal job loss, we report the results with respect to the spousal loss of a job, as well.

In assessing the presence of the labor supply response to an income shock, we use the labor force participation status as our dependent variable (see also Prieto-Rodriguez and Rodriguez-Gutierrez 2003; Başlevent and Onaran 2003). The dependent variable was constructed by first identifying individuals who were employed for pay at the time of the survey. Next, out of the individuals who did not have a job, we identified those who were looking for a job and classified them as unemployed. The employed and unemployed then together comprised the labor force. The individuals who held no jobs and were not looking for one were classified as out of the labor force.

In our estimation, the dependent variable y_i takes the value 1 if individual i is active in the labor force and 0 if individual i is inactive. We estimate a binomial logit model, in which y_i, conditional on the vector of regressors X_i, follows the logistic distribution:

$$\Pr(y_i = 1 \mid X_i) = \frac{\exp(X_i'\beta)}{1 + \exp(X_i'\beta)} = \Lambda(X_i'\beta). \tag{1}$$

In this specification, the marginal effect with respect to continuous variables for individual i can be defined as:

$$ME_i = \frac{\partial \Lambda(X_i'\beta)}{\partial X_i} = \Lambda(X_i'\beta)(1 - \Lambda(X_i'\beta)\beta. \tag{2}$$

The marginal effects with respect to a binary variable d for individual i can be defined as:

$$ME_i = \Pr(y_i = 1 \mid \overline{X}_{i \backslash d}, d = 1) - \Pr(y_i = 1 \mid \overline{X}_{i \backslash d}, d = 0), \tag{3}$$

where $\overline{X}_{i \backslash d}$ is the mean of the variables in the sample, excluding d.

We report the marginal effects as the average of the individual marginal effects (Greene 2003, p. 668). Note, however, that individual marginal effects with respect to a binary variable (such as household-specific unemployment shock) are evaluated at the means of other variables before being averaged.

A positive marginal effect of the shock reflects a higher likelihood of labor force participation for individuals who experienced the loss of another household member's job. Conversely, the negative marginal effect is indicative of the lower likelihood of labor force participation among individuals who experienced another household member's job loss. To the extent that the only difference between individuals identical in terms of observable characteristics is the loss of another household member's job, the higher (lower) likelihood can be interpreted as an indication that the person who, without the household member's job loss, would have been out of (in) the labor force, had entered (exited) the labor force as a result of this shock. And it is in this sense that a positive result can be viewed as the evidence of the added worker effect. This can be viewed as an indirect approach to assessing the added worker effect, with the direct one using a transition from inactive to active status as the dependent variable.

Other individual and household variables in the estimation include gender, age group, marital status, the level of educational attainment, and the number of children in the household. Macroeconomic characteristics account for country-level heterogeneity and include unemployment rate, per capita GDP in constant 2000 US dollars, service share, industry share, government share, and export share, the last four all as percentages of GDP, based on the World Bank's World Development Indicators (WDI). Although their primary function in the estimation is to control for country-level heterogeneity, the inclusion of the unemployment rate and per capita GDP also allows us to evaluate the impact of macroeconomic environment on the probability of labor force participation separately from the impact of household specific shocks. In order to make such inferences, we exploit the cross-country variation in the unemployment rate and per capita GDP (Aguiar *et al.* 2011).

Due to the unavailability of the unemployment rate data for all the countries, we derive the unemployment rates from the dataset itself (the correlation coefficient between the survey-based unemployment rates and the available WDI-based unemployment rates is 75 percent). We use both unemployment rate and GDP per capita as indicators of macroeconomic environment because of a somewhat weak relationship between per capita GDP and unemployment rate in transition countries (EBRD 2012, p. 30). The use of service and industry shares is intended to capture the impact of sectoral differences on the labor force participation, as these differences can be important determinants of the variation in labor force participation rates. The government share serves as a proxy for the social safety net due to its potentially important role in explaining the presence of the need for secondary employment responses. Finally, the export share captures the variation in openness of the economies. In combining both household-level and macroeconomic data, this chapter is similar in spirit to Cho and Newhouse (2013) and Bhalotra and Umaña-Aponte (2010).

5 Data summary

The unweighted sample consists of 60 percent women and 40 percent men, heavily skewed toward women. EBRD (2012) attributes the overrepresentation of females in the sample to the fact that the household members permanently away from home for work or studies, and hence excluded from the sample, are males. To correct for this feature of the data, EBRD introduced weights approximating the gender (and age) breakdown within each country's population. We use these weights in all our estimations.

The labor force participation rates vary among men and women. The rate is 71.31 percent for women and 87.21 percent for men. The survey-based rates overestimate the labor force participation rates for 15–64 year olds from the WDI database, which are 60.01 percent for women and 73.71 percent for men.[10] One reason for such overestimation might be the substantially lower labor force participation rates of 15–18 year olds dragging the WDI-based rate down because the WDI rates are based on 15–64-year-old individuals, whereas in our case the age range is 18–64 by survey design.

Survey responses reveal that a substantial portion of the households has been hurt by the crisis. In the final sample, 47.1 percent of the households report being affected a fair to a great deal by the crisis. The crisis was transmitted to them via several channels, the two most important ones being the drop in wages (26.49 percent of the total sample) and the employment loss of at least one household member (11.83 percent of the total sample) (Table 8.1).

As can be seen from Table 8.2, about 15 percent of respondents experienced a household member's loss of a job (note that 11.83 percent reported that to be the main shock they experienced). About 67 percent of the respondents are married. The proportion of female respondents reporting having one or more children is higher for women than for men. This finding likely reflects a higher incidence of single motherhood compared to single fatherhood. Women are proportionately more educated compared to men, with 24.2 percent of females having tertiary education and only 21.66 percent of males, consistent with other evidence from the region (World Bank 2012).

Table 8.1 Household income shocks listed as the main way in which the crisis was experienced during the two years prior to the interview

Type of a shock	*Percentage*
Reduced wages[a]	26.49
At least one member lost a job	11.83
Reduced remittances	8.27
Delayed wages	7.61
Reduced working hours	4.42
A person who did not have a job found one or someone who had a job took another one[b]	3.78
Increased working hours	3.17
Family business lost	2.24
Family member returned from abroad	1.70
Not applicable (not affected at all)	30.47

Notes
Weighted proportions.

a Household labor supply response may vary depending on the nature of the household-specific income shock. Given their pervasive nature, the responses that reduced wages initiate may have important implications for the analysis of labor force participation rates. Unfortunately, due to data limitations, we are unable to pursue this question. The reason is that we do not know the identity of the household members whose wages are reduced. As a result, we cannot argue that the labor force participation status of respondents is a response to another household member's wage reduction. In this context, the finding of a positive relationship between the wage reduction and the likelihood of labor force participation may be simply an outcome of the respondents experiencing wage reduction being employed to begin with.

b The response to this question could allow us to directly evaluate the added worker effect in employment (although not in labor force). However, similar to the wage reduction question, we are unable to identify the household member making the transition.

Table 8.2 Summary statistics

	Female	Male
Labor force	0.7131	0.8721
Job loss other	0.1447	0.1357
Marriage	0.6727	0.6621
No children	0.4917	0.5632
1 child	0.2432	0.2181
2 or more children	0.2650	0.2187
Age 18–24	0.1144	0.1357
Age 25–34	0.2942	0.3117
Age 35–44	0.2594	0.2458
Age 45–54	0.2373	0.2088
Age 55–64	0.0947	0.098
Secondary	0.3475	0.3674
Vocational	0.1837	0.1665
Tertiary	0.2420	0.2166

Note
Weighted proportions.

Women's labor force participation rates are especially sensitive to individual and household characteristics (Table 8.3). For example, whereas labor force participation rates of married and unmarried men are similar, married women have a lower labor force participation rate than unmarried women. Similarly, men's labor force participation rates hardly vary in response to the number of children; however, for women, the rate drops, especially if there are two or more children in the household. Men have a wide peak age range, whereas women reach their peak labor force participation rates only after passing the child-bearing years. In sum, women's labor force participation appears to be much more strongly affected by their household responsibilities. With respect to educational attainment, labor force participation rates of men increase from 86.88 percent for complete secondary to 93.44 percent for tertiary education; however, the sensitivity is once again much higher among women. Female labor force participation rate increases from 67.54 percent for women with secondary education to 85.23 percent, a 17.69 percentage point variation, compared to 6.56 percentage points for men. This appears to suggest that women's labor force returns to education are higher than men's.

Pertinent to our analysis, the labor force participation rate of women who experienced another household member's job loss is lower compared to the corresponding rate of women who did not. This seems to refute the hypothesis of the added worker effect. However, this pattern is reversed for married women, those who were 45–54 years old and women with secondary education. For men, across all categories, there is an unequivocal decrease in the labor force participation rate as a result of the loss of another household member's job. Next, we test these preliminary predictions in a multivariate framework.

Table 8.3 Labor force participation rates, by gender, demographic group, and the job loss of another household member

	Women		Men	
	No job loss	Job loss	No job loss	Job loss
Total	0.7156	0.6985	0.8781	0.8339
Unmarried	0.8215	0.7743	0.8723	0.8012
Married	0.6614	0.6716	0.8811	0.8474
No children	0.776	0.7711	0.8813	0.8418
1 child	0.7216	0.7126	0.8872	0.8174
2 or more children	0.5949	0.5713	0.8602	0.8327
Age 18–24	0.6192	0.6094	0.8389	0.7507
Age 25–34	0.6734	0.6498	0.8964	0.8466
Age 35–44	0.7616	0.7064	0.8958	0.8621
Age 45–54	0.7651	0.7800	0.8824	0.8741
Age 55–64	0.7193	0.6720	0.8181	0.7623
Secondary	0.6717	0.6976	0.8774	0.8190
Vocational	0.7771	0.7654	0.9003	0.8819
Tertiary	0.852	0.8551	0.9393	0.8817

Note
Weighted proportions.

6 Results

6.1 Loss of another household member's job

6.1.1 Women

After controlling for individual, household, and country-level characteristics, we find the presence of a mild added worker effect among women. Having experienced the loss of another household member's job raises the probability of women's labor force participation by 2.9 percentage points. The result is largely driven by *married* women, for whom the loss of another household member's job results in a 3.58 percentage point higher probability of labor force participation (Table 8.4). Furthermore, if we evaluate the added worker effect of married women with respect to the husband's loss of a job, the magnitude is substantially higher at 10.51 percentage points, on a par with the estimates from other countries (e.g., Fernandes and de Felicio 2005; McKenzie 2004).

Age appears to play an important role in determining the likelihood of labor force participation as a result of a household income shock. The added worker effect is present among the 25–34-year-old women, with their probability of labor force participation increasing by 3.63 percentage points (although only at 10 percent significance level). The second age group, in which we observe the evidence of the added worker effect, is the group of 45–54-year-old women. For them, the probability of labor force participation in response to another household member's job rises by 4.32 percentage points. These women have passed

Table 8.4 Marginal effects of the job loss of another household member, by gender and subsamples (except for the second row results, which are the marginal effects of the spousal job loss)

	Women	Men
Overall	0.0290	−0.0229
	(0.0117)**	(0.0118)*
Overall (with spousal loss of a job)	0.1051	−0.0294
	(0.0310)***	(0.0174)*
Married	0.0358	−0.0195
	(0.0149)**	(0.0133)
Unmarried	0.0035	−0.0411
	(0.0221)	(0.0238)*
Age 18–24	0.0444	−0.0510
	(0.0390)	(0.0421)
Age 25–34	0.0363	−0.0325
	(0.0207)*	(0.0241)
Age 35–44	−0.0015	−0.0225
	(0.0227)	(0.0204)
Age 45–54	0.0432	0.0083
	(0.0188)**	(0.0183)
Age 55–64	0.0103	−0.0605
	(0.0297)	(0.0427)
Secondary	0.0534	−0.0444
	(0.0206)***	(0.0225)**
Vocational	−0.0038	−0.0019
	(0.0240)	(0.0290)
Tertiary	0.0131	−0.0496
	(0.0221)	(0.0307)
No children	0.0370	−0.0219
	(0.0138)***	(0.0163)
1 child	0.0217	−0.0470
	(0.0214)	(0.0256)*
2 children or more	0.0187	−0.0104
	(0.0276)	(0.0222)
Credit card	0.0153	−0.0217
	(0.0207)	(0.0241)
No credit card	0.0352	−0.0224
	(0.0138)**	(0.0153)
Secondary residence	0.0132	−0.0580
	(0.0420)	(0.0486)
No secondary residence	0.0308	−0.0205
	(0.0128)**	(0.0117)*
GDP per capita less than $1,000	−0.0122	−0.0148
	(0.0363)	(0.0351)
$1,000–$2,000	0.0246	−0.0193
	(0.0220)	(0.0247)
$2,000–$3,300	0.0557	−0.0544
	(0.0185)***	(0.0224)**
GDP per capita $3,300 or higher	0.0165	−0.0049
	(0.0192)	(0.0193)
Unemployment rate 13 percent or higher	0.0322	−0.0283
	(0.0138)**	(0.0138)**
Unemployment rate <13 percent	0.0011	−0.0085
	(0.0231)	(0.0198)
Non-EU countries	0.0437	−0.0234
	(0.0131)***	(0.0150)
EU countries	0.0039	−0.0211
	(0.0191)	(0.0195)

Notes
*** p-value < 0.01, **p-value < 0.05, * p-value < 0.10; average marginal effects reported; cluster-adjusted standard errors.

their prime child-bearing age and are likely to have older children. Consequently, the lower level of child care responsibilities reduces their opportunity cost of work hence raising their odds of entering the labor force in response to a household income shock.

The conjecture that child-rearing serves as a formidable barrier for female labor force participation is further supported by the finding that the added worker effect is statistically significant only among women in the households without *children*. It is only in their case that the probability of labor force participation is higher, by 3.7 percentage points. For women with one or more children in the household, there is no evidence of the added worker effect.

An equally important role for women is played by their level of *education*, as the added worker effect is dominant only among the women with secondary education, potentially due to their higher vulnerability. Their probability of labor force participation rises by 5.34 percentage points in the case of a job loss of a household member. Women with vocational or tertiary education do not exhibit the added worker effect, their education likely serving as a proxy for the greater security against household income shocks.

We further explore the role that greater vulnerabilities might play in amplifying the impact of household income shocks on women's labor force participation. In particular, we investigate the possibility that the added worker effect is stronger among the households that face financial constraints, forcing them to increase their labor supply as a coping strategy (Lundberg 1985). We use two variables as proxies for financial constraints: owning a secondary residence and having a credit card. Owning a secondary residence likely reflects greater financial security as does having a credit card, which, in the absence of the earnings information, serves as an indicator of moderate and stable household income.

We find that women from the households that own secondary residences (8.32 percent of the sample) do not exhibit the added worker effect. In contrast, the effect is present among the women in households without secondary residence as their probability of being in the labor force increases by 3.08 percentage points in response to the loss of a household member's job. Further emphasizing the influence of financial constraints, women from households in which someone owns a credit card (22.78 percent of the sample) do not exhibit the added worker effect. On the other hand, among the women from the households in which no one owns a credit card, the probability of labor force participation increases by 3.52 percentage points in response to the loss of a household member's job. In sum, microeconomic vulnerabilities indeed amplify the impact of household income shocks.

In turn, in order to evaluate the extent to which macroeconomic conditions influence the presence of the added worker effect, we group the countries of the region into different categories, based on EU membership, unemployment rates, and per capita GDP. We find that the added worker effect among women is absent in the EU countries but is present in the non-EU countries (4.37 percentage point increase), potentially due to the presence of stronger social insurance systems in the EU transition countries. This result is present even though government share in the GDP is included in the estimation, implying that it only partially accounts for the differences in social infrastructure. To a strong extent, the presence of the added worker effect appears to depend on economic factors. We find that in countries with the unemployment rate above 13 percent (mean unemployment rate in the region), the magnitude of the added worker effect is 3.22 percentage points, whereas the evidence in the countries with the below average unemployment rates is inconclusive. Further nuances emerge by grouping countries according to their per capita GDP. We find that it is the countries in the middle of the distribution ($2,000–$3,300) that drive the results, with the dominant added worker effect of 5.57 percentage points. The absence of the added worker effect in the countries with per capita GDP above US$3,300 (regional average in 2010) could potentially be attributed to the presence of stronger social insurance mechanisms. Indeed, Vodopivec *et al.* (2005) argue that in these transition countries, unemployment benefits protected many households from falling into poverty. On the other hand, the absence of the added worker effect at the bottom of the regional distribution could be attributed to the weaker prospects of finding a job. Hence, on a macro-economic scale, although weaker institutional and macroeconomic environment may contribute to a stronger female added worker effect, by depressing the prospects of finding a job, greater vulnerabilities can also negatively affect the decision to join the labor markets. Our findings appear to reveal an inverted-U relationship between the added worker effect and the level of economic development, measured by per capita GDP.

6.1.2 Men

In contrast to women, there is no evidence of the added worker effect among men. In fact, the opposite is the case: the loss of another household member's job is associated with a 2.29 percentage point decrease in the probability of labor force participation. This negative effect is especially pronounced among unmarried men with secondary education with one child in the household.

What can potentially explain the finding of the negative relationship? It is unlikely that men's greater involvement in household responsibilities in order to substitute for market goods is the culprit.[11] The possibility that respondents increase their leisure time at the expense of searching for a job when another household member loses a job might not be a plausible explanation, either. A more likely explanation lies in spurious correlation in male household members' labor force status. The negative labor supply responses of men may be a manifestation of the first-round effects of the crisis that men experienced more painfully than women because their employment was concentrated in industries that were hit the most. That is, the negative marginal effects could reflect not so much the response to the unemployment shock, but the correlation in employment status among men, which applies only to men and not to women due to the nature of their industrial segregation.

Further support for this possibility is rendered by the role that financial constraints play in men's labor force participation in relation to unemployment shocks. To the extent that greater household vulnerabilities are also associated with more vulnerable forms of employment and hence a higher likelihood of multiple male household members losing a job, financial constraints will amplify the negative relationship between the labor force participation of respondents and the unemployment shock. Indeed, although the evidence based on the ownership of a credit card is somewhat inconclusive (marginal effect is negative but insignificant), the evidence based on the ownership of a secondary residence reveals the presence of a negative relationship between labor force participation and unemployment shocks among the men whose households do not own a secondary residence.

Similar to microeconomic vulnerabilities, a weaker macroeconomic environment results in a stronger negative relationship, as we observe among the countries with unemployment rates above 13 percent. Furthermore, the negative association is present only in the countries that are in the middle of the per capita GDP distribution ($2,000–$3,300). Its absence among the richest countries of the region might be attributed to men in more affluent countries choosing to remain in the labor force instead of withdrawing from it because of the presence of a stronger unemployment insurance system. The absence of the negative correlation among the poorest countries of the region could potentially be attributed to their greater dependence on agriculture, which serves as a default employment type in many households in these countries.

6.2 Macroeconomic factors

Unlike the gender-varying responses to household-specific unemployment shocks, the association between labor force participation and unemployment rates is negative for both women and men, revealing the presence of the discouraged worker effect (Table 8.5). Furthermore, the discouraged worker effect is almost twice as strong for women as it is for men. Indeed, a 1 percentage point increase in the unemployment rate lowers the probability of labor force participation by 0.22 percentage points and by 0.12 percentage points for women and men, respectively.

For women, the marginal effect with respect to per capita GDP reinforces the finding of the discouraged worker effect, as a 1 percent decrease in per capita GDP is associated with a 0.0662 percentage point decrease in the probability of labor force participation.[12] For men, this relationship is insignificant.

The differences in the relationship of labor force participation rates to unemployment rates and to per capita GDP underscore a very weak connection between unemployment rates and per capita GDP in the transition countries (EBRD 2012). They also seem to reveal that weaker labor markets exert a stronger depressing pressure on the labor force participation rates than the drop in the GDP. The link between per capita GDP and labor force participation rates appears to be much looser for men, in particular.

Our findings hence indicate that men's drop in the labor force participation rate was likely a result of the initial unemployment shock due to their industrial

Table 8.5 Complete logit results, by gender

	Women	Men
Job loss incidence	0.0290	−0.0229
	(0.0117)**	(0.0118)*
Marriage	−0.1156	0.0195
	(0.0103)***	(0.0100)*
Age 18–24	−0.1602	−0.0382
	(0.0195)***	(0.0190)**
Age 25–34	−0.0997	−0.0039
	(0.0126)***	(0.0125)
Age 45–54	−0.0292	−0.0184
	(0.0119)**	(0.0135)
Age 55–64	−0.122	−0.0946
	(0.0186)***	(0.0186)***
Secondary	0.0876	0.0452
	(0.0112)***	(0.0086)***
Vocational	0.1488	0.0604
	(0.0113)***	(0.0097)***
Tertiary	0.2151	0.0924
	(0.0107)***	(0.0092)***
No. of children	−0.0335	−0.0062
	(0.0051)***	(0.0041)
Unemployment rate	−0.0022	−0.0012
	(0.0005)***	(0.0005)**
Log GDP per capita	0.0662	−0.0081
	(0.0087)***	(0.0088)
Service share	0.0007	0.0013
	(0.0014)	(0.0012)
Industry share	−0.0035	0.0007
	(0.0014)**	(0.0012)
Government share	−0.0025	−0.0059
	(0.0014)*	(0.0015)***
Exports	0.0011	0.0015
	(0.0003)***	(0.0003)***
N	18,243	18,243

Notes
*** p-value < 0.01, **p-value < 0.05, * p-value < 0.10; average marginal effects reported; cluster-adjusted standard errors in parentheses.

concentration, but it was further compounded by the discouraged worker effect. For women, on the other hand, the discouraged worker effect was dominated by the added worker effect, contributing to an increase in the female labor force participation rate.

6.3 Individual and household factors

Our results also shed light on the impact of individual and household characteristics on the labor force participation rates of men and women. They reveal patterns similar to the ones exhibited in other parts of the world (Sabarwal *et al.* 2011). Focusing on women's results, we observe that marriage lowers their probability of labor force participation by 11.56 percentage points (Table 8.5). The prime age window of women is rather narrow: 35–44-year-old women exhibit the highest labor force participation rates. The lowest rates are present among the youngest and the pre-retirements groups. This result also provides another explanation for why 45–54-year-old women are the primary drivers of the added worker effect, as their initial labor force participation rates are lower than the rates for 35–44-year-old women. Education increases the probability of labor force participation among women: completing secondary education raises the probability of labor force participation rate by 8.76 percentage points and these returns increase to 14.88 percentage points for vocational education and 21.51 percentage points for tertiary education. Hence, the finding that the added worker effect is the strongest among women with secondary education could be partly driven by their lower initial labor force participation rates. Each additional child in the household reduces the probability of labor force participation of women by 3.35 percentage points.

For men, the picture is somewhat different. Marriage plays a slightly positive role in explaining their labor force participation, whereas having children has no effect on it. Men's prime age window is much wider than women's and includes individuals between the ages of 25 and 55, i.e., three age groups. On the other hand, similar to women, the youngest and the pre-retirement groups have the lowest probabilities of labor force participation. Education increases the probability of labor force participation, but its effect for men is substantially smaller than it is for women. Completing secondary education increases the probability of men's labor force participation only by 4.52 percentage points. The increase in men's labor force participation rate is only 6.04 percentage points as a result of completing vocational education and 9.24 percentage points as a result of completing tertiary education. Hence, the returns to education in terms of labor force participation are indeed higher for women.

6.4 Caveats and robustness checks

In interpreting our results, several caveats need to be kept in mind. One such caveat is that the presence of a relationship between the job loss of another household member and labor force status in principle only implies correlation rather than causation. For example, if household members operate in similar industries, the job loss of another household member may be associated with although not cause a transition from employment to inactive status for the respondent. In such a case, we will observe a negative relationship and, we argue, it is this reason that explains the negative association between the male labor force participation rate and the household employment shock.

Furthermore, the use of the labor force participation status rather than the transition between statuses necessitates caution when interpreting the presence of the marginal effect as a sign of the transition into and out of the labor force.

For example, if individuals from minority ethnic groups have a higher job loss probability (e.g., due to industrial or occupational segregation) as well as a higher initial probability of labor force participation, the positive marginal effect may be purely driven by the ethnic factor rather than the employment shock. In such a case, the coefficient will be overestimated and, for the purposes of our interpretation, although some transition might still take place, at least a portion of the higher likelihood could be attributed to the ethnic differences.

Another issue might arise from the fact that the precise cause for the job loss is not known. It is possible, for example, that another household member's loss of a job is a reaction to the respondent's change in the labor force status, potentially biasing the results. This could happen if a husband exits the labor force voluntarily as a response to his wife entering the labor force. However, given the challenging economic environment during this period, it is reasonable to assume that for the vast majority of the households, the job loss was involuntary. Finally, we do not know whether the household member who lost the job has found a new one. If so, our coefficient will underestimate the magnitude of the dominance of the added worker effect, since some of the individuals who lost a job may have found it, no longer requiring that the respondents enter the labor market.

We assess the robustness of our findings by re-estimating the model using several different specifications. We estimate it by no longer excluding the data for the inactive individuals who were retired or students, with no significant change in the results. To assess the sensitivity of the results to the measures of macroeconomic environment, we conduct the estimation using the WDI-based unemployment rate data instead of the survey-based unemployment rates. The impact of the unemployment rate on the labor force participation rate using either measure was similar, confirming the validity of our results. However, the inclusion of the full sample countries increases the efficiency of our results, rendering support to the preferred specification that includes survey-based unemployment rate data.

In addition, in order to analyze whether the added worker effect is driven by the entry into agricultural labor force, we limit the observations to individuals not involved in agricultural activities. We do so by taking advantage of the survey question, which asks whether sales or bartering of farm products constitutes a source of livelihood for the households. This re-estimation potentially reduces the possibility of a bias due to the ambiguous classification of unpaid workers since the employment is defined in terms of the work for pay. Our findings confirm the presence of an added worker effect among women and, once again, of a negative correlation among men.

Finally, due to the nature of the dataset, which includes individual and country-level variables, we account for the possibility that the error-terms within countries are correlated by clustering for countries (rather than survey-based PSUs). The added worker results remain significant. Our preferred specification is the one that clusters for the survey-based PSUs in order to allow for comparability when regional subsamples are analyzed.

7 Conclusions

The recent crisis was associated with a spike in women's labor force participation rate and a dip in men's labor force participation rate. Different mechanisms may have played a role in contributing to or counteracting these shifts. In this chapter, we investigated the extent to which these changes may have been due to the distress response to the crisis using the data from 28 transition countries.

We find the presence of the added worker effect among women, indicating that the added worker effect is indeed a likely factor explaining the increase in the labor force participation rate of women. The added worker effect among women is present in the context of both spousal relationships and in the context of a general household setup in contrast to other studies (e.g., Cunningham 2001), highlighting the importance of a more extended household structure than seen in advanced and many developing economies. The added worker effect among women is driven by married 45–54-year-old women with secondary education who have no children in the household. Having children remains a formidable barrier to joining the labor force even when households experience income shocks. Individual and household-level vulnerabilities strengthen the female added worker effect, in line with the findings from other countries (Sabarwal et al. 2011). We find that variations in both institutional and economic characteristics play a role in determining the presence of the female added worker effect. Indeed, the evidence of the added worker effect is found only in the non-EU countries. Furthermore, the added worker effect is stronger in weaker labor market environments, modeled in terms of above-average unemployment rates. On the other hand, in terms of per capita GDP, the added worker effect is present only among the countries in the middle of the per capita GDP distribution. We conjecture that the appearance of the inverted-U relationship can be explained by the presence of a well-developed social insurance system among the more affluent countries of the region and by the low odds of finding a job in the poorer countries of the region.

In the case of men, there is evidence of a negative correlation between the loss of another household member's job and labor force participation rate, driven by unmarried men with secondary education and one child in the household. The negative correlation is present among men who are financially more vulnerable. Furthermore, the correlation is stronger in the countries with higher unemployment rates and per capita GDP in the middle of the distribution. We contend that the negative relationship is less likely to indicate their withdrawal from the labor force as a response to the loss of another household member's job. A more likely explanation is that it is a result of a greater correlation in the labor force status of men because they tend to concentrate in the industries that experienced greatest job losses during this crisis.

Unlike the responses to household-specific income shocks that differ between the two genders, weak macroeconomic conditions appear to depress the labor force participation outcomes of both men and women. In particular, higher unemployment rates result in lower labor force participation rates among both men and women, hinting at the presence of the discouraged worker effect on a macroeconomic scale that cuts across genders. For women, this effect is also present with respect to per capita GDP, as their labor force participation rate increases in per capita GDP.

Addressing the original goal of this chapter, our findings reveal that the decrease in men's labor force participation during this crisis is likely a combined result of the first-round sectoral contraction and the second-order discouraged worker effect as a response to the weaker labor market environment. For women, on the other hand, the added worker effect appears to have outweighed the discouraged worker effect, contributing to an increase in their labor force participation rate.

These findings underscore that the responses to household-specific microeconomic shocks cannot be divorced from the macroeconomic context in which individual and household decisions are made. The need for and hence the magnitude of the responses is conditional on macroeconomic characteristics.

Future work needs to explore the long-term consequences of the added worker effect especially due to its distress connotation, as some studies have found that the work experience gained by female added workers improved their competitiveness in the labor market (Posadas and Sinha 2010). More work is needed to understand the role that variations in institutional characteristics, such as unemployment insurance schemes and financial systems, may play in determining the strength of the added worker effect in transition countries. Beyond the added worker effect, it will be important to assess the extent to which the added workers in transition countries have been able to realize their desire to work and evaluate the quality of the created employment opportunities.

Notes

1 There are 29 countries in the region: Albania, Armenia, Azerbaijan, Belarus, Bosnia and Herzegovina, Bulgaria, Croatia, Czech Republic, Estonia, Georgia, Hungary, Kazakhstan, Kosovo, Kyrgyz Republic, Latvia, Lithuania, Macedonia FYR, Moldova, Montenegro, Poland, Romania, Russian Federation, Serbia, Slovakia, Slovenia, Tajikistan, Turkmenistan, Ukraine, and Uzbekistan.
2 The energy-exporting countries include Azerbaijan, Kazakhstan, Russian Federation, and Turkmenistan. Their inclusion diminishes the magnitude of the contraction to a still sizable 3.84 percent.
3 The numbers are expressed in constant 2000 US dollars.
4 This definition is an extension of the original definition of the added worker effect, which entails the increase in wives' labor force participation in response to the spousal loss of a job (e.g., Lundberg 1985). More recent work studies the responses of household members as opposed to wives only (Cerrutti 2000), and considers the change in the working hours of those experiencing the initial shock and of those responding to it as opposed to employment loss and entry from inactivity into labor force (Gong 2011).
5 In a related finding, the evidence from Spain reveals the presence of a threshold unemployment rate beyond which the discouraged worker effect dominates the added worker effect (their estimate of the threshold for Spain for the recent crisis is 11.7 percent) (Congregado *et al.* 2011).

6 Estimating our model using their sample of transition countries, we also find no evidence of the added worker effect. Cho and Newhouse (2013) use Bulgaria, Latvia, Lithuania, Macedonia, Poland, and Romania.
7 To match the approach of Bhalotra and Umaña-Aponte (2010), we re-estimate our model using employment status (instead of the labor force participation status) as the dependent variable and per capita GDP as the economy-wide shock variable (in addition to the household-specific loss of another household member's job). Similar to these authors, our findings reveal no evidence of the added worker effect into employment with respect to per capita GDP. Bhalotra and Umaña-Aponte (2010) use Albania, Azerbaijan, Armenia, Kazakhstan, Kyrgyzstan, Moldova, Turkmenistan, Uzbekistan, and Ukraine in their estimation.
8 We drop the observations for Turkmenistan, for which variables for only 27 households are available. Therefore, our estimation includes data from 28 countries of the transition region. In addition to the transition region, the dataset includes data for France, Germany, Italy, Mongolia, Sweden, the United Kingdom, and Turkey, which are not used in this study.
9 Shared households are defined as households that contain an "additional adult" (a resident aged 18 and older who is neither the householder, the householder's spouse, nor the householder's cohabiting partner) (US Census Bureau 2012).
10 The WDI-based averages are based on 26 of the 29 transition countries, for which the data are available. The averages exclude Kosovo, Montenegro, and Serbia. Re-estimating the survey-based labor force participation rate for these 26 countries results in labor force participation rates of 72.65 percent for women and 87.77 percent for men, even higher than for the full sample.
11 The finding of the negative marginal effect among married couples has been attributed to the assortative mating hypothesis, according to which, spouses share characteristics that make both more likely to experience similar shocks (Spletzer 1997).
12 Note that the marginal effect with respect to ln(per capita GDP) is the same as semielasticity defined as $dy/d\ln(x)=dy/((1/x)dx)=(dy/dx)*x$, where $x=\ln$(per capita GDP). Hence, in this case, a doubling of per capita GDP is associated with 6.62 percentage point increase in female labor force participation.

References

Aguiar, M., Hurst, E., and Karabarbounis, L. (2011) "Time use during recessions," National Bureau of Economic Research Working Paper 17259, Cambridge.
Antonopoulos, R. (2009) "The current economic and financial crisis: the gender perspective," Levy Economics Institute Working Paper 562, Annandale-on-Hudson, NY.
Başlevent, C. and Onaran, Ö. (2003) "Are married women in Turkey more likely to become added or discouraged workers?" *Labour*, 17: 439–58.
Bhalotra, S. and Umaña-Aponte, M. (2010) "The dynamics of women's labour supply in developing countries," IZA Discussion Paper 4879, Bonn.
Cerrutti, M. (2000) "Economic reform, structural adjustment and female labour force participation in Buenos Aires, Argentina," *World Development*, 28: 879–91.
Cho, Y. and Newhouse, D. (2013) "How did the Great Recession affect different types of workers? Evidence from 17 middle-income countries," *World Development*, 41: 31–50.
Congregado, E., Golpe A.A., and van Stel, A. (2011) "Exploring the big jump in the Spanish unemployment rate: evidence on an 'added worker effect'," *Economic Modelling*, 28: 1099–105.
Cunningham, W. (2001) "Breadwinner or caregiver? How household role affects labour choices in Mexico?" World Bank Policy Research Working Paper 2743, Washington, DC.

EBRD (European Bank for Reconstruction and Development) (2009) *Transition in Crisis?* Annual Report, London: European Bank for Reconstruction and Development.

EBRD (2012) *Life in Transition: after the crisis*, London: European Bank for Reconstruction and Development.

EBRD (2013) "Regional economic perspectives in EBRD countries of operations: January 2013," EBRD Office of the Chief Economist, London: European Bank for Reconstruction and Development.

Fernandes, R. and de Felicio, F. (2005) "The entry of the wife into the labour force in response to the husband's unemployment: a study of the added worker effect in Brazilian metropolitan areas," *Economic Development and Cultural Change*, 53: 887–911.

Gong, X. (2011) "The added worker effect for married women in Australia," *The Economic Record*, 87: 414–26.

Greene, W.H. (2003) *Econometric Analysis*, 5th edn., Upper Saddle River, NJ: Prentice Hall.

Heltberg, R., Hossain, N., Reva, A., and Turk, C. (2012) "Anatomy of coping: evidence from people living through the crises of 2008–11," World Bank Policy Research Working Paper 5957, Washington, DC.

İlkkaracan I. and Değirmenci, S. (2013) "Economic crises and the added worker effect in the Turkish labour market," in R. Antonopoulos (ed.), *Gender Perspectives on the Global Economic Crisis*, London: Routledge.

ILO (International Labour Organization) (2010) *Women in Labour Markets: measuring progress and identifying challenges*, Geneva: International Labour Office.

ILO (2012) *Global Employment Trends for Youth 2012*, Geneva: International Labour Office.

Juhn, Ch. and Potter, S. (2007) "Is there still an added worker effect?" Federal Reserve Bank of New York Staff Report 310, New York.

Karaoglan, D. and Okten, C. (2012) "Labour force participation of married women in Turkey: is there an added or a discouraged worker effect?" IZA Discussion Paper 6616, Bonn.

Lokshin, M. and Yemtsov, R. (2004) "Household strategies for coping with poverty and social exclusion in post-crisis Russia," *Review of Development Economics*, 8: 15–32.

Lundberg, S. (1985) "The added worker effect," *Journal of Labour Economics*, 3: 11–37.

McKenzie, D. (2003) "How do households cope with aggregate shocks? Evidence from the Mexican Peso crisis," *World Development*, 31: 1179–99.

McKenzie, D. (2004) "Aggregate shocks and urban labour market responses: evidence from Argentina's financial crisis," *Economic Development and Cultural Change*, 52: 719–58.

McLaren, Z.M. (2012) "Coping with intrahousehold job separation in South Africa's labour market," IZA Working Paper 6811, Bonn.

Posadas, J. and Sinha, N. (2010) "Persistence of the added worker effect: evidence using panel data from Indonesia?" mimeo, Washington, DC: World Bank.

Prieto-Rodriguez, J. and Rodriguez-Gutierrez, C. (2003) "Participation of married women in the European labour markets and the 'added worker effect'," *Journal of Socio-Economics*, 32: 429–46.

Rubery, J. (ed.) (1988) *Women and Recession*, London: Routledge.

Sabarwal S., Sinha, N., and Buvinic, M. (2011) "How do women weather economic shocks? A review of the evidence," World Bank Research Working Paper 5496, Washington, DC.

Serneels, P. (2002) "The added worker effect and intrahousehold aspects of unemployment," Centre for the Study of African Economies Working Paper 2002-14, Oxford.

Singh, A. and Zammit, A. (2000) "International capital flows: identifying the gender dimension," *World Development*, 28: 1249–68.

Skoufias, E. and Parker, S.W. (2004) "The added worker effect over the business cycle: evidence from urban Mexico," *Applied Economics Letters*, 11: 625–30.

Spletzer, J.R. (1997) "Reexamining the added worker effect," *Economic Inquiry*, 35: 417–27.

Stephens, M., Jr. (2002) "Worker displacement and the added worker effect," *Journal of Labour Economics*, 20: 504–37.

Unal, F.G., Dokmanovic, M., and Abazov, R. (2010) "The economic and financial crises in CEE and CIS: gender perspectives and policy choices," Working Paper 598, Annandale-on-Hudson, NY: The Levy Economics Institute of Bard College.

UN (United Nations) (2013) *World Economic Situation and Prospects 2013: global outlook*, New York: United Nations.

UN (2009) *Gender Gap and Economic Policy: trends and good practices from the ECE region*, Geneva: United Nations.

United States Census Bureau (2012) "Census bureau reports more adults living in shared households, more receiving food stamps, public assistance unchanged," press release, November 28, 2012. Online: www.census.gov/newsroom/releases/archives/american_ community_survey_acs/cb12-224.html.

Vodopivec, M., Woergoetter, A., and Raju, D. (2005) "Unemployment benefit systems in central and eastern Europe: a review of the 1990s," *Comparative Economic Studies*, 47: 615–51.

World Bank (2012) *Opportunities for Men and Women: emerging Europe and Central Asia*, Washington, DC: World Bank.

9 Economic crises and the added worker effect in the Turkish labor market

Serkan Değirmenci and İpek İlkkaracan*

1 Introduction

As the repercussions of the global economic crisis in Turkey triggered a sharp increase in the national unemployment rate from 10 percent in 2007 to 14 percent in 2009, the Minister in Charge of Economic Affairs, Mehmet Şimşek, was reported to point to "housewives" deciding to look for jobs as an important source of the unemployment problem. He stated during a public speech at a conference entitled "The Global Financial Crisis and the Turkish Economy":

> You know why the unemployment rate has been increasing? Because more women than before start looking for jobs in times of economic crises ... [of the 50 million people who are the potential labor force in Turkey] more than half do not search jobs because they are housewives or students.... Hence it is important to have a correct reading of the implications of rising unemployment rates for the real economy. If there is unemployment because people have lost jobs, this means they are pushed out of the market, and of course this will create a negative impact on the economy. But if the person did not have a job before starting to look for one and that is what causes unemployment to rise, this would have a more limited impact on the economy. Hence we should not pump up the pessimism and try to have a correct reading of what this rise in unemployment means.
>
> (*Milliyet Daily Newspaper*, March 18, 2009)

Şimşek's unfortunate statement received much public uproar and criticism both for its gender discriminatory content as well as the unrealistic perspective that it offered on the unemployment problem. Nevertheless, the gendered labor force participation pattern that the minister referred to is one of the two distinct labor supply effects of economic downturns, one being the "added worker" effect, the other being the "discouraged worker" effect. Both effects are plausible responses

* The authors are grateful for insightful and careful reviews by Rania Antonopoulos of earlier versions of this chapter and also for comments by the participants of the session titled "The Great Recession: Gender Perspectives and Gender Impacts of the Global Economic Crisis" at the June 2012 IAFFE Conference in Barcelona, Spain.

to unemployment shocks, yet each affects labor force participation (and unemployment) in diametrically opposite directions.

The added worker effect refers to the case where household members who are not labor market participants or who are employed only as secondary earners of the household choose to increase their own labor supply in order to compensate for the income losses incurred due to involuntary job loss or reduction in the earnings of the primary worker who is usually the household head. This labor supply response of secondary workers is a transitory way of smoothing intertemporal income and consumption for a family. In the context of extended models, the added worker effect may also be influenced by other relevant factors such as unemployment insurance, employment uncertainty, and household liquidity constraints.[1] To the extent that the movements of added workers entail transitions from non-participation to unemployment, it can be said that the effect creates additional pressure on an already contracted labor market in the short run. On the other hand, economic crises can also culminate in the so-called "discouraged worker effect" (DWE), which refers to the case where previously active labor market participants give up looking for jobs and withdraw from the labor market altogether when they experience failed job searches or when their expectation to find a job is gravely reduced. Women's status as secondary earners makes them relatively more vulnerable to both effects.[2]

Ehrenberg and Smith (2000) report that the added worker effect becomes relatively weaker as women become increasingly integrated into the labor market through regular employment, and as unemployment insurance benefits provide incentives to remain out of the labor force. The Turkish labor market provides a weak example by both criteria and is therefore a candidate, in fact, for a strong added worker effect. Women in Turkey can be hardly considered to be integrated into the market; when the crisis hit in 2008, female labor force participation rate was only 24.5 percent, one of the lowest rates globally. Consequently, the male breadwinner household is still highly prevalent.[3] The unemployment insurance scheme, on the other hand, introduced in 2002, has only limited coverage. In the first half of 2009, at the peak of the crisis, as the unemployment rate hit record highs at 16.1 percent with 3.8 million people unemployed (February 2009), only about 8 percent of the unemployed received unemployment benefits.[4] Hence, by both criteria, the Turkish labor market appears to provide an ample setting for an added worker effect in response to economic downturns.

At the same time, however, the female employment rate has remained very low throughout the past three decades of market liberalization in Turkey despite a relatively high growth rate. This is reflective of deeply embedded structural factors, both on the supply and demand side, which create a disabling environment for women's integration into the labor market. The lack of work–family reconciliation mechanisms such as preschool child care centers or elderly care services, or employed women's poor access to maternity leave due to informal employment practices, creates bottlenecks on women's labor supply (İlkkaracan 2010). On the other hand, the growth process under trade and financial

liberalization since the 1980s has been one with limited capacity to generate sufficient employment demand vis-à-vis a growing population plus rural-to-urban
migration. To the extent that jobs have been created, the work conditions for
workers with lower education have entailed long work hours and low wages.
These poor labor market demand conditions have also played a crucial role in
the inability of the economic growth process to pull women into the labor market
(İlkkaracan 2012).

Hence, while Turkey does seem to provide an ample setting for the female
added worker strategy as a coping mechanism for households where the primary
male earner suffers from job loss, the structural factors against women's entry
into the labor market are also likely to weaken such potential. Against this background, this chapter aims to investigate the extent of the added worker effect in
Turkey, particularly in response to the recent economic crisis of 2008–09.

To the best of our knowledge, there are three studies on the added worker
effect in Turkey. Başlevent and Onaran (2003), based on an analysis of 1988 and
1994 Household Labor Force Survey micro data, report a statistically significant
added worker effect by married women in response to the 1994 currency crisis.
Their empirical analysis relies on a bivariate choice model of couples who live
in the same household and an estimation of a pair of probit equations, one on the
employment status of the husband and the other one on the participation status
of the wife. The study suggests that a negative (positive) correlation between the
error terms of the two equations will be indicative of an added worker (discouraged worker) effect. While they do not find any statistically significant correlation using 1988 data, they find a negative correlation for 1994, which they
interpret as an added worker effect dominating a discouraged worker effect. A
working paper by Polat and Saraceno (2010) adopts an identical methodology to
Başlevent and Onaran (2003) on a sample of married couples aged 24–54 from
the Household Budget Surveys for 2002–05 to explore the effects of the 2001
financial crisis in Turkey. Finding a statistically significant negative correlation
between the two probit estimations for 2002–04, they suggest this as evidence of
a strong added worker effect by married women as triggered by the 2001 crisis.[5]
Finally, another working paper by Karaoglan and Okten (2012), using a sample
of urban married couples aged 20–54 from Household Labor Force Survey data
for 2000–10, estimates a labor force participation equation for women, where
husband's unemployment and as well as regional unemployment rates are among
explanatory variables. They find a statistically significant positive coefficient on
husband's unemployment status whereby they also report on the extent of this
effect, such that husband's unemployment increases the probability that the wife
will enter the labor market by 4–8 percent varying across yearly cross-section
estimations. The study also finds a negative coefficient on the regional unemployment rate, which they interpret as evidence of a discouraged worker effect.[6]

In investigating evidence for an added worker effect among women using
Household Labor Force Survey (HFLS) micro data for 2004–10, this chapter
differs from the earlier studies in a number of respects. First of all, rather than
simply basing the analysis on a static association between women's observed

S. Değirmenci and İ. İlkkaracan

participation status and men's observed unemployment status in the survey period, we explore whether there is a dynamic relationship between transitions of women and men across labor market states. To do this, we make use of a question introduced to the HLFS in 2004 on previous year's labor market status. This allows us to explore transitions by female members of households from non-participant in the previous year to participant status in the current year, in response to male members making a transition from employed in the previous period to unemployed in the current period. Using this transition data, we explore whether and to what extent primary male earners moving from employed to unemployed status determines the probability of married or single female full-time homemakers entering the labor market. Second, we explore the female added worker effect not only for the overall sample as is the case in the previous studies, but also for different groups of women. Hence, we are able to demonstrate that the effect varies widely depending on particular characteristics of the woman, such as her education level, age, urban/rural residence, and marital and parental status.

The identification of the transitions of women and men between labor market states also allows us to estimate the extent of the female added worker effect at an aggregate level. Hence, unlike the above-mentioned earlier studies, which simply report at the individual micro level, whether an added worker effect exists in Turkey or not (like in Başlevent and Onaran 2003; Polat and Saraceno 2010), we are able to report estimates on absolute numbers of female added workers and shares of households that use female added workers as a coping strategy against unemployment shocks. Using these weighted numbers we are also able to report our estimates of the impact of the female added worker phenomenon on the unemployment rate or labor force participation rate in the 2008–09 economic crisis.

The rest of the chapter is organized as follows. Section 2 provides an overview of the gendered patterns in the Turkish labor market as well as the signs of the added worker effect as deduced from an examination of aggregate data on gender-disaggregated employment and unemployment rates. Section 3 describes the data, construction of the operational sample, and methodology. The findings are presented in Section 4, while we draw out our conclusions in Section 5.

2 Gendered patterns in employment and unemployment under economic crises

Structural transformation of the Turkish economy from agriculture toward industry and services has been an ongoing process since the start of the industrialization drive in the first half of the twentieth century. The accompanying population shift from rural to urban residence has resulted in a long-term declining trend in women's labor market activity rates. While men were transformed from a rural agricultural work force to urban industrial and service workers, women shifted from a rural agricultural work force of unpaid family workers to predominantly urban full-time homemakers. As a background, it is worth noting a number of manifestations of the gendered structure of the labor markets in Turkey.

First, the labor force participation gap is striking and remains persistent through time. The female participation rate remains under 30 percent versus an above 70 percent male participation rate. The gap exists both for rural and urban populations, but particularly so for the latter (Figure 9.1). Female rural participation rates are generally higher than urban ones, given the dominance of small-scale family farming in rural areas and women's participation in agricultural production in such settings. Yet, under the agricultural reform process in the 2000s as part of the World Bank structural adjustment program, public subsidies to agriculture were withdrawn and replaced by a temporary cash transfer scheme to alleviate the negative income impact. This resulted in a massive withdrawal of rural population from the labor force, particularly of women, who were previously employed as unpaid family workers in agriculture (İlkkaracan and Tunalı 2010). Hence, as can be seen in Figure 9.1, the decline in rural participation rates has narrowed the gender and within-group (that is, among women) difference with the urban labor market in the 2000s. Nevertheless, dominance of agricultural activities in rural areas continues to provide relatively more opportunities for rural women's participation, albeit at the cost of vulnerable employment, in the status of unpaid family workers. Small-scale family farming also provides a buffer for low-income households in response to economic fluctuations. This becomes particularly visible with the turnaround of the declining trends in rural participation rates since the start of the crisis in 2008.

Second, given the lack of subsidized child care centers and preschool education, reservation wages of women, which are influenced by the value they attribute to their unpaid household production, remain high. On the other hand, under unstable economic growth marked by frequent crises since financial liberalization in the

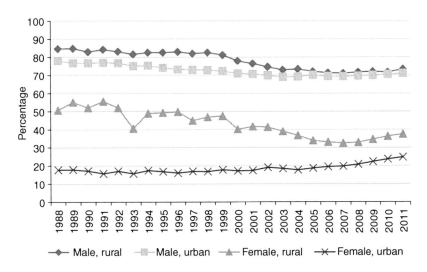

Figure 9.1 Labor force participation rates by gender and rural–urban residence 1988–2011 (source: TSI, HLFS data, www.tuik.gov.tr/VeriBilgi.do?alt_id=25).

early 1990s, labor market conditions have deteriorated; long working hours, low wages, and employment without social security coverage have become the standard working conditions particularly for lower-qualified workers. Hence, from an analytical point of view, the expected market value of wages for particularly lower-than-university educated urban women have remained lower than of their reservation wages conditioned by domestic care responsibilities.

In this context, it is expected that the gender participation gap varies widely by socioeconomic as well as marital status. A disaggregation of the gender participation gaps for urban prime working age population (age 20–44) by education level and marital status (Figure 9.2) indeed shows that for elementary school graduates, the participation rates for married (single) men is 70 (50) percentage points higher than for married (single) women; in the case of married (single) high school graduates the gap begins to narrow somewhat, at 50 (30) percentage points; and for married (single) university graduates, the gender gap narrows further down to (disappears at) 30 (0) percentage points (Figure 9.2). Given these widely varying patterns of female employment by education and marital status, the presence or magnitude of the added worker effect could also vary along the same lines. A stronger effect can be expected for more highly educated women as well as single women for whom the above-explained structural constraints are relatively less binding. For more highly educated women, the constraints are less binding because their expected market wages are higher. For single women, the constraints are less binding because their reservation wages are lower. Similarly, one can expect a weaker added worker effect for less educated and married women for whom structural constraints are truly disabling because they not only face lower expected market wages but also have higher reservation wages due to their marital and parental status. Variations in the added worker effect among different groups of women is one of the issues that we explore below in our analytical section.

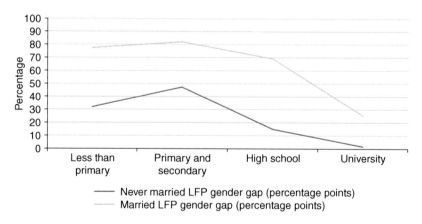

Figure 9.2 Gender labor force participation (LFP) gap by education and marital status (source: İlkkaracan 2010, based on HLFS micro data for 2008 for Urban Population of Prime Working Age (20–44)).

Third, an emerging characteristic of the labor market is the prevalence of informal employment. As of 2011, approximately 43 percent of the employed do not have any social security coverage. This is for some part due to the relatively large numbers of people employed in small-scale family farming. The competitive pressures of export-led growth have been another factor at work sustaining informal employment patterns in non-agricultural sectors: 24 percent of men and 27 percent of women employed in non-agricultural sectors do not have any social security coverage as of 2012 (TurkStat 2012). Yet, the switch from import substitution to export orientation in the early 1980s in Turkey did not trigger any secular increasing trend in female employment rates, as has been observed in many other developing economies under export-led growth. Female labor force participation rates remained around a meager 20 percent for most of the 1980s and 1990s.[7]

Following the financial liberalization reforms in the early 1990s, the Turkish economy went through periodic crises, including the 1994 and 2001 currency crises, and the 2008–09 crisis, which was triggered by the global downturn.

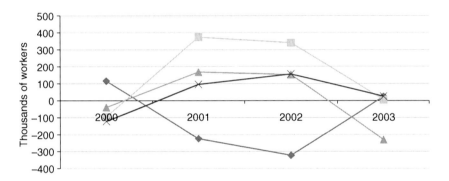

Figure 9.3a Change in numbers of employed and unemployed by gender: 2000–01 crisis (source: TSI, HLFS dataweb site, www.tuik.gov.tr/VeriBilgi.do?alt_id=25).

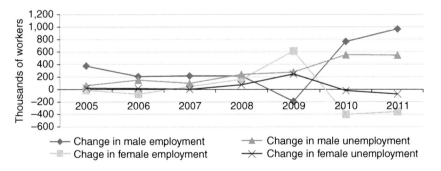

Figure 9.3b Change in numbers of employed and unemployed by gender: 2008–09 crisis (source: TSI, HLFS data, www.tuik.gov.tr/VeriBilgi.do?alt_id=25).

These recessions had the expected negative labor market effects in terms of increasing unemployment for men and women alike, but surprisingly, female employment registered a substantial increase in both periods. This was not the case for men.

The changes in the numbers of employed and unemployed men and women during the 2000–01 and 2008–09 crises are shown in Figure 9.3 (also see Appendix Table A1). Accordingly, in 2001 and 2002, the number of unemployed men rose by 374,000 (a 34 percent increase) and 341,000 (a 23 percent increase), respectively. During the same period, there was also a drop in the number of employed men by 225,000 persons in 2001 and 323,000 in 2002. The number of unemployed women also increased in both years (by 95,000 and 156,000 workers corresponding to an increase of 25 and 32 percent, respectively). The 2008–09 crisis had a more dramatic impact on unemployment. The number of unemployed men rose by 161,000 in 2008 and a phenomenal 614,000 in 2009, while male employment declined by 192,000 persons. This corresponded to an almost 4 percentage point increase in the male unemployment rate (from 10 percent in 2007 to 13.9 percent in 2009). The number of unemployed women increased by 74,000 in 2008 and 245,000 in 2009, marking an increase in the female unemployment rate of over 3 percentage points (from 11 percent in 2007 to 14.3 percent in 2009). Yet, what is striking is that while there is a substantial decline in male employment in both crises, we observe a net increase in female employment rates with around 150,000 women entering the labor market per year in 2001 and 2002, and around 250,000 per year in 2008 and 2009.

Put simply, we observe an increasing trend of female labor force participation rates in crisis periods. These aggregate figures do seem to indicate a possible added worker effect.[8] In the following sections, we present evidence from micro data of household labor force surveys to explore the extent to which such a female added worker effect has been at work in the recent economic crisis.

3 Data and methodology

In this study, we utilize HLFS micro data for the period 2004–10. To identify the added worker effect, we take advantage of the question on "previous year's labor market status," which was added to the survey from 2004 onwards. The HLFS have been conducted by the Turkish Statistical Agency (TurkStat) since 1988,[9] and over the years both the survey questionnaire as well as the sampling base have undergone a number of improvements. One of the most significant revisions was undertaken in 2004, whereby the number of questions in the survey almost doubled and the sampling was expanded to enable reporting on a regional basis by 26 NUTS2 regions.[10] The questions of particular interest for our purposes have also been integrated into the HLFS since 2004. These are questions on past year's labor market status (inquiring about the work status of the person in the previous year); identifying whether s/he was employed at the same job, at another job, or looking for a job; or, if declaring to be not a labor market participant, then providing non-participant status information according to a list of five options: homemaker, retired, student, ill or disabled, and other. Using the answers to these questions, it becomes possible to follow the transitions across the states of non-participant, employed, and unemployed.

Hence, the following analysis makes use of the annual HLFS for seven years from 2004 to 2010. There are 472,837 individual observations in 121,622 households in the 2004 HLFS. From 2004 onwards, there is a slight increase in the sample size of each year's HLFS that reflects population growth. Accordingly, the 2010 HLFS consists of 522,171 individual observations in 143,871 households.

Making use of the question on past year's labor market status, the analysis proceeds in two steps. The first step entails an attempt to identify the extent and profile of the added worker effect. We identify for each year of analysis the transitions by women from non-participant to participant (employed or unemployed) in households that suffer an unemployment shock and in households where no such shock takes place. What we call the "unemployment shock households" are those where the primary male earner (the male reference person) has made a transition from being employed in the previous year to unemployed in the current year.[11] In these households, we identify the women of working age (15–65) who, in the previous year, had full-time homemaker or retired status.[12] Given the very low female labor force participation rates in Turkey, the retired make up as little as 2.5 percent (2004) to 3.5 percent (2010) of the non-participant females in our operational sample; hence, the analysis below pertains primarily to transitions out of full-time homemaking to labor market participation.[13] Hence, from here onwards, we refer to the non-participant status as homemakers. These constitute our pool of potential female added workers. Out of this pool, we identify the ones who actually make a transition into employed or unemployed status in the current year. These are the women who can be qualified as added workers, yet with a number of caveats.

First of all, limiting the scope of the analysis only to unemployment shocks to male primary earners suffers from an underestimation of the added worker effect. It is possible that some of the transitions in the non-shock households also entail an added worker effect, whereby the transition is triggered by falling earnings or increasing job loss risk by the male primary earner as well as any other members of the household suffering from similar unemployment shocks, earnings declines, or increasing job loss risk. Also, beyond entry of non-participant women into the labor market, the added worker effect can also entail an increase of working hours by those already in employment.

On the other hand, to the extent that some of the labor market transitions by women in the unemployment shock households are independent of the male reference person becoming unemployed, it would be an overestimation. To enable a comparison, we also identify women making similar transitions (from full-time homemaking to participant status) in the households where the reference person is male but who does not experience a similar unemployment shock. In other words, these are the households where the male reference person either did not change labor market status since the previous year or made a transition across participant and non-participant states but not from employed to unemployed.[14] Through a comparison of these two types of households, those exposed to an unemployment shock and those that were not, we argue that any significant difference in female transition ratios would be indicative of an added worker effect.

Hence, it can be said that while the question on past labor market status provides a useful tool for some approximate estimation of added workers, it does not permit a perfect identification given the nature of available data. Labor force surveys do not pose any questions as to why the respondents move between different labor market states. Hence, it is not possible to identify those who enter the labor market in order to compensate for the loss of labor income by other members of the household. At best, the transitions by women to the labor market in these different types of households can be said to provide some estimate of the range of the added worker effect by female homemakers. In the analysis that follows, we use the weighted numbers of women making the transition into the labor market in the unemployment shock households and the non-shock households to provide a rough estimate of the impact of female added worker effect on the increase in the aggregate employment and unemployment rates observed during the crisis year. We also provide a comparison of the transition ratios in Turkey to those reported for 11 EU countries in an earlier study of the added worker effect in Europe. Finally, we present demographic and employment profiles of the women making the transition in the two groups.

The second step of the analysis entails a logit regression analysis to identify the isolated effect of a household unemployment shock at instigating a transition from non-participant to participant status by women after controlling for a range of other determinants of transitions. We conduct cross-section estimations of annual data for each year using the following model:

$$y_i = \alpha_0 + \alpha_1\ Ushock_i + \alpha_2\ X_i + \alpha_3 U_r + + \alpha_4 A_r + \alpha_5 S_r + \mu_i$$

The dependent variable y is a binary variable that takes on the value 1 if woman i has made a transition into the labor market from non-participant (homemaker or retired) status in the previous year to the labor market in the current year and 0 if not. *Ushock*, our explanatory variable of interest, is again a binary variable that takes on the value 1 if woman i is a member of a household that experienced an unemployment shock (i.e., the male reference person has moved from employment in the previous year to unemployment in the current year) and 0 if no such shock has taken place. X_i entails a series of control variables for labor and household heterogeneity, such as woman's demographic (age, education, and marital and parental status) and household characteristics (education and social security status of household head, presence of other employed household members, household size, rural/urban residence). We also include a series of demand side controls for regional variations in labor demand: U_r is the unemployment rate in region r; A_r and S_r are shares of agricultural and service sector employment in total regional employment. The regional disaggregation entails 26 regions at the NUTS2 level. μ_i is the error term independently distributed across individuals. Our operational sample consists of women of working age (15–65) who were in homemaker or retired status in the previous year and living in households with a male reference person. This makes up approximately 50 percent of the total female sample of working age.

Based on the results of the logit regression above, we are able to estimate the marginal effects of an unemployment shock to the household (i.e., the primary male earner moving from employed to unemployed) on increasing/decreasing the probability of the dependent variable (i.e., the probability of a female homemaker making the transition to the labor market). In logit analysis, with a binary dependent variable, it is hypothesized that the probability of the occurrence and non-occurrence of an event is determined by the following functions:

$$\text{Prob}(Y = 1 \mid x) = F(x, \beta)$$

$$\text{Prob}(Y = 0 \mid x) = 1 - F(x, \beta)$$

The set of parameters β reflects the impact of changes in x on the probability. The problem at this point is to devise a suitable model for the right-hand side of the equation. For a given regressor vector, we would expect

$$\lim_{x'\beta \to +\infty} \text{Prob}(Y = 1 \mid x) = 1$$

$$\lim_{x'\beta \to -\infty} \text{Prob}(Y = 1 \mid x) = 0$$

The normal distribution has been used in many analyses, giving rise to the probit model,

$$\text{Prob}(Y = 1 \mid x) = \int_{-\infty}^{x'\beta} \varphi(t)dt = \Phi(x'\beta)$$

The function $\Phi(t)$ is a commonly used as notation for the standard normal distribution function. Partly because of its mathematical convenience, the logistic distribution,

$$\text{Prob}(Y = 1 \mid x) = \frac{\exp(x'\beta)}{1 + \exp(x'\beta)} = \Lambda(x'\beta)$$

has also been used in many applications. The notation $\Lambda(\cdot)$ indicates the logistic cumulative distribution function and the model is called the logit model which is used in the following analysis.

The marginal effect of an explanatory variable X is the partial derivative of the prediction with respect to X and measures the expected change in the response variable as a function of the change in X with the other explanatory variables held constant. Presenting marginal effects often brings more information than just looking at coefficients. So the marginal effect measurement is required to interpret the effect of the regressors on the dependent variable. For the logistic distribution, we calculate the marginal effect as

$$\frac{d\Lambda(x'\beta)}{d(x'\beta)} = \frac{\exp(x'\beta)}{[1+\exp(x'\beta)]^2} = \Lambda(x'\beta)[1-\Lambda(x'\beta)]$$

So, in the logit model,

$$\frac{\partial E(y\mid x)}{\partial x} = \Lambda(x'\beta)[1-\Lambda(x'\beta)]\beta$$

When x_j is a continuous variable, its partial effect on $\Pr(y=1|x)$ is obtained from the partial derivative:

$$\frac{\partial \Pr(y=1\mid x)}{\partial x_j} = \frac{\partial F(x\beta)}{\partial x_j} = f(x\beta)\beta_j,$$

where

$$f(z) \equiv \frac{dF(z)}{dz}$$

is the probability density function associated with F. Because the density function is non-negative, the partial effect of x_j will always have the same sign as β_j.

When x_j is a dichotomous independent variable, the marginal effect is the difference in the adjusted predictions for the two groups. If x_2 is binary, the partial effect of changing x_2 from 0 to 1, holding all other variables fixed, is

$$F(\beta_1 + \beta_2 \cdot 1 + \cdots + \beta_K x_K) - F(\beta_1 + \beta_2 \cdot 0 + \cdots + \beta_K x_K)$$

Or keeping the notation in terms of probabilities, we can express the appropriate marginal effect for a binary independent variable, say d, as follows:

$$\text{Marginal Effect} = \Prob[Y=1-|\bar{x}(d), d=1] - \Prob[Y=1-|\bar{x}(d), d=0]$$

where $\bar{x}(d)$, denotes the means of all the other variables in the model. Simply taking the derivative with respect to the binary variable as if it were continuous provides an approximation that is often surprisingly accurate. Hence, based on the results of the logit regression, we are able to estimate the marginal effects of an unemployment shock to the household, which is a binary variable (i.e., taking on the value 1 if the primary male earner has moved from employed status in the previous year to unemployed status in the current year or 0 otherwise) on increasing the occurrence probability of the dependent variable (i.e., taking on the value 1 if the woman who was a homemaker in the previous year has moved to participant status in the current year) based on mean values of all the other explanatory variables.

4 Empirical analysis

4.1 Identifying the added worker effect through transitions between labor market states: numbers and shares of female added workers

Table 9.1 displays the numbers and shares of transitions by male household reference persons from employment to unemployment (what we call the unemployment shock households) and the transitions in these households by women from non-participant (homemaker) status to participant (employed or unemployed) status. The number of male reference persons moving from employment to unemployment is stable, close to 300,000 people per year in 2004–07 (around 2.6 percent of all households with an employed male reference person). 2008 records a rise by almost 30 percent, to 373,000 (increasing to 3.3 percent of all households with an employed male reference person). This is followed by an even more dramatic increase by 42 percent in 2009 to over half-a-million male household reference people leaving employment and starting to look for a job (peaking at 5 percent of all households with an employed male reference person). 2010, the recovery year after the crisis, records a decline in these numbers, but they are still above the pre-2008 figures.

The last column of Table 9.1 shows the numbers and shares of women who make the transition from non-participant (homemaker) status to labor market participant (employed or unemployed) status in these unemployment shock households. Two observations stand out. First, they are generally quite low, ranging from a minimum of 5 percent of all female homemakers living in these households in 2004 (13,454 women) to a peak of 8.3 percent in 2009 (36,209 women) and 9 percent in 2010 (27,661 women), exhibiting an increase under the economic crisis.[15] These shares are not as substantial as we had expected against a background of very low female participation rate as well as very low coverage by unemployment insurance in Turkey. The second observation is that almost equal shares of women enter the labor market through employment (starting to work at a job) as unemployment (starting to look for a job).

Table 9.2 juxtaposes the transitions by women in unemployment shock households that were displayed in Table 9.1 to similar transitions by women in non-shock households. Women's transition ratios in the unemployment shock households are stable over the time period observed but also consistently and substantially higher (almost double the rate) than those in the non-shock households, which is indicative of the presence of an added worker effect. The gap between the shares of transitions grows wider in 2009–10 as the crisis deepens. Another difference between the two groups' transitions is that in the unemployment shock

Table 9.1 Transitions between labor market states by men and women in households experiencing an unemployment shock

Year		Male reference persons moving from employed to unemployed	Female homemakers moving from non-participant to employed	Female homemakers moving from non-participant to unemployed	Female homemakers moving from non-participant to participant (employed + unemployed)
2004	No.*	297,731	7,034	6,420	13,454
	%	2.6**	2.6	2.4	5.0***
2005	No.	293,541	11,082	8,457	19,539
	%	2.6	4.2	3.2	7.4
2006	No.	286,721	9,429	8,478	17,907
	%	2.5	4.0	3.6	7.6
2007	No.	289,652	11,433	6,497	17,930
	%	2.7	4.5	2.6	7.1
2008	No.	372,766	9,255	11,010	20,265
	%	3.3	2.9	3.5	6.4
2009	No.	530,463	19,373	16,836	36,209
	%	4.8	4.4	3.8	8.3
2010	No.	376,409	14,849	12,812	27,661
	%	3.4	4.8	4.2	9.0

Source: TurkStat (2012), HLFS micro data 2004–10.

Note
* The numbers are weighted numbers. ** Percent of all employed male household reference people. *** Percent of all female homemakers living in the unemployment shock households.

Table 9.2 Transitions to the labor market by women in unemployment shock and non-shock households 2004–10

Year	Type of household		Female homemakers moving from non-participant to employed	Female homemakers moving from non-participant to unemployed	Female homemakers moving from non-participant to participant (employed + unemployed)
2004	Unemployment shock HHs	No.*	7,034	6,420	13,454
		%**	2.6	2.4	5
	Non-shock HHs	No.	199,236	133,132	332,368
		%	1.5	1.1	2.6
2005	Unemployment shock HHs	No.	11,082	8,457	19,539
		%	4.2	3.2	7.4
	Non-shock HHs	No.	385,979	165,804	551,783
		%	2.9	1.3	4.2
2006	Unemployment shock HHs	No.	9,429	8,478	17,907
		%	4.0	3.6	7.6
	Non-shock HHs	No.	404,180	178,740	582,920
		%	3.0	1.3	4.3
2007	Unemployment shock HHs	No.	11,433	6,497	17,930
		%	4.5	2.6	7.1
	Non-shock HHs	No.	360,331	151,605	511,936
		%	2.8	1.2	4.0
2008	Unemployment shock HHs	No.	9,255	11,010	20,265
		%	2.9	3.5	6.4
	Non-shock HHs	No.	354,623	173,795	528,418
		%	2.8	1.5	4.3
2009	Unemployment shock HHs	No.	19,373	16,836	36,209
		%	4.4	3.8	8.3
	Non-shock HHs	No.	343,851	196,042	539,893
		%	2.8	1.7	4.5
2010	Unemployment shock HHs	No.	148,49	12,812	27,661
		%	4.8	4.2	9.0
	Non-shock HHs	No.	412,495	208,481	620,976
		%	3.4	1.8	5.2

Source: TurkStat (2012), HLFS micro data 2004–10.

Note

* The numbers are weighted numbers. ** Percentage of all female homemakers living in the relevant household category.

households, almost half the women who enter the labor market move into unemployment, while in the non-shock households only about 30 percent enter unemployment, while the majority moves from non-participant status directly into employment. This can be taken as indicative of the distress conditions under which the female added worker effect takes place in the unemployment shock households

As far as the absolute weighted numbers are concerned, the number of women who make a transition to the labor market in 2009 at the peak of the crisis reaches a high of 36,209 women in unemployment shock households, and over half-a-million in non-shock households. As far as the effect on the labor force participation or unemployment rate is concerned, the impact is very little if we limit the added worker effect to only transitions in unemployment shock households. If the 36,209 female homemakers living in the households where the primary male earner lost his job had not entered the labor market, the female labor force participation rate would have decreased from 26 percent (the rate reported in official statistics for 2009) to only 25.9 percent. As for the unemployment rate, if the 16,836 women who made a transition to unemployed status were to continue in their homemaking status, the unemployment rate would decrease only by 0.05 percentage point from 14.02 percent as reported in official statistics to merely 13.97 percent.[16]

This is, however, an underestimation as explained above, since some of the transitions in the non-shock households possibly entail some added worker effect due to declining income or increasing instability of the primary male earner or due to job loss, declining earnings, or increased job risk faced by members of the household other than the male reference person. At a maximum, if we were to consider the counterfactual situation that all the female homemakers of working age living in households with a male reference person that we identified as making the transition in 2009, this constitutes a total of 576,102 women (539,893 + 36,209). If all of them were to remain in full-time homemaking rather than entering the labor market, then the female participation rate would have declined by a non-negligible 2 percentage points (from 26 to 24 percent). The total number of unemployed would be lower by 212,878 people; hence, the aggregate unemployment rate would have declined only by half a percentage point from 14 to 13.5 percent. Hence, even at a gross overestimation of the female added worker effect, the "housewives starting to look for jobs" in the minister's words seems to have played a very limited role in raising unemployment rates under the crisis.

4.2 Demographic and employment profiles of transitions from homemaker to the labor market

The demographic profiles of the transitions are outlined in Figures 9.4a–9.4d for two selected years, 2007 as a non-crisis year and 2009 as the crisis year.[17] The homemakers we identified as making a transition into the labor market are predominantly lower-educated women (more than two-thirds have primary or

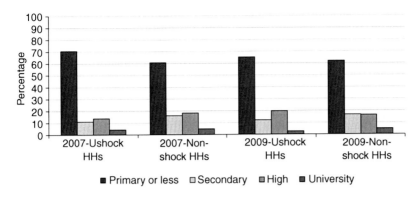

Figure 9.4a Homemakers entering the labor market by level of education.

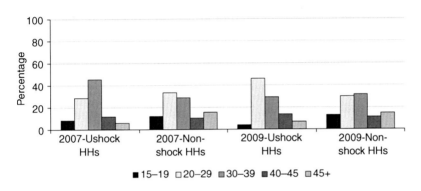

Figure 9.4b Homemakers entering the labor market by age group.

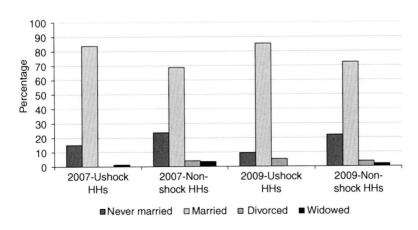

Figure 9.4c Homemakers entering the labor market by marital status.

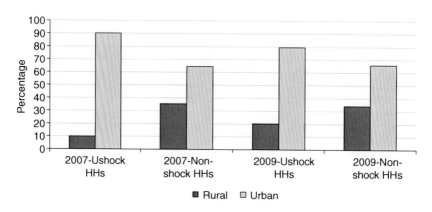

Figure 9.4d Homemakers entering the labor market by urban/rural residence (source: TSI, HLFS micro data 2007 and 2009).

less schooling), younger (under 40 years old), married (about 70–80 percent), mostly in urban residence (two-thirds). This general profile reflects average population characteristics. Yet there are some noteworthy differences between the transitions depending on whether the household has been exposed to an unemployment shock or not. The education profile of the homemakers entering the labor market in unemployment shock households is more skewed toward lower levels of education than those in the non-shock households. There is a relatively larger share of those above age 40 in unemployment shock households. Married women have a relatively larger share (85 percent) of transitions in unemployment shock households than in non-shock households (70 percent). In 2009, for instance, 22 percent of transitions in non-shock households are by never-married (younger) women versus only 9.4 percent in unemployment shock households.

As far as the employment profiles are concerned (Figures 9.5a–9.5e), in non-shock households a striking one-third of the transitions into employment are in the agricultural sector, which is also reflected in the higher shares of unpaid family workers and self-employed. Hence, a non-negligible number of transitions in non-shock households reflect entry–exit in and out of small-scale family farming characteristic of rural women. By contrast, in unemployment shock households, female transitions into agriculture are under 10 percent. They are predominantly in industry (40 percent), trade (10–20 percent), and services (20–30 percent). It is striking that of those who make a transition in unemployment shock households in the crisis year of 2009–10, it is overwhelmingly in full-time (79 percent), salaried (87 percent), and permanent (64 percent) jobs. Yet, only one-third (36 percent) have social security coverage. Social security coverage for women entering employment in non-shock households is even less (about one-fifth), reflective of the dominance of agricultural work in this category.

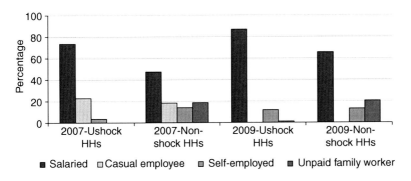

Figure 9.5a Homemakers entering employment by work status.

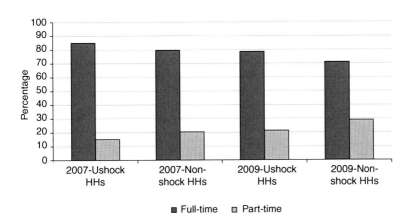

Figure 9.5b Homemakers entering employment by work time.

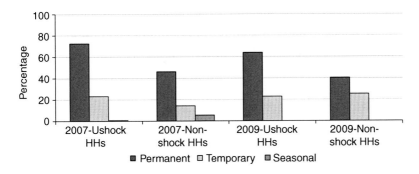

Figure 9.5c Homemakers entering employment by type of contract.

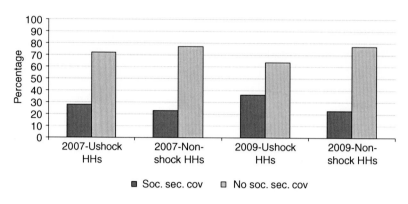

Figure 9.5d Homemakers entering employment by social security coverage.

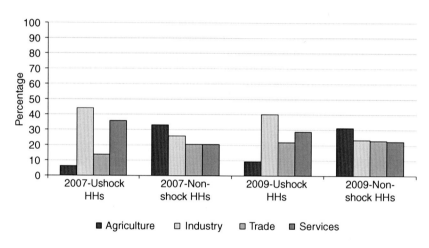

Figure 9.5e Homemakers entering employment by sector (source: TSI, HLFS micro data 2007 and 2009).

4.3 Estimating the marginal effect of the unemployment shock on transitions to the labor market

In order to estimate the marginal effects of a household unemployment shock on probability of a female homemaker making a transition into the labor market, we ran two sets of yearly cross-section estimations: those including only labor supply-side variables, as is common in most studies on labor supply, and also estimations adding demand-side controls such as the regional unemployment rate and the regional shares of agriculture and services in total employment. These demand-side variables are meant to control for regional variations in employment demand rather than reflect the effects of a demand-side shock over time, since the regressions are cross-section estimations. The marginal effects of the unemployment shock variable for different estimations are presented in Table 9.3, while the results for all the other controls are presented in the Appendix Tables A2i, A2ii, A3a.i, A3a.ii, and A3b.

All estimations show that a household unemployment shock is a statistically significant and economically meaningful determinant of women's transitions into the labor market after controlling for a range of other supply- and demand-side variables. Table 9.3 displays the estimated marginal effects of an unemployment shock on the probability that a female homemaker makes a transition to the labor market; the results are displayed for the entire sample as well as for different subgroups.

For the overall sample, we find that a household unemployment shock (male reference person moving from employment to unemployment) increases the probability that a female homemaker will enter the labor market by 3 percent at a minimum observed for 2004; but for the rest of the annual cross-sections by around 6–8 percent.[18] The results of estimations, including demand-side control, are reported for two years, 2007 as a non-crisis year and 2009 as the crisis year.[19] We observe that introducing the demand-side controls for regional variation – such as the regional unemployment rate, regional share of agriculture, and services in total employment – does not change the sign or magnitude of the marginal effect of the unemployment shock in any substantial manner.

The estimations for different subgroups of women in the rest of Table 9.3 show that the marginal effects of the unemployment shock vary substantially across different demographic profiles. A household unemployment shock increases the probability that a rural homemaker will enter the labor market by 11 percent in 2009 versus 6 percent for an urban homemaker with average characteristics. Restricting the operational sample to the 20–45 age group, we observe a higher marginal effect of the unemployment shock than the overall sample (age 15–65). A household unemployment shock increases the probability that a university graduate homemaker in the 20–45 age group will enter the labor market by 34 percent, while the marginal effect is 17 percent for a high school graduate, only 7 percent for a secondary school graduate, and 13 percent for a primary school graduate in the same age group. The marginal effect of an unemployment shock is larger for a married woman in the 20–45 age group with no small child (13.2 percent) than for her counterpart with a small child (11.5 percent). These differences in added worker effects for different groups of women parallel the differences in employment patterns by education and marital status that were presented in the second section. As discussed above, such varying patterns among women are reflective of the structural constraints against their labor market engagement. Our findings here show that the added worker effect is similarly conditioned by the same structural constraints conditioning women's labor force participation patterns and hence result in varying magnitudes of the effect by education level (determining women's expected market wages) and marital status (determining women's reservation wages).

Table 9.3 Marginal effects of a household unemployment shock on female homemakers' transitions into the labor market

	2004	2005	2006	2007	2008	2009	2010
All sample Supply-side variables only	0.0331*** (0.00540)	0.0589*** (0.00773)	0.0652*** (0.00884)	0.0699*** (0.00879)	0.0634*** (0.00776)	0.0695*** (0.00674)	0.0750*** (0.00820)
All sample Including demand-side variables				0.06880 (0.00859)		0.0713 (0.00684)	
Urban	0.0322*** (0.00570)	0.0505*** (0.00754)	0.0575*** (0.00866)	0.0580*** (0.00830)	0.0658*** (0.00847)	0.0575*** (0.00667)	0.0667*** (0.00828)
Rural	0.0255** (0.0121)	0.0674*** (0.0204)	0.0640*** (0.0230)	0.0821*** (0.0251)	0.0368** (0.0158)	0.110*** (0.0202)	0.107*** (0.0262)
Age 20–45	0.0438*** (0.00852)	0.0670*** (0.0106)	0.0722*** (0.0118)	0.0993*** (0.0134)	0.0842*** (0.0121)	0.104*** (0.0111)	0.117*** (0.0138)
Age 20–45 and...							
Primary graduate	0.0398*** (0.0109)	0.0599*** (0.0131)	0.0973*** (0.0178)	0.106*** (0.0191)	0.0791*** (0.0158)	0.125*** (0.0173)	0.128*** (0.0202)
Secondary graduate	0.127** (0.0525)	0.0502 (0.0355)	0.0832* (0.0447)	0.0990* (0.0581)	0.0783** (0.0393)	0.0668** (0.0300)	0.166*** (0.0457)
High school graduate	0.0955** (0.0395)	0.147*** (0.0451)	0.0929** (0.0411)	0.146*** (0.0436)	0.167*** (0.0470)	0.166*** (0.0354)	0.157*** (0.0468)
University graduate	0.253 (0.184)	0.0590 (0.127)	0.311 (0.212)	0.275* (0.143)	0.121 (0.125)	0.335*** (0.122)	0.200 (0.129)
Married with child 0–4				0.153*** (0.0323)	0.0883*** (0.0232)	0.115*** (0.0218)	0.165*** (0.0296)
Married with NO child 0–4				0.107*** (0.0204)	0.113*** (0.0195)	0.132*** (0.0182)	0.129*** (0.0203)

Another interesting aspect of our findings is that marginal effects of the unemployment shock are not necessarily higher in the crisis years (2008–10) compared to non-crisis years. The marginal effect that we pick up through the logit estimation is that of a micro-level unemployment shock specific to the observed household. It is likely that a macro shock may enhance further the marginal effect of the micro-level shock due to deteriorating labor market conditions and the lower likelihood of the male primary earner finding another job in a crisis context. On the other hand, it is also possible that such a negative macro shock can also trigger a discouraged worker effect through decreasing possibilities for finding jobs and deteriorating work conditions and weaken the added worker effect at the micro level. The lack of any significant differences in marginal effects between crisis and non-crisis years can possibly be attributed to counteracting forces of both effects at work in a simultaneous manner.[20]

We should also note that the other coefficients on supply-side controls have the expected signs (Tables A2i, A2ii, A3a.i, A3a.ii, and A3b): the probability that the woman will make a transition to the labor market increases with her education level and age (but at a decreasing rate with age); it is lower for urban women, given the option of working as an unpaid family worker in agriculture for rural women; it is also lower for married women and those with small children, as well as larger household size, due to heavier domestic work load. The probability also decreases with higher education of the household reference person, his social security coverage and presence of other employed household members. The negative association of women's transitions into the labor market with this last set of controls can be interpreted as indicative of better income access (and hence fall back) options of higher socioeconomic status households.

Considering the findings above, there seems to be a well-defined female added worker effect in Turkey, but it is of limited scope. Table 9.4 juxtaposes our findings of transition ratios in Turkey (this time modified for married women only) for 2009 when they reach the highest levels with those reported for 11 EU countries in a study by Prieto-Rodriguez and Rodriguez-Gutierrez (2003). Married women's transitions are disaggregated here for two types of husbands' transitions, namely, husband remains employed and husband moves from employed to unemployed or non-participant. Among the EU countries, the Netherlands (26.4 and 41.6 percent) and Denmark (30.1 and 33.4 percent) have the highest female transition ratios for both categories of husbands' transitions, while Ireland has the lowest (6.4 and 7 percent). Italy has the second lowest female transition ratio (8 percent) after Ireland for the case of husbands remaining in employment, and Portugal has the second lowest share (3.3 percent) for the case of husbands moving into unemployment or non-participation. Turkey, even at the highest level of transitions in 2009, displays the lowest female transition ratio at 4.4 percent for the case of husbands remaining in employment. For the case of husbands moving out of employment, it has the second lowest share at 5.8 percent after Portugal.

Table 9.4 Comparison of married women's transition ratios in Turkey with 11 EU countries

	Husband-work to work			Husband-work to unemployment or inactivity			Total number of Transitions
	Woman remains inactive	Woman-inactivity to-work	Woman-inactivity to-unemployment	Woman remains inactive	Woman-inactivity to-work	Woman-inactivity to-unemployment	
Turkey	95.6	2.9	1.6	94.2	3.3	2.5	330
Belgium	85	8.9	6.1	100	–	–	427
Denmark	68.9	14.3	16.8	66.6	11.1	22.3	170
France	87.9	8.9	3.2	81.2	6.2	12.6	1,066
Germany	90.2	7.5	2.3	80.1	6.6	13.3	1,228
Great Britain	83.6	14.9	1.5	85.7	14.3	–	626
Greece	85.7	4.9	9.4	80.7	8.8	10.5	1,145
Ireland	93.6	5.4	1	93	4.2	2.8	1,030
Italy	92	4.4	3.6	84.8	5.5	9.7	2,319
Holland	73.6	7.7	18.7	58.4	33.3	8.3	1,107
Portugal	86.9	7.5	5.4	96.7	3.2	–	1,008
Spain	90.8	4	5.2	81.8	5.8	12.4	2,256

Source: The transition ratios for Turkey have been calculated by the authors from HLFS micro data for the year 2009. The figures for the EU countries reproduced from Prieto-Rodriguez and Rodriguez-Gutierrez (2003) were derived from European Community Household Panel (ECHP), for the years 1994–96.

5 Conclusion

Given very low labor force participation rates of women and the dominance of single-male earner households, combined with limited scope of unemployment insurance, one would expect Turkey to provide a setting conducive to a potential added worker effect as a household strategy to cope with economic downturns. At the same time, we noted that there are strong structural constraints on both the supply and demand sides that create a disabling environment for women's labor market engagement. The lack of child care facilities or elderly care services and limited access to maternity leave impose binding constraints on the supply side. Poor employment generation, low wages, long working hours, and informal employment practices on the demand side provide poor prospects for expected returns from participation. Such structural constraints are likely to weaken any potential for the female added worker effect to emerge as a household coping strategy in cases of job loss by the primary male earner.

Our analysis of HLFS micro data for 2004–10 shows that there is definitely evidence of a female added worker effect in Turkey but that it is of limited scope. Comparing transitions in households that suffer from an unemployment shock to those that do not, we find that in the former the share of women moving from homemaking to participant status are almost double those in the latter and also the share of those who enter directly into unemployed status are much higher. Yet even in the crisis years only 8–10 percent of the prime working age female homemakers living in a household where the primary male earner experienced job loss is observed to move from full-time homemaking status to labor market participation. A comparison with married women's transitions to labor market ratios (juxtaposed to male transitions to unemployment) from a sample of EU countries shows that Turkey displays much lower female transition tendency even at the peak of the crisis when the shares of women moving from homemaking to labor market reaches their highest levels. Given the limited possibilities for women to compensate for income loss by the primary male earner, do Turkish households revert to other coping mechanisms or are they simply worse off than their counterparts in other countries? This remains a question to be explored.

Cross-section yearly regressions with woman's transition as the dependent variable shows that, after controlling for a whole range of supply- as well as regional demand-side variables, an unemployment shock to the primary male earner is a statistically significant and positively associated determinant of women's moving from full-time homemaking to labor market participation. The male primary earner experiencing job loss increases the probability that a female homemaker will enter the labor market by 6–8 percent. However, estimations for different subsamples of the operational sample yield wide-ranging estimates of marginal effects. For instance, a household unemployment shock increases the probability that a university graduate homemaker in the 20–45 age group will enter the labor market by as much as 34 percent, for a high school graduate by 17 percent, while for her counterpart with a secondary education by only

7 percent. We should note, however, that university graduates constitute only as little as 11 percent of the female adult population (age 25+) and high school graduates only 18 percent (TurkStat 2012). In other words, the overwhelming majority of adult women in Turkey have secondary or lower education and hence face poor employment prospects (long working hours and low wages) in that they were to enter the labor market in a context where there is no public provisioning of care services to alleviate their domestic workload.

We conclude that while the female added worker strategy is evidently a coping mechanism of some households in Turkey in the context of an economic crisis, such a strategy is of limited accessibility for many households when the primary earner becomes unemployed and there are eligible working age women with the potential to enter the labor market. We attribute this finding for Turkey to the deeply embedded structural constraints on women's integration into the labor market. The disabling factors both on the labor supply and demand sides are particularly hindering for married women with lower labor market qualifications, a group that constitutes the majority of the female adult population. This means that in households of lower socioeconomic status, which are also the households that are more fragile vis-à-vis unemployment shocks, women have only limited ability to enter the labor market to compensate for income losses by the primary male earner.

Table A1 Changes in number of employed and unemployed by gender: 2000–01 and 2008–09 crises

Change in (in 1000s)	Employed men	Unemployed men	Employed women	Unemployed women
2000–01 crisis				
2000	115	−95	−40	−122
2001	−225	374	168	95
2002	−323	341	153	156
2003	24	4	−231	25
2008–09 crisis				
2005	374	−16	61	20
2006	206	−75	150	16
2007	217	45	98	2
2008	216	161	239	74
2009	−192	614	276	245
2010	764	−403	554	−20
2011	967	−358	548	−74

Source: TSI, HLFS data (www.tuik.gov.tr/VeriBilgi.do?alt_id=25).

Table A2.i Logistic regressions on transitions 2004–10 (logit coefficients)

VARIABLES	2004 coefficient	2005 coefficient	2006 coefficient	2007 coefficient	2008 coefficient	2009 coefficient	2010 coefficient
UshockHH	1.276***	1.208***	1.248***	1.440***	1.324***	1.330***	1.278***
	(0.125)	(0.100)	(0.106)	(0.107)	(0.0995)	(0.0802)	(0.0883)
urban	0.0155	−0.383***	−0.258***	−0.240***	−0.126***	−0.229***	−0.110***
	(0.0526)	(0.0369)	(0.0363)	(0.0394)	(0.0395)	(0.0381)	(0.0372)
primarysch	0.520***	0.167***	0.451***	0.476***	0.342***	0.296***	0.292***
	(0.0858)	(0.0532)	(0.0543)	(0.0600)	(0.0566)	(0.0537)	(0.0499)
secondarysch	0.948***	0.527***	0.661***	0.660***	0.439***	0.362***	0.381***
	(0.103)	(0.0691)	(0.0682)	(0.0720)	(0.0679)	(0.0646)	(0.0594)
highsch	1.331***	0.851***	1.074***	1.193***	1.013***	0.934***	0.856***
	(0.102)	(0.0732)	(0.0711)	(0.0747)	(0.0717)	(0.0692)	(0.0663)
vocationalsch	1.758***	1.118***	1.262***	1.415***	1.232***	1.124***	1.055***
	(0.111)	(0.0804)	(0.0776)	(0.0811)	(0.0779)	(0.0751)	(0.0719)
university	2.365***	1.744***	1.878***	2.161***	1.962***	1.799***	1.710***
	(0.131)	(0.102)	(0.0961)	(0.0977)	(0.0948)	(0.0906)	(0.0856)
married	−1.115***	−0.981***	−1.085***	−0.750***	−0.684***	−0.652***	−0.515***
	(0.0693)	(0.0508)	(0.0509)	(0.0577)	(0.0568)	(0.0561)	(0.0550)
age	0.168***	0.108***	0.107***	0.0933***	0.0965***	0.125***	0.122***
	(0.0156)	(0.0106)	(0.0103)	(0.0117)	(0.0116)	(0.0114)	(0.0108)
age2	−0.00285***	−0.00168***	−0.00168***	−0.00168***	−0.00183***	−0.00220***	−0.00212***
	(0.000226)	(0.000144)	(0.000141)	(0.000160)	(0.000159)	(0.000156)	(0.000145)
child0_4	NA	NA	NA	−0.393***	−0.344***	−0.325***	−0.301***
	NA	NA	NA	(0.0456)	(0.0445)	(0.0427)	(0.0395)
child5_11	NA	NA	NA	0.0578	0.0444	0.0364	0.0821**
	NA	NA	NA	(0.0406)	(0.0401)	(0.0383)	(0.0360)

continued

Table A2.i Continued

VARIABLES	2004	2005	2006	2007	2008	2009	2010
	coefficient	coefficient	coefficient	coefficient	coefficient	coefficient	coefficient
child12_14	NA	NA	NA	0.0757*	0.270***	0.272***	0.297***
				(0.0456)	(0.0439)	(0.0419)	(0.0386)
child0_14	NA	0.166***	0.0697	—	—	—	—
		(0.0428)	(0.0427)				
HHsize	−0.154***	−0.146***	−0.148***	−0.152***	−0.160***	−0.173***	−0.171***
	(0.0155)	(0.0107)	(0.0110)	(0.0134)	(0.0132)	(0.0130)	(0.0124)
Ref_primary	0.329***	0.00310	0.0299	0.0915	−0.0830	0.0466	0.0838
	(0.0928)	(0.0601)	(0.0605)	(0.0688)	(0.0637)	(0.0639)	(0.0605)
Ref_secondary	0.252**	−0.0149	−0.165**	−0.0239	−0.201**	−0.00900	−0.0163
	(0.111)	(0.0765)	(0.0772)	(0.0837)	(0.0794)	(0.0770)	(0.0728)
Ref_high	0.00917	−0.443***	−0.362***	−0.299***	−0.367***	−0.267***	−0.289***
	(0.119)	(0.0888)	(0.0859)	(0.0942)	(0.0887)	(0.0868)	(0.0811)
Ref_vocational	0.0585	−0.256***	−0.259***	−0.157*	−0.182**	−0.129	−0.133*
	(0.127)	(0.0892)	(0.0857)	(0.0925)	(0.0870)	(0.0858)	(0.0806)
Ref_university	−0.269**	−0.835***	−0.564***	−0.536***	−0.728***	−0.496***	−0.788***
	(0.133)	(0.103)	(0.0944)	(0.101)	(0.0973)	(0.0929)	(0.0898)
past_homemaker	0.0526	0.455***	0.117***	−0.369***	−0.362***	−0.486***	−0.735***
	(0.0574)	(0.0388)	(0.0387)	(0.0456)	(0.0423)	(0.0379)	(0.0358)
Member_emp	1.196***	1.455***	1.472***	1.643***	1.648***	1.552***	1.699***
	(0.0827)	(0.0687)	(0.0672)	(0.0748)	(0.0725)	(0.0644)	(0.0664)
Ref_socialsec	−0.405***	−0.414***	−0.336***	−0.296***	−0.442***	−0.419***	−0.412***
	(0.0510)	(0.0393)	(0.0381)	(0.0405)	(0.0403)	(0.0389)	(0.0361)
Constant	−6.010***	−4.468***	−4.562***	−4.518***	−4.167***	−4.343***	−4.443***
	(0.273)	(0.189)	(0.187)	(0.212)	(0.208)	(0.205)	(0.196)
Observations	93,652	96,757	97,670	95,577	93,195	92,203	91,721

Table A2.ii Logistic regressions on transitions 2004–10 (marginal effects)

VARIABLES	2004	2005	2006	2007	2008	2009	2010
	mfx	mfx	mfx	mfx	mfx	mfx	mfx
UshockHH	0.0331***	0.0589***	0.0652***	0.0699***	0.0634***	0.0695***	0.0750***
	(0.00540)	(0.00773)	(0.00884)	(0.00879)	(0.00776)	(0.00674)	(0.00820)
urban	0.000209	-0.0114***	-0.00785***	-0.00607***	-0.00327***	-0.00677***	-0.00364***
	(0.000709)	(0.00120)	(0.00117)	(0.00105)	(0.00106)	(0.00119)	(0.00127)
primarysch	0.00698***	0.00454***	0.0131***	0.0115***	0.00874***	0.00839***	0.00954***
	(0.00113)	(0.00144)	(0.00158)	(0.00147)	(0.00146)	(0.00154)	(0.00166)
secondarysch	0.0195***	0.0178***	0.0247***	0.0206***	0.0132***	0.0116***	0.0141***
	(0.00299)	(0.00283)	(0.00322)	(0.00283)	(0.00237)	(0.00234)	(0.00250)
highsch	0.0330***	0.0333***	0.0489***	0.0482**	0.0397***	0.0389***	0.0395***
	(0.00411)	(0.00393)	(0.00473)	(0.00460)	(0.00407)	(0.00407)	(0.00418)
vocationalsch	0.0578***	0.0509***	0.0641***	0.0653***	0.0547***	0.0522***	0.0543***
	(0.00697)	(0.00557)	(0.00619)	(0.00619)	(0.00544)	(0.00529)	(0.00545)
university	0.111***	0.110***	0.132***	0.149***	0.128***	0.118***	0.122***
	(0.0138)	(0.0118)	(0.0125)	(0.0133)	(0.0118)	(0.0109)	(0.0107)
married	-0.0231***	-0.0379***	-0.0460***	-0.0236***	-0.0222***	-0.0232***	-0.0201***
	(0.00208)	(0.00266)	(0.00299)	(0.00233)	(0.00233)	(0.00250)	(0.00257)
age	0.00228***	0.00295***	0.00307***	0.00223***	0.00244***	0.00349***	0.00393***
	(0.000196)	(0.000284)	(0.000291)	(0.000274)	(0.000284)	(0.000307)	(0.000337)
age2	-3.87e-05***	-4.58e-05***	-4.81e-05***	-4.02e-05***	-4.63e-05***	-6.17e-05***	-6.83e-05***
	(2.77e-06)	(3.81e-06)	(3.94e-06)	(3.69e-06)	(3.83e-06)	(4.09e-06)	(4.43e-06)
child0_4	NA	NA	NA	-0.00886***	-0.00827***	-0.00868***	-0.00928***
				(0.000975)	(0.00102)	(0.00109)	(0.00117)
child5_11	NA	NA	NA	0.00139	0.00113	0.00102	0.00267**
				(0.000980)	(0.00102)	(0.00108)	(0.00118)

continued

Table A2.ii Continued

VARIABLES	2004	2005	2006	2007	2008	2009	2010
	mfx	mfx	mfx	mfx	mfx	mfx	mfx
child12_14	NA	NA	NA	0.00185	0.00733***	0.00818***	0.0104***
				(0.00113)	(0.00128)	(0.00135)	(0.00146)
child0_14	NA	0.00472***	0.00198*	—	—	—	—
		(0.00126)	(0.00120)				
HHsize	−0.00210***	−0.00397***	−0.00424***	−0.00364***	−0.00405***	−0.00483***	−0.00551***
	(0.000213)	(0.000289)	(0.000313)	(0.000321)	(0.000334)	(0.000364)	(0.000402)
Ref_primary	0.00443***	8.44e−05	0.000857	0.00219	−0.00210	0.00130	0.00271
	(0.00124)	(0.00164)	(0.00173)	(0.00164)	(0.00162)	(0.00179)	(0.00195)
Ref_secondary	0.00377**	−0.000403	−0.00446**	−0.000568	−0.00472***	−0.000251	−0.000523
	(0.00184)	(0.00206)	(0.00197)	(0.00197)	(0.00174)	(0.00214)	(0.00232)
Ref_high	0.000125	−0.0102***	−0.00905***	−0.00637***	−0.00806***	−0.00675***	−0.00837***
	(0.00163)	(0.00172)	(0.00186)	(0.00179)	(0.00169)	(0.00198)	(0.00210)
Ref_vocational	0.000815	−0.00631***	−0.00674***	−0.00354*	−0.00428**	−0.00345	−0.00408*
	(0.00181)	(0.00198)	(0.00201)	(0.00196)	(0.00191)	(0.00217)	(0.00235)
Ref_university	−0.00328**	−0.0166***	−0.0131***	−0.0105***	−0.0141***	−0.0115***	−0.0193***
	(0.00146)	(0.00147)	(0.00175)	(0.00160)	(0.00143)	(0.00179)	(0.00166)
past_homemaker	0.000727	0.0142***	0.00346***	−0.00802***	−0.00845***	−0.0126***	−0.0221***
	(0.000808)	(0.00139)	(0.00119)	(0.000903)	(0.000912)	(0.000922)	(0.00102)
Member_emp	0.0122***	0.0282***	0.0301***	0.0276***	0.0295***	0.0321***	0.0386***
	(0.000667)	(0.000923)	(0.000954)	(0.000883)	(0.000931)	(0.00101)	(0.00107)
Ref_socialsec	−0.00538***	−0.0110***	−0.00942***	−0.00693***	−0.0109***	−0.0114***	−0.0130***
	(0.000671)	(0.00103)	(0.00105)	(0.000929)	(0.000972)	(0.00103)	(0.00112)
Constant	—	—	—	—	—	—	—
Observations	93,652	96,757	97,670	95,577	93,195	92,203	91,721

Table A3a.i Logistic regressions on transitions including demand-side controls (2007) (logit coefficients)

VARIABLES	2007	2007	2007	2007	2007
	coefficient	*coefficient*	*coefficient*	*coefficient*	*coefficient*
UshockHH	1.440***	1.397***	1.498***	1.425***	1.449***
	(0.107)	(0.107)	(0.107)	(0.107)	(0.107)
urban	-0.240***	-0.248***	-0.177***	-0.245***	-0.161***
	(0.0394)	(0.0394)	(0.0399)	(0.0395)	(0.0400)
primarysch	0.476***	0.403***	0.505***	0.456***	0.384***
	(0.0600)	(0.0609)	(0.0600)	(0.0605)	(0.0609)
secondarysch	0.660***	0.577***	0.707***	0.637***	0.573***
	(0.0720)	(0.0729)	(0.0721)	(0.0725)	(0.0730)
highsch	1.193***	1.123***	1.230***	1.174***	1.114***
	(0.0747)	(0.0754)	(0.0748)	(0.0751)	(0.0755)
vocationalsch	1.415***	1.331***	1.455***	1.393***	1.311***
	(0.0811)	(0.0819)	(0.0812)	(0.0816)	(0.0820)
university	2.161***	2.062***	2.239***	2.132***	2.084***
	(0.0977)	(0.0987)	(0.0979)	(0.0984)	(0.0988)
married	-0.750***	-0.772***	-0.732***	-0.758***	-0.762***
	(0.0577)	(0.0577)	(0.0577)	(0.0577)	(0.0576)
age	0.0933***	0.0941***	0.0961***	0.0935***	0.0988***
	(0.0117)	(0.0117)	(0.0117)	(0.0117)	(0.0118)
age2	-0.00168***	-0.00171***	-0.00170***	-0.00169***	-0.00176***
	(0.000160)	(0.000160)	(0.000160)	(0.000160)	(0.000161)
child0_4	-0.393***	-0.385***	-0.391***	-0.391***	-0.374***
	(0.0456)	(0.0456)	(0.0456)	(0.0456)	(0.0457)
child5_11	0.0578	0.0610	0.0670*	0.0583	0.0778*
	(0.0406)	(0.0405)	(0.0407)	(0.0406)	(0.0406)

continued

Table A3a.i Continued

VARIABLES	2007	2007	2007	2007	2007
	coefficient	coefficient	coefficient	coefficient	coefficient
child12_14	0.0757*	0.0832*	0.0750	0.0773*	0.0889*
	(0.0456)	(0.0456)	(0.0457)	(0.0456)	(0.0456)
HHsize	-0.152***	-0.140***	-0.162***	-0.148***	-0.145***
	(0.0134)	(0.0135)	(0.0135)	(0.0135)	(0.0135)
HHref_primarysch	0.0915	0.0504	0.119*	0.0804	0.0536
	(0.0688)	(0.0691)	(0.0688)	(0.0689)	(0.0693)
HHref_secondarysch	-0.0239	-0.0485	-0.0212	-0.0285	-0.0685
	(0.0837)	(0.0839)	(0.0837)	(0.0838)	(0.0841)
HHref_highsch	-0.299***	-0.308***	-0.311***	-0.298***	-0.338***
	(0.0942)	(0.0944)	(0.0943)	(0.0943)	(0.0946)
HHref_vocationalsch	-0.157*	-0.188***	-0.179*	-0.163*	-0.248***
	(0.0925)	(0.0927)	(0.0926)	(0.0926)	(0.0929)
HHref_university	-0.536***	-0.544***	-0.559***	-0.535***	-0.588***
	(0.101)	(0.101)	(0.101)	(0.101)	(0.101)
pastwrk_homemaker	-0.369***	-0.395***	-0.380***	-0.377***	-0.426***
	(0.0456)	(0.0457)	(0.0457)	(0.0457)	(0.0458)
HHmember_emp	1.643***	1.624***	1.663***	1.637***	1.639***
	(0.0748)	(0.0748)	(0.0749)	(0.0748)	(0.0750)
HHref_socialsec	-0.296***	-0.317***	-0.286***	-0.302***	-0.322***
	(0.0405)	(0.0407)	(0.0406)	(0.0406)	(0.0408)
SERVICE				-0.00200**	0.00713***
				(0.000780)	(0.00207)
AGRICULTURE			0.0132***		0.0154***
			(0.00105)		(0.00118)
REGIONUNEMP	-0.0220***				-0.0636***
	(0.00303)				(0.00780)
Constant	-4.518***	-4.299***	-5.025***	-4.443***	-4.782***
	(0.212)	(0.214)	(0.216)	(0.214)	(0.217)
Observations	95,577	95,577	95,577	95,577	95,577

Table A3b.i Logistic regressions on transitions including demand-side controls (2009) (logit coefficients)

VARIABLES	2009	2009	2009	2009	2009	2009
	coefficient	coefficient	coefficient	coefficient	coefficient	coefficient
UshockHH	1.330***	1.340***	1.387***	1.378***	1.367***	
	(0.0802)	(0.0803)	(0.0806)	(0.0805)	(0.0806)	
urban	−0.229***	−0.207***	−0.170***	−0.171***	−0.184***	
	(0.0381)	(0.0383)	(0.0385)	(0.0384)	(0.0386)	
primarysch	0.296***	0.261***	0.317***	0.281***	0.277***	
	(0.0537)	(0.0540)	(0.0537)	(0.0537)	(0.0546)	
secondarysch	0.362***	0.331***	0.391***	0.359***	0.356***	
	(0.0646)	(0.0648)	(0.0647)	(0.0647)	(0.0654)	
highsch	0.934***	0.904***	0.966***	0.945***	0.945***	
	(0.0692)	(0.0694)	(0.0693)	(0.0693)	(0.0699)	
vocationalsch	1.124***	1.079***	1.144***	1.115***	1.118***	
	(0.0751)	(0.0755)	(0.0752)	(0.0752)	(0.0761)	
university	1.799***	1.769***	1.863***	1.848***	1.849***	
	(0.0906)	(0.0907)	(0.0907)	(0.0907)	(0.0916)	
married	−0.652***	−0.653***	−0.638***	−0.640***	−0.641***	
	(0.0561)	(0.0560)	(0.0561)	(0.0561)	(0.0562)	
age	0.125***	0.126***	0.127***	0.128***	0.128***	
	(0.0114)	(0.0115)	(0.0115)	(0.0115)	(0.0115)	
age2	−0.00220***	−0.00222***	−0.00221***	−0.00224***	−0.00224***	
	(0.000156)	(0.000156)	(0.000156)	(0.000156)	(0.000156)	
child0_4	−0.325***	−0.317***	−0.325***	−0.323***	−0.326***	
	(0.0427)	(0.0427)	(0.0428)	(0.0428)	(0.0428)	
child5_11	0.0364	0.0382	0.0345	0.0350	0.0344	
	(0.0383)	(0.0383)	(0.0384)	(0.0384)	(0.0384)	

continued

Table A3b.i Continued

VARIABLES	2009	2009	2009	2009	2009
	coefficient	coefficient	coefficient	coefficient	coefficient
child12_14	0.272***	0.276***	0.269***	0.270***	0.270***
	(0.0419)	(0.0419)	(0.0419)	(0.0419)	(0.0420)
HHsize	-0.173***	-0.170***	-0.176***	-0.170***	-0.169***
	(0.0130)	(0.0130)	(0.0130)	(0.0130)	(0.0130)
HHref_primarysch	0.0466	0.0314	0.0710	0.0506	0.0460
	(0.0639)	(0.0639)	(0.0639)	(0.0639)	(0.0642)
HHref_secondarysch	-0.00900	-0.0288	-0.00605	-0.0124	-0.00826
	(0.0770)	(0.0770)	(0.0770)	(0.0770)	(0.0771)
HHref_highsch	-0.267***	-0.281***	-0.272***	-0.264***	-0.255***
	(0.0868)	(0.0869)	(0.0868)	(0.0869)	(0.0869)
HHref_vocationalsch	-0.129	-0.158*	-0.135	-0.150*	-0.146*
	(0.0858)	(0.0860)	(0.0859)	(0.0859)	(0.0861)
HHref_university	-0.496***	-0.517***	-0.507***	-0.504***	-0.495***
	(0.0929)	(0.0929)	(0.0928)	(0.0928)	(0.0929)
pastwrk_homemaker	-0.486***	-0.496***	-0.500***	-0.521***	-0.526***
	(0.0379)	(0.0380)	(0.0380)	(0.0380)	(0.0381)
HHmember_emp	1.552***	1.547***	1.557***	1.551***	1.550***
	(0.0644)	(0.0644)	(0.0645)	(0.0645)	(0.0645)
HHref_socialsec	-0.419***	-0.425***	-0.409***	-0.413***	-0.413***
	(0.0389)	(0.0390)	(0.0390)	(0.0390)	(0.0391)
SERVICE	—	—	—	-0.0204***	-0.0290***
				(0.00149)	(0.00299)
AGRICULTURE	—	—	0.0102***	—	-0.00494**
			(0.000968)		(0.00206)
REGIONUNEMP	—	-0.0266***	—	—	0.00964*
		(0.00430)			(0.00557)
Constant	-4.343***	-3.976***	-4.744***	-3.479***	-3.053***
	(0.205)	(0.213)	(0.209)	(0.215)	(0.297)
Observations	92,203	92,203	92,203	92,203	92,203

Table A3a.ii Logistic regressions on transitions including demand-side controls (2007) (marginal effects)

VARIABLES	2007	2007	2007	2007	2007
	mfx	mfx	mfx	mfx	mfx
UshockHH	0.0699***	0.0659***	0.0735***	0.0686***	0.0680***
	(0.00879)	(0.00847)	(0.00908)	(0.00870)	(0.00859)
urban	-0.00607***	-0.00623***	-0.00432***	-0.00620***	-0.00383***
	(0.00105)	(0.00105)	(0.00102)	(0.00106)	(0.000990)
primarysch	0.0115***	0.00969***	0.0120***	0.0110***	0.00891***
	(0.00147)	(0.00147)	(0.00145)	(0.00148)	(0.00143)
secondarysch	0.0206***	0.0173***	0.0220***	0.0196***	0.0165***
	(0.00283)	(0.00267)	(0.00288)	(0.00280)	(0.00258)
highsch	0.0482***	0.0436***	0.0496***	0.0469***	0.0417***
	(0.00460)	(0.00438)	(0.00466)	(0.00456)	(0.00423)
vocationalsch	0.0653***	0.0585***	0.0672***	0.0635***	0.0553***
	(0.00619)	(0.00583)	(0.00628)	(0.00612)	(0.00559)
university	0.149***	0.134***	0.157***	0.144***	0.133***
	(0.0133)	(0.0126)	(0.0138)	(0.0132)	(0.0125)
married	-0.0236***	-0.0243***	-0.0224***	-0.0238***	-0.0231***
	(0.00233)	(0.00235)	(0.00225)	(0.00234)	(0.00225)
age	0.00223***	0.00224***	0.00226***	0.00224***	0.00227***
	(0.000274)	(0.000272)	(0.000269)	(0.000264)	(0.000264)
age2	-4.02e-05***	-4.06e-05***	-4.00e-05***	-4.04e-05***	-4.05e-05***
	(3.69e-06)	(3.67e-06)	(3.63e-06)	(3.69e-06)	(3.56e-06)
child0_4	-0.00886***	-0.00864***	-0.00866***	-0.00882***	-0.00813***
	(0.000975)	(0.000970)	(0.000959)	(0.000974)	(0.000943)
child5_11	0.00139	0.00146	0.00158	0.00140	0.00180*
	(0.000980)	(0.000973)	(0.000965)	(0.000979)	(0.000943)
child12_14	0.00185	0.00202*	0.00180	0.00189*	0.00209*

continued

Table A3a.ii Continued

VARIABLES	2007	2007	2007	2007	2007
	mfx	mfx	mfx	mfx	mfx
	(0.00113)	(0.00113)	(0.00111)	(0.00113)	(0.00110)
HHsize	-0.00364***	-0.00334***	-0.00380***	-0.00355***	-0.00334***
	(0.000321)	(0.000320)	(0.000315)	(0.000322)	(0.000310)
HHref_primarysch	0.00219	0.00120	0.00279*	0.00192	0.00123
	(0.00164)	(0.00164)	(0.00161)	(0.00164)	(0.00159)
HHref_secondarysch	-0.000568	-0.00113	-0.000494	-0.000675	-0.00154
	(0.00197)	(0.00193)	(0.00194)	(0.00196)	(0.00184)
HHref_highsch	-0.00637***	-0.00649***	-0.00647***	-0.00634***	-0.00682***
	(0.00179)	(0.00176)	(0.00174)	(0.00179)	(0.00167)
HHref_vocationalsch	-0.00354*	-0.00416**	-0.00392**	-0.00366*	-0.00517***
	(0.00196)	(0.00190)	(0.00189)	(0.00195)	(0.00176)
HHref_university	-0.0105***	-0.0105***	-0.0106***	-0.0104***	-0.0108***
	(0.00160)	(0.00158)	(0.00154)	(0.00160)	(0.00148)
pastwrk_homemaker	-0.00802***	-0.00847***	-0.00808***	-0.00816***	-0.00877***
	(0.000903)	(0.000888)	(0.000883)	(0.000901)	(0.000849)
HHmember_emp	0.0276***	0.0272***	0.0274***	0.0275***	0.0265***
	(0.000883)	(0.000882)	(0.000869)	(0.000884)	(0.000860)
HHref_socialsec	-0.00693***	-0.00735***	-0.00658***	-0.00705***	-0.00722***
	(0.000929)	(0.000924)	(0.000915)	(0.000930)	(0.000897)
SERVICE	—	—	—	-4.77e-05**	0.000164***
				(1.87e-05)	(4.76e-05)
AGRICULTURE	—	—	0.000311***	—	0.000353***
			(2.48e-05)		(2.73e-05)
REGIONUNEMP	-0.000523***	—	—	—	-0.00146***
	(7.21e-05)				(0.000179)
Constant	—	—	—	—	—
Observations	95,577	95,577	95,577	95,577	95,577

Table A3b.ii Logistic regressions on transitions including demand-side controls (2009) (marginal effects)

VARIABLES	2009	2009	2009	2009	2009	2009
	mfx	mfx	mfx	mfx	mfx	mfx
UshockHH	0.0695***	0.0702***	0.0738***	0.0724***	0.0713***	
	(0.00674)	(0.00678)	(0.00700)	(0.00690)	(0.00684)	
urban	−0.00677***	−0.00608***	−0.00490***	−0.00490***	−0.00526***	
	(0.00119)	(0.00118)	(0.00116)	(0.00115)	(0.00116)	
primarysch	0.00839***	0.00737***	0.00890***	0.00780***	0.00767***	
	(0.00154)	(0.00154)	(0.00153)	(0.00151)	(0.00153)	
secondarysch	0.0116***	0.0104***	0.0125***	0.0113***	0.0111***	
	(0.00234)	(0.00229)	(0.00237)	(0.00230)	(0.00232)	
highsch	0.0389***	0.0371***	0.0405***	0.0389***	0.0388***	
	(0.00407)	(0.00398)	(0.00414)	(0.00404)	(0.00407)	
vocationalsch	0.0522***	0.0489***	0.0531***	0.0507***	0.0508***	
	(0.00529)	(0.00512)	(0.00533)	(0.00517)	(0.00523)	
university	0.118***	0.114***	0.125***	0.122***	0.122***	
	(0.0109)	(0.0107)	(0.0113)	(0.0111)	(0.0112)	
married	−0.0232***	−0.0232***	−0.0224***	−0.0223***	−0.0223***	
	(0.00250)	(0.00249)	(0.00245)	(0.00244)	(0.00243)	
age	0.00349***	0.00352***	0.00351***	0.00353***	0.00352***	
	(0.000307)	(0.000307)	(0.000305)	(0.000303)	(0.000302)	
age2	−6.17e−05***	−6.21e−05***	−6.13e−05***	−6.15e−05***	−6.15e−05***	
	(4.09e−06)	(4.09e−06)	(4.06e−06)	(4.04e−06)	(4.03e−06)	
child0_4	−0.00868***	−0.00844***	−0.00858***	−0.00847***	−0.00852***	
	(0.00109)	(0.00109)	(0.00108)	(0.00107)	(0.00107)	
child5_11	0.00102	0.00107	0.000960	0.000966	0.000947	
	(0.00108)	(0.00108)	(0.00107)	(0.00106)	(0.00106)	

continued

Table A3b.ii Continued

VARIABLES	2009	2009	2009	2009	2009
	mfx	*mfx*	*mfx*	*mfx*	*mfx*
child12_14	0.00818***	0.00828***	0.00798***	0.00797***	0.00793***
	(0.00135)	(0.00135)	(0.00134)	(0.00133)	(0.00132)
HHsize	−0.00483***	−0.00476***	−0.00488***	−0.00468***	−0.00462***
	(0.000364)	(0.000363)	(0.000361)	(0.000357)	(0.000358)
HHref_primarysch	0.00130	0.000876	0.00197	0.00139	0.00126
	(0.00179)	(0.00178)	(0.00177)	(0.00175)	(0.00176)
HHref_secondarysch	−0.000251	−0.000796	−0.000167	−0.000339	−0.000226
	(0.00214)	(0.00211)	(0.00212)	(0.00210)	(0.00210)
HHref_highsch	−0.00675***	−0.00704***	−0.00679***	−0.00656***	−0.00635***
	(0.00198)	(0.00195)	(0.00195)	(0.00195)	(0.00195)
HHref_vocationalsch	−0.00345	−0.00415*	−0.00356*	−0.00389*	−0.00378*
	(0.00217)	(0.00212)	(0.00214)	(0.00210)	(0.00211)
HHref_university	−0.0115***	−0.0119***	−0.0116***	−0.0115***	−0.0113***
	(0.00179)	(0.00176)	(0.00176)	(0.00175)	(0.00176)
pastwrk_homemaker	−0.0126***	−0.0128***	−0.0128***	−0.0132***	−0.0133***
	(0.000922)	(0.000920)	(0.000913)	(0.000903)	(0.000901)
HHmember_emp	0.0321***	0.0319***	0.0318***	0.0315***	0.0314***
	(0.00101)	(0.00100)	(0.000998)	(0.000992)	(0.000991)
HHref_socialsec	−0.0114***	−0.0115***	−0.0110***	−0.0110***	−0.0110***
	(0.00103)	(0.00103)	(0.00103)	(0.00102)	(0.00102)
SERVICE				−0.000560***	−0.000795***
				(4.11e−05)	(8.22e−05)
AGRICULTURE			0.000282***		−0.000135**
			(2.70e−05)		(5.65e−05)
REGIONUNEMP		−0.000742***			0.000264*
		(0.000120)			(0.000153)
Constant	−	−	−	−	−
Observations	92,203	92,203	92,203	92,203	92,203

Table A4a Homemakers entering the labor market by demographic and job characteristics – unemployment shock households

	2004		2005		2006		2007		2008		2009		2010	
	No.	*%*	*No.*	*%*	*No.*	*%*	*No.*	*%*	*No.*	*%*	*No.*	*%*	*No.*	*%*
No. moving from homemaker into participant (employed or unemployed) status	**13,454**		**19,539**		**17,907**		**17,930**		**20,265**		**36,209**		**27,661**	
No. moving from homemaker into employed status	7,034	**100**	11,082	**100**	9,429	**100**	11,433	**100**	9,255	**100**	19,373	**100**	14,849	**100**
Education levels														
No school	688	**9.8**	969	**8.7**	1,034	**11.0**	1,902	**16.6**	2,332	**25.2**	2,087	**10.8**	2,128	**14.3**
Primary school (5 years)	3,542	**50.4**	7,346	**66.3**	5,508	**58.4**	6,181	**54.1**	4,108	**44.4**	10,567	**54.5**	7,197	**48.5**
Secondary school (8 years)	1,210	**17.2**	1,097	**9.9**	1,037	**11.0**	1,271	**11.1**	1,174	**12.7**	2,356	**12.2**	3,722	**25.1**
High school	744	**10.6**	720	**6.5**	896	**9.5**	710	**6.2**	713	**7.7**	2,683	**13.8**	879	**5.9**
Vocational or technical high school	546	**7.8**	804	**7.3**	807	**8.6**	867	**7.6**	780	**8.4**	1,146	**5.9**	608	**4.1**
Graduate or above	304	**4.3**	146	**1.3**	147	**1.6**	502	**4.4**	147	**1.6**	533	**2.7**	314	**2.1**
Age groups														
Aged 15–19	1,204	**17**	1,321	**11.9**	2,005	**21.3**	962	**8.4**	1,425	**15.4**	786	**4.1**	1,682	**11.3**
Aged 20–24	732	**10**	2,012	**18.2**	772	**8.2**	1,270	**11.1**	564	**6.1**	3,314	**17.1**	1,903	**12.8**
Aged 25–29	877	**12**	1,319	**11.9**	1,891	**20.1**	2,007	**17.6**	2,749	**29.7**	5,608	**28.9**	2,235	**15.1**
Aged 30–34	1,734	**25**	2,722	**24.6**	1,552	**16.5**	2,775	**24.3**	1,156	**12.5**	2,704	**14.0**	3,758	**25.3**
Aged 35–39	1,354	**19**	1,056	**9.5**	1,397	**14.8**	2,411	**21.1**	1,763	**19.1**	2,974	**15.4**	2,282	**15.4**
Aged 40–44	700	**10**	1,313	**11.8**	965	**10.2**	1,335	**11.7**	567	**6.1**	2,629	**13.6**	2,226	**15.0**
Aged 45–49	319	**5**	866	**7.8**	576	**6.1**	539	**4.7**	511	**5.5**	651	**3.4**	105	**0.7**
Aged 50–54	114	**2**	114	**1.0**	144	**1.5**	133	**1.2**	290	**3.1**	528	**2.7**	658	**4.4**
Aged 55–59	0	**0**	359	**3.2**	126	**1.3**	0	**0.0**	228	**2.5**	179	**0.9**	0	**0.0**
Aged 60–64	0	**0**	0	**0.0**	0	**0.0**	0	**0.0**	0	**0.0**	0	**0.0**	0	**0.0**
Marital status														
Never married	1,376	**20**	2,214	**20.0**	2,336	**24.8**	1,718	**15.0**	1,602	**17.3**	1,826	**9.4**	1,758	**11.8**
Married	5,658	**80**	8,633	**77.9**	6,797	**72.1**	9,564	**83.7**	7,261	**78.5**	16,537	**85.4**	13,091	**88.2**
Divorced	0	**0**	114	**1.0**	297	**3.1**	0	**0.0**	163	**1.8**	1,009	**5.2**	0	**0.0**
Widowed	0	**0**	121	**1.1**	0	**0.0**	150	**1.3**	228	**2.5**	0	**0.0**	0	**0.0**

continued

Table A4a Continued

	2004 No.	2004 %	2005 No.	2005 %	2006 No.	2006 %	2007 No.	2007 %	2008 No.	2008 %	2009 No.	2009 %	2010 No.	2010 %
Rural/urban														
Rural	1,024	15	2,757	24.9	2,367	25.1	1,132	9.9	1,111	12.0	3,947	20.4	2,559	17.2
Urban	6,010	85	8,325	75.1	7,062	74.9	10,301	90.1	8,144	88.0	15,426	79.6	12,290	82.8
Sector of employment														
Agriculture	1,044	15	1,497	13.5	1,437	15.2	710	6.2	2,446	26.4	1,802	9.3	1,182	8.0
Industry	2,845	40	4,494	40.6	3,393	36.0	5,037	44.1	2,992	32.3	7,767	40.1	7,393	49.8
Trade	1,477	21	1,881	17.0	2,606	27.6	1,583	13.8	966	10.4	4,218	21.8	3,727	25.1
Services	1,668	24	2,476	22.3	1,993	21.1	4,102	35.9	2,849	30.8	5,586	28.8	2,548	17.2
Work status														
Salaried	4,823	69	5,671	51.2	5,388	57.1	8,414	73.6	5,466	59.1	16,849	87.0	12,935	87.1
Casual employee	1,811	26	2,090	18.9	2,379	25.2	2,601	22.8	2,880	31.1	0	0.0	0	0.0
Employer	0	0	0	0.0	209	2.2	0	0.0	0	0.0	0	0.0	0	0.0
Self-employed	400	6	2,375	21.4	1,453	15.4	417	3.7	798	8.6	2,290	11.8	1,760	11.9
Unpaid family worker	0	0	211	1.9	0	0.0	0	0.0	111	1.2	234	1.2	153	1.0
Full-time/part time														
Full-time	6,844	97	8,519	76.9	7,489	79.4	9,707	84.9	8,334	90.0	15,235	78.6	11,657	78.5
Part-time	190	3	1,828	16.5	1,940	20.6	1,726	15.1	921	10.0	4,138	21.4	3,192	21.5
Type of job contract														
Permanent	5,218	74	7,993	72.1	5,191	55.1	8,289	72.5	5,422	58.6	12,412	64.1	9,416	63.4
Temporary	1,203	17	368	3.3	2,053	21.8	2,646	23.1	2,014	21.8	4,437	22.9	3,519	23.7
Seasonal	613	9	1,987	17.9	522	5.5	80	0.7	910	9.8	0	0.0	0	0.0
Work place														
Field, garden	1,044	15	1,497	13.5	1,237	13.1	710	6.2	2,279	24.6	1,680	8.7	897	6.0
Regular workplace	5,074	72	6,369	57.5	6,128	65.0	7,967	69.7	5,776	62.4	12,771	65.9	10,432	70.3
Marketplace	0	0	0	0.0	0	0.0	123	1.1	0	0.0	0	0.0	0	0.0
Mobile	196	3	163	1.5	382	4.0	348	3.0	135	1.5	798	4.1	359	2.4
Home	720	10	2,129	19.2	1,483	15.7	2,210	19.3	878	9.5	3,485	18.0	2,859	19.3
Social security coverage														
Yes	1,896	27	1,220	11.0	1,961	20.8	3,195	27.9	3,657	39.5	7,031	36.3	5,428	36.6
No	5,138	73	9,128	82.4	7,468	79.2	8,238	72.1	5,597	60.5	12,342	63.7	9,421	63.4

Table A4b Homemakers entering the labor market by demographic and job characteristics – non-shock households

	2004		2005		2006		2007		2008		2009		2010	
	No.	%	No.	%	No.	%	No.	%	No.	%	No.	%	No.	%
No. moving from homemaker into participant (employed or unemployed) status	**386,309**		**634,759**		**664,311**		**605,925**		**617,048**		**629,831**		**724,843**	
No. moving from homemaker into employed status	228,527	100	441,771	100	457,702	100	419,633	100	407,611	100	394,308	100	470,802	100
Education levels														
No school	26,130	11.4	81,864	18.5	76,153	16.6	63,316	15.1	69,511	17.1	71,321	18.1	92,631	19.7
Primary school (5 years)	122,485	53.6	229,293	51.9	233,777	51.1	192,101	45.8	183,777	45.1	173,485	44.0	207,764	44.1
Secondary school (8 years)	29,553	12.9	54,642	12.4	56,025	12.2	67,369	16.1	59,256	14.5	65,490	16.6	79,920	17.0
High school	27,393	12.0	34,368	7.8	43,321	9.5	46,099	11.0	43,557	10.7	38,993	9.9	36,702	7.8
Vocational or technical high school	12,244	5.4	25,089	5.7	28,113	6.1	30,110	7.2	30,991	7.6	25,623	6.5	32,097	6.8
Graduate or above	10,722	4.7	16,515	3.7	20,314	4.4	20,637	4.9	20,519	5.0	19,397	4.9	21,688	4.6
Age groups														
Aged 15–19	29,793	13.0	51,105	11.6	56,871	12.4	50,785	12.1	54,114	13.3	50,926	12.9	51,422	10.9
Aged 20–24	40,566	17.8	67,565	15.3	62,766	13.7	69,844	16.6	65,846	16.2	59,220	15.0	70,636	15.0
Aged 25–29	43,847	19.2	68,744	15.6	68,277	14.9	70,268	16.7	62,094	15.2	58,232	14.8	71,665	15.2
Aged 30–34	34,357	15.0	67,622	15.3	67,661	14.8	64,005	15.3	64,071	15.7	63,920	16.2	71,995	15.3
Aged 35–39	31,970	14.0	62,352	14.1	68,647	15.0	56,650	13.5	62,612	15.4	60,096	15.2	72,255	15.3
Aged 40–44	21,090	9.2	50,890	11.5	51,431	11.2	43,223	10.3	37,551	9.2	43,986	11.2	53,263	11.3
Aged 45–49	13,067	5.7	31,688	7.2	37,871	8.3	28,919	6.9	29,035	7.1	27,266	6.9	37,536	8.0
Aged 50–54	8,426	3.7	21,038	4.8	22,711	5.0	16,872	4.0	19,048	4.7	17,832	4.5	23,217	4.9
Aged 55–59	4,015	1.8	12,076	2.7	12,493	2.7	12,308	2.9	7,895	1.9	8,933	2.3	12,291	2.6
Aged 60–64	1,396	0.6	8,690	2.0	8,974	2.0	6,757	1.6	5,344	1.3	3,896	1.0	6,522	1.4
Marital status														
Never married	58,431	25.6	100,714	22.8	101,020	22.1	99,226	23.6	96,141	23.6	86,751	22.0	93,963	20.0
Married	152,648	66.8	306,830	69.5	323,208	70.6	289,253	68.9	283,188	69.5	285,619	72.4	348,994	74.1
Divorced	8,449	3.7	20,027	4.5	18,845	4.1	16,945	4.0	16,305	4.0	14,563	3.7	16,636	3.5
Widowed	8,999	3.9	14,201	3.2	14,629	3.2	14,208	3.4	11,977	2.9	7,376	1.9	11,209	2.4

Table A4b Continued

	2004		2005		2006		2007		2008		2009		2010	
	No.	%	No.	%	No.	%	No.	%	No.	%	No.	%	No.	%
Rural/urban														
Rural	75,924	33.2	213,057	48.2	201,922	44.1	149,044	35.5	137,556	33.7	134,663	34.2	151,974	32.3
Urban	152,603	66.8	228,714	51.8	255,780	55.9	270,589	64.5	270,055	66.3	259,646	65.8	318,828	67.7
Sector of employment														
Agriculture	57,057	25.0	120,584	27.3	136,073	29.7	139,060	33.1	123,496	30.3	123,384	31.3	151,820	32.2
Industry	70,933	31.0	101,764	23.0	104,597	22.9	108,856	25.9	106,663	26.2	92,327	23.4	116,264	24.7
Trade	48,808	21.4	64,432	14.6	80,695	17.6	85,887	20.5	86,259	21.2	90,308	22.9	95,745	20.3
Services	51,729	22.6	77,452	17.5	78,713	17.2	85,829	20.5	91,193	22.4	88,290	22.4	106,975	22.7
Work status														
Salaried	114,168	50.0	162,124	36.7	176,210	38.5	198,797	47.4	188,222	46.2	259,068	65.7	310,248	65.9
Casual employee	46,256	20.2	64,168	14.5	77,077	16.8	77,408	18.4	90,102	22.1	0	0.0	0	0.0
Employer	2,264	1.0	2,527	0.6	5,630	1.2	6,036	1.4	3,429	0.8	3,323	0.8	3,818	0.8
Self-employed	25,733	11.3	70,707	16.0	64,657	14.1	59,368	14.1	48,188	11.8	51,344	13.0	64,539	13.7
Unpaid family worker	40,106	17.5	64,706	14.6	76,504	16.7	78,023	18.6	77,670	19.1	80,574	20.4	92,198	19.6
Full-time/part-time														
Full-time	205,896	90.1	302,080	68.4	315,994	69.0	334,078	79.6	319,270	78.3	279,927	71.0	330,022	70.1
Part-time	22,631	9.9	62,151	14.1	84,085	18.4	85,554	20.4	88,341	21.7	114,381	29.0	140,780	29.9
Type of job contract														
Permanent	171,941	75.2	236,770	53.6	169,695	37.1	193,851	46.2	182,035	44.7	159,540	40.5	181,743	38.6
Temporary	26,714	11.7	73,342	16.6	57,737	12.6	59,254	14.1	68,037	16.7	99,528	25.2	128,504	27.3
Seasonal	29,872	13.1	54,119	12.3	25,855	5.6	23,100	5.5	28,252	6.9	0	0.0	0	0.0
Work place														
Field, garden	57,057	25.0	120,057	27.2	133,778	29.2	137,692	32.8	120,979	29.7	119,905	30.4	146,817	31.2
Regular workplace	134,055	58.7	175,561	39.7	193,780	42.3	218,148	52.0	216,633	53.1	192,479	48.8	216,897	46.1
Marketplace	915	0.4	1,417	0.3	1,657	0.4	739	0.2	648	0.2	1,666	0.4	1,399	0.3
Mobile	6,128	2.7	7,643	1.7	9,300	2.0	8,314	2.0	12,292	3.0	5,821	1.5	7,529	1.6
Home	30,372	13.3	46,992	10.6	51,251	11.2	44,292	11.2	47,562	11.7	64,284	16.3	82,186	17.5
Social security coverage														
Yes	59,064	25.8	77,091	17.5	77,398	16.9	96,145	22.9	95,371	23.4	89,881	22.8	108,824	23.1
No	169,463	74.2	287,140	65.0	322,680	70.5	323,488	77.1	312,240	76.6	304,427	77.2	361,979	76.9

Source: TSI, HLFS micro data 2004–2010

Notes

1 For theoretical discussions, see Mincer (1962, 1966), Ashenfelter (1980), Killingsworth and Heckman (1986), Rosen (1992), and Lundberg (1985).

2 Both added and discouraged worker effects pertain to labor-supply-side responses by women to unemployment shocks as identified in the orthodox labor economics literature. Feminist economics, on the other hand, often approaches the gendered implications of economic downturns on women's employment from a demand-for-labor-side perspective. Rubery (1988) advances three distinct possibilities: the buffer hypothesis, the segmented labor market hypothesis, and the substitution hypothesis. To the extent that women workers play a "buffer role" in the labor market, hired under expansionary periods as male labor supply runs short, they can also be the first to be let go in a contractionary period, "last hired – first fired." If there is a segmented labor market, however, with substantial occupational/industrial gender segregation, then women's employment can be more or less affected in economic downturns relative to men's depending on the sectors and occupations they are concentrated in. Finally, the substitution effect refers to the possibility that women workers can be preferred to men as lower-cost alternatives, with the effect being more pronounced particularly in economic downturns. It is possible to argue that the supply- and demand-side effects interact with and condition one another, determining the concrete outcomes. For instance, in the case of a segmented labor market or substitution effect from the demand side favoring female labor, one can expect any added worker effect to be more pronounced than it would be otherwise. The analysis in this chapter focuses on the added worker effect, i.e., on the supply side. While we do introduce some demand-side controls to the extent that data is available, these control for regional variations in labor demand and we do not attempt to test for the interaction of supply- and demand-side effects.

3 İlkkaracan and Değirmenci (2013) report using 2010 SILC data that of all households (HHs), 33 percent are single-earner male breadwinner HHs; 11 percent are multiple-earner male breadwinner HHs; 22 percent are dual earner HHs; 10 percent are female-headed HHs, and 24 percent are in some other category, predominantly jobless HHs. Excluding the small-scale family farming HHs where the dual-earner structure is relatively more common, of non-farming households, 38 percent are single-earner male breadwinner HHs; 11 percent are multiple-earner male breadwinner HHs; only 12 percent are dual-earner HHs; 11 percent are female-headed HHs, and 28 percent are in some other category.

4 This is calculated based on the numbers reported in Uysal (2012).

5 They report that the correlation coefficient turns insignificant in 2005, which they suggest implies that the effect of the crisis is over by then and shocks at the household level are absorbed by other means than buffer labor supply.

6 İlkkaracan's (2012) study (of which the primary objective was to explore the reasons behind women's low rates of labor force participation in Turkey) also reports results from three cross-section regressions on HLFS micro data in 1988, 2000, and 2008 that unemployment of the husband emerges as a statistically significant determinant of female labor supply.

7 See İlkkaracan (2012) for an account of the limited impact of export-oriented growth on female employment.

8 From the standpoint of demand for labor, to what extent this increase was triggered by a substitution effect versus growth of employment in female-dominated sectors remains to be explored. A contributing factor that might have triggered a substitution effect under the recent crisis was the announcement by the government in June 2008 of a series of precautionary policies against the emerging unemployment problem. These included a subsidy applied toward social security premiums of newly employed young people and women on the condition that they were not in formal employment in the previous year. In other words, the social security premiums of newly employed

women and young workers, which are normally paid by the employer, were paid under the subsidy scheme by the government. The government contribution was at a rate of 100 percent in the first year of employment and was reduced by 20 percent each year starting in the second year of employment, eventually expiring after the fifth year. Government officials claimed this positive discriminatory measure was respons- ible for the increasing trend in female employment despite the crisis. Official figures indicated that by the end of 2009, approximately 50,000 women had been hired under this subsidy scheme. Yet, it was unclear as to what share of these women were simply pulled out of informal employment into formal employment rather than creating new female employment.

9 The HLFS was conducted bi-annually from 1988 to 1999, quarterly from 2000 to 2004, and monthly since 2005.

10 NUTS (Nomenclature of Territorial Units for Statistics) is a geocode standard for ref- erencing the subdivisions of countries for statistical purposes. The standard is developed and regulated by the European Union. Turkey comprises 12 NUTS1 regions, 26 NUTS2 regions, and 81 NUTS3 regions (corresponding to 81 provinces).

11 We confine the analysis to households where the reference person is male because the focus of the chapter is on a female added worker effect. This is contextualized as one where the primary earners are male and the female household members react to eco- nomic downturns in their secondary earner roles. The overwhelming majority of house- holds in Turkey have a male reference person, though on a declining trend, in the period of analysis from 88.08 percent in 2000 to 84.52 percent of all households in 2010.

12 Those who do not participate in the labor market (either as employed or unemployed) are categorized in the following status: student, homemaker, retired, ill or disabled, or other. Our operational sample of potential added workers includes homemakers and retired only.

13 We leave out students because the group that we are really concerned with is the women who are pushed to secondary latent earner role through gendered patterns such as full-time homemaking or early retirement, both almost exclusively female phenom- ena in Turkey. Also, transitions to the labor market from student status are more likely to be independent of the household unemployment shock.

14 The households that we categorize as non-unemployment-shock households are the ones where the male reference person could have remained either in the same status since the previous year, i.e., employment, unemployment, or non-participant status. Or he could have made a transition from employment or unemployment to non- participant, from non-participant to employment or unemployment, from unemploy- ment to employment or non-participant.

15 While 2010 is the year of post-crisis recovery, the transitions that we observe in 2010 entail the homemakers in 2009 who live in households where the male reference person lost his job some time in the past year.

16 By TurkStat statistics, the total female labor force is 26,317,000, female unemployed is 979,000, and total unemployed is 3,470,000 people in 2009 (www.tuik.gov.tr/Veri- Bilgi.do?alt_id=25.)

17 The profiles for the entire period of analysis, 2004–10, are shown in Tables A4a and A4b in the Appendix.

18 Note that as explained in Section 3, these marginal effects refer to the specific case where all other explanatory variables are taken at their mean values.

19 See Tables A3a.i–A3b.ii for detailed results on demand-side variables. Regional unemployment rates carry a negative sign in all estimations for 2007 (Tables A3a.i and A3a.ii). For 2009 (Table A3b.i and A3b.ii), however, when they are entered in the model by themselves, they carry a negative sign indicative of a discouraged worker effect, yet when the other labor market controls are introduced, such as the regional agricultural and service shares of employment, the coefficient on regional unemploy- ment turns positive pointing to an added worker effect at the aggregate level.

20 Note, however, that Tables 9.1 and 9.2 showed that in crisis years, the number of female added workers was substantially higher parallel to the increase in the number of households facing the unemployment shock. The share of added workers as a ratio of total homemakers remained largely stable across the crisis and non-crisis years similar to the marginal effects.

References

Ashenfelter, O. (1980) "Unemployment as disequilibrium in a model of aggregate labor supply," *Econometrica*, 48: 547–64.

Başlevent, C. and Onaran, O. (2003) "Are married women in Turkey more likely to become added or discouraged workers?" *Labour*, 17: 439–58.

Ehrenberg, R.G. and Smith, R.S. (2000) *Modern Labor Economics: theory and public policy*, New York: Addison-Wesley.

İlkkaracan, I. (2012) "Why so few women in the labor market in Turkey: a multi-dimensional analysis," *Feminist Economics*, 18: 1–36.

İlkkaracan, I. (ed.) (2010) *Emek piyasasında toplumsal cinsiyet eşitliğine doğru: iş ve aile yaşamını uzlaştırma politikaları* (*Towards Gender Equality in the Labor Market: work and family life reconciliation policies*), Istanbul: Women for Women's Human Rights and Istanbul Technical University, WSC-SET.

İlkkaracan, I. and Değirmenci, S. (2013) "Household labor supply structure and family well-being: the case of Turkey," Working Paper, Istanbul Technical University, Faculty of Management.

İlkkaracan, I. and Tunalı, I. (2010) "Agricultural transformation and the rural labour market in Turkey," in B. Karapinar, F. Adaman, and G. Ozertan (eds.), *Rethinking Structural Refom in Turkish Agriculture: beyond the World Bank's strategy*, New York: Nova Science Publishers.

Karaoglan, D. and Okten, C. (2012) "Labor force participation of married women in Turkey: is there an added worker or a discouraged worker effect?" IZA Discussion Paper, No. 6616, Bonn: Institute for the Study of Labor.

Killingsworth, M. and Heckman, J. (1986) "Female labor supply: a survey," in O. Ashenfelter and R. Layard (eds.), *Handbook of Labor Economics*, Vol. I, Amsterdam: North Holland.

Lundberg, S. (1985) "The added worker effect," *Journal of Labor Economics*, 3: 11–37.

Mincer, J. (1962) "Labor force participation of married women: a study of labor supply," in H.G. Lewis (ed.), *Aspects in Labor Economics*, Princeton: Princeton University Press.

Mincer, J. (1966) "Labor force participation unemployment: a review of recent evidence," in R.A. Gordon and H.S. Gordon (eds.), *Prosperity and Unemployment*, New York: Wiley.

Milliyet Daily Newspaper (2009) "Şimşek: İşsizlik oranı niye artıyor biliyor musunuz?" March 18. Online: www.milliyet.com.tr/Ekonomi/SonDakika.aspx?aType=SonDakika&ArticleID=1072654 (accessed May 22, 2013).

Polat, S. and Saraceno, F. (2010) "Macroeconomic shocks and labor supply in emerging countries: some lessons from Turkey," OFCE Working Paper, No. 2010-36, Paris: Observatoire Français des Conjonctures Économiques.

Prieto-Rodriguez, J. and Rodriguez-Gutierrez, C. (2003) "Participation of married women in the European labor markets and the 'added worker effect'," *Journal of Socio-Economics*, 32: 429–46.

Rosen, S. (1992) "Distinguished fellow: mincering labor economics," *Journal of Economic Perspectives*, 6: 157–70.

Rubery, J. (1988) *Women and Recession*, New York: Routledge & Kegan Paul.

TurkStat (Turkish Statistical Agency) (2012) *Household labor force survey*, Online: www.tuik.gov.tr/VeriBilgi.do?alt_id=25 (accessed May 23, 2013).

Uysal, G. (2012) "Turkey," in N. Foster, D. Hanzl, S. Leitner, F. Sanoussi, and N. Rabemeafara (eds.), *Study on "Monitoring of Sectoral Employment,"* European Commission Report.

10 Agricultural innovation for food security and environmental sustainability in the context of the recent economic crisis

Why a gender perspective?

Diana Alarcón and Christina Bodouroglou*

1 Introduction

The recent interlinked food, fuel, and financial crises have aggravated poverty and food insecurity, particularly in the developing world. International food prices have surged in the past half-decade, making food less affordable to many, and drawing attention to the deeper structural flaws in the global food production system. In addition, the technology and agricultural practices of the last 40 years have led to the degradation of productive land, large greenhouse gas (GHG) emissions, and extensive water pollution; all of these factors have threatened the sustainability of food production.

A major technological upgrade of agriculture will have to take place to open the space for the adoption of sustainable technologies and land management practices to increase food production with environmental sustainability.

At the heart of the food security challenge are small scale farmers – many of whom are women – as around 90 percent of food consumed in developing countries is locally produced. In Africa and East and South-East Asia, women account for over 40 percent of the agricultural work force, but they have restricted access to land, credit, markets, and technology. This chapter argues that meeting the food security challenge while protecting the environment will require explicit policies to build sustainable agricultural innovation systems with a strong gender perspective to make knowledge and technology available to female farmers.

This chapter sets out by providing an overview of the state of global food insecurity. It proceeds by outlining the structural and environmental constraints

* At the time of writing, the authors worked for the Development Policy and Analysis Division of the United Nations Department of Economic and Social Affairs (UN-DESA); Christina Bodouroglou is now working for UNCTAD. This chapter was part of the research done for the World Economic and Social Survey 2011: The Great Green Technological Transformation. The authors also wish to acknowledge the valuable contributions of Sylvie I. Cohen and Andres Figueroa of the United Nations Entity for Gender Equality and the Empowerment of Women (UN Women). The views expressed in this chapter are those of the authors and do not represent the official position of UN-DESA or its Member States.

to increasing food production and access, before identifying multiple interventions aimed at addressing these constraints. The study then revisits the "Green Revolution" experience of the 1960s–1970s to draw lessons on paving the way toward a second radical transformation of agriculture to expand food production, while protecting the environment. Focus shifts to the central role of small-scale farmers, and particularly women, in enhancing sustainable food production, followed by the obstacles faced by female farmers. The chapter concludes with policy implications, calling for the building of gender-sensitive sustainable agricultural innovation systems at the national level, as well as supporting actions in the international arena.

2 Persistent food insecurity

The 2007–08 food crisis and the renewed surge in food prices in 2010–11 have exposed deep structural problems in the global food system and the need to increase resources and foster innovation in agriculture to accelerate food production. The dramatic food price increases in 2007–08 and the ensuing economic crisis did not help to reduce the number of people suffering from hunger. According to the Food and Agriculture Organization's (FAO) latest estimates, the global number of undernourished people was 867 million in 2007–09, signaling a threat to world economic, social, and political stability.[1] In 2010–12 the number of hungry people increased further to reach 868 million worldwide (FAO 2012) (Figure 10.1).[2]

The overwhelming majority (98 percent) of the world's undernourished people live in developing countries, with almost two-thirds of them concentrated in seven nations (Bangladesh, China, the Democratic Republic of the Congo, Ethiopia, India, Indonesia, and Pakistan). Most hungry people (almost 563

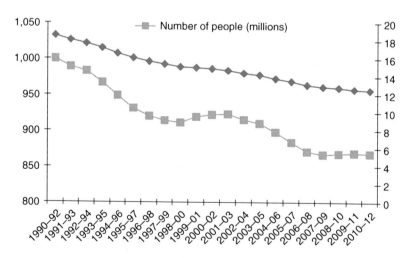

Figure 10.1 Undernourished populations worldwide, 1990–2012 (source: FAO 2012).

million) reside in Asia, although Sub-Saharan Africa has the highest share of undernourished people when compared to the total population (almost 27 percent or around 234 million people) (FAO 2012) (Figure 10.2).

While progress varies from country to country, developing countries as a group have not moved closer to the food security target established at the World Food Summit of halving the number of undernourished people by 2015; instead, the number of undernourished people decreased slightly from one billion in 1990–92 to 868 million in 2010–12.[3] Based on the revised estimates from the FAO, progress toward the less ambitious target in the Millennium Development Goal (MDG) 1 of halving the proportion of people who suffer from hunger seems within reach. With appropriate actions to reverse the slowdown in 2007–08, it will still be possible to reduce by half the share of undernourished people from 23.2 percent in 1990. In 2012, it stood at 14.9 percent.

The 22 countries regarded as facing a "protracted food security crisis" are home to over 162 million undernourished people (about 19 percent of the world's total).[4] The proportion of undernourished people ranges from 17 percent in Guinea to 73 percent in Burundi (FAO 2012). Patterns of food security vary not only *between* but also *within* countries. Aggregate data typically mask inequalities at the regional, local, and household level. For instance, although China has achieved food security at the national level, there remain pockets of poverty and food insecurity, with 158 million people (or 12 percent of the population) still undernourished.[5] Nutritional patterns differ along geographical, social, ethnic, and gender lines. In developing countries, a higher share of children living in rural areas are underweight (20 percent), compared to those residing in urban areas (14 percent). Income is also an important determinant of undernutrition. In Africa, the share of underweight children from the lowest household wealth quintile (28 percent) is twice as high as that from the highest quintile (14 percent). Though overall prevalence rates of undernutrition are similar for male and female populations, there are regional differences. In Africa,

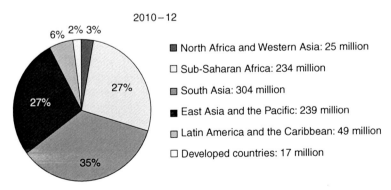

Figure 10.2 Undernourished populations by region, 1969–2010 (source: FAO 2012).

the share of underweight children is slightly higher in boys (21 percent) than in girls (19 percent); in Southern Asia the reverse is true. In certain countries and communities, gender differences in the prevalence of undernutrition are exceptionally large. For instance, in India, 49 percent of female children are underweight compared to 46 percent of male children (FAO 2011).[6]

3 Agricultural context: high food prices and environmental degradation

The unsettling reality is that one in eight people on the planet lack access to sufficient food and an equal number are overfed, when sufficient food is produced globally to feed the world's population. This is evidence of serious shortcomings in the functioning of the global food system (Godfray et al. 2010).

This is largely the result of structural imbalances in food demand and supply. Demand for food has risen owing to continued global population growth, rising incomes, and altered dietary patterns in an increasingly urbanized world. Use of food crops for bio-fuels is increasingly adding to this demand. Agricultural output has not kept pace with this growing demand owing to competition for land, adverse climatic conditions (possibly linked to climate change[7]), high oil and farm input prices, and dwindling public investment in rural infrastructure, agricultural research and extension, and food price supports.

Tighter food supply and demand conditions have led to the prevalence of higher and more erratic world food prices in recent years. This has been aggravated by the significant increase in financial speculation in commodity futures markets over the past decade, which has contributed to the persistence of high and volatile food prices (Gilbert 2008; UN 2011b). International prices for corn, wheat, and rice more than doubled between 2006 and 2008. While prices declined in late 2008, food prices have since rebounded, attaining new record highs in February 2011. Despite conflicting evidence, it would appear that recent price rises have also been accompanied by higher volatility, which increases uncertainty, thereby hindering investment in human and physical capital, technology, and innovation (FAO 2009).

The severe impact of the recent food price crises on living conditions is attested by the riots that have broken out in more than 30 countries. Increasing food prices have had a particularly negative impact on the poor, who spend 50–70 percent of their income on food (von Braun 2009). Higher food prices are estimated to have pushed over 150 million people into poverty since 2007 (World Bank 2008, 2011). Although higher prices provide incentives to increase production, many small farm holders are unable to respond owing to lack of access to finance, agricultural inputs, markets, and technology (UN 2008).

While the expansion of food production is vital for achieving food security and reducing poverty, it is also associated with negative environmental consequences. Agricultural activities that underpin food production have been recognized as a major contributor to GHG emissions, water scarcity and pollution, land degradation, and biodiversity loss.

Unsustainable natural resource management also has adverse socioeconomic impacts. In particular, land degradation can lead to substantial productivity losses, thereby posing risks to food security. It is also a predominant factor in the migration of people. Use of inorganic fertilizers and pesticides, and the spread of pests and livestock diseases, can further adversely affect human health (IAASTD and McIntyre 2009). Natural resource degradation may also exacerbate gender inequalities by increasing the time requirement for fulfillment of female responsibilities such as food production, fuel-wood collection, and soil and water conservation. For instance, in rural Rajasthan, India, approximately 50 person-hours per month are required for households gathering fuel-wood (Laxmi *et al.* 2003). In Malawi, women spend between 4 and 15 hours per week collecting firewood (Rehfuess *et al.* 2006).

4 Many roads to food security

Achieving the goal of food security requires explicit interventions to address the specific constraints that restrict the *availability*, *accessibility*, and/or proper *utilization* of food for nutrition. Countries with a poor natural resource base for agriculture may have to rely on imports to guarantee food availability; in these cases, the development of foreign currency earning activities and fair international trade practices are critical for food security. In other contexts, sufficient food production may not be enough to guarantee food security if people (or groups of people) do not have the resources to purchase enough food for consumption; job creation and policies to guarantee decent employment may be needed to improve income generation and sustainable access to food. Finally, the link between access to food and adequate nutrition may require specific interventions in at least two areas. First, extended infrastructure for water and sanitation coupled with improvements in people's health would be needed to make sure food intake translates into appropriate nutrition. Second, appropriate regulation and technical innovation may be needed to guarantee the safety and adequate nutrient content of food crops.

Safety nets and emergency food distribution mechanisms have been used extensively in response to natural catastrophes (droughts, floods, and so on) but also in response to civil war and political conflict. Safety nets and other forms of social protection have also been used to ensure minimum consumption levels of people at times of economic crisis or in countries with large income inequality. Conditional cash transfers and emergency employment programs have contributed to preventing food insecurity and to reduce extreme poverty.

The specific context of each country will dictate different policy combinations to guarantee food security for all citizens. There is little that can be said in general, except that food security is a complex phenomenon that requires well-designed interventions to guarantee the availability and accessibility of food and appropriate nutrition (Figure 10.3). Food security remains an urgent global, national, and local challenge. It requires the design and implementation of policy initiatives as part of the national development strategies of countries, as well as better governance of global trade and food distribution systems.

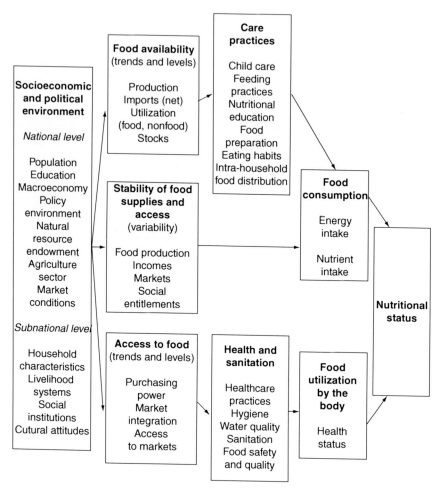

Figure 10.3 Elements in achieving food and nutrition security (source: World Bank, FAO, and IFAD 2009).

In the remainder of this chapter, the focus of attention is the first policy challenge identified above: how to increase the availability of food for all. Current patterns of undernutrition and the need to increase food production to feed a growing population require an increase in food production by an estimated 70 percent globally and 100 percent in developing countries by mid-century. If the goal of environmental sustainability is to be attained, increasing food production will have to be achieved without placing additional stress on natural resources and with the use of eco-friendly technology.

Combating hunger and malnutrition in a sustainable manner and guarding against high and volatile food prices will require a radically different approach addressing the structural constraints on food production. This would entail both the establishment of an integrated national framework for sustainable natural resource management, and a harnessing of the technology and innovation needed to increase the productivity, profitability, resilience, and climate change mitigation potential of rural production systems and forests.

In thinking about the conditions to induce a new transformation in agriculture, the experience of the first green revolution in agriculture may provide important policy guidance.

5 The Green Revolution in the 1960s and 1970s

In response to a similar food security crisis in the 1950s, the "Green Revolution" experience of the 1960s–1970s in Asia and Latin America brought about dramatic increases in productivity and production of staple crops through the adoption of a specific package of technologies – namely, higher-yielding varieties of wheat, rice and maize, chemical fertilizers, and irrigation (UNCTAD 2010).

The Green Revolution of the 1960s and 1970s was a response to widespread poverty and food insecurity in developing countries at a time when close to one-third of the world's population (one billion people) were vulnerable to hunger and malnutrition (Spielman and Pandya-Lorch 2009). High dependence on food aid in Asia and the risk of repeated famines in India prompted a concerted international effort for the radical transformation of agriculture through the development of high-yielding seed varieties (IFPRI 2002).

The technological innovations that gave rise to the green revolution were based on the breeding of new varieties of wheat, rice, and maize; and later on extended to millet, sorghum, maize, cassava, and beans. The new seed varieties were more resistant to pests and disease, more responsive to chemical nutrients, and had shorter agricultural cycles that allowed double and even triple cropping (IFPRI 2002; Lipton 2010).

Results were impressive; in the period 1970–95, there was a rapid expansion in the production of cereals in Latin America and Asia (Figure 10.4). Cereal production in Asia increased from about 310 million tons a year in 1970 to 650 million in 1995 and, although the population increased by 60 percent, food production rose faster, with the result that cereal and calorie availability per person increased by nearly 30 percent, and wheat and rice became cheaper (Hazell 2009). Real per capita income more than doubled in Asia from 1970 and 1995 and poverty decreased (IFPRI 2002).

In Latin America, the price of cereals decreased, making them more accessible to the poor in urban and rural areas. The consumption of calories per person also increased in spite of rapid population growth.

The research and development (R&D) that supported the Green Revolution was based on a large and interconnected system of international research centers sustained through large contributions from governments in developed and developing countries and from private foundations. The original research conducted in the International Center for Maize and Wheat Improvement (CIMMYT) in

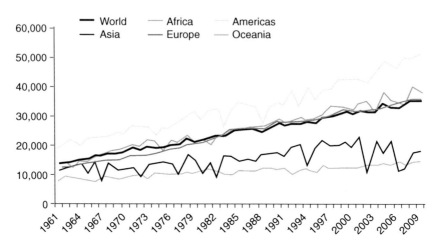

Figure 10.4 Cereal yields, 1961–2009 (Hg/Ha) (source: FAOStat).

Mexico and the International Rice Research Institute (IRRI) in the Philippines was rapidly expanded to other research centers, and in 1971, the Consultative Group on International Agricultural Research (CGIAR) was created to coordinate research. These centers were able to attract unprecedented long-term international support to sustain research operations, gene banks, and nursery programs within an environment of open and free exchange of information and plant genetic materials under a shared research agenda for food security (Dubin and Brennan 2009). In the first two decades of operation, the budgets available to the centers that are part of the CGIAR grew fast, from US$15 million in 1970 to US$305 in 1990 (Pardey and Beintema 2001).

But the success of the Green Revolution must also be placed in the historical context that facilitated a global consensus to fight poverty and hunger. Internationally, the Green Revolution emerged in the context of the Cold War where poverty and hunger were perceived by Western governments as a source of social tensions and the expansion of communism in Asia and Latin America (Hazell 2009).

In Asia and Latin America, governments gave priority to investments in infrastructure to expand rural roads, irrigation and electrical power, and the construction of facilities to improve the storage and distribution of cereals. Basic education, agricultural research, and extension services to support farmers also improved, and international lending for agricultural development was prioritized – in the 1980s, around a quarter of the total lending from the World Bank was for agriculture (Pardey and Beintema 2001).

There are important lessons to learn from the experience of the Green Revolution in Asia and Latin America on paving the way toward a second large transformation of agriculture:

1   The development of new technology and management systems in agriculture does not occur overnight; it requires long-term support for R&D and an environment of cooperation, experimentation, and learning with efficient and free flow of information, as well as a shared research agenda. Adequate and long-term financial support from national and international public sources is most important.

2   The adoption of new technology and innovative practices in production requires an enabling policy framework and adequate investment in infrastructure, capacity development among farmers, as well as access to inputs, credit, and markets in a process where governments play a key role in directing resources and creating incentives to ensure these conditions.

3   Radical transformation of agriculture for food security is possible when there is political will and long-term commitment – from national and international stakeholders – around a common agenda for food security.

To the extent that the technology behind the Green Revolution helped to intensify food production, it made a positive contribution to the preservation of forest and wetlands from conversion to cropping (Hazell 2009). But this positive contribution was partly offset by the over-extended use of chemical fertilizers and water and the extension of mono-cropping.

The technology from the Green Revolution relied on improved seeds, heavier use of fertilizers and chemical pesticides, and intensive use of water. The accumulation of chemical residues depleted the soil micronutrients while intensive use of water eventually led to the depletion of water tables and the build-up of salt in the most productive land; the combination of all these factors led to land degradation, the contamination of water sources, and increased risk of occupational poisoning. At the same time, the expansion of monocultures led to the loss of biodiversity, including the decimation of beneficial insects and wildlife and the growth of new pest biotypes (Lipton 2010).

6 Toward a true green technological revolution in agriculture

The challenge of increasing agricultural production for food security nowadays is far more complex than in the past and will require strengthened systems of innovation with the flexibility to respond to the specific needs of farmers in a variety of ecological and socioeconomic contexts (Lipton 2010), without expanding the agricultural frontier and with sustainable use of natural resources. Achieving these objectives simultaneously will require a great transformation in agriculture and land management. There are at least five areas where technology and innovation are needed to accelerate the transitions toward sustainable agriculture: improve pest management to reduce the contamination of water sources, soil erosion, and human poisoning; improve weed control to reduce the use of herbicides; make more efficient use of water to avoid depletion of water sources and contamination; reverse land degradation; and protect biodiversity and natural ecosystems.

Water conservation, soil protection and biodiversity enhancement need to form part of an integrated approach of sustainable land and forest management, which must also integrate biophysical with sociocultural, institutional, and behavioral variables while recognizing the multifunctional nature of agriculture. A holistic, cross-sectoral approach should consider trade-offs and build on synergies between sectors to prioritize and promote technically available and economically feasible "win–win" options that ensure food security, poverty reduction, and environmental sustainability. In this endeavor, a sustainable agricultural innovation system (SAIS) perspective provides a useful framework for policymaking. By recognizing the dynamic nature of learning and innovation in addition to the multiplicity of actors engaged in the innovation process and the institutional contexts within which they interact helps to identify the kind of policies and incentives to stimulate innovation to increase food productivity while protecting the environment (UN 2011a).

It is important to recognize that there is an abundance of successful experiences of localized innovation to address these issues, often in response to weather and other shocks (see, for example, Pretty *et al.* 2006). The policy challenge is how to identify and support the scaling-up of these local instances of agricultural innovation in poor and food insecure countries and regions. In doing so, important lessons can be drawn from several well-known examples of rural innovations with large-scale impacts such as the integrated pest management (IPM) approach, the Farm Field Schools (FFS), the System of Rice Intensification (SRI), the networks of millers and politicians that popularized the use of New Rice for Africa (NERICA), the diffusion of micro-irrigation in Bangladesh, and watershed management in India (Hall *et al.* 2010; Brooks and Loevinsohn 2011). Common features among these widespread efforts in sustainable agriculture intensification include explicit support from governments, multilateral and civil society organizations, and/or direct involvement of local farmers, including women, in donor-led initiatives.

7 Central role of small-scale farm holders in the battle against poverty and hunger

In supporting a new transformation in agriculture for food security and sustainable management of natural resources, it is important to take into account the specific context in developing countries. In recent years, there has been growing international consensus over the centrality of small-scale farm holders (of whom a large proportion are women) in improving food security. The need to support small-scale farming stems from the fact that they are the mainstay of food production in most developing countries. Between 75 and 90 percent of staple foods in developing countries are locally produced and consumed (UNCTAD 2010). Almost 90 percent of all farmers in developing countries cultivate plots of two hectares or less, and are often net buyers of food (IFPRI 2005).

Increasing productivity of small-scale farms would not only directly enhance food security, but would also contribute to poverty reduction by raising farm incomes and freeing labor resources for industrial development. Small-scale farming, which tends to be more diversified in crop cultivation, has several advantages over large-scale monoculture systems. There is empirical evidence showing that for certain crops, small-scale production is more efficient than large scale (20–60 percent higher yields) and also less damaging for the environment (including climate change mitigation) (Altieri 2008).

However, realization of these advantages is conditional upon small farm holders having adequate access to technology and knowledge relevant to the diversity of agro-ecological conditions and local crop varieties, as well as appropriate access to rural infrastructure (such as irrigation and roads), to affordable credit and farm inputs (such as quality seeds, fertilizers, and pesticides), weather insurance, and education. Such conditions are a requisite for the successful adaptation of sustainable farming techniques and this is where the new revolution in agriculture represents a major departure from the previous Green Revolution: there is no standard "technical package" that will be able to respond to the technical requirements of the large variety of food requirements and agro-ecological conditions of very diverse local contexts of regions and countries with food deficits. Instead, a menu of technological options and supporting services needs to be made available to small-scale farmers in countries and regions facing food insecurity.

8 Innovation in agriculture and the role of women

Women account for a significant share of the agricultural work force and have the potential of making important contributions to increasing food production and improving natural resources management, provided a supportive policy framework sensitive to the specific needs of female farmers and rural workers is put in place.

In Africa, women account for more than half of the agricultural output, 60 percent of marketing and almost all food production in Sub-Saharan Africa (Mehra and Rojas 2008). In Africa and East and South-East Asia, women make up over 40 percent of the agricultural work force. Estimates of the share of female employment in that work force range from around 35 percent in Côte d'Ivoire and the Niger to over 70 percent in Lesotho (FAO 2011). In Latin America there is an increasing presence of women in small-scale agriculture.

Women also constitute a large share of employment in export-oriented agriculture and food production in developing countries. As reported by Mehra and Rojas (2008), women make up almost 80 percent of workers in flower exporting activities in Zimbabwe, 75 percent in the cotton industry in Tajikistan, and over 60 percent in shrimp processing in Bangladesh.

The growing presence of women in agricultural production in developing countries is being referred to as the "feminization" of agriculture. Largely driven by trends of male out-migration, there are an increasing number of female-headed households around the world and changing patterns of gendered division of farm labor. In Africa, a quarter of households are headed by women, although the share varies significantly among countries, ranging from under 10 percent in Burkina Faso to close to 50 percent in Namibia, South Africa, and Swaziland (FAO 2011).

In creating the conditions necessary to increase food production with environmental sustainability, women have a crucial role to play, not only as food producers, but also as those chiefly responsible for food processing and preparation in developing countries. Their traditional position as primary family care-takers – with tasks including gathering fuel and fetching water, cleaning, cooking, child rearing, and caring for the sick – is critical in ensuring household-level improvements in food and nutritional security.

Women's responsibility for providing food for their families also extends to their role as wage earners. Both rural and urban women in waged labor dedicate a substantial portion of their income to purchase food. Notably, empirical research confirms gender-differentiated patterns in the disposal of income, with women having a higher marginal propensity than men to spend on goods that benefit children and for collective household consumption.[8]

Women further contribute to food security through the preservation of biodiversity and plant genetic resources. Women farmers are skilled in biodiversity management and are major repositories of traditional knowledge upon which many indigenous populations' survival strategies depend (World Bank *et al.* 2009). Women often experiment with and adapt indigenous species and thus become experts in plant genetic resources (Karl 1996; Bunning and Hill 1996). Women's experience with traditional knowledge for sustainable agriculture is evidenced, for instance, in the West Usambara highlands of Tanzania, where soil conservation was adopted by almost 60 percent of female-headed households but less than 40 percent of male-headed households (Tenge *et al.* 2004).

9 Constraints faced by female farmers

Despite their central role in agriculture and food security, women in developing countries often face constraints that limit their capacity to improve food production and enhance food and nutritional outcomes. These include gender inequalities in accessing resources such as land, credit, rural organizations, agricultural inputs and technology, education and extension services, as well as the "gender blindness" of agricultural development policies and research.

Women often face discrimination in accessing agricultural inputs and support services, which hinders their ability to improve farm productivity and market their goods. This is owing to a confluence of factors, including gender-blind development policies and research; discriminatory legislation, cultural attitudes, and norms; and lack of participation in decision-making and policy design.

A mere 5 percent of landholders in North Africa and West Africa are women, only 15 percent in Sub-Saharan Africa are women, and 25 percent in a sample of countries in Latin America are women. Furthermore, their average farm size is significantly smaller (FAO 2011). Small farm holders around the world face constraints in accessing loans and other financial services, but in most developing countries, the share of female smallholders who can access credit is 5–10 percentage points lower than for their male counterparts (FAO 2011). Insufficient credit and lack of membership in rural organizations, in turn, denies women access to modern agricultural inputs and technologies such as improved seeds, fertilizer, pesticides, and mechanical tools and equipment. Gender inequalities are also documented in terms of access to rural education and training. Only 5 percent of all agricultural extension resources worldwide were found to be directed at female farmers, and only 15 percent of the extension personnel were female (FAO 1993).

Gender differentials in terms of access to productive agricultural resources present an important obstacle to raising global food production and productivity. Notably, it has been estimated that if women enjoyed equal access to agricultural land, inputs, and technologies, they could increase farm yields by 20–30 percent. This would translate to a rise in agricultural production in developing countries by 2.5–4 percent and a decline in the number of people with hunger by 12–17 percent (FAO 2011).

As outlined previously, inequitable access to productive resources partly stems from the reality that women's contributions are often unrecognized in mainstream agricultural policies and research agendas. Much of women's work relating to agricultural production and food security remains "invisible." Women have traditionally held the major responsibility for carrying out unpaid care-taking activities (such as food preparation, health care, cleaning and sanitation, and collection of fuel and water) and other non-remunerative work (including subsistence agriculture). These activities are not typically accounted for in national accounts, surveys, censuses, and policies (see Floro 1995; Cagatay 1996).

Despite a growing supply of gender disaggregated data and studies on women's contributions to agriculture and food security, household-level data tend to ignore the intra-household distribution of agricultural responsibilities and resources. Research and policies thereby fail to account for conflict of interests and patriarchal power relations within the family, which often lead to detrimental impacts for rural women and girls. Notably, there is ample evidence of the existence of gender-related differentials in household health-seeking and nutritional behavior.[9]

This relates to a body of work testifying to the existence of a "geography of gender" – that is, regional differences in the forms and magnitude of gender inequality associated with variations in patriarchal regimes, particularly among the poorer countries of the world. The most marked forms of gender inequality are associated with regimes of extreme forms of patriarchy – or so-called "male farming systems" characteristic of North Africa and much of Asia (Boserup 1970). Restrictions on female mobility, patrilineal inheritance, and patrilocal marital practices have meant the economic devaluation of women and their overall dependence on men in much of this region. In contrast, research in Sub-Saharan Africa points to the prevalence of highly complex, lineage-base homesteads with considerable gender segmentation (or "female farming systems," whereby spouses may work on separate fields and maintain individual accounting units).

In practice, there are also gender-related rigidities in the intra-household division of labor, with limited "substitutability" between the labor of women and men, particularly in the "reproductive" sphere (Folbre 1986). With the commercialization of agriculture, increasing opportunities for women to undertake paid rural activities have often led to a "double burden," whereby women are expected to undertake remunerative work as well as maintain their traditional care-taking responsibilities, often with detrimental impacts of their health. For instance, in the Philippines, increases in women's market participation was accommodated by reductions in their leisure time, with the time devoted to domestic work and child care remaining roughly the same (Folbre 1986). When farm and domestic tasks are combined, women typically work an average of 13 hours more than men each week in Asia and Africa.[10]

Women also bear a disproportionate part of the HIV/AIDS burden; not only are they more likely than men to be infected, but they are also more likely to be the ones caring for those suffering from HIV/AIDS (UNAIDS 2006).

> In agrarian societies, the HIV/AIDS epidemic is intensifying existing labour bottlenecks, increasing widespread malnutrition; providing a barrier to traditional mechanisms of support during calamities, *massively adding to the problems faced by rural women, especially female-headed farm households arising from gender division of labour and land rights/resources*, and deepening macroeconomic crises by reducing agricultural exports. In extremis, it is creating the new variant famine.
>
> (de Waal and Tumushabe 2003, p. 2; emphasis added)

By ignoring women's unpaid household burden and the intra-household distribution of labor and resources, rural policies can be designed in a "gender-blind" manner and have serious consequences for women. For instance, structural adjustment programs (SAPs) and trade liberalization policies, which have been widely implemented since the 1980s in several developing countries, can affect women negatively through the impact of changes in income, prices, public expenditures, and working conditions (Young 1993).[11] SAP policies have expanded the extraction and production of natural resources to be traded on the international market; this has favored large over small producers and men over women. Gender-insensitive policies have, in the view of various researchers, contributed to past food crises in Africa (Gladwin 1991; Gordon 1996) and the increased domestic and subsistence burdens of women (Nyoni 1991; Sen 1996). Unequal gender divisions of labor and resource control in agriculture (especially in Sub-Saharan Africa) may constitute barriers to the achievement of macroeconomic objectives by constraining the response of peasant farmers to new incentives provided by SAPs. In principle, the incentives under SAPs should shift women in agricultural labor away from food production. But women continue to engage in subsistence production as family responsibilities make them less mobile than men. Men control and benefit most from cash crops; often redefining (women's) food crops into ("their") cash crops, when the former become major sources of cash income (Gordon 1996). In addition, by ignoring women's unpaid reproductive labor, such policies fail to account for the fact that public expenditure cuts have resulted in many activities such as health services being shifted from the public sphere to the female reproductive sphere (especially in the case of poor families). Increasing women's burdens not only has negative implications for their own health and well-being, but it also jeopardizes the welfare of the next generation (Darity 1995).

Agricultural research, too, pays insufficient attention to female farmers and their particular needs. Agendas tend to be focused on improving rural production technologies and techniques for more lucrative export-oriented crops (which tend to fall under the realm of male responsibility) while neglecting staple food crops for domestic consumption traditionally cultivated by women. This is partly caused by the lack of female representation and decision-making in agricultural research. Women's participation in agricultural research is less than 20 percent in developing countries, although there are large differences across regions. The percentage of women engaged in agricultural research ranges from 3 percent in Eritrea and Pakistan, to circa 40 percent in Argentina, Botswana and Uruguay, and 55 percent in Myanmar (FAO 2011).

10 Building gender-sensitive SAIS

The preceding analysis suggests that it is critical to recognize the different roles and circumstances of men and women in food production and markets in order to design informed research agendas, projects, and programs, improve agricultural output and incomes, and enhance food and nutrition security. Reducing gender inequalities in access to productive resources and technological opportunities in agriculture is a necessary condition to increasing the sector's contribution to sustainable development, poverty reduction, and food security (World Bank *et al.* 2009).

The SAIS framework has the potential to contribute to mainstreaming gender perspectives by taking into account the many actors involved in the value chain, the diverse organizations that facilitate education, research, and extension systems, as well as the policies, attitudes, and practices that frame agricultural research, education and training, production, and trade. The SAIS framework attaches great importance to matters of equality in access to technology, inputs, services, and decision-making processes (UN 2011b) (Figure 10.5).

The technological transformation for sustainable agriculture will require the creation of enabling conditions at all levels of agricultural research, policy, and value chain to support a full, fair, and viable participation of women in sustainable systems of food production.

Since the 1980s, national and international support for agricultural research has decreased, with expenditures for agricultural R&D in Africa, East and South-East Asia (excluding China), and the Middle East remaining low. The development and adaptation of new technology required to increase sustainable food production demands significant long-term public and private funding

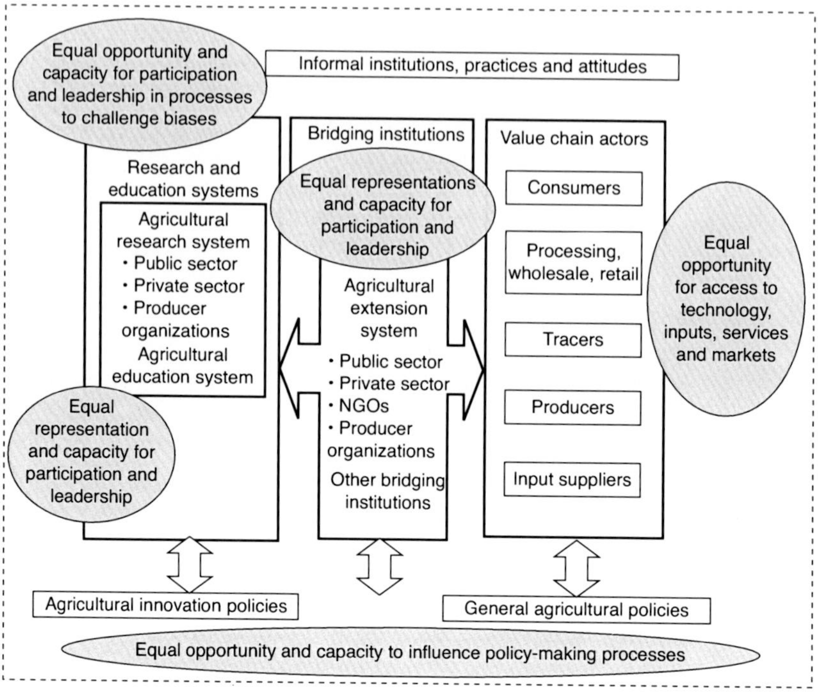

Figure 10.5 Interrelations among the elements of agricultural innovation systems (source: World Bank *et al.* 2009).

toward agricultural R&D. Further, the model of operation of research institutions needs to become more flexible and inclusive so as to improve its responsiveness to the needs of small-scale farmers. Joint experimentation and learning, as well as adoption of a multidisciplinary focus would greatly contribute to that end. Agricultural research also demands closer and more direct collaboration among public research institutions, the private sector, and small-scale farmers through innovative partnerships, which may include, for instance, patent buyouts, prizes, joint ventures, co-financing and advance-purchase agreements, comprehensive risk assessments, and suitable regulatory schemes (Pardey and Beintema 2001; Bhagwati 2005; Elliot 2010; Lipton 2010).

Agricultural research and policies must also be drafted through a gender-sensitive lens by focusing on the needs and capabilities of resource-constrained rural women. Research and policies need to examine how the envisaged applications could potentially reduce or aggravate gender-based differences such as the work burden of women and access to markets and income (Schierbinger 2010). An increasing number of female scientists and decision-makers must also be represented in agricultural research institutions. Research should, further, incorporate the repertory of knowledge and skills that local communities, including women farmers, have developed over time to sustain their livelihoods and resolve their environmental challenges. Tapping into traditional knowledge can usefully complement and contribute to the development of modern science and technology. There are important benefits to be found in recognizing and supporting rural women innovators by fostering the production of innovations that are context-appropriate and have a greater chance of uptake by low-income households. As an example, Prolinnova, a civil society multi-stakeholder international network engaged in participatory and localized innovation development, illustrates a gender-responsive, pro-poor agriculture innovation model that uses local expertise. The Prolinnova network supports local innovators, including farmers or other natural resources users, to find ways of improving their livelihoods, building on existing local, indigenous knowledge with minimum external interference. It provides grants to male and female inventors for purchasing inputs, materials, and equipment, and offers technical assistance. Women farmers are part of the grant steering committee and thus influence the direction of local research (Letty and Waters-Bayer 2010).

Increasing awareness and stimulating the adoption of sustainable technology and crop management practices – particularly in light of the potential trade-offs between increasing food production and halting environmental degradation – will also require a wider dissemination of knowledge, information, information and communications technology, and technical support for small-scale farmers, including women, through quality education in rural areas. This includes support for adult literacy and innovative peer-to-peer learning programs and adequate extension services. The experience of the Farm Field Schools – operating in 87 countries – shows that innovation and flexible natural resource management can be advanced through farmer-to-farmer learning, with participation from formal and informal research institutions. Education, publicity, advocacy, and legislation are also important with respect to reducing food waste and promoting the adoption of sustainable diets and consumption practices.

Making sustainable agriculture technologies available to small-scale farmers in diverse agro-climatic regions further requires substantial investments in rural infrastructure, including roads, irrigation, electricity, and storage facilities. This must be complemented by measures to improve market access – including to credit, inputs, and insurance – for small-scale farm holders, with a particular emphasis on improving access for female farmers. Of note is that such policies need to be context specific. For instance, in regions such as Asia and Latin America, where over-use of fertilizers has caused depletion of natural resources, governments may need to reconsider their continued subsidization. This is contrary to the case of Sub-Saharan Africa, where small-scale farm holders generally use a fraction of the recommended fertilizer levels. In addition, introduction of risk reduction mechanisms (such as grants, tax incentives, innovative insurance policies, and new forms of venture capital) can be critical in averting devastating income losses of small farm holders, which undermine investment in many areas, including in technology and innovation (Leeuwis and Hall 2010).

Improving women's access to productive resources, technologies, and markets will require gender analysis in policy-making and targeted support. However, such efforts cannot be confined to economic and technological solutions. In order to ensure that women producers benefit from a more dynamic agricultural sector linked to food security and sustainable development, other gender inequalities related to income and time poverty have to be addressed. Combating gender bias in rural contexts will require changes in legislation, policies, and institutions – including changes in deeply rooted patriarchal attitudes and norms. Strategies to open new opportunities for women farmers thus have to address intra-household distributions of income and assets, the sharing of paid and unpaid work and domestic responsibilities, and the rise in number of female-headed households in rural areas linked to male out-migration.

Enhancing income and food security among small-scale farm holders in developing countries may also necessitate improved access to land through redistribution practices and more secure property rights.

In implementing these policies, governments will have to overcome political obstacles and build stronger partnerships and coalitions among the multiple stakeholders within a SAIS. For example, through regulation to prevent monopolistic practices in food markets and adoption of ethical and environmental certification processes, new opportunities emerge for linking small farm holders to larger exporting markets along global food value chains.

11 International action

The international community has much to contribute to a global agenda for food security and environmental sustainability. Delivering on the financial pledges made in the aftermath of the food crisis of 2007–08 would constitute an important down-payment on realizing the commitment to the goal of eradicating hunger.

International action is also needed to reform agricultural subsidies in Organisation for Economic Co-operation and Development (OECD) countries, which undermine the ability of farmers in developing countries to compete. This includes rethinking subsidies to biofuels and supporting new-generation biofuels to reduce the diversion of agricultural land use from food production. Non-tariff measures on food trade must be reformed so that these are truly science based and adequate assistance is provided for small-scale producers to meet their needs. The WTO Agreement on Trade-Related Aspects of Intellectual Property Rights (TRIPS) and other bilateral and regional trade agreements that incorporate TRIPS-based provisions – which introduce monopolistic and exclusive rights regimes into plants and seed varieties – may also need to be modified to permit knowledge and seed sharing in developing countries.

Reconstituting the global, regional, and national capacities for agricultural R&D with international financial support can further result in a rapid increase in agricultural productivity. New financing mechanisms should also be developed to expand payments to small-scale farm holders, especially women, in developing countries for environmental services that help protect natural resources, preserve biodiversity, and increase carbon sequestration in agriculture and forestry. Finally, effective regulation of commodity futures markets can help minimize unwarranted price volatility, which dilutes incentives to invest and undermines the viability of poor farmers and rural workers around the world.

Notes

1 The World Food Summit Plan of Action considered food security as existing "when all people, at all times, have physical and economic access to sufficient, safe and nutritious food to meet their dietary needs and food preferences for an active and healthy life" (FAO 1996). Based on this definition, undernourishment is thus a key indicator of food insecurity. Undernourishment exists when caloric intake is below the minimum dietary energy requirement, which is the amount of energy needed for light activity and a minimum acceptable weight for attained height. It varies by country and over time, depending on the gender and age structure of the population.
2 Estimates of undernutrition in this chapter have been updated to reflect the latest figures reported by FAO in October 2012 Data can be accessed online at: www.fao. org/publications/sofi/food-security-indicators/en. The FAO's latest estimates involved a major revision in the methodology to improve the parameters for the estimation of dietary energy requirements, those for food access and a new function to estimate the prevalence of undernutrition. These estimates also incorporate the new revisions of the world population; the demographic characteristics of households from recent surveys and estimates for food losses at the distribution level. In spite of these improvements, the figures reported are considered to be a lower bound in the actual prevalence of undernutrition. Aspects of nutrition other than energy availability are not considered; no adjustment is made to energy requirements at different levels of activity; and short-term food price variations are not taken into account. Thus the 870 million figure is likely to be overly optimistic (FAO 2012).
3 Commitments agreed to at the 1996 World Food Summit included the call for at least halving the number of undernourished people in the world by the year 2015 (FAO 1996, Para. 7). This goal was reinforced by the Millennium Declaration adopted by Heads of State and Government in September 2000, which resolved to halve by 2015 the proportion of the world's people who suffer from hunger (UN 2000).
4 Protracted crisis situations are characterized by recurrent natural disasters and/or conflict, longevity of food crises, breakdown of livelihoods, and insufficient institutional capacity to respond. Countries in protracted crisis include Afghanistan, Angola, Burundi, Central African Republic, Chad, Congo, Côte d'Ivoire, the Republic of Korea, the Democratic Republic of the Congo, Eritrea, Ethiopia, Guinea, Haiti, Iraq, Kenya, Liberia, Sierra Leone, Somalia, Tajikistan, Uganda, and Zimbabwe (FAO 2010). Although there is no data for Sudan in the latest revision made by FAO, the formerly unified country was believed to have experienced a protracted crisis situation.
5 See: www.fao.org/hunger/en (accessed October 13, 2012).
6 This level of disaggregation has not been updated by FAO to reflect the latest aggregate estimates published in 2012.
7 Climate change impacts agriculture in many ways, with changes in temperature, precipitation, and climatic variability affecting the timing and length of growing seasons and yields and thereby exacerbating land degradation and contributing to water scarcity (Agrawala and Fankhauser 2008). For instance, it is estimated that in Southern Africa, yields could fall by up to 50 percent between 2000 and 2020 (Parry *et al.*

2007) and that by 2080, 600 million additional people could be at risk of hunger as a direct consequence of climate change (UNDP 2007).
8 Male income is more strongly associated with "adult" or "bad" goods such as alcohol, cigarettes, and "female companionship" (Alderman *et al.* 1995; Duflo and Udry 2004).
9 See, e.g., Sen (1990), Sen *et al.* (2002), Osmania and Sen (2003).
10 See: http://web.unfpa.org/intercenter/food/womenas.htm (accessed July 29, 2011).
11 For feminist work on structural adjustment see, inter alia, Cornia *et al.* (1987), Bourguignon *et al.* (1991), Elson (1995), Gladwin (1991), Haddad (1991), Beneria and Feldman (1992), Sparr (1994), Bakker (1994), Stromquist (1999).

References

Agrawala, S. and Fankhauser, S. (eds.) (2008) *Economic Aspects of Adaptation to Climate Change: costs, benefits and policy instruments*, Paris: Organisation for Economic Co-operation and Development.
Alderman, H., Chiappori, P.A., Haddad, L., Hoddinott, J., and Kanbur, R. (1995) "Unitary versus collective models of the household: is it time to shift the burden of proof?," *World Bank Research Observer*, 10: 1–19.
Altieri, M.A. (2008) "Small farms as a planetary ecological asset: five key reasons why we should support the revitalization of small farms in the global South," *Food First: Institute for Food and Development Policy*, May 9. Online: www.foodfirst.org/en/node/2115 (accessed October 2, 2012).
Bakker, I. (eds.) (1994) *The Strategic Silence: gender and economic policy*, London: Zed Books with the North–South Institute.
Beneria, L. and Feldman, S. (1992) *Unequal Burden: economic crises, persistent poverty and women's work*, Boulder, CO: Westview Press.
Bhagwati, J. (2005) "Development aid: getting it right," *OECD Observer*, 249. Online: www.oecdobserver.org/news/archivestory.php/aid/1579/Development_aid.html (accessed October ,2 2012).
Boserup, E. (1970) *Women's Role in Economic Development*, New York: St. Martin's.
Bourguignon, F., de Melo, J., and Morrisson, C. (1991) "Poverty and income distribution during adjustment: issues and evidence from the OECD project," *World Development*, 19: 1485–508.
Brooks, S. and Loevinsohn, M. (2011) "Shaping agricultural innovation systems responsive to food insecurity and climate change," background paper prepared for *World Economic and Social Survey 2011.*
Bunning, S. and Hill, C. (1996) *Farmers' Rights in the Conservation and Use of Plant Genetic Resources: a gender perspective*, Rome: FAO.
Cagatay, N. (1996) "Gender and international labor standards in the world economy," *Review of Radical Political Economics*, 28: 92–101.
Cornia, G.A., Jolly, R., and Stewart, F. (1987) *Adjustment with a Human Face: protecting the vulnerable and promoting growth* (2 vols.), Oxford: Oxford University Press.
Darity, W. (1995) "The formal structure of a gender-segregated low-income economy," *World Development*, 23: 1963–8.
de Waal, A. and Tumushabe, J. (2003) "HIV/AIDS and food security in africa: a report for DFID," unpublished paper. Online: www.sarpn.org/documents/d0000235/P227_AIDS_Food_Security.pdf (accessed October 2, 2012).
Dubin, H.J. and Brennan, J.P. (2009) "Fighting a 'shifty enemy': the international collaboration to contain wheat rusts," in D.J. Spielman and R. Pandya-Lorch (eds.), *Millions

Fed: proven successes in agricultural development, Washington, DC: International Food Policy Research Institute.

Duflo, E. and Udry, C. (2004) "Intrahousehold resource allocation in Côte d'Ivoire: social norms, separate accounts and consumption choices," NBER Working Paper No. 10498, Cambridge, MA: National Bureau of Economic Research.

Elliot, K.A. (2010) "Pulling agricultural innovation and the market together," Working Paper No. 215, Washington, DC: Center for Global Development.

Elson (1995) "Gender awareness in modeling structural adjustment," *World Development*, 23: 1851–68.

Floro, M. (1995) "Economic restructuring, gender and the allocation of time," *World Development*, 23: 1913–29.

Folbre, N. (1986) "Hearts and spades: paradigms of household economics," *World Development*, 14: 245–55.

FAO (1993) *Agricultural Extension and Women Farm Workers in the 1980s*, Rome: Food and Agriculture Organization of the United Nations.

FAO (1996) *Report of the World Food Summit, 13–17 November 1996*, WFS 96/REP, Rome: Food and Agriculture Organization of the United Nations.

FAO (2009) *Investing in Food Security*, Rome: Food and Agriculture Organization of the United Nations.

FAO (2010) *The State of Food Insecurity in the World 2010: addressing food insecurity in protracted crises*, Rome: Food and Agriculture Organization of the United Nations.

FAO (2011) *The State of Food and Agriculture 2010/2011: women in agriculture – closing the gender gap for development*, Rome: Food and Agriculture Organization of the United Nations.

FAO (2012) *The State of Food Insecurity in the World 2012: economic growth is necessary but not sufficient to accelerate reduction of hunger and malnutrition*, Rome: Food and Agriculture Organization of the United Nations.

Gilbert, C.L. (2008) "How to understand high food prices," Discussion Paper No. 23, Trento, Italy: Department of Economics, University of Trento. Online: www.unitn.it/files/23_08_gilbert.pdf (accessed October 2, 2012).

Gladwin, C.H. (ed.) (1991) *Structural Adjustment and African Women Farmers*, Gainesville, FL: University of Florida Press.

Godfray, H.C.J., Crute, I.R., Haddad, L., Lawrence, D., Muir, J.F., Nisbett, N., Pretty, J., Robinson, S., Toulmin, C., and Whiteley, R. (2010) "The future of the global food system," *Philosophical Transactions of the Royal Society B: Biological Sciences*, 365: 2769–77.

Gordon, A. (1996) *Transforming Capitalism and Patriarchy: gender and development in Africa*, Boulder, CO: Lynne Rienner.

Haddad, L. (1991) "Gender and adjustment: theory and evidence to date," mimeo, Washington, DC: International Food Policy Institute.

Hall, A., Dijkman, J., and Sulaiman, R. (2010) "Research into use: investigating the relationship between agricultural research and innovation," UNU-MERIT Working Paper Series No. 2010-44, Maastricht: United Nations University – Maastricht Economic and Social Research and Training Center on Innovation and Technology.

Hazell, P.B.R. (2009) "Transforming agriculture, the green revolution in Asia," in D.J. Spielman and R. Pandya-Lorch (eds.), *Millions Fed: proven successes in agricultural development*, Washington, DC: International Food Policy Research Institute.

IAASTD and McIntyre, B.D. (2009). *Agriculture at a Crossroads: global report*, Washington, DC: Island Press.

IFPRI (2002) *Green Revolution, Curse or Blessing?* Washington, DC: International Food Policy Research Institute.

IFPRI (2005) "The future of small farms," proceedings of a research workshop, Wye, United Kingdom, June 26–29, 2005, jointly organized by International Food Policy Research Institute (IFPRI)/2020 Vision Initiative, Overseas Development Institute (ODI), and Imperial College, London.

Karl, M. (1996) *Inseparable: the crucial role of women in food security*, Manila: Isis International.

Laxmi, V., Parikh, J., Karmakar, S., and Dabrase, P. (2003) "Household energy, women's hardship and health impacts in rural Rajasthan, India: need for sustainable energy solutions," *Energy for Sustainable Development*, 7: 50–68.

Leeuwis, C. and Hall, A. (2010) *Facing the Challenges of Climate Change and Food Security: the role of research, extension and communication institutions – final report*, Rome: Food and Agriculture Organization of the United Nations, Wageningen University, and UNU-MERIT.

Letty, B.A. and Waters-Bayer, A. (2010) "Recognising local innovation in livestock-keeping: a path to empowering women," *Rural Development News*, 1: 27–31.

Lipton, M. (2010) "From policy aims and small-farm characteristics to farm science needs," *World Development*, 38: 1399–412.

Mehra, R. and Rojas, M.H. (2008) *A Significant Shift: women, food security and agriculture in a global marketplace*, Washington, DC: International Center for Research on Women.

Nyoni, S. (1991) *Women and Energy: lessons from the Zimbabwe experience*, Harare: Zimbabwe Environmental Research Organisation.

Osmania, S. and Sen, A. (2003) "The hidden penalties of gender inequality: fetal origins of ill-health," *Economics and Human Biology*, 1: 91–104.

Pardey, P.G. and Beintema, N.M. (2001) *Slow Magic: agricultural R&D a century after Mendel*, Washington, DC: International Food Policy Research Institute.

Parry, M.L., Canziani, O.F., Palutikof, J.P., van der Linden, P.J., and Hanson, C.E. (eds.) (2007) *Climate Change 2007: impacts, adaptation and vulnerability – contribution of working Group II to the fourth assessment report of the intergovernmental panel on climate change*, IPCC Fourth Assessment Report (AR4), Geneva: Intergovernmental Panel on Climate Change.

Pretty, J.N., Noble, A.D., Bossio, D., Dixon, J., Hine, R.E., Penning de Vries, F.W.T., and Morison, J.I.L. (2006) "Resource-conserving agriculture increases yields in developing countries," *Environmental Science and Technology (Policy Analysis)*, 40: 1114–19.

Rehfuess, E., Mehta, S., and Prüss-Üstün, A. (2006) "Assessing household solid fuel use: multiple implications for the Millennium Development Goals," *Environmental Health Perspectives*, 114: 373–8.

Schiebinger, L. (2010) "Gender, science and technology," background paper prepared for the UN Division for the Advancement of Women (DAW) and UNESCO. Online: www.un.org/womenwatch/daw/egm/gst_2010/Schiebinger-BP.1-EGM-ST.pdf (accessed October 4, 2012).

Sen, A. (1990) "More than 100 million women are missing," *New York Review of Books*, 37. Online: www.nybooks.com/articles/archives/1990/dec/20/more-than-100-million-women-are-missing/?pagination=false (accessed October 2, 2012).

Sen, G. (1996) "Gender, markets and state: a selected review and research agenda," *World Development*, 24: 821–9.

Sen, G., George, A., and Ostlin, P. (eds.) (2002) *Engendering International Health*, Cambridge, MA: MIT Press.

Sparr, P. (1994) *Mortgaging Women's Lives: feminist critiques of structural adjustment*, London: Zed Books for the United Nations.

Spielman, D.J. and Pandya-Lorch, R. (2009) "Fifty years of progress," in D.J. Spielman and R. Pandya-Lorch (eds.), *Millions Fed: proven successes in agricultural development*, Washington, DC: International Food Policy Research Institute.

Stromquist, N.P. (1999) "The impact of SAPs in Africa and Latin America," in C. Heward and S. Bunwaree (eds.), *Gender, Education and Development*, London: Zed Books Ltd.

Tenge, A.J., Graaff, J.D., and Hella, J.P. (2004) "Social and economic factors affecting the adoption of soil and water conservation in West Usambara highlands, Tanzania," *Land Degradation and Development*, 15: 99–114.

UNAIDS (2006) *Fact Sheet: women, girls, gender equality and HIV*. Online: www.unaids.org/en/media/unaids/contentassets/documents/factsheet/2012/20120217_FS_WomenGirls_en.pdf (accessed October 4, 2012).

UN (United Nations) (2000) *United Nations Millennium Declaration*, A/RES/55/2.

UN (2008) *Comprehensive Framework for Action*, report prepared by the High-level Task Force on the Global Food Crisis, July 15, New York: United Nations.

UN (2010) *Access to Land and the Right to Food*, report presented to the 65th General Assembly of the United Nations [A/65/281], October 21.

UN (2011a) *The World Economic and Social Survey 2011: the great green technological transformation*, New York: United Nations.

UN (2011b) *World Economic Situation and Prospects 2011*, New York: United Nations.

UNCTAD (2010) *Technology and Innovation Report 2010: enhancing food security in Africa through science, technology and innovation*, United Nations Conference on Trade and Development. Sales No. E.09.II.D.22.

UNDP (2007) *Human Development Report 2007/2008: fighting climate change – human solidarity in a divided world*, Basingstoke: Palgrave Macmillan.

von Braun, J. (2009) "Overcoming the world food and agriculture crisis through policy change and science," prepared for the Trust for Advancement of Agricultural Sciences (TAAS), Fourth Foundation Day Lecture, organized by International Food Policy Research Institute, New Delhi, March 6, 2009. Online: www.ifpri.org/publication/overcoming-world-food-and-agriculture-crisis-through-policy-change-and-science (accessed October 2, 2012).

World Bank (2008) "Food price crisis imperils 100 million in poor countries," World Bank News and Broadcast. Online: http://web.worldbank.org/WBSITE/EXTERNAL/NEWS/0,,contentMDK:21729143~pagePK:64257043~piPK:437376~theSitePK:4607,00.html (accessed January 12, 2011).

World Bank (2011) "Food price watch," February. Online: www.worldbank.org/foodcrisis/food_price_watch_report_feb2011.html (accessed March 24, 2011).

World Bank, FAO, and International Fund for Agricultural Development (IFAD) (2009) *Gender in Agriculture Sourcebook*, Washington, DC: World Bank.

Young K. (1993) *Planning Development with Women: making a world of difference*, London: Macmillan.

Index

Page numbers in *italics* denote tables, those in **bold** denote figures.

Caribbean 75; Mexican 76, 79, 81;
negative 25, 39, 87; per capita 13, 185,
190, *197*, 198–200, *201*, 204–5, 206n7,
206n12; percentage of **106**, 110; real
128; share of 35; South African 127

Hall, A. 264, 271
Hazell, P. 261–3
health insurance 147, 175, 181, 182n11
Heckman, J.J. 51, 68n10
Hirway, I. 1112, 160
HIV/AIDS 268
household 4–5, 7, 12, 60, 77, 111, 137,
150, 153n11, 166–8, 189, 199, 200, 203,
217, 219, 231, 273n2; consumption
reduced 172; coping mechanism 211;
dual-earner 63; education **168**; female-
headed 100n11, 265–6, 268, 272; female
members 14, 212; fuel-wood collection
259; health expenditures 34; hurt by
crisis 194; male reference person 221,
224, 229, 252n11, 252n14–15; needs 74,
188; non-unemployment-shock 252n14;
poor 56, 67, 78, 148, 158; rural 125,
181n10; in Russia 190; shared 191,
206n9; tension increased 170; Turkish
233–4, 252n11; Turkmenistan 206n8;
unemployment shock *222*, 226, *247*,
253n20; unpaid work increased 169;
vulnerable 13; without children 198;
workers' 180
household income 4, 18, 60, **63**, *64*, 88–90,
94; decreasing 78; low 8, 52–3, 63, 213,
271; middle-income 67; reduced 93;
shock 9, 12– 13, *194*, 196, 198, 204;
shrinking 134; single-male earner 233,
251n3
Household Labor Force Survey (HLFS)
14, 211–12, **213–15**, 216–17, *222–3*,
226, **228**, *232*, 233, **234**, *250*, 251n6,
252n9
Hsu, S. 1011, 137
hukou 145–6, 150, 152n4; rural 136, 139,
142; urban hukou 136, 139–40, *142*, 151
Human Development Index (HDI) 159
Hungary 205n1
hunger 15, 133, 256–7, 260–2, 264, 267,
272, 273n3, 273n7; *see also*
malnutrition; nutrition; undernourished
people

Ilkkaracan, I. 13–14, 189, 210–11, 213,
214, 251n3, 251n6–7
India 5, 9–11, 105, 107, 115, 120, 129,

129n3, 129n8, 162, 175, 177, 264; blood
diamonds 180; capital account 159;
crisis effects 123, 125, 134, 160;
economic development 129n1;
education 110, 129n11; employment
decline 106, 114; employment effects
112–13, 116, 124; famines 261; gender
bias **121**; globalized industry 157;
imports 109; informal workers 22; job
loss 134; Reserve Bank of India 161;
rural 259; SAMs 108, 111; skills bias
122; undernutrition 256, 258
Indian Central Bank 161; Diamond
Institute 177; economy 11, 158–60, 173;
equity markets 159; exports **107**, 159;
rupee 159, 162
Indian Government 104, 123, *124*, 125,
128, 173, 175, 180, 181n1, 181n10;
Government of Gujarat 178;
Government of India Labor Bureau 160
Indonesia 2, 30, *31*, 135, 177; male worker
31; undernourished people 256; wives
190; women workers 134
INEGI 79, *82*
inflation 43, 73, 93–4; in Argentina 45;
curbing 99; targeting 79
input–output (IO) 53, 108, 129n3; analysis
53, 56–8; framework 64
Instituto Nacional de Estadística y
Geografía (INEGI) 79, *82*
Instituto Nacional de las Mujeres
(INMUJERES) 85–6, 97
International Assessment of Agricultural
Science and Technology for
Development (IAASTD) 259
International Center for Maize and Wheat
Improvement (CIMMYT) 261
International Food Policy Research
Institute (IFPRI) 261, 264
International Fund for Agricultural
Development (IFAD) **260**
International Labour Organization (ILO) 1,
17, 23, 29, *31*, 36, *37*, 77–8, 81, 84,
101n21, 125, 127, 132, 135, 139;
employment rates *21–2*; Global
Employment Trends *18*; Global
Employment Trends for Women 4, 19,
134, 187; ILO/UN 77–8, 81; Research
Conference in Geneva 104; survey
144–5; unemployment rates *19*, 4950;
youth employment 40–1, 186
International Monetary Fund (IMF) 35,
4950, 80, 92, 128
International Rice Research Institute 262

National Home Health Aide Survey
(NHHCS) 54
National Plan for Work Regularization 44
National Rural Employment Guarantee
Act (NREGA) 125, 172, 175, 181n10
National Sample Survey Organisation 123
NEDLAC 127
New Rice for Africa 264
nongovernmental organization (NGO) 166,
270
North Africa *18*, 19, *21*, 32, **257**;
landholders 266; patriarchy 267
North American Free Trade Agreement
(NAFTA) 79
North American Industry Classification
System (NAICS) 58, 65
nutrition 17, 35, 259, **260**, 269, 273n2;
malnutrition 15, 260–1, 268;
undernutrition 257–8, 260, 273n2; *see
also* hunger; undernourished people
nutritional 266; behavior 267; patterns 257

Ocampo, J.A. 76, 100n7–8
OECD (Organisation for Economic
Co-operation and Development) 25,
27–8; agricultural subsidies 272; gender
wage gaps **27**; labor force participation
rates **26**; part-time work **28**
Ortiz, I. 3, 17, 20, 34–5

Pakistan 256, 269
Pardey, P.G. 262, 270
pension 36, *37–8*, 44, 137, 165, 175, 178;
non-contributory programs 42; non-
taxable 89, 101n32; pilot scheme 146;
plans 138; private funds 89; rural
insurance 137; schemes 151; system 11,
44, 89; transfers 45; universal 150;
pest management (IPM) 263; integrated
264
PHI 55
Poland 186, 205n1, 206n6
Polat, S. 211–12
Pollin, R. **62**
Portugal 3, 25, 27, 49, 231, *232*
Posadas, J. 189, 205
poverty 41, 52, 83, 100n11, 135, 159, 171,
255, 257–8; below poverty level 54;
decreased 261; Ecuadorian rate 93;
escaping 12, 174; exacerbating 14;
extreme 78, 94, 99, 100n10; falling into
67, 199; global fight against 262;
household 68; incidence 88, 100n10;
incidence doubled 42; levels 87;

mitigation 98; reduced 15; reduction
258–9, 264, 269; status 56; time 148,
272; women at risk 4
poverty line 78, 83, 94, 159; federal 54,
63, 69n24; official 36, 55–6
Prieto-Rodriguez, J. 189, 192, 231, *232*
primary sampling unit (PSU) 191, 203
Productive Recovery Program (REPRO)
45, 88
Programa de Empleo Transitorio (PET) 86,
101n22
Program to Promote Growth and
Employment (PICE) 84
pro-poor 135; agriculture innovation
model 271
public works 7, 45, 50, 96, 125, 127
Puyana, A. 76, 80, 83

Qian, Z. 146–7

recession 6, 25, 40, 50–1, 74, 77, 80, 85,
87, 96, 171, 186; Great Recession 1, 42,
49, 61, 68; pre-recession level 51, 54;
transitional 184
reference person 221, 231; male 217–19,
221, *222*, 224, 229, 252n11, 252n14–15
registered employment **43**, 44; female
employment 216; non-registered
employment 45; private enterprises 42;
workers 42, 78; as unemployed 138;
units 160–1, 178; unregistered 161, 173,
179
registered wage workers 78
Reinhart, C.M. 3, 17
renminbi (RMB) 34, 146–7
research and development (R&D) 15, 261,
263; agricultural 269–70, 272
Reserve Bank of India task force 161, 170,
174, 181n9
Rojo Brizuela, S. 45–6
Romania 205n1, 206n6
Rubery, J. 105, 120, 184, 187–8, 251n2
Russian Federation 205n1–2

Sabarwal, S. 185, 188, 202, 204
safety nets *38*, 41, 190, 259
Seguino, S. 22, 147
self-employment 17, 28, 32, 78, 158, 168
Sen, A. 51–2
Sen, G. 268
Serbia 205n1, 206n10
Serneels, P. 190–1
shock absorbers 12, 169, 174, 176